VOLUME THREE

# TRENDS IN POLICING

## Interviews with Police Leaders Across the Globe

## International Police Executive Symposium Co-Publications

**Dilip K. Das, *Founding President-IPES***

**Global Trafficking in Women and Children**
By Obi N.I. Ebbe and Dilip K. Das
ISBN: 978-1-4200-5943-4

**Contemporary Issues in Law Enforcement and Policing**
By Andrew Millie and Dilip K. Das
ISBN: 978-1-4200-7215-0

**Trends in Policing: Interviews with Police Leaders Across the Globe, Volume Two**
By Dilip K. Das and Otwin Marenin
ISBN: 978-1-4200-7520-5

**Criminal Abuse of Women and Children: An International Perspective**
By Obi N.I. Ebbe and Dilip K. Das
ISBN: 978-1-4200-8803-8

**Urbanization, Policing, and Security: Global Perspectives**
By Gary Cordner, AnnMarie Cordner and Dilip K. Das
ISBN: 978-1-4200-8557-0

**Global Environment of Policing**
By Dilip K. Das, Darren Palmer, and Anthony L. Sciarabba
ISBN: 978-1-4200-6590-9

**Trends in Policing: Interviews with Police Leaders Across the Globe, Volume Three**
By Dilip K. Das and Otwin Marenin
ISBN: 978-1-4398-1924-1

**Police Without Borders: The Fading Distinction between Local and Global**
By Cliff Roberson and Dilip K. Das
ISBN: 978-1-4398-0501-5

**Terrorism, Counterterrorism, and Internal Wars: Examining International Political Violence**
By Austin Turk, Dilip K. Das, and James Ross
ISBN: 978-1-4398-2104-6

**Effective Crime Reduction Strategies: International Perspectives**
By James F. Albrecht and Dilip K. Das
ISBN: 978-1-4200-7838-1

**Strategies and Responses to Crime: Thinking Locally, Acting Globally**
By Dilip K. Das, Mintie Das, and Larry French
ISBN: 978-1-4200-7669-1

**Justices of the World: Their Views, Opinions, and Perspectives**
by Cliff Roberson and Dilip K. Das
ISBN: 978-1-4200-9978-2

**Cross Cultural Profiles of Policing**
By Dilip K. Das and Osman Dolu
ISBN: 978-1-4200-7014-9

VOLUME THREE

# TRENDS IN POLICING

## Interviews with Police Leaders Across the Globe

Edited by

OTWIN MARENIN AND DILIP K. DAS

International Police Executive Symposium
Co-Publication

CRC Press
Taylor & Francis Group
Boca Raton London New York

CRC Press is an imprint of the
Taylor & Francis Group, an **informa** business

CRC Press
Taylor & Francis Group
6000 Broken Sound Parkway NW, Suite 300
Boca Raton, FL 33487-2742

First issued in paperback 2017



ISBN-13: 978-1-4398-1924-1 (hbk)
ISBN-13: 978-1-138-11321-3 (pbk)



**Library of Congress Cataloging-in-Publication Data**

Das, Dilip K., 1941-
Trends in policing : interviews with police leaders across the globe / Dilip K. Das and Otwin Marenin.
p. cm.
Includes bibliographical references and index.
ISBN 978-1-4200-7520-5
1. Police--Cross-cultural studies. 2. Police administration--Cross-cultural studies. 3. Police-community relations--Cross-cultural studies. 4. Police chiefs--Interviews. I. Marenin, Otwin. II. Title.

HV7921.D38 2009
363.2--dc22 2008036396

**Visit the Taylor & Francis Web site at**
**http://www.taylorandfrancis.com**

**and the CRC Press Web site at**
**http://www.crcpress.com**

# Contents

# Foreword

BRUCE BAKER

In international police training circles, there is a widespread belief that policing by and large is the same worldwide: that the universal challenge is to maintain law and order and social peace in a lawful and humane way. But the narrative of universalism looks far less convincing under this volume's close inspection of senior police managers across six continents. Like its two predecessors in the series, this volume of interviews demonstrates that context matters; indeed, it molds police services into very different organizations.

Those with responsibility for state policing are revealed in these pages to be responsible for very diverse entities: some very large organizations and some small (just 1,050 police officers for the Solomon Islands); some with the latest high-tech equipment and some with little or outdated equipment; some manage organizations where political interference is routine and others manage those where it is only sporadic; some enjoy popular confidence and others are widely despised.

These differences are not insignificant. And, again, the police forces described are not *all* doing the same activities. Yes, there are thieves, brawlers, and prostitutes in Rio, Oslo, Sarajevo, Melbourne, Mexico City, Kinshasa, and Honiara, but not all face private militia, ethnic violence, large-scale no-go areas, and significant community-based policing organizations. And none has an identical culture to others. The senior managers of the developed and developing world may have attended the same courses, use the same police-speak, and wear uniforms, but they manage very different entities and, off the record (and off *this* record), have organizational aims that may go beyond democratic policing and employ offices that go beyond democratic policing guidelines. It is a reminder, should we need it, that policing is peculiarly difficult to export and peculiarly difficult to analyze globally when it is uncertain whether like is being compared with like.

Not only does this volume demonstrate that context matters for police services, but it is also a living demonstration of the importance of contingent factors such as the personalities and prejudices of the senior officers. Once again, in this as in the other volumes in this series, it is clear that organizational priorities are influenced by personal priorities. Some of the interviewees put their faith in training, some in management restructuring, some in forensic science, some in computerization, and some in the morality with which they were brought up. The narrowness of their focus and the intensity (and good fortune) of the implementation have played their part in producing distinct organizational configurations.

In the final analysis, this book is a sociology of police leaders. We enter (as much as they allow their guard to be lowered) the mindset of those whose decisions affect the lives of tens of thousands of citizens who are subject to or ignored by the officers these leaders supervise. That, of course, is to make the unproven assumption that what these senior experienced officers decide actually happens on the ground of the local police station—a dangerous assumption in many cases. Nevertheless, the conceptualization of this book and its companion volumes is an important contribution to policing studies.

We are indebted to IPES for conceiving and seeing through this project. The interviews will not teach the reader how to be a good senior police officer in any police service, but it will force the aspirant to high office to reflect on his or her own values, commitment to public service, the nature of what is possible in the inevitably constrained circumstances of real life, and what he or she thinks the police are for and should be like.

# Introduction

Otwin Marenin and Dilip Das

This is the third volume in a series of interviews with police leaders across the world. It is worth restating the idea and purpose behind these books, which take time and serious hard work by the interviewers, the leaders interviewed, and the editors.

There exists an abundance of scholarly work on the police, their institutions, their policies and practices, their successes and failures. But there is very little published writing available on what the practitioners who are the subjects of scholarly interest and research think about their work: their concerns, their opinions and evaluations of what works and what does not, their conceptions of success and failure, their experiences and insights gained from living the police life.

These volumes are created under the aegis of the International Police Executive forum (IPES), an organization founded by Dilip Das on the principle and belief that there should be greater interaction and exchange of information and ideas among scholars and practitioners than currently existed. This belief and the effort to record the views of practitioners are not designed as a critique of, alternative to, or substitute for scholarly work, but rather as a complement to it. It is our firm belief that, when combined, these two different realms of information—knowledge and wisdom—will lead to more accurate understanding and better theorizing about policing; more effective, humane, and, yes, democratic policing and better security; improved justice; and increased well-being of communities.

Almost unavoidably and by habit, there is some distrust among scholars and practitioners about the value of knowledge gained and held by others. We do not share that distrust. We do not believe that, unless one has done policing, one cannot understand or interpret what policing is like, nor do we believe that practitioners cannot think theoretically about issues other than their pressing operational and managerial needs. Scholars know policing from the outside in and practitioners from the inside out. Both perspectives are valuable, and they provide reciprocal correctives to potential misunderstandings and misinterpretations of the realities of policing or conceptions of needed reforms.

The goal in recording, translating, transcribing, and publishing these interviews is just that: to record and not judge (at least right away) what the leaders are telling the interviewers. The fact that one might have answered a question differently is not an issue for us. We know what we think but we want to record as accurately as possible what police leaders think, as stated in their own words.

The interviews in this volume, as in the past two, reflect a wide diversity of opinions among the police leaders, with some consistent overlaps. Police leaders deal with a basically similar job: how to manage an organization and how to ensure that the job is done as planned. However, they do so in contexts that are fundamentally different in terms of political life, economic resources, social structures, police–community relations, and transnational interactions.

Still, within these vastly different contexts, the leaders discuss political influences on policing and tend to reject them; profess an adherence to the ideology of community policing while noting the problems that stand in the way of institutionalizing this style of policing; are aware of the need to interact with the international environment from which come transnational crime, advice and assistance by states, NGOs, IGOs, and the traveling horde of consultants; and seek to improve the performance, as defined by local and international standards, of the agencies that they lead. It is also obvious that some leaders are more practically oriented and concerned mostly with managerial and administrative issues, while others have a more philosophical bend, which seeks to place and understand the roles of the police within the wider order, justice, and security contexts. As elsewhere, policing reflects the interplay of personalities, political pressures, public demands or apathy, professional norms, and the concrete dynamics of (in)security.

In the end, it is our hope, as editors, that readers will find the views expressed by leaders in this and the other volumes interesting, useful, and complementary to their own understanding of police and policing. That has been our experience.

*On a personal note,* I (Marenin) have to note that this will be my last editing partnership with Dilip in these books. I have thoroughly enjoyed doing the editing, learned a lot, and think I am a better scholar for having done this work. Editors have a firsthand look at new information, insights, and the felicitous, quotable expression of an idea or policy. Being, as it were, ahead of the curve of learning has its rewards. Of course, editing is only a small part of the production process. The heavy lifting has been done by the interviewers who agreed to talk with leaders, to translate, transcribe, and send the interviews to us, and to do this on their own time and with their own resources. It is their work that has made these books possible. Ultimately, though, it is the police leaders who agree to have their views recorded and published that made it possible to convert the belief that complementary knowledge is a good thing into reality. We thank them all.

I would be remiss not to mention the support received from the publisher, Taylor & Francis, for this work and to its support staff and editors, specifically Carolyn Spence, who have been immensely helpful in getting these volumes published.

Cheers.

# Contributors

**Jasmin Ahić** holds the position of assistant professor in the Security Studies Department at the Faculty of Criminal Justice Science at the University of Sarajevo and University of AAB, Kosovo. He graduated from the Faculty of Political Sciences, University of Sarajevo, and has an MSc and PhD in political sciences. He is assistant editor of *Criminalistic Themes*—a scientific magazine for criminology, criminalistic and security studies published by the University of Sarajevo. He was scholar of the Royamont Process of the National and Kapodistrian University of Athens, Greece.

Ahić is a part-time research fellow at the Geneva Center for the Democratic Control of Armed Forces (DCAF), Switzerland, and contributor to *Police Practice and Research,* an international journal. His research is focused on political and security problems in Bosnia and Herzegovina and the Western Balkans, reform and transition of the security sector, security policies, private security sectors, police integrity and the control of policing. His work is published in Bosnian, Croatian, Serbian and English. Telephone/office: +387 33 561 272. Contact jahic@fknbih.edu, www.fknbih.edu, or jahic@fkn.unsa.ba.

**Elena Azaola** is a senior investigator at the Center for Advanced Studies and Research in Social Anthropology in Mexico City, where she received her PhD degree in social anthropology. She also graduated as a psychoanalyst. She was an advisor at the National Commission of Human Rights (1991–1993) and is a current council member at the Commission of Human Rights of Mexico City. She has published more than 125 articles and books in Mexico, as well as in other countries.

Most of Dr. Azaola's research has been in the field of juvenile and women's justice institutions, human rights, and violence. Her research on commercial sexual exploitation of children (1999–2003) was sponsored by the United Nations Children's Fund (UNICEF). She co-coordinated a national report (2004) on violence sponsored by the World Health Organization (WHO) and the European Commission project for street children in Mexico (1997–1999). Since 2001 she has conducted several research projects on Mexico's police forces. She is the board chair of the Institute for Security and Democracy, which won the 2007 McArthur Award for Creative and Effective Institutions. She can be reached at eazaola@ciesas.edu.mx.

**Bruce Baker** is professor of African security and director of the African Studies Center at Coventry University, UK. His published articles and books cover African democratization, governance, policing, security sector reform, popular justice, and informal justice. His current research focus is informal and formal policing in postconflict African states and has led to *Multi-Choice Policing in Africa* (Nordiska Afrikainstitutet, 2007), *Security in Post-Conflict Africa: The Role of Non-State Policing* (CRC Press 2009), and numerous articles (see www.africanpolicing.org). He has conducted fieldwork in Zimbabwe, Mozambique, South Africa, Rwanda, Uganda, The Gambia, Sierra Leone, Cape Verde, Seychelles, Liberia, Southern Sudan, and Comoros. He can be reached at lsx103@coventry.ac.uk.

**David Baker** is a senior lecturer of criminal justice at the School of Humanities, Communications and Social Sciences, at Monash University. From 2001 to 2005, he was a senior lecturer of criminal justice and criminology at the School of Political and Social Inquiry. From 1991 to 2000, he was a lecturer in the Department of Police and Justice Studies at Monash University. Previous to his Monash lecturing appointment, he was a training instructor at the Victoria Police Academy for 5 years.

Dr. Baker's main area of research is public order policing. His most significant contribution is a single-authored book, *Batons and Blockades: Policing Industrial Disputes in Australasia*, 2005. This original book, which examines and analyzes changes in the way police services in Australia and New Zealand control the workplace dynamics of industrial conflict, is based on public order policing theory and practice within an industrial relations context. He is a member of the International Policing Research Consortium that is nearing completion of the "International Comparative Research Project on Police Use of Force."

Dr. Baker has researched and published a number of interdisciplinary articles and chapters in relation to police history, the strategic role of the Australian Federal Police, South Pacific policing, police unionism, criminal justice, labor history, industrial relations, and politics. He is an associate investigator for the ARC Research Center of Excellence for Policing and Security from 2007 to 2111 that is centered at Griffith University. His involvement focuses on Project 1.2, "Understanding Conflict in Vulnerable Communities."

Contact information: Criminal Justice, Monash University, Gippsland Campus, Northways Road, Churchill, Victoria 3842; Ph: 61 3 9902 6387 (Gippsland), Ph: 61 3 9903 2819 (Caulfield), Mobile: 0439110811; David.Baker@arts.monash.edu.au.

**Bruno M. Baltodano** is a PhD candidate in the political science department at Washington State University. He received his BA degree from Eastern Washington University and his MA degree from Washington State University. His research focuses on the behavior of insurgency groups in Nicaragua, Colombia, and Iraq as well as the development of nationalism and political autonomy of indigenous communities in the Caribbean Coast of Nicaragua. He has conducted field research in Nicaragua and is currently part of a research team conducting work in the Middle East.

**Dilip Das** served as a police chief before joining academia. He is the founding president of International Police Executive Symposium (IPES, www.ipes.info), which brings police researchers and practitioners together to facilitate cross-cultural, international, and interdisciplinary exchanges for the enrichment of the profession. Dr. Das also serves as the founding editor-in-chief of *Police Practice and Research: An International Journal,* which is affiliated with IPES. His publications include more than two dozen books and numerous articles. He is a professor of criminal justice and a human rights consultant to the United Nations.

Dr. Das's address is Norman Vale, 6030 Nott Road, Guilderland, New York 12084; tel. (518) 452-7845; cell (802) 598-3680; fax (518) 456-6790; dilipkd@aol.com.

**Melchor C. de Guzman** is currently an assistant professor of criminal justice at the College of Brockport at the State University of New York. He earned his doctorate degree in criminal justice from the University of Cincinnati in Ohio. Dr. de Guzman's research includes the examination of citizen participation in the control of the police primarily through the civilian review boards. He also investigates organizational factors that influence police behavior and community-oriented policing. His most recent research includes the utilization of Web sites by police departments in the delivery of police services. Prior to joining academia, Dr. de Guzman was a senate secretary for the Senate Committee on National Defense and Security in the Philippines. He also lectured in the National Police College of the Philippines' program for a master's in public safety administration. In addition he lectured on research and leadership courses to Philippine police officers taking the Officers' Senior Executive Course (OSEC). He was also a director of the Philippine Veterans Affairs Office in the Philippines. Dr. de Guzman can be reached by phone at (585) 395-5785 and by e-mail at mdeguzman@brockport.edu.

**Laurence Armand French** is a police psychologist and criminologist with over 40 years experience in the field. He holds BA, MA, and PhD degrees in sociology/criminology from the University of New Hampshire-Durham, a second MA degree in school psychology from Western New Mexico University, and a second PhD degree in cultural psychology from the University of Nebraska-Lincoln. He is a former U.S. Marine who served during the Vietnam era with both the 6th and 7th Fleets and the 3rd Marine Division. Dr. French is a professor emeritus of psychology from Western New Mexico University, a senior research associate with the Justiceworks Institute at the University of New Hampshire, and a senior Fulbright scholar at the University of Sarajevo. He is a fellow of the American Psychological Association and has over 270 publications, including 15 books.

**Rune Glomseth** is a police superintendent and an assistant professor at Norwegian Police University College. He has many years of experience in law enforcement, including police patrolling, investigations, police intelligence, proactive work, and administration. He teaches organizational development and leadership to undergraduate and graduate students as well as law enforcement executives.

**Robert F. J. Harnischmacher** was born in 1948 in Lippstadt (West Germany). In 1967 he earned Abitur in economic sciences at Kolleg Burg Eringerfeld. Throughout his course of military service, he served as an instructor. He authored close combat and self defense learning material for special units of police (e.g., GSG 9, etc.), units of the military police (Feldjäger of the German Bundeswehr), and units in foreign countries. He studied jurisprudence at the Westphalian Wilhelms University of Münster. Currently he is the owner and managing director of the firm International Security and Media Consulting (ISMC) in Lippstadt.

Harnischmacher is very active in many fields such as economy, security, juridical sciences, police affairs, coaching, and writing (www.ismc-harnischmacher.de), both national and international. He authors, edits, and coauthors a variety of publications such as juridical essays, books for studying law, commentaries of law, and documents in Europe and worldwide in many languages. He is an associate editor of and contributor to the *World Police Encyclopedia*, and lectures at academies, technical high schools of public administration, universities, conferences, and symposia, both national and international. As an expert, he teaches criminology, criminal policy, and police science; moreover, he is also a consultant in security and intelligence matters, especially business intelligence.

**George Howell** has been at the front of ICOS's endeavors in Brazil, forging partnerships with Brazilian and international institutions, and working to catalyze security and development approaches to public security policy strategies. Currently, Howell is the coordinator of the Center of Excellence on Public Security, established by ICOS in 2008, which works with governments to develop pragmatic responses to pressing social crises.

Howell has an interest in developing responses to twenty-first century security and development challenges, counternarcotics intelligence, and integrated approaches to governance. His background is in political economy. He holds a BA degree in social anthropology from Goldsmith's University and an MSc degree in development studies from the School of Oriental and African Studies in London.

**Ronald D. Hunter** holds the rank of professor and is the first full-time faculty member within the criminal justice/criminology program at Georgia Gwinnett College. He received his PhD degree in criminology from Florida State University. He previously taught at Western Carolina University, the University of West Georgia, Jacksonville State University, and the University of North Carolina at Charlotte. Dr. Hunter has held administrative positions of program coordinator, department head, and associate dean.

Prior to entering academia, Dr. Hunter was a sergeant with the Tallahassee (Florida) Police Department. Assignments included supervising the joint Tallahassee–Leon County Robbery Task Force, the Managing Criminal Information Unit, the Career Criminal Unit, the Records Section, and officers within Uniformed Patrol. He also served 7 years as a part-time municipal judge in Cave Spring, Georgia. Dr. Hunter is a past president of the Southern Criminal Justice Association and of the Academy of Criminal Justice Sciences. His research interests are primarily in the areas of crime prevention and law enforcement. He has published textbooks on research methods, criminological theories, robbery prevention, and police–community relations as well as published articles and has presented numerous papers on a myriad of criminal justice issues.

His professional affiliations include the Academy of Criminal Justice Sciences (Section on Police and Section on Security and Crime Prevention), Southern Criminal Justice Association, and International Police Executive Symposium. His contact information is Professor of Criminal Justice and Criminology, School of Liberal Arts, Georgia Gwinnett College, 1000 University Center Lane,

Lawrenceville, GA 30043; e-mail: rhunter@ggc.edu or Justician@comcast.net; phone: 678-524-6476.

**Santiago Iniguez Flores** is a recent graduate from the University of Tampa. He has conducted research on police and the courts in Mexico, including video documentaries. He currently serves as a law clerk in Mexico City. Contact info: Medanos 198-B Col. Las Águilas, Mexico D.F. 01710; siniguezflores@ut.edu, 0445528954069.

**Nedžad Korajlić** has been an assistant professor and head of the criminalistic department at the Faculty of Criminal Justice Science at the University of Sarajevo since 2002. He graduated from Faculty of Criminal Justice Sciences, University of Skopje, Macedonia. He earned a master's degree in criminalistics at the University of Sarajevo and a PhD in criminology at Faculty of Criminal Justice Science at the University of Sarajevo. He was deputy minister of the Ministry of Interior of the Zenica-Doboj Canton, Bosnia, and Herzegovina. He is a holder of a silver police badge (1996) and golden police badge (1997). His area of research and specialization is criminalistics and the United States of America. In the framework of his scientific and expert education, he has been engaged in numerous projects in the country and abroad. His work is published in Bosnian, Croatian, Serbian, and English. Telephone/office: +387 33 561 276. Contact: nkorajlic@fknbih.edu.

**Peter C. Kratcoski,** PhD, emeritus professor of justice studies, Kent State University, and adjunct professor of justice studies at Kent State University's regional campuses, served as chairperson of the Department of Criminal Justice Studies at Kent State. He completed research and served as a consultant for numerous juvenile justice and social service agencies. He has authored a number of books, written numerous book chapters and articles for professional journals, and presented many papers at national and international professional conferences. He served as editor of *The Journal of Crime and Justice* and is currently North America editor of *Police Practice and Research.* He is the official recorder for the International Police Executive Symposium and has authored a number of articles and book chapters based on the topics that were the focuses of the IPES meetings. He is the coauthor (with Dilip K. Das) of *Meeting the Challenges of Global Terrorism* (2003) and *Police Education and Training in a Global Society* (2007). His current research and writing focus on juvenile justice, school violence, and international policing.

**Anthony P. LaRose,** PhD, is a 2004 Fulbright Scholar who holds a bachelor's degree in political science from the University of Massachusetts at Amherst, a master's in criminal justice, and a PhD in political science (administration of justice and applied policy studies from Washington State University). He has published numerous manuscripts in English and Spanish in the areas of international policing, police corruption, and court processes of the U.S. district courts. His latest manuscript has been accepted for an upcoming volume of the *International Criminal Justice Review*. He is currently an associate professor at the University of Tampa and a research fellow at Statistical Systems, Inc. Contact info: Anthony P. LaRose, Department of Criminology, University of Tampa, 401 W. Kennedy Blvd., Tampa, FL 33606; (813) 257-3807; alarose@ut.edu.

**C. M. Jessica Li** is currently a lecturer at the department of applied social studies, City University of Hong Kong. She received her BA degree in social work and PhD degree from the City University of Hong Kong, and MPhil in criminology from Cambridge University, UK. Before teaching at the City University of Hong Kong, she had been a social worker providing services to at-risk youth, young offenders, and their families for 15 years. Dr. Li has worked on several local and overseas projects related to juvenile offenders, workplace violence prevention, female drug abusers, juvenile theft, community policing, and domestic violence. She is the author and coauthor of 2 books (including *Theft and Delinquency: Juvenile Crime Prevention Theories and Practice*, published in 2008) and over 16 book chapters and journal articles.

**Sean Maddan,** PhD, is an assistant professor in the department of criminology at the University of Tampa. His research areas include criminological theory, statistics, research methods, and the efficacy of sex offender registration and notification laws. Articles by Dr. Maddan have appeared in *Justice Quarterly* and the *Journal of Criminal Justice.*

Most recently, he coauthored the textbook, *Statistics in Criminology and Criminal Justice*. Contact info: Sean Maddan, Department of Criminology, University of Tampa, 401 W. Kennedy Blvd., Tampa, FL 33606; (813) 257-3859; smaddan@ut.edu.

**Otwin Marenin** is a professor in the criminal justice program at Washington State University. He received his BS degree from Northern Arizona University and his MA and PhD degrees (in comparative politics) from UCLA. He has taught at Ahmadu Bello University and the University of Benin in Nigeria and the Universities of Baltimore, California, Colorado, and Alaska-Fairbanks in the United States. His research and publications have focused on policing systems in Native American communities in the United States and communities in Africa, especially Nigeria. More recent, he has done research and written on developments in international policing, police in UN peacekeeping operations, transnational police assistance programs, and efforts to reform the policing systems in failed, transitional, and developing states. Recent publications include *Policing Change, Changing Police: International Perspectives* (editor, 1996), *Transforming the Police in Central and Eastern Europe* (coeditor Marina Caparini, 2002), *Challenges of Policing Democracies* (coeditor Dilip Das, 2004), and *Borders and Security Governance: Managing Borders in a Globalized World* (coeditor Marina Caparini, 2006).

**James E. McCabe** is an assistant professor of criminal justice at Sacred Heart University in Fairfield, Connecticut. He took on this position after completing 21 years of service with the New York City Police Department. In the NYPD, he held numerous command-level assignments, including the commanding officer of labor relations, commanding officer of the training bureau, commanding officer of the police academy, and the commanding officer of the 110th precinct in Elmhurst/Corona, Queens. He was also assigned as the executive officer of the police commissioner's office and the 113th precinct in South Jamaica, Queens. He retired from the NYPD in 2006 with the rank of inspector to assume a new career in academia at Sacred Heart.

Dr. McCabe has a BA in psychology from Queens College, an MA in labor studies from Empire State College, an MA in criminal justice from John Jay College, and a PhD in criminal justice from the CUNY

Graduate Center. He is a graduate of the 189th session of the FBI National Academy and executive programs at Columbia University's Not-for-Profit Management Institute (Police Management Institute) and the JFK School of Government at Harvard University.

His dissertation examined the relationship between drug enforcement and serious crime in Queens, New York City, and he is actively continuing this line of research in the academic community. He has published numerous scholarly articles and book chapters on the subject of police effectiveness and is also active with local police departments in improving their operations. He has lectured around the country to both police and academic audiences about organizational behavior, leadership, supervisory communications, and the impact of police operations on public safety and neighborhood satisfaction with police services.

Dr. McCabe has received numerous awards from civic, academic, and law enforcement agencies. He is the 1999 recipient of the prestigious Arthur Niederhoffer Award for Criminal Justice Research and has been featured in a documentary on policing on the History Channel and in the *New York Times* section on "public lives." He can be reached at mccabej@sacredheart.edu.

**Richard Mears** is currently the executive director of the Maine Institute for Public-Safety Innovation (MIPSI) and an associate professor of justice studies with tenure. Prof. Mears is responsible for grant administration, program development, and training delivery of all MIPSI projects and technical assistance issues. He is a retired deputy chief of police for Brunswick, Maine, with over 20 years of management experience, training, and education at the executive level.

In 1984 Prof. Mears was appointed the director of regional in-service training for 17 law enforcement agencies in the mid-coast Maine area. Those agencies included state, county, and municipal law enforcement services. He has created many new and innovative law enforcement training strategies and is a recipient of the Robert Quinn Award issued by the New England chiefs of police for "outstanding contributions to law enforcement training." Upon his retirement from police service in 1996, he was offered an appointment at the University of Maine at Augusta as a criminal justice faculty member. As a faculty member, he was assigned the task of developing a bachelor's degree program in the administration of justice. Upon the completion of that task, he was assigned to assist in the development of the Maine Community Policing Institute at the University of Maine at Augusta. His academic experience includes the development and teaching of upper level justice studies courses and teaching courses on the statewide educational network.

Prof. Mears has conducted research on a number of law-enforcement-related issues and is considered an expert in police civil liability. He has published a number of articles related to criminal justice practices and has experience in developing subject forums on justice-related topics including antiterrorism issues and mass transportation security. He has delivered training and papers at numerous national and international conferences and for government agencies.

Prof. Mears holds various positions related to justice issues, including chair of the Regional Centers for Public-Safety Innovation (RCPI) Network, 2007–2008, chair of the International Association of Chiefs of Police Section on International Managers of Police Academies and College Training Programs (IMPACT), 2005–2009; and former secretary of the North East Association of Criminal Justice Sciences (NEACJS). He is also a member of the Maine Criminal Justice Commission. He has held a variety of positions at the executive level in social service organizations and nongovernmental organizations. He can be reached at the University of Maine, 46 University Drive, Augusta, Maine 04330; tel. (207) 621-3281, fax (207) 621-3301.

**Eldan Mujanović,** MA in criminal justice, is senior lecturer assistant at the Faculty of Criminal Justice, Criminology and Security Studies, University of Sarajevo. At present, he is a PhD student conducting research in the area of international police cooperation. He is a former police officer who worked in the Criminal Investigation Department. Basic areas of interest are issues of international police cooperation, criminal investigation, money laundering, financial investigations, confiscation of illegally obtained property, juvenile delinquency, and property crime. Contact information: e-mail: emujanovic@fkn.bih.edu, tel: +387 33 56 12 69.

**Chantal Perras** teaches in the criminology department at the University of Montreal. She received her MA degree from the same university. Her research and publications focus on cooperation and partnership among police organizations at both the national and international levels. Recently, she also has done research and written about international trafficking in drugs and on the convergence between antiterrorism and antigang models. Recent publications include "Convergent Models of Police Cooperation in Antiorganized Crime and Antiterrorism Activities" (cowritten with Frédéric Lemieux, George Washington University, 2010), a chapter in *International Police Cooperation: Emerging Issues, Theory and Practice* (editor Frédéric Lemieux, 2010); "Police Cooperation in International Drug Investigations in North America," a chapter in *Urbanization, Policing, and Security: Global Perspective* (editors Gary Cordner, Ann Marie Cordner, and Dilip K. Das, 2010); and "Une Histoire de l'Entrepreneuriat Illicite: Des Ajustements et Des Strategies Innovantes dans les Marchés de la Drogue en Colombie," an article included in *Cahiers de la Sécurité 10,* Oct–Dec 2009.

**Branislav Simonovic** is a full-time professor of criminalistics at the School of Law, the University of Kragujevac. He is a professor of community policing at Police College in Banja Luka (Republika Srpska—Bosnia and Herzegovina) as well. He is engaged in practical community policing initiatives. His primary fields of interest are community policing, strategic planning, some aspects of interrogation in police and court settings, forensic aspects of DNA, etc. He has published more than 60 papers and some books: *Providing and Assessing a Statement in Police and Court* (1997), *Criminalistics Handbook* (2004), and *Community Policing* (2006). In 1991, he was awarded his PhD degree for a thesis on criminal motivation. He likes to play chess. He lives in Kragujevac. His e-mail address is simonov@eunet.rs, or duda@jura.kg.ac.yu.

**André Matheus e Souza** has worked in the Brazilian Ministries of Health and Education, assisting the management of projects and doing research for international negotiations. He has been a policy analyst at the International Council on Security and Development's (ICOS) office in Rio de Janeiro since last year and is now working in its fund-raising efforts and the development of new projects. Souza holds a BA and an MSc in international relations from the University of Brasília, with a focus on International Security. Currently, he studies project management in an MBA program at Getúlio Vargas Foundation.

**Kate Storey-Whyte** is a senior forensic consultant, trainer, and linguist. After completing a PhD degree in modern Irish morphophonology at Monash University, she joined the Speaker Identification Program there, before moving to private practice. She has researched and published extensively in the field of the forensic applications of language and linguistic and acoustic data and has been involved in many high-profile cases, including two royal commissions. In 2008 she was appointed as an expert advisor to the National Policing Improvement Agency, UK, and also completed assessor training for the CRFP (Council for the Registration of Forensic Practitioners).

Dr. Storey-Whyte's casework has made her increasingly aware of the problems facing non-English speakers in criminal investigations and court proceedings and of the need for a far greater appreciation of the role of interpreters—situations that often impinge on the human rights of both suspects and defendants and of victims and witnesses—and is founding chair of the Forensic and Military Linguist, Interpreter and Translator Executive Group. She organizes the annual Forensic Summer School and Workshop at the University of Novi Pazr (Serbia) and is an invited speaker/advisor internationally at forensic science laboratories and police headquarters, security organizations, counterterrorism units, schools, universities, and conferences. She has just produced two online police education courses in best practice in the use of language evidence and in the use of interpreters.

She has particular interests in police and forensic practice; the establishment of forensic systems, protocols, information management, training, and the implementation of forensic programs in conflict, postconflict, postcolonial, emergent, and transitional states; and in the history and theory of forensic science. She is principal of AudioLex Forensic and of the UK/Balkans-based NGO JCAAT Consulting. Her address is Agincourt House, Llangunllo, Knighton LD7 1SU, UK; tel: 01547 550 263 or 0116 263 3253 (+44) fax: 0844 77 44 543; cj@audiolex.co.uk.

**Morgan Gareth Tanafon** is currently a senior pursuing a BA degree in criminology at the University of Tampa. Morgan is active in student government and holds the positions of junior congressman, vice president of finance, and treasurer. He was involved in writing a new student government constitution and will compete in the National Moot Court competition finals in 2010. His research has also included investigating the impact of social science on the decisions of the Supreme Court of Mexico. Contact info: Morgan Tanafon, Writing Center, University of Tampa, 401 W. Kennedy Blvd., Tampa, FL 33606; (813) 253-3333; mtanafon@ut.edu.

**Dominique Wisler,** PhD, has been trained at universities in Switzerland, Germany, and the United States. A full-time consultant, founder, and codirector of a Swiss-based nongovernmental organization (coginta.org) dedicated to police reforms, he has managed, evaluated, or designed police and Ministry of Interior restructuring programs in transitional countries, including Sudan, Iraq, Turkey, Mozambique, Haiti, Bosnia and Herzegovina, and the Democratic Republic of Congo. He is a standing member of security sector reform expert groups of the United Nations and the Swiss Foreign Office.

A former professor in political sociology at the University of Geneva, Dr. Wisler has published 9 books and over 50 peer-reviewed academic articles on civilian oversight, community policing, and protest policing, among others. His latest book is a coedited volume on comparative community policing with case studies in Africa, Asia, Europe, and the Americas (CRC Press, London, 2009). He is a member of advisory committees of academic associations (South Asia Association of Criminology), academic journals (*Police Practice and Research*), and editor-in-chief of a working paper series for the International Police Executive Symposium. Tel. +41 (0)22 784 68 80; e-mail: wisler@coginta.org. Visit the Justice and Police Reform Forum at www.jprforum.ning.com.

# 1

# Interview With Commissioner Mal Hyde

## South Australia's Long-Serving, Reformist Police Commissioner

INTERVIEWED BY DAVID BAKER

**Contents**



**Background**

White settlement of South Australia commenced in 1836. It was destined for free British settlers in order to avoid the stigma of the convict origins of the other colonies and also that civil liberties and religious tolerance could flourish. Although idealistically such a colony of respectable settlers, based on the principles of systematic colonization, was envisaged without the need for an organized police force, the South Australian Police (SAPOL) was established in 1838 to provide order to the fledgling colony. Unlike in the other states of Australia, SAPOL has always been centrally administered, although its mandate encompasses vast and diverse geography.

Today, the jurisdiction extends for just over one million square kilometers ranging from the cosmopolitan capital city of Adelaide to remote mining and desert regions. The 170 years of continuous existence and service make SAPOL one of the oldest police agencies in the world. Often viewed by those in the eastern seaboard states as a relatively quiet state, South Australia today has been subjected to the spectrum of crime from drug trafficking to recent bikie (outlaw motorcycle gang) violence.

South Australia is one of the six states within Australia, each with its own autonomous police organization. It has a population of almost 1.6 million people (less than 10% of Australia's population) and is policed by approximately 4,500 sworn police officers supported by 1,150 auxiliary staff. SAPOL has an annual budget of approximately $A550 million.

In April 2009, Mal Hyde had his contract renewed for a further 3 years as commissioner of the South Australian Police. Mal was originally appointed to the state's prime policing office in February 1997. During his 12 years to date (in 2009) as commissioner, he was credited with maintaining stability and integrity within SAPOL and its community dealings and fostering a strong customer orientation and service philosophy.

Major reforms have been implemented during Commissioner Hyde's tenure. Philosophical, structural, and operational changes have drastically transformed policing and its relationship with the community. These changes are discussed in this interview. When the interview took place in 2009, South Australia had recorded its lowest levels of crime since 1996, with a 7.5% reduction in the first 4 months of 2009.

Mal Hyde is a proud policeman who was raised in a distinguished police family. His father was a police officer who mainly worked in rural areas where the police house adjoined the police station. A week prior to his 17th birthday in 1967, Mal joined the Victoria Police under the cadet training system. He undertook various roles as detective, district patrol officer, and superintendent of an inner city division. He worked his way through the ranks to become a deputy commissioner in the Victoria Police in 1993. As deputy commissioner, he had a leading role in organizational restructuring, flattening management levels, and maximizing resources available for operational policing, while also overseeing personnel and industrial issues. He had a strong anticorruption profile in Victoria and worked closely with three Victorian chief commissioners.

In February 1997, he was appointed the 20th commissioner of SAPOL. He was the initial chair of the board of management of the Australian High Tech Crime Center that fostered police relationships and assisted high-tech crime management by referrals, training, intelligence, target development, and investigations. Mal is a highly decorated police leader: In 2004, he was awarded the Australian Police Medal and in 2008 the Order of Australia for service to policing and law enforcement, especially for work in the fields of developing improved service delivery methods, the detection and prevention of illicit drug use and electronic crime, and contributions to national law enforcement policies. He has bachelor of law (honors) and master of business administration degrees; he describes the latter study as "the best education I ever received."

### The Interview

This interview was conducted on May 7, 2009, in the office of Commissioner Hyde at SAPOL headquarters, located in Adelaide's central business district. Commissioner Hyde openly and enthusiastically talked about SAPOL and his reforming role within the organization. The interview was digitally recorded and transcribed.

*DB:* Tell me about your early police career and how you progressed through the ranks with Victoria Police.

*MH:* I have always had a passion for policing in the sense of really believing in the essential value of policing because I grew up in a police family. I grew up living on police stations. I can't remember any time where I wasn't exposed in some way to policing. My father was a police officer in Victoria and he tended to work in country areas where we lived in the police house alongside the police station. I grew up in the context of a police family and a police life and so I always had this very strong interest in policing and I never, never really contemplated doing anything different. When the opportunity arose, I joined the cadet system in Victoria. That state had a program in place which took young people in and exposed them to policing and then at a certain stage they went into mainstream training.

I joined the police cadets on February 7 and my birthday is February 13, so I was 16 but really almost 17 when I went into the cadets. I graduated as a normal recruit in Victoria at 18½. I think 18½ is much too young to be an effective police officer and we wouldn't be doing that sort of thing today and that is why there is a tendency toward more mature people with life experience. In those days it was almost full employment, so they wanted to get young people into the organization; people joined for life and so all of those things happened.

Not long after I graduated, I really immersed myself in the operational side of policing. I also had an interest in further study. I had left schooling at year 11 and I wanted to study law, so I spent some time getting my year 12 qualification to be admitted into studying law. I wasn't intending to leave policing but I just saw a law degree as an important part of being a better police officer and knowing more about the law. I spent some time doing law part-time.

I had been a constable at South Melbourne (inner suburb of Melbourne) in the 60s and I returned in the 70s as a sergeant. I was invited to be part of a fledgling prosecutions division. Senior officers Kel Glare and Bill Horman, whom you would know, were inspectors at the time and they had been given a task of setting up a prosecutions division. I became involved with a few other officers who had law degrees doing prosecuting work, which I really enjoyed. I continued doing my studies but I also kept a police career going with promotional exams. I ended up having a fair bit of involvement in prosecuting. I was also interested in being a detective, but this tended to take my career off as a prosecutor because I was studying law. I was also interested in reform and innovation, so I started doing some work in that field and I kept getting projects to do. I would do one and I suppose I did reasonably well, so the way that they reward you for doing a bad job well is that they give you another difficult job.

Other opportunities emerged—for example, in the 80s the commissioner at the time wanted to have people with more business qualifications. He sent me off to Melbourne Business School to do an MBA and I must say that was probably the best education that I ever received because that enabled me to synthesize corporate management arrangements and I have used a lot of that quite extensively. Just the thinking and the understanding as I have moved forward have been a terrific education in going forward.

*DB:* What did you learn from working with senior police like Victorian Chief Commissioners Miller, Glare, and Comrie?[1]

*MH:* I watch people and I think about what they are doing and why and I had an interest in continuing education so I spent time reading articles, looking at things, reading biographies, so I am a bit of a watcher in a sense. I think it is important that you don't become static and that you learn from others and you learn about your environment as you move forward. So there are things that I saw with "Mick" Miller, which I found over time to be very solid and you could use those even in a more modern context. The fundamental approaches that he took to some issues were really very insightful, very reliable sort of approaches, so they go in the back of your mind. Like a lot of things in life, you know things don't become readily apparent immediately but when you are in the right set of circumstances or situation then you draw upon what you have seen with people.

I would have to say one of the big advantages in life is to have people who have trust and confidence in you to give you opportunities, and Kel Glare and Neil Comrie were two instrumental people in my career because they had that trust and confidence in me and gave me things to do. They were quite instrumental in helping me to go forward in the organization. I probably learned much from "Mick" Miller, even though I wasn't directly involved with him, by just observing even from afar some of the really good lessons that came from him. A very big intellect, he was quite a deep thinker and he had a persona around him which gained a lot of respect. He was well regarded and respected in the community, not only within policing but within the community as well.

*DB:* Why did you move to South Australia in February 1997?

*MH:* February '97. I had always had a great deal of interest in South Australia. I always had a high regard for the South Australian Police and the South Australian community. It's a place where people really do want to do well and have pride. Back in the '60s as a cadet, when I spent a couple of weeks in the South Australian Academy at Fort Largs,[2]

I was really struck by the pride people had and who they were and what they were doing. When an opportunity arose while I was a deputy commissioner in Victoria, I applied for the commissioner's position in SA and was fortunate enough to be able to come over here.

*DB:* What would you see as the highlight of your policing career to date?

*MH:* First, when you do this sort of job, you don't actually sit back and think about what you might or might not have achieved, because there is so much to do in front of you that when you do things you tend to then push them behind you and you are focusing on the things that need to be done. Second, so much happens that it is very hard to narrow it down to one. But probably in terms of highlights, well, obviously, having a position like I have is a highlight. It's the pinnacle of a police career.

The thing about not only having the position is what you can also do with the position and here I was fortunate enough to be able to start a reform program which we have been able to continue through for more than a decade now. It has been a very significant reform program. Most major reform that occurs within policing has an external stimulus to give it the leverage that it needs—a royal commission or a public inquiry or something of that nature. What we did here was to be able to make those sorts of fundamental major changes without having the leverage and being really given the mandate to do it. The organization had been a little bit static and hadn't kept up to date, so the government of the day actually wanted it to be modernized and reformed.

So, I had a mandate to do that. There wasn't any interference in terms of what should be done. Sometimes with policing, politicians get nervous about what's being done and that nervousness translates into some sort of "don't do it" type of arrangement. On the one hand, they want police to reform but on the other hand they don't like the impact, which often comes from the workforce creating pressure on them through the community, so there is a bit of a tension there. Now that didn't happen. We had the opportunity to make these major changes and they have carried through, so if there is any highlight it was really being able to be a part of doing all that because I had some wonderful people who were really willing to travel the same road over time.

*DB:* What are the most important changes that you have experienced in your policing career—things like philosophy, organizational structure, policies, and programs? What would you see as significant changes?

*MH:* There have been enormous changes in policing. Policing is a profession where some things change and some things remain the same. The dynamics of policing, the problem of policing, the art of policing, what policing is all about don't change because it's a mixture of the behavior of people (its innate human behavior that might vary because of different cultures) and then also the way authority interplays with that behavior. That's the essence of what policing is about; now that doesn't change, it's the same today as it was 20 years ago and 30 years ago. The detail changes—we get more drugs or less drugs or more mental impairment or less mental impairment—the detail does change but the actual dynamics of policing doesn't. What has changed enormously is the way police go about doing their job and it's far more professional, it's far more accountable, it's far more proactive about trying to problem solve and prevent rather than simply reacting to the issue.

It's like chalk and cheese in terms of professionalism. I have just come from a regular meeting of a local service area (LSA), a geographic area. These LSAs have tactical coordination groups where police leaders are looking at their problems and working on solutions to fix them and reflecting on how they were operating. Comparing 20 years ago in policing, such groupings never existed, so there is far more professional accountability for delivering the right sort of service to the community today than there was previously. There have been enormous changes within communities (illicit drug use was nowhere near the problem 20 years ago). Technology, communications—all those things have drastically transformed policing.

*DB:* If you could make a judgment, do you think policing has improved or declined?

*MH:* I have got absolutely no doubt [that it has improved]. There are different styles of policing. One style of policing is simply a law enforcement model, a traditional model which takes the rule of law and enforces that rule of law in the community. It's more reactive in terms of managing the rule of law. Another model is more about service: Why do police exist? What sort of service do they provide to the community? I am squarely an advocate of that model.

*DB:* I have gained that impression.

*MH:* The rule of law is an important part of policing but it's not the only part. My view is that police are more than law enforcers. Ultimately, I take the view that police are here to provide a service to the community at the broad level. It's the measure of safety and security that the community needs in order to function as a community. That is why we are there and a rule of law is part of that safety and security but policing is more than that. We are like a platform; people say, "Oh, police are the thin blue line between criminals and the community." That is true. However, a better way of looking at it is that the community stands on the police's shoulders—that the police should be there underneath the community supporting the community in what they do. If you want a metaphor, it is better to say the police hold the community on their shoulders rather than the thin blue line type of concept.

When you take that approach, the marketing discipline is important. I don't mean marketing in the sense of selling; I mean marketing in the sense of saying you have customers and you deliver a service to customers and that service to customers needs to be based on what they need—not necessarily on what they want, but on what they need. (This concept was really reinforced through my business administration study as I was very impressed by the marketing discipline.)

As a starting point for understanding what you are doing, you are going to stand a better chance of getting the actual service delivery right. I used that concept when we were setting up a program for change here. We took the community as our customer and we said, "Well, what do we need to do in terms of satisfying our community's needs?" We established a change program on that basis and that is what we have been doing for more than a decade: building and building and building so that when you look at that sort of model and you compare it to the service that police might have been giving 20, 30 years ago under a law enforcement type of model, [they are] "chalk and cheese."

Police in Australia have always operated on the English model, which says that the police and the community are one in a sense. As a concept, we have been influenced by that model, so there always has been a reasonably close connection between the policing style and the community. In smaller communities, the police will know what is happening in those communities; police are both reactive but also have proactive elements because they know where the problems are and who the problem people are.

*DB:* Is policing more difficult today than in the past?

*MH:* No, I don't think so. I think one of the good things of our system is that senior police started on the bottom, so they should understand the business of policing, the dynamics of policing. It's very important to understand the business of policing so that, as you go up to more senior levels, you are going to make, hopefully, the right decisions. I think that the young people today who are on the street have a far more complex service delivery environment than we ever had, and to that extent, it is more difficult today than it used to be.

However, on the other side, the new police grow up with that type of new-age policing environment, so they don't know anything different. This is just the environment that they have got to deal with; it's a far more accountable and challenging environment than it was decades ago. There is absolutely no doubt about that. They operate in a far more challenging and accountable environment, but so too do the senior managers in the organization, who work in the same environment. We want managers in the organization who are in tune with what is happening so that they can initiate the right action to get the right results. Senior managers should not be far removed from their service delivery; we hold them to account for service delivery and we have a very strict accountability model which drives service. Our senior people are really closely connected with the workforce. It's a challenging environment for all of them and I wouldn't say that any part has a more or less difficult job than the others. You never know what's coming next. You try to anticipate and you get much of it right, but you can't get 100% of it.

*DB:* You have touched already on your personal policing philosophy. Have your ideas about policing changed over the years?

*MH:* Yes, to some extent they have because, when you are a junior person in the organization, you see that your future or your immediate problems are really in front of your face. It's not until you go up to more senior levels that you start to see things from a more strategic, longer term and broader perspective. Your understanding of things does change over time and therefore your perspectives of it change.

*DB:* As commissioner, how do you see your relationships with government and political groups?

*MH:* You need to understand the key elements to success. I'm very big on this, that almost every problem or situation can be broken down to find the essence of what it is you need to do to be successful. We are very big here on setting future directions and other strategies, to try to make sure that the fundamentals are right. We work on those key essential things to success. The commissioner's job includes the management of a range of stakeholders and you need to understand the fundamentals in terms of how you should successfully handle those. The media is a key area that you need to manage and you need to handle that in a way which achieves success in terms of how it reflects on the organization and how you communicate with the community. Your relationship with the government and other politicians needs to be on a sound basis as well to be successful.

Some years ago, fortuitously, I researched the relationship between the chief commissioner of Victoria and the government. I studied the fundamentals of police–government relations: its derivation and dimensions and why and how they operated. If you go back to the fundamentals of that relationship and why it is there in our sort of society and if you stick to the fundamentals, you manage relationships in a sense of knowing individuals have ways of thinking about things. I am concerned about how, in some jurisdictions (and I won't name them), police leaders are becoming more political in the way they are managing the relationship with governments of the day. That is really fraught with danger and can cause them trouble.

I believe that you should have a professional working relationship with the government of the day and the minister to whom you report. There needs to be a clear understanding of where the boundaries are and why it is important for police to have a measure of independence because that actually works to the advantage of both sides at the end of the day. It's an advantage for the government of the day to be able to say, "Well, that is an operational matter that the commissioner should make a decision about." They don't become involved and equally the police commissioner should recognize what is legitimately of interest to government. I've had no political involvement or engagement or influence at any time.

*DB:* How would you describe your relationship with the police union or association?[3]

*MH:* They are a key stakeholder and you need to have a professional working relationship with the police association, so that should be worked on. This is not a new phenomenon; this is a fundamental thing that needs to be worked on. I always treat the police association with respect, having regard for the role it plays. Its role is different from your role, so don't expect it to behave in the same way or think the same way as you do about a problem. I try to gain a "win–win" outcome.

If you avoid having a "win–loss" attitude to working with the association, you achieve better outcomes. You will get better cooperation from the association if it can see that you're genuine in trying to obtain outcomes that suit all parties.

Sometimes you can't compromise and that is just the nature of things. Often you and the association can compromise and you can achieve an outcome which suits both parties. It's a very important part of the working relationship because 98 or 99% of your police staff will be members of the police association. It is a foolish approach to be at loggerheads with them. If you can avoid it, you should and you should work on avoiding it.

*DB:* How significant are crime prevention programs and techniques in the fight against crime?

*MH:* Okay, now sometimes people think that crime prevention is somewhat different from what policing is actually about in dealing with crime. I don't see it that way. I see our role as reducing the level of crime within the community; whether you use techniques which could be regarded as crime prevention or techniques which could be regarded as police techniques, I don't see the difference. I think our task is about reducing the level of crime in the community, making the community safer, making the community feel safer. Feeling safer is sometimes more important than actually being safer and the techniques that policing has been employing have been quite successful around mainly targeting problems, targeting patterns of crime, targeting hotspots, targeting times of crimes and types of crime and targeting repeat offenders. The reality of life is that certain people commit a crime in the community and they are largely repeat offenders. Certain ones of those repeat offenders commit more of your crime, so it is not rocket science to actually target those people; if you can deter or apprehend them and disable them in terms of committing crime, you are going to be more successful.

We have been pushing a problem-solving approach; we take the view that the best philosophy underpinning police operations should be about problem solving—that we should be identifying and understanding problems and introducing the right sort of measures to deal with them. Now, under that, there is no difference between what might be seen as more traditional policing and what might be seen as more traditionally in the crime prevention category. I see it all together. We are here trying to push forward what has worked well in the past that we need to keep doing, but if we don't keep finding new ways of reducing crime, we will be like others in the past, standing still and the world will go past us. So it's a continuous improvement process and, in the process of doing that, we are pushing more into mainstream crime prevention models. They might be on a continuum, but it is all part of the same approach.

*DB:* How are crime rates in South Australia?

*MH:* Going extremely well! We are down 7.5% this year. People are talking about the global financial crisis and that feeds into pressure on crime rates going up. South Australia hasn't seen that yet. We haven't felt the impacts yet of the global financial crisis in a way which could push into that. I think the criminologists are quite divided on whether economic changes do feed into increases or reductions in crime; so, as a phenomenon, the jury is still out in terms of how that might actually work.

We have had reductions of crime over a number of years. There is a bit of a "J" curve in introducing major change. It doesn't just flick in immediately; sometimes it takes a bit of time for it to bite and sometimes it actually gets a little worse before it bites. If you take that base year 2000 [a few years after introducing changes], break-ins, for example, were 38,000 in that year; last financial year, we had 19,000, so its 50% less. Two thousand nine will probably come in at around 16,000, so the reductions are greater than 50%. If you think about crimes that affect the community, house break-ins are one of those because you know people's houses are their castle and there's a sanctity about them, which, if disturbed, means not only loss of property but also their feelings of well being.

We have had significant reductions, but crime is just part of it. When you look at why police are here and what we do, crime is part of it, of course. Road safety is another part, public order is another, but we also manage major events and we do a number of other functions. You have got to manage a range of things.

*DB:* What are some of the biggest challenges facing the police organization?

*MH:* All things don't work perfectly, that's a truism. Part of policing is to be flexible. You need to be flexible in structures and you need to be flexible in approaches because there is a dynamic about policing which is not 100% predictable. In terms of satisfying the needs of the community, delivering a service, you need to have a little flexibility about you, and you need to develop people who are flexible in their approach. Starting from constables on the street through to leaders and managers, one needs to be adaptive to be successful.

You start with a plan. We introduced "Future Directions Strategies,"[4] a broad road map, which we use for 3 to 4 years, and we renew [and] adjust on the way forward. The organization finds that things that worked well yesterday don't necessarily work well today, so we are constantly making changes. The biggest achievement of any leader or manager is to change the way people think, because ultimately that is what leadership is about. If you can change the thinking into the direction that you want to go as an organization, you can overcome all sorts of challenges. So, the first challenge is to make sure that you have a vision, a direction, people who understand and who are thinking about it the way you want them to think about it. It is a constant process because you have new people coming into the organization—people with different responsibilities—and they are moving around. The greatest challenge is to get people thinking the way that is necessary to deliver the best service to the community.

The more immediate challenges are quite broad and, in fact, you can pick a shopping list of them. Operational challenges here will be reflected in other places. The current topical debate is around organized crime and bikies.

South Australia is introducing a raft of legislative changes and we have made organizational changes and are making more. We have prepared a serious organized crime strategy to channel efforts in the right place and there has been a bit of creative thinking around it.

The challenge around the bikies is really twofold. The first is that they commit serious crime and much of it is organized type of crime, so you have to deal with that. There are other organized crime groups as well, but the bikies have a public face, which most organized criminals don't have and which is about their persona: how they use violence, how they dress, how they behave, and how they like to be above the law. There is a great deal of public concern that may not necessarily match the serious crime that they are committing. And the fact that there is serious concern about their behavior is an issue in itself that police have to deal with. In terms of bikies, we actually don't have a major problem here in the sense that it exceeds the problem in other states and territories. When you count the number of bikies, South Australia only has about 6% of the national figure and we have 8% of the population of Australia, so we are actually underrepresented in bikies.

Indigenous offending—here is a major problem. They are grossly overrepresented in the crime figures and the concern about that is that the social conditions that are producing that sort of outcome will continue. If we don't make changes, we will continue to have a major crime problem. Not only are indigenous people overrepresented as offenders, they are over-represented as victims as well, so the indigenous community stands as a very challenging social problem to fix. We have a lot of mental impairment in the community that stems partly from the de-institutionalization policies that we have had over the last few decades, putting mentally ill persons back into the community. Drug and alcohol abuse in the community is feeding into the problem.

A lot of policing is around mental impairment, the haves and have-nots, the polarization between the rich and the poor. The polarization is there and becoming more distinct and pronounced and therefore feeding in as a crime problem. The organizational challenges need to be properly directed, properly focused, correct structures in place, a continuous improvement model, the right philosophies like problem solving and customer orientation, recruiting the appropriate people, developing the model, and making sure the police are well led and disciplined.

*DB:* Is there anything about policing that is easy?

*MH:* No, there isn't, and it is a challenging job, but the rewards come from doing a difficult job. It is like anything in life. The things that are difficult to do have the greatest rewards because you get a great deal of satisfaction from doing that. There is the satisfaction of both helping people in need and of providing a service that is really fundamental to the well-being of the community. However, we have to deal with criminals and people who are quite dysfunctional. Police deal with it within a justice system which, in everyone's mind, doesn't always produce the results it should.

*DB:* You mentioned the reform process earlier. Could you elaborate on that?

*MH:* We changed the whole lot; we changed everything, including the philosophy. We adopted the seven "S" model [possibly the Boston Consulting Group model]. You can conceive an organization in terms of seven Ss and the first one is what you are trying to achieve as an organization, what they call a superordinate goal. That is where you must start.

You have another six sets of Ss which relate to how you construct the process of achieving that goal and to the strategy of the organization, structure, the staffing, the skills, the style, and so on. We have changed the whole lot in terms of that. When I was an assistant commissioner in Victoria, I was working on some reform projects and was responsible for policy and research. I analyzed what the structure of policing was all about in my mind. It was about customer orientation, what our role is and how should we do it and all of those things. I constructed a model for me which made sense of all the things that we had to do in South Australia and that is what we used.

*DB:* Where do you go for theory and research about policing?

*MH:* We look at what others do, at what works, and what doesn't work. I am not in favor of doing things that don't work. We take a concept and say, "All right, is that actually going to work?" and we look and analyze it. We hardly used a consultant in all SAPOL reform; we used internal people.

First, they do know the business better and if they are properly directed on what they should be looking at and how they should look at it, then they are going to really understand it a lot better and give you better answers. I never let an area review themselves though. I always use an externality when we look at something. Not that I don't think people are fair in what they do, it is just that mentally they will have a view of the situation which is just mutually reinforcing. You need to get somebody outside with a better understanding and more objectivity.

Second, the organization is actually the one that is going to implement changes; they have to make it work. We have always wanted things here that are going to work, so we take a concept, look at it, and make sure it is actually going to work. That doesn't mean we operated within a comfort zone; we didn't, I can tell you. We were beyond our comfort zone nearly all the time, but we had a measure of confidence that we had analyzed and looked at something enough to know where and how it was going to work. If it needed tweaking, we could tweak it.

*DB:* Is outside expertise utilized?

*MH:* We brought people in from other police services. One of the impediments to success is success. If you do something well, you think, "Well, this is the way you do it," and you keep trying to do it that way. But if the world changes, then you will actually fail, so you have got to be careful of success in going forward. So what I say to police here is that if you think you are the best in the world, you are actually starting to go backward because you are closing your mind off to the way you should see things.

From the start we tried to introduce an externality; we wanted people to be outward looking. First, for a number of years, we hosted international conferences here and we had five or six hundred people come to these international conferences. They worked really well; I could send two or three hundred of my staff to these conferences, whereas if I were sending them interstate or overseas I could only send one or two. Cost-wise, I could expose more people.

Second, we have had exchange programs with other police services; the one with Kent in England is a classic. We have had this program for 10 years. We bring an officer from there to here and we send one over there, not necessarily at the same time. They get sworn in, they get put into a position they actually have to manage, they are there for 3 months, and they wear the uniform of the police service of the exchange. They are at chief inspector or superintendent level. The officer, whom we bring here, every day will rub off on other staff, the people around—Like throwing a stone in a pond, the ripples go out. We tried to create more of an outward looking approach to things and to really get people seeing things in a different way.

Because of this relationship with Kent, now we do this with New Zealand and Singapore (we don't actually have the exchange model with Singapore). I have done it with Royal Canadian Mounted Police and Ontario and so on. In the relationship we developed with Kent, we supported each other. We wanted to look closely at our intelligence model that we had in place, so an officer from Kent came out and spent time looking at it, an expert from intelligence to have a look at it. Also, when we were reviewing our recruit training, we got an officer from Kent to come out and examine recruit training. It is not as if we wouldn't get outsiders looking into the organization; rather, it is just that with the right sort of clear thinking, you should be able to generate many things within the organization as well.

*DB:* To what extent have transnational and global issues, such as human rights demands and terrorism, affected police thinking in South Australia?

*MH:* We need to be in tune with what is happening in the community and the community is affected by what is happening not only nationally, but internationally as well. So the terrorism threat, for example, meant that we had to put measures into place here so that we were prepared and had an increased capability. I had to change the structure of the organization; I have an assistant commissioner now whose major responsibility is taking care of that portfolio. We have had to put resources into investigative capabilities and dealing with threats of terrorism; we have had to put into place plans and arrangements.

We need to understand what is happening and, if there are changes in human rights issues, then we have to reflect that as well in the organization. We are influenced by, anticipate, and are sensitive to the signals that are coming and try to understand those signals in order to prepare. You don't always get it right because the signals are sometimes a bit too soft and you don't actually see them before you should have made a change.

*DB:* Criminologists use the term "democratic policing." Would you like to comment?

*MH:* Policing is not democratic in the sense that the police commissioner is elected and it is not a popularity vote. It's more about doing what is right and being respected for it. If you are popular in the process, then that is a bonus. Whether you are a constable or a commissioner, you can't chase popularity in terms of what you do, so from that democratic point of view it doesn't work.

"Democratic" in the sense of reflecting the community's aspirations is probably more of what you are talking about. If you take it in a way that I suggested and if you cater to the community's needs and provide that platform under which the community can operate, that's the first dimension. The other dimension is that police are at the front end of social tensions, so whatever is happening in that community in a socially tense way tends to be where police are. If it's protests on the street, if it's concerns about bikies, if it's concerns about migrants or if it's whatever—where those social tensions are, you generally find police are there because it is just the nature of the job.

*DB:* What do you see as the likely future developments in policing?

*MH:* People will always be people, so there is that dynamic of policing that won't change and there is an increased volatility in the community and it is probably a mix of things, you know—particularly mental illness, particularly drugs. You will find more highly volatile incidents so that the crime might reduce, but what I don't see reductions in highly volatile incidents that occur, of people getting killed or seriously injured. That could be a real, continuing problem in terms of that dynamic of people. In terms of the delivery of service, we are probably going to get into more technology and there is going to be a much greater sophistication in the use of technology to enable us to do our job better.

Now, that can only go so far because you still need to be in contact with the community, you need to be specialists but you can't forget being generalists and that is what they did in England. They had this heavy focus on crime because they believed that would best serve the community. In the process in England, they lost contact with the community and in the last few years they are putting back reassurance policing, neighborhood policing, because they are trying to get in contact with the community again. When we looked at England over 10 years ago, we said, "No, we are not going to do that." While you need to get more sophisticated on one end, you need to keep your connections going on the other. Technology is going to play a big part of where we go in the future. I believe in being a watcher, being a studier and looking at things and then practicing to see how they work and how they don't work. In the process, you work out what suits you best and in many cases it's an individual thing; at the end of the day, what works for you won't necessarily work for someone else.

*DB:* Are there any other observations about the commissioner's role that you would like to make?

*MH:* A lot of your job is around problem solving and it seems in the organization that problems keep percolating up to the top. And sometimes you say to yourself, "I wish you guys would fix these problems instead of walking in my door all the time with your problems." But over time, I have just come to appreciate that that is the nature of the job; that's the nature of the way organizations work and people need somebody who can be more definitive in solving problems.

The other thing that has intrigued me, and I have felt a bit of frustration about this, is that there are strategic changes that you need to put into place, but people think incrementally. So officers will come to you with continuous improvement, the "how to make a better mouse trap" type of approach. They can push the boundaries on that because they are thinking incrementally. People don't necessarily think in a discontinuous way—that is, changing something completely and saying this is no longer going to be the paradigm, that there is a lack of continuity between what happened in the past and what you need to do in the future. I find that people don't do that. It is left to the commissioner to actually say that the officer is bringing an incremental change, when we need to completely change our view about how this is done. Very, very rarely is a completely new paradigm advocated. Human nature doesn't necessarily think like that. Police probably don't feel as though they have the authority or the mandate to think like that as well—that is, think outside the square. The commissioner often has to really create the situation of thinking outside the square and do something in a more strategic and different way.

*DB:* Would you like to add any final remarks?

*MH:* In a service model like that of SAPOL, you are saying the community has a stake in what you are actually doing, but the community is actually a part of the solution as well. The service model says that the community needs are to have less crime; they need a safe and secure environment. If they are going to have less crime, how do you make less crime? You need a problem-oriented approach. The problems occur in the community, so if you don't engage the community in problem solving, you are actually not going to reduce crime; therefore, you are not going to satisfy the community needs. The community needs certainty and a structure and a security in their environment, so you don't throw out the rule of law, police being law enforcers.

We are getting good results in South Australia. When we started, police were not regarded very highly by the government or the public sector. Now police are actually held up as a model and I think that is a little bit remarkable.

## Summary

Commissioner Hyde is a vehement advocate of the police providing customer orientation and focus through an expansive service delivery model. The ongoing reform process has been extensive and the commissioner highlights evidence of its workability and successes. Despite 12 years at the helm of SAPOL, he remains enthusiastic about his philosophy of policing and his role as commissioner; he was proud to have his contract renewed for a further 3 years and ready to meet the challenges ahead.

## Endnotes

1. Chief Commissioners Sinclair Imrie ("Mick") Miller (1971–1987), Kel Glare (1987–1992), and Neil Comrie (1993–2001) held that position in the following years. It is an interesting and novel fact that Victoria has a chief commissioner, whereas the other five states of Australia have a commissioner. This unusual nomenclature stems historically from the formation of the Victoria Police in 1853 as an amalgamation of the seven small police forces that operated prior to Victoria's constitutional separation from New South Wales.
2. In April 2009, the South Australian premier revealed the design plans for a new, technologically advanced $59 million police academy at Fort Largs.
3. The police profession throughout Australia is heavily unionized; approximately 96% of sworn police officers belong to their relevant state association or union.
4. See the "Future Directions Strategy 2007–2010" at the SAPOL Web site (www.sapolice.sa.gov.au/sapol/about_us/publications.jsp>).

# 2

# Interview With Mag. Maximilian Edelbacher (Ret.), Federal Police of Austria

## INTERVIEWED BY PETER C. KRATCOSKI

**Contents**



**Background**

Maximilian Edelbacher studied law at the University of Vienna, completed a traineeship at the courts as a candidate for attorney, and became a legal expert in the Bundespolizeidirektion, the headquarters of the Austrian Federal Police, in 1972. From 1976 to 1986 he was an expert for burglary, forgery, and prostitution in the Viennese Major Crime Bureau. In 1986 he became head of the homicide squad and was chosen chief of the Major Crime Bureau in 1988. He has also been involved in leadership education of the Federal Police of Austria and the training of criminal investigators and executives.

Edelbacher served as a teacher for the Middle European Police Academy and as a lecturer at the University of Vienna's School of Economics and Business Administration. He is a member of the

Academy of Criminal Justice Sciences (United States) and of the International Association of Financial Crime Investigators. He was a consultant to the United Nations, has written numerous book chapters and articles, and has engaged in collaborative research and writing on community policing and comparative juvenile justice. His books include *Viennese Criminal Chronicle,* in the Applied Criminalistics Series (three volumes), *History of Insurance Fraud in Austria,* and *Organized Crime in Europe.*

**The Interview**

*Personal Background*

*PCK:* Max, please explain in some detail why you became a police officer. Be as personal as you want. For example, were there experiences in your childhood that had an influence on your decision?

*ME:* As a young man, it was not my wish to become a police officer at all. I wanted to become a teacher. Because of family circumstances, I had to work while I was pursuing my education. I had to drop my wish to become a teacher and studied law instead. That was easier to combine with work. When I had finished my studies, military service, and justice service and was working in a financial institution, a friend of mine, whom I have known from our studies, advised me to get a job with the police. In the '70s this was a very well paid opportunity for a young legal advisor, and I moved.

*PCK:* Please explain how your formal education had an effect on your career choice. As you progressed through your career, did you ever have doubts about your career choice? Were there times that you thought about quitting and going into some other type of work?

*ME:* In the 70s there was an advantage to having studied law if you wanted to work in the police force. You could start as a legal advisor and did not have to start as a street cop and work your way up the ladder. Of course, this could create some difficulties. The street cops watched the legal advisors very carefully. They wanted to know that you showed a realistic sense of what the job was all about, whether you could put the book knowledge into practice, and, most important, if they could count on you. It was a hard time to learn about the real life of the cop on the street, to survive and be respected. I was lucky to find willing and experienced officers who accepted my will to learn and to improve; otherwise, I would probably have failed.

Very soon, in my second year, I had an identity crisis. As a young legal advisor you had to deal mainly with administrative law cases. This was not really my main interest. I preferred being confronted with criminal cases. Fortunately, I had the opportunity to work with experienced investigators on criminal cases. I learned so much from them. The experience was tremendous and I never had any more doubts about my career choice.

*Work Experiences*

*PCK:* What were some of the major high points of your career—for example, promotions, solving important cases, being recognized for leadership, having responsibility to see some new policy or organizational plan implemented?

*ME:* Starting as a young legal advisor, my first promotion was the move from a district position to the central unit, the Major Crime Bureau. As a legal advisor, you are regularly promoted: You start with a uniform with two golden stars, are promoted to three stars, and so on. The career is *Kommissär, Oberkommissär, Rat,* and *Oberrat* and you can become a *Hofrat* or *Polizeipräsident.* I became a *Hofrat.* Becoming the chief of the Major Crime Bureau meant I was number six in the Austrian Police organization. But this promotion does not necessarily mean that you are really good and experienced.

The real success only can be measured by solving important, spectacular crime cases. If you succeed in solving such crime cases, then you will be respected. Such work was the basis for my career. I became a good investigator; my field of expertise especially was interrogation. In 1986 I became deputy chief and chief of the homicide squad team. After Chief Dr. Matthaus Tuschi retired in 1988, I became chief.

Being responsible as a leader, my duties changed completely. This was an enormous challenge. When I became chief, I immediately was confronted with a whole bunch of administrative problems. In the beginning, I was not trained and did not have the experience to solve these problems. I had to learn very fast what it means to be a leader. Many of my decisions were based on gut feelings. It was a difficult time, but I was lucky to be supported by older, more experienced and knowledgeable chiefs, like the president, who gave me good advice and helped me to survive. But it was not easy.

*PCK:* Max, as head of the bureau or as chief, did you follow a specific management model (leadership style)? Explain.

*ME:* It was very important that I had studied at the Vienna University of Economics and Business Administration. There I had the chance to learn a lot about management theories. I learned how to plan, to solve crisis situations, and to regulate conflicts. Project management was the basis to implement the modernization of our old system, to motivate employees, and to bring visions into reality. You can learn by failures and by training on the job, and you can prepare theoretically at universities. I did all of that. I decided to install a rather open style. For me, it was important to offer the same level of knowledge to all leading employees. There always existed differences in knowledge between the leading criminal officers and the legal advisors. This was a bad situation and weakened the whole system. My first structural change was the implementation of a daily meeting of legal advisors and leading officers under my command. By this routine I changed the level of understanding and knowledge immediately. This measure increased our operational successes.

*PCK:* Why were you chosen to be the head of the Major Crime Bureau? Explain some of the factors and circumstances that led to the decision.

*ME:* To be truthful, I was not the first choice of the political authorities. The police president was looking for another leader. I had a high reputation as a criminal expert, but even though I had, politically speaking, a social democratic background, I was not the first choice. When the minister of the interior and the police president had to decide who would be the next chief of the Major Crime Bureau, my problem was that I had arrested two judges. They were under suspicion to have committed insurance fraud. One of them was the son of a representative to the National Assembly. Immediately, there was some resistance toward choosing me as a future leader of the Major Crime Bureau.

My strengths were professionalism, being rather young (43 years), and being a hard worker. Another advantage was that the criminal investigators respected me. My great weakness was I had no political lobby behind me. The decision process took about half a year until the minister of interior and the police president came directly to my office and told me that they selected me. This was the greatest day in my life, except for the day I married my wife, Edith.

Today I can say that, after 15 years of leadership, my strongest contribution was to have acted independently, not to have been influenced politically and that I just simply followed the rule of law. For example, I had to lead as a police chief an investigation against the police president himself and ended it successfully; the president had to resign afterward.

*PCK:* Compare police work during the early part of your career with police work at the present time.

*ME:* If I think about the changes in police work, comparing the strengths and weaknesses of the "old police" compared to the "new police," I became more and more aware about all of the improvements and technical advantages of the new police, but also the fact that human resources were the strength of the "old police." Police have to work with people. You have to listen to victims and offenders, you have to speak with them, and it seems in some way we are losing this capacity. Some young officers cannot communicate with and listen to people.

*PCK:* Discuss the major changes in the way in which police officers and administrators work.

*ME:* Police work has changed dramatically. It is becoming more and more technical and formalistic. In the 70s you had to fill in a half-page paper, if you had arrested a suspicious person, to fulfill all the formalistic issues. Today you have to fill in eight pages of dense questions. It comes out that basically the system is engaged with itself so densely that less time is left for the important part, to deal with people. On the other side, the police system is improving its professionalism by more technique, more knowledge, more forensics, more analytic background. But on the other side, police are confronted with less ability to care for human beings when they are dealing with victims and offenders.

*PCK:* Are the goals of police work the same or have they changed? Has the use of modern technology led to improvements in police efficiency and effectiveness?

*ME:* Generally, the goals of police work have not changed dramatically. Police always had to care for safety, help, and support. The background philosophy changed because, for many centuries, police cared for state power, the emperor or the government. Since 1990, officially it was written down in the Security Police Act that police have to care about people. This looked much more dramatic than it was in reality. Police simply always had to care for people.

Of course, modern technology has increased police effectiveness. For example, the Vienna police have to handle 3,000 daily emergency calls. Out of these calls, about 1,000 calls lead to a police reaction. This work can be handled much better by new technology. The main goals of police work are support, help, and assistance. There, police act much more professionally. In the field of crime and prevention you need human resources. There I can see weaknesses because police structures suffer by cutting down resources.

*Explanation of the Job*

*PCK:* Max, with reference to your former position as head of the Major Crime Bureau, explain your specific job tasks.

*ME:* The Major Crime Bureau was the largest criminal investigation department in Austria. Austria is a rather small country with 8.2 million inhabitants. The bureau was responsible for solving major crime cases in Vienna. Vienna is the capital, with about 1.7 million people, and approximately 40% of all crimes in Austria are committed in Vienna. The Major Crime Bureau became a well known institution in Austria as well as in Europe and the United States. It was created in 1858 and was eventually dismantled in 2002. I served as chief from 1988 to 2002. Being the chief of this prestigious policing agency was a great honor, even through there were times when the job was very demanding and stressful.

*PCK:* How many people did you have working in the bureau?

*ME:* The Major Crime Bureau employed 204 criminal investigators (men and women) and 54 administrative employees. There were 12 legal advisors, including the chief and his deputy, 10 referent secretaries, and other administration staff.

*PCK:* Provide an outline of the organizational structure of the Major Crime Bureau. What types of crimes were considered major crimes?

*ME:* The Major Crime Bureau was part of the Bundespolizeidirektion Wien (Federal Police of Vienna), which was split into five general departments:

Department 1: Staatspolizei (State Police, somewhat like the U.S. Secret Service) was responsible for security issues of embassies, political institutions—for example, the parliament, the presidency and other governmental agencies and official buildings.

Department 2: Kriminalpolizei (Criminal Investigations), centralized in the Sicherheitsbüro (Major Crime Bureau), was responsible for all major crimes in Vienna (murder, robbery, hostage taking, organized burglary, white-collar crime and drug trafficking, prostitution, gambling, crime prevention).

Department 3: Sicherheits und Verkehrsabteilung (Security and Traffic Department) was responsible for all traffic issues—for example, all Viennese had to ask for their driving licenses at this department.

Department 4: Fremdenpolizei (Foreigner Police) was responsible for dealing with all problems of foreigners.

Department 5: Kommissariatsabteilung (department for 23 districts) was the headquarters for all police organizations in the 23 districts of Vienna. In each district there existed police (Polizeikommissariat) with uniformed, civil, and administrative suborganizations responsible for the area within their district. In 2001, the organizational structure changed and the number of districts was reduced from 23 to 14.

*PCK:* What were the jurisdictional boundaries? Was your authority limited to Vienna or did it extend to entire Austria? Were there other major crime bureaus located in other cities in Austria?

*ME:* My authority was limited to Vienna. But if an offender was arrested in Vienna who had committed crimes outside Vienna, we investigated these cases too. Since Vienna is so important to the entire country of Austria, very often crimes were being committed in other regions of Austria or even in other countries and criminals were crossing borders and coming to Vienna. In such cases, we assumed the leadership in the investigation because the investigators in the Major Crime Bureau had the knowledge, skills, and equipment to complete thorough investigations. During the time I served as head of the bureau, cooperation with the judicial authorities of our jurisdiction was expanded. We worked together on cases. We cooperated with Interpol on all international cases.

*PCK:* Explain how the Austrian Federal Police was structured and where the Major Crime Bureau was located in the organizational structure. Base your answer to this question on how the police department was structured before it was reorganized.

*ME:* The Austrian Police and former Gendarmerie always were federally organized. On the top there was the minister of the interior, the structure of the Ministry of the Interior with about 2,000 employees, and at the lower level there were gendarmerie and police (since July 1, 2005, only police in the nine provinces of Austria). The number of employees in 2008 was about 30,000, including 14,000 in the police force, 13,000 in the force of gendarmerie (after the 2005 reform, only police), and the rest administrative personnel.

Austria is divided into nine federal states: Vienna, Lower Austria, Upper Austria, Burgenland, Styria, Carinthia, Salzburg, Tyrolia, and Vorarlberg. While the gendarmerie was responsible for the rural areas, the responsibility for the 14 large cities lay with the police (2.8 million people live in cities such as Vienna, Graz, Salzburg, Linz, and Innsbruck). After the police reform in 2005, the gendarmerie and the police were united in one force.

The federal police force in Vienna is a subdivision of the Ministry of the Interior. It is the largest division. Before 2002 the Vienna Police had about 9,500 employees. This number was dramatically reduced and now there are about 8,500 employees; about 5,800 are uniformed police officers, 800 are criminal investigators, and about 1,900 are administrative staff. It still is a large organization. This organization is headed by the police president. The vice president (now a woman) also serves as the chief of the presidential department.

Until 2002, the Major Crime Bureau was located in Department II. It was the largest criminal investigation bureau in Austria, although it was only responsible for Vienna. In October 2002, the Major Crime Bureau was abolished. The Economic Police unit was also abolished. Since November 2002, there exists only a Kriminaldirektion1. This unit is closely organized along the lines of the former Major Crime Bureau. It has similar duties, but lost its importance because of the 2003 newly established Bundeskriminalamt in Austria.

*PCK:* Explain why the Federal Police was reorganized.

*ME:* In autumn 1999 we had elections in Austria. The governing Social-Democratic Party lost its position and in January 2000 we had a new government, a conservative one. The new government's goals were reducing administration and cutting down the budget expenses. Therefore, the number of police personal was reduced in the following years from 33,000 to 30,000 (gendarmerie, police, administration).

Officially, they wanted to bring in more efficiency; unofficially, they started a dramatic political change of the leadership. The Austrian police always tended to be headed by Social-Democratic leaders, while the gendarmerie was generally headed by rather conservative leaders. After the police reform was finished, almost all of the top positions in the police were in the hands of the Conservative leaders.

*PCK:* Do you think this reorganization was an improvement? Why?

*ME:* The basic idea was OK. Austria is a small country. The structures should have been modernized a long time ago. To integrate police and gendarmerie made sense. The effects of synergies were clear by building one institution, one education system, one leadership—abolishing the differences between gendarmerie and police. The reality was different. Police and gendarmerie were melted under the name "police," but inside there is only the old military system of gendarmerie. This fact was not accepted by a lot of the employees and leadership.

*PCK:* Did the police become more efficient? Did they become more professional?

*ME:* If you look at the performance, crime increased between 2000 and 2008 from about 500,000 to about 600,000 offenses per year. The clearance rate decreased from 51 to 27%. Total personnel was reduced from 30,000 to 27,000 officers. Motivation of the employees is generally low; there are enormous problems related to leadership, quality performance, insecurity, and job satisfaction. Political influence and an increase of administrative work exist. Operative efficiency appears to have declined rather than having improved.

Professionalism was increased in the field of forensic evidence. Special units, like Bundeskriminalamt Austria in 2003 or Bundesamt für Verfassungsschutz und Terrorismusbekämpfung in 2002 (a new unit to fight terrorism and to protect constitutional institutions) were created, but on the whole, the reforms neglected to strengthen a scientific approach of police work.

*PCK:* Explain your duties and tasks as a police chief after the reorganization. Discuss how your responsibilities changed.

*ME:* After reorganizing the leadership in the police force, the legal advisors were eliminated from operational duties. Before this change, legal advisors, who were trained in law, went to the crime scenes, interrogated criminals and victims, had an active role in the operational leadership, and wrote reports sent to the prosecutor's service and investigative judges.

After July 1, 2005, all these activities were handled by police officers. Legal advisors only were allowed to control the written material after all of the initial steps in the investigations had been completed. Immediately, there was a loss of quality performance. This is validated by the fact that the clearance rate for crimes dropped from 51 to 27%.

*PCK:* In Austria, who is responsible for developing policies and operational strategies for the police—for example, Ministry of the Interior, bureau or police chiefs?

*ME:* Developing policies and operational strategies happens on different levels. The difficulty of acting as a chief is that decisions on the top level, like by the minister of the interior, the police president, or political decisions of the government or the city (the mayor of a city), can be influenced by public opinion—especially by media, surprisingly.

Besides the top level you have to be aware that decisions on the middle level can be influenced by regional interests. For example, I had to learn that dealing with drug problems you always had to respect regional problems and proposals. For all kinds of problems you had to be aware of special groups of interests, like schools, elderly people, health problems, traffic issues, etc.

Each Monday, in the beginning of the week, the police leadership met and discussed main issues in the Bureau of the Presidential Department (Bureau of Police Chiefs). The important leaders, about 18 persons, described their activities and plans and they were discussed with the president and vice president.

*PCK:* As head of the Major Crime Bureau and as police chief, do you think you had enough authority to establish policies and to develop operational procedures?

*ME:* Basically I had enough authority, although a chief wishes always to have more power. Formally, my legal power was restricted. It was restricted by the fact that I was responsible for everything, but had no direct power over the people. Criminal investigators were promoted by their direct leading officers, who reported to the chief of the Major Crime Bureau, but decided on their own. Basically, I could decide policies and develop my operational ideas. As chief, you always had to watch tendencies of higher levels, like the minister of the interior, the police president, or the mayor of the city of Vienna, and had to adapt your measures to the personal limitations of your staff. It is a fact that if you don't lead a "dream team," you are limited.

In the 1990s, as a young, progressive, somewhat idealistic police officer, I recognized some important weaknesses in the operation of the police and I wanted to bring in some basic changes. Even the minister of the interior supported my ideas. But at this time change was not possible because of the strong influence of the unions. Later on in the Strasser era (the minister of interior of the Conservative government), there was no discussion and unions were deprived of their power. This was a strategy where Social-Democratic leaders failed.

It has to be recognized that the power to change anything in the organization was activated by conservative persons. You can argue about the way, but you cannot neglect the fact that they did it. Although I am very critical about what has happened since 2000, especially in 2005, you have to accept that something had to happen.

*PCK:* Can you give examples of situations in which the official policies conflicted with your personal opinions on how a matter should be handled?

*ME:* Basically, we could work without much interference of the minister of interior or the police president. You always had to watch the thin line of duty to report to your masters and to care for the strategic line of your investigation, especially if you were dealing with very sensitive cases that implicated political issues. For example, we had to deal with serial killings in a hospital in Vienna, where elderly people were cared for. The fact that four nurses killed elderly people was politically very sensitive and the mayor of the city of Vienna was not very much pleased with our investigations.

*PCK:* Police administration has become more formal and bureaucratic. In your opinion, has this change resulted in an improved police organization or one that is not as effective as it was in the past?

*ME:* Formalism and bureaucratic burdens can be accepted as contributions to democratic standards. To inform a suspicious person about rights and duties of police has to be respected as a basic part of human rights standards. To fill in all kinds of reports for centralized analysis systems has to be seen as improvement of the organization because it offers intelligent capacity for line officers. These formalisms reduce the effectiveness of practical work. The point of no return is the fact that sometimes there arises the impression that formalism is more important than the output of practical daily work.

*PCK:* Compare police officers entering the police service at the present time with the police who entered the service at the time you entered and during different periods of your career.

*ME:* Many elder police officers still active in the system or just retired are happy not to start again. Very often elder officers recognize that it is much harder to start now than it was in former times. Elder officers had experienced a well-balanced period of time. They enjoyed work, the freedom of improvisation, friendship, and partnership and even could remember funny experiences they will never forget. Young officers, male or female, miss a lot of these well known experiences. Today they come in, work on their job, and leave.

*PCK:* Do you think current police officers are better educated, trained, and more professional than those of the past?

*ME:* In some ways, yes. Police officers are educated very professionally. They are much more technically equipped, have a much better theoretical and computerized understanding.

What they miss is building their personality, individuality, and character. These "old" typical police officers with their strong personalities were very important in the daily contacts with people in former times. I miss them. The system misses them. Police work has a strong tendency to teamwork. Very often I have the feeling young officers come in, work, but have no interest or possibility to build intensive partnerships or relationships with each other. In former times, it was no question that after ending your job you were sitting together with colleagues, drinking a beer and talking to each other. Today this happens very rarely.

*PCK:* Are the entrance requirements for a federal police position about the same today as they were in the past?

*ME:* What seems to be better are the objective requirements, like body tests, psychological tests, intellectual checking. Who is choosing police work always depends very much on the economic situation and on the general level of education. If the economy runs nicely and offers well paid jobs, fewer people are interested in choosing a police job. Nowadays, it is very hard for young people to get a job. Today, police can select whom they are taking or not. More than 40% of young people asking for a police job offer higher education standards, as this is necessary to become a police officer.

*PCK:* What are the educational requirements for those who enter the force at the supervisory/administrative level? Is an academic degree required? If not, should an academic degree be required as a prerequisite for these positions?

*ME:* Today, you have to be a minimum of 19 years old, have to have served military, have to have finished job education or have to have attended and finished high school or Matura. In our country, that means attending basic school, 8 years of higher education finishing with final tests, which we call Matura. Entering the supervisory/administrative level, you have to have finished a minimum standard higher education (Matura) or an academic education. What has changed is that legal advisors are not required any more for executive duties. They are only allowed to start in the administrative level. I criticized this development as choosing the "cheap police model" because this tendency is contrary to all other high-standards countries. They try to implement an academic education level at the police academy, but still this academic education does not exist in Austria's police academy. There was long discussion about whether police should cooperate with universities or educate their personnel on their own. Just now, people with university education are rather rare in the police system.

*PCK:* Is the current police officer as motivated to service as in the past?

*ME:* Young officers who have just finished school are highly motivated. If they come out into the system, they are rather quickly influenced by bad circumstances. The general features of the system do not guarantee high permanent motivation.

*PCK:* In the past, did politics, influence, or corruption have any importance in the selection of federal police officers? Are any of these factors important today in the selection of police?

*ME:* For many decades, to become a police officer was influenced very much by politics. That changed very much with the newly designed selection mechanism. Nowadays, it depends solely on your own capacities if you enter the system. If you pass all the requirement tests, you will become a police officer, independent of whether you are male, female, poor or rich, social-democratic or conservative, or none of these.

It is highly problematical how someone is promoted. It is still very important to belong to a political party or to have "good friends." It is very important to be supported by important politicians or leaders.

Promotion higher and higher in the system is even worse. I always said, "I was a bad Catholic and a bad Social-Democrat, because I preferred to play tennis instead of attending churches or political meetings." I tried to be good on the job. With all my weaknesses, I was lucky enough to get a chance to be promoted, because they did not care as much as the leadership does nowadays.

A good friend of mine, the retired chief of the forensic institution of the Vienna University Department of Medicine, said, "I was lucky because of all my handicaps.

I was promoted frequently. I even became chief of the Forensic Unit."

*PCK:* Is it worse than it was?

*ME:* I would answer "yes." It is easy to become a police officer. It is difficult to become and stay as a leader. Because of the merging of the police and gendarmerie, there immediately existed too many leaders. It was easier for gendarmerie officers to get promoted because the conservative members of the government and the Ministry of the Interior prefer people from their own background. This is not corruption, but it is subjective selection. Maybe you can understand it as political interference—is this corruption?—but in no way is it a fair procedure of promoting young, talented employees.

*Theory and Practice*

*PCK:* Max, I can see from your curriculum vitae that you have considerable experience in teaching and completing research and that you have written extensively on police and criminal justice topics. Did you have these interests in academics and theory throughout your career or did these develop sometime later in your career?

*ME:* When I was young, I wanted to become a teacher. Because of my family background I had chosen police as my working profession. I studied law at the Vienna University, at the Legal Department. There I made contacts in the Institute of Criminology, Sociology and Forensics. Confronted with crime cases, I learned that clearing up such cases is a very interesting challenge, especially white-collar crime cases. But all this was just rather practical work, nothing theoretical.

In 1991, Professor Dilip K. Das from the United States visited Austria and did a comparative study on policing in several European countries. This was the beginning point for my interests in police theory. By his contacts I met Professor Peter C. Kratcoski from the United States in 1994. We became good friends, did several studies, and were teaching together. That changed my academic background completely. Although I am primarily a practitioner, these contacts opened up possibilities of theoretical discussion with police topics. I became a member of the ACJS [Academy of Criminal Justice Sciences], of IPES [International Police Executive Symposium], visited meetings of the American Society of Criminology, and had the chance to write book chapters and to present papers about police topics at conferences.

Because of all these international activities, I organized together with my American partners in 1997 a symposium on "International Police Cooperation" and later I was invited as an international expert by United Nations, Council of Europe, and OSCE several times.

*PCK:* Have you been able to integrate the research and theoretical information you obtained from participation in conferences, reading of research reports, and from your own research into your administrative and applied work in the field?

*ME:* This was very difficult. I was very open to and desired theoretical experiences and knowledge, but it was difficult to bring all this knowledge to the officers on the front line. As I already mentioned, I myself started in 1991 to become interested in these things. I was chief of the Major Crime Bureau between 1988 and 2002. Only very little of my theoretical knowledge could be transferred to practical work. It was easier to use these materials for teaching in the police academy or in the Middle European police academy. It was complicated to motivate criminal investigators or top leaders in our organization to be interested in new international developments in policing. There are many causes why. It would have been so important to succeed in bringing this knowledge and integrating it, especially when police reform started in Austria. There I failed completely. I was not able to make political or police leaders aware of new police theories. Our police reform brought the very old system of a "military police," which is very limited in understanding policing in modern democratic countries. The conservative powers leading our police organization could not be convinced to drop their ideas on policing Austria.

*PCK:* What type of information from academic or scientific research sources is the most useful?

*ME:* If I look into my library, I love all the books I gathered about police theories and research. Of course, books about international police cooperation, terrorism, organized crime, community policing and crime prevention, juvenile crime, and corrections are very oriented to the practical. Police theory opens up your mind for a much deeper insight into all problems connected to fear of crime, questions of life quality, what makes policing attractive for people, and what they expect from policing their societies. Very useful for police work were the developments in the fields of forensics, DNA, profiling, new methods of analyzing, insights of sociology and psychology, and general developments in science and technology. There is no question that modern computer technology improved police work immensely.

*PCK:* Police administrators are often very reluctant to change once they feel comfortable with the way things are. However, academic research on police often points out some of the weaknesses in the current system as well as provides suggestions for change and improvement. Please give me several examples from your own experiences of a significant change in police work—for example, changes in police organizational structure, changes in the mission of police work, changes in the way the police and citizens interact, changes in the techniques and methods used in their work—that were made as a result of research or writings coming from academics.

*ME:* A very significant change in police work brought the Anglo-Saxon experience in crime prevention to Austria. In 1974, my former chief visited an exhibition in London on crime prevention and wrote a report about his experiences, and this was the starting point of a new philosophy of understanding police work. It took nearly 20 years before the slogan of police work changed from "serving the authorities" to "serve the community." In 1991, this new slogan was written down in the Security Police Law Act, which was empowered in 1993.

My personal experience happened in the 1990s. We had to deal with several serial killers and we learned about the FBI approach of profiling. Another lesson was learned from new DNA technologies.

As I mentioned already, we should have learned about new theories of policing in Austria. It was never asked and researched what people were expecting of police in our country. When we reformed police in Austria, we moved backward to the "good old military model." This model is not bad, but we did not even discuss whether this was the best solution for policing Austria in the twenty-first century.

*PCK:* Have academically educated nonsworn personnel been integrated into the Austrian Federal Police? If yes, in what types of positions or types of work are they utilized? Possible examples would be researchers, forensic experts, scientists, psychologists.

*ME:* No, we have only sworn academic educated personnel. When I criticized the police reform I had to write a proposal: "How to Make Academic Cooperation More Efficient." I visited several universities and professors and worked out three models of cooperation. My proposal was not accepted.

The professors of different Austrian universities proposed to cooperate ad hoc, if something interesting has to be researched, to research special issues of interest, and to cooperate steadily. None of these ideas was accepted. Still, we have enormous problems because of too little cooperation with academic institutions.

Reviewed from the historical standpoint, the "Viennese school of criminology" became famous because of a strong cooperation with the Vienna University Institute of Forensics. At the end of the nineteenth century and the beginning of the twentieth century, Austrian criminal investigators were invited to the United States and to China because of their expertise and knowledge. The Vienna Institute of Forensics was closed down in spring 2008.

*PCK:* In your opinion, should there be a concerted effort to civilianize some of the more technical tasks associated with police work?

*ME:* Yes, to become more and more professional is the main issue in policing. All the important background work can be fulfilled by civilians.

*PCK:* Are there some specific tasks that must be completed by sworn officers? If yes, what are they?

*ME:* In my understanding, traditional police work has to be done by sworn officers. Traditional police work is the kind of work where police officers have to show up as witnesses at the court procedure; therefore, crime scene works or interrogations have to be performed by them. Public order and state security issues like protection of members of the government or ambassadors, for example, are typical duties of sworn police officers.

*PCK:* Based on your experiences, have there been times when the research materials or input from academics caused more harm than good? If possible, give a concrete example.

*ME:* It the last decade it was very popular that private management advisors (firms) advised the minister of the interior on his ambition for reforming police. It happened that this advice was rather bad and inefficient. They were just driven by the knowledge they gathered in the private industry, but had no idea about police work.

The last ministers brought in members of their cabinet, who are very often academics, but strongly driven by their goals rather than by learning and understanding job issues. They failed because they were all young, "innovative, and cool," but were not willing to learn.

### *Women in Police*

*PCK:* Police work throughout the world has traditionally been dominated by men. Even at the present time less than 20% of the total number of police officers are women and a smaller proportion of supervisors and administrators are women. What is the situation in Austria?

*ME:* For many decades, police work was a man's job. It changed in the 1970s. The first wave of women employees increased the percentage of women to about 7 or 8%. A lot of these women became pregnant and the percentage decreased to 5%. Nowadays we have a percentage of about 12% women in police. The increase in the percentage of women in the police reduced the danger of police power abuse. Women in the organization stabilize the public appearance of police. There is more communication, more citizen-friendly orientation, but still the number of women officers is small. Again the same problem arises: Women at the age of 20 to 30 become pregnant and there are no organizational solutions to employ other women for the pregnant ones.

*PCK:* During your career, has there been a significant increase in the number of female police officers in the federal police? What changes have you observed in the types of work female officers are assigned? Are there certain departments (types of work) from which female officers are excluded?

*ME:* I started police work in the 1970s. When I finished my police career, the number of female police officers had doubled. Women acting as uniformed police officers are very productive in dealing with violence in families, abuse-of-children investigations, and peace-keeping activities in the regular life of citizens.

In criminal cases, my experience is that violent crime cases (again, violence against women and children, sexual abuse) and fraud cases are covered very well by female officers. We have some excellent women working in these fields.

*PCK:* What are some of the problems you have observed that female police officers encounter when trying to obtain an equal status in the force? Give a few specific situations involving female officers that you dealt with in your capacity as head of the Major Crime Bureau or during the time you served as police chief.

*ME:* When I was starting as police chief we had only two female criminal investigators out of 160 investigators. In 1988 we only had these two ladies, 12 secretaries, and nine women working with the administrative staff in the Major Crime Bureau. In my era the number of female investigators increased from two to 23 women and I brought in the first two female legal advisors. Problems arose with questions of acceptance by men, but we could overcome these problems rather quickly. Leadership problems were more difficult to solve. It was much easier for male officers to cooperate with females than to accept their leadership role. Today we have a female police vice president in Vienna, but this was a big surprise for the male leadership society.

*PCK:* Some police organizations have established policies for female officers with young children, allowing them to continue working part time and thus providing the mothers with an opportunity to spend more time with their children, while still being able to continue their police careers. Do the Austrian police have any such policy? If yes, is it a good policy? Does it create any problems? Do you have examples from your experiences to draw on?

*ME:* Part-time jobs are difficult to install. We have such policewomen, but it seems they have difficulties having the same career opportunities as full-time officers. The main problem is that police officers are acting as public officials. The system is not flexible enough to react to the private wishes of employees. They are trying to change the whole system now and maybe that will create more flexibility to solve such problems.

### *Disciplining Officers and Handling Corruption*

*PCK:* As an administrator, I assume you had to become involved in disciplinary cases and perhaps some cases involving corruption. What is the typical procedure that was followed when officers were accused of committing infractions of rules or/and policies?

*ME:* When I was a young legal advisor in the Major Crime Bureau, I had to investigate criminal offenses of police officers in Vienna. Basically, the procedure was performed in two ways. The investigation of crime cases of officers was performed by the Major Crime Bureau, while the disciplinary procedure was performed by the personnel authority in the police headquarters. If a police officer of the Major Crime

Bureau became a criminal, the whole procedure was performed by the police headquarters.

In 2001, a special unit was created under the command of the police president himself, the so-called Office for Special Investigations [BBE—Büro für Besondere Angelegenheiten] and all criminal and disciplinary cases in Vienna are performed by this unit.

In 2003, the Office for Internal Affairs [BIA—Büro für Interne Angelegenheiten] was established on the level of the Ministry of the Interior, which deals with so-called important cases of corruption in Austria. Therefore, if a Vienna case is an important one it moves from the BBE to the BIA. All investigations are supervised by the prosecutor's office in Vienna.

Now it is being discussed whether general structure of investigations of criminal, disciplinary, and corruption cases should be changed, because a bad picture is revealed to the public if police investigate police. This is a political decision and we don't know how it will be decided.

*PCK:* Were the same procedures followed when the person was accused of violating the law—for example, being involved in corruption?

*ME:* Basically, yes. If only disciplinary offenses were committed, then the case was or is handled by police or the Ministry of the Interior. If crime appears, it is handled by the justice system.

*PCK:* Are there provisions in the policies regulating the Austrian police for use of external oversight to investigate complaints against police officers? If yes, explain the procedure.

*ME:* See my answer to the first question on corruption. Besides disciplinary or criminal cases, there is a procedure if an Austrian citizen complains about police. If bad behavior happened or an exculpation is necessary, the Ministry of the Interior or the police headquarters of the province will deal with it.

*PCK:* What is your position on the issue of external oversight versus in-house responsibility for investigating complaints and applying discipline?

*ME:* My personal view is that a bad picture is shown to the public if police investigate police. My personal experience was and is that so-called “little police corruption” is on the increase. There are a lot of external and internal causes, and it seems to be necessary that an independent institution should investigate police failures and corruption on the level of the prosecution service—on the justice level.

*Professionalism and Unionization*

*PCK:* Are Austrian police represented by labor unions (professional organizations)? If yes, explain how the union becomes involved in administrative matters (promotions, disciplining, recruitment, salaries, and benefits).

*ME:* The Austrian police have strong unions. The unions act as one institution but are divided into interest groups of the political parties, like the social-democratic party or conservative party. They have strong influence in discussing salaries and benefits. The former influence in promotion, disciplining, and recruitment was reduced by the fact that the Conservative government reduced their influence dramatically.

*PCK:* During the time you served as an administrator, what type of relationship did you have with the police union (professional organization)?

*ME:* When I was a young police employee, I worked for the unions. I was a member of the unions, became elected as a representative, and worked very hard for other employees, to improve working conditions, promotion, etc.

In my time of leadership, I basically was confronted with a strong police union. Sometimes the unions acted too strongly. Although I myself worked for the unions, seen from the standpoint of a police leader, it was difficult to compromise with them. Especially, personnel decisions could have been very complicated, if we did not find the right person for the right job.

*Problems and Change*

*PCK:* Max, now that you are retired and can step out of the environment a bit and reflect on policing in Austria, what do you think are the major concerns (problem areas) that will confront the administrators in the future? You can include present problems in your answer.

*ME:* On June 9, 2008, a book came out where I wrote down the problems of policing in Austria today. My statement was that you can learn so much by history, but we did not. The police still are acting professionally and showing quality. What has happened in Austria is the fact that by reforming the police in 2001 to 2005, political powers decided to implement a more centralistic, military system that is not adequate to temporary issues in policing. Motivation, professionalism, academic approach, and leadership suffered too much and it is time for evaluation, rethinking, and consolidation.

The goal of policing is that police have to work with people, for people, and not against people. This is my main concern in today's policing. In 1991 this goal was implemented in the Police Security Act, but in 2008 it seems we have forgotten this important statement.

*PCK:* Max, reflecting on your career, if you had a chance, would there be anything you would have done differently?

*ME:* What I have learned and understood, I acted as I did and wouldn't change it even if I would have a second chance. My weakness was not to be as diplomatic as I should have been, and I should have gained more political clout.

Police work is connected with failures, because decisions have to happen quickly. You have to be aware that failures happen, but you have to analyze them and you have to learn by them. You cannot act without the capacity to learn steadily and to try to improve. It would be wonderful to avoid failures, but this is not a realistic picture of daily police work. This is the challenge of the job.

*PCK:* Thanks, Max.

# 3

# Interview With Major General Fazil Balahasan oglu Guliyev, Head, Organizational-Inspection Department, Azerbaijan Ministry of Internal Affairs

## INTERVIEWED BY RONALD D. HUNTER

**Contents**



**Background**

Major General Fazil Balahasan oglu Guliyev has served as head of the Organizational-Inspection Department of the Azerbaijan Ministry of Internal Affairs since 2001. General Guliyev's insights are particularly interesting in light of the many significant events that have impacted the Republic of Azerbaijan since he began his career in 1983. I met General Guliyev at the 16th Annual International Police Executive Symposium in Ohrid, Macedonia. During the symposium, General Guliyev graciously consented to allow me to interview him regarding the police in Azerbaijan, his career, and his insights regarding policing. The interviews were conducted through a series of e-mails in which questions and responses were exchanged.

*Personal Background*

Following conscripted service in the Soviet military, then Officer Guliyev joined the Azerbaijan militia (which performed police services) in 1983. He steadily advanced through the ranks. Since Azerbaijan gained independence from the former Soviet Union, in 1991, General Guliyev has held increasingly important positions within the Ministry of Internal Affairs, including director of the Headquarters Division, head of the Division of Economic Crimes, director of management, and, since 2001, head of the Organizational-Inspection Department. In 2002 he was awarded the Azerbaijani Banner Order for Achievement. In 2004 he was promoted to the rank of major general. General Guliyev is a graduate of Baku State University. He is married with two children.

**The Interviews**

*RH:* General, thank you for taking the time to discuss your career and sharing your insights regarding policing. This is indeed an honor. May I begin by asking what influenced you to join the police?

*FG:* To tell the truth, service in the police was not my childhood dream and I had never thought of it. I went in for sports training for about 12 years at a young age. That time, I was mainly thinking of myself as a specialist in this area—as a trainer. Upon completion of secondary school, I was admitted to the sport institute and graduated from it. My engagement with militia activities took place purely by chance, when I received an offer—as I had a pedagogical background—to work for the service which was responsible for organizing character-strengthening activities for the prevention of delinquency in minors. I hesitated more than a year when I received the offer, but life turned out in a way that later I started service by giving my consent. Today, I recall with a great sense of gratitude those who in time advised me to pursue this opportunity. I would say it determined my destiny.

*RH:* When you began your career in 1983, Azerbaijan was a republic within the Soviet Union. How were the police forces within Azerbaijan organized?

*FG:* First, let me note that the history of emergence of the Ministry of Internal Affairs, which carries out the functions of ensuring public security and the fight against criminality in the Republic of Azerbaijan, takes its beginning from the activity of public order protection groups founded by decree of the government of Azerbaijan Democratic Republic dated July 2, 1918. Despite difficulties of the period and a lack of national personnel, the police played an important role in formation of the state of Azerbaijan (which was the first democratic republic in the East) and securing internal public order. After the fall of the Democratic Republic, the militia, during the era of Soviet Union, in essence, had a class character and was the state entity responsible for implementation of state policy. Despite this, the internal affairs bodies of Azerbaijan gained much experience, knowledge, and professionalism and strengthened their organizational structures.

At the time when I started my service, the militia was an organizational agency of the Ministry of Internal Affairs (MIA) carrying out broad and huge functions. The ministry, along with ensuring public security and organizing the fight against criminality, also was carrying out the functions of penitentiary service and fire protection. Although the ministry formally was part of the government of the Republic, in reality it was under command of USSR Ministry of Internal Affairs and decisions on all issues were taken in Moscow. Appointments to managerial posts had to be approved by Moscow.

However, I would not like to create an impression as if everything was awful at that time and that there was not a proper fight against criminality. The fight against criminality and, in general, against infringements of legal order was organized in a systematic form and there were sufficient significant results in this area. Especially after the election of National Leader Heydar Aliyev in Azerbaijan as a leader in 1969, state support to the Ministry of Internal Affairs was strengthened and special attention and care started to be given to issues such as the purification of corrupt personnel, the promotion of personnel dedicated to their duties and nation, and the training of employees in the spirit of national moral values and patriotism. In 1983 when I started my career in internal affairs, the national composition of personnel completely reflected the national composition of the Republic's population.

*RH:* You were a ranking officer when Azerbaijan gained independence in 1991. What were the impacts of independence on the structure and administration of the police forces? What were some of the challenges in creating a new police force after Soviet times?

*FG:* A very complicated public–political situation indeed emerged in Azerbaijan at the beginning of its independence. Such a situation was mainly related to unjustified land claims and the military invasion of Armenia into Azerbaijan. Due to a lack of military bodies at that time, the duty of protecting the peaceful lives of citizens was placed on the shoulders of internal affairs bodies. Personnel in front rows fighting to repulse Armenian aggression fought with bravery and hundreds of colleagues perished in these battles.

In 1994, upon declaration of the ceasefire, national leader Heydar Aliyev started to carry out huge building measures and fundamental reforms based on the principles of legality and statehood. Personnel policies and working environments necessary for a professional fight against criminality were created. Laws on the police and operational-investigative activity and statutes on Ministry of Internal Affairs of the Republic of Azerbaijan, service in internal affairs bodies of the Republic of Azerbaijan, and other normative legal acts were adopted. Penitentiary and fire-extinguishing services were taken from the structure of the ministry and placed, respectively, under the Ministries of Justice and Emergency Cases. Services to fight against organized crime, the illegal market in drugs, human trafficking, internal security, personnel management, international cooperation, and public relations were founded.

Nowadays, the Ministry of Internal Affairs of the Republic of Azerbaijan and the police are passing through a period of development and improvement in their organizational structures. The activities of the police are organized based on international norms and standards combined with a new lifestyle and modern social and economic relations of the society. The Ministry of Internal Affairs is headed by a minister who is appointed (and may also be dismissed) by the president of the Republic of Azerbaijan. In order to discuss separate, important issues and determine the ways for their solution, a board of the ministry, which is a consultative body composed of high ministry officials, currently functions in the ministry. The head of the ministry board is the minister for internal affairs, due to the post held, and other members are determined based on high positions within the ministry. The composition of the ministry board is approved by president of the Republic of Azerbaijan.

The organizational structure of the Ministry of Internal Affairs is divided into operation, public security, and maintenance services according to functions and duties determined by appropriate statute. The ministry executes the tasks assigned to it by bodies subordinate to it. Sixteen major departments (15 departments and one section) are included within the structure of the ministry, which was approved by the president of the Republic of Azerbaijan. The Ministry of Internal Affairs of Nakchivan Autonomous Republic; internal forces; regional and specialized police bodies; standing police divisions; education, training, and health institutions; the National Central Bureau of Interpol in the Republic of Azerbaijan; support society; and other bodies comprise the unique system of the ministry.

Certainly, as a result of reforms carried out in response to contemporary challenges, the extent of tasks defined for internal affairs bodies has expanded. Along with the prevention of crimes, the protection of human rights and freedoms is considered to be a main priority in the activities of police, which executes its service duties currently in a completely different public–political environment in this new period of the existence of democratic institutions and their significant share in life of society in the country. In order to achieve delegated objectives, complex organizational, legal, and character training measures are carried out for the humanization of the police, making it an apolitical organization which carries out its activities based on principles of the rule of law and human rights and freedoms.

*RH:* Did Azerbaijan receive any assistance from other countries in making the transition from a state militia within the Soviet Union to a national police force?

*FG:* Certainly. It was inescapable because, at that time, the Azerbaijani police bodies did not have enough experience to work in conditions of independence, especially in a democracy and openness to the world. But countries having rich democratic traditions have assisted in the transition from which our country obtained huge experience. From this perspective, the higher administration of the ministry paid special attention to establishment and development of international relations.

Within recent years, strong cooperation and friendship ties were established among the Ministry of Internal Affairs and the relevant institutions of many foreign countries, and these ties are constantly expanding. Currently, existing relations on bilateral, multilateral, and regional levels with the United States, Turkey, Austria, Germany, France, Czech Republic, Hungary, Poland, Israel, China, several Arabic countries, CIS [Commonwealth of Independent States] countries including the Russian Federation, Ukraine, Kazakhstan, Georgia, Moldova, Uzbekistan, and other countries are developing according to the interests of all parties.

Working relations were also established with the UN and Council of Europe committees on "human rights protection" and "against torture." We carry out active work within the authorities defined by law with the UN, Council of Europe, CIS, Guam, the Economic Cooperation Organization, and other organizations due to membership of Azerbaijan in these organizations. At the same time, regular meetings are held with delegations of international organizations visiting our country and local representatives of these organizations, including representatives of the diplomatic corps of foreign countries accredited in Azerbaijan.

Employees are sent to foreign countries, including the United States and European states for training. Along with these seminars, training and courses are organized in Azerbaijan with the participation of experienced international experts. They take part in different forums and conferences organized by Council of Europe, OSCE [Organization for Security and Cooperation in Europe], and other international organizations in order to increase the efficiency of the application of foreign practice. For example, in outdoor services where police personnel are in regular contact with citizens, fundamental changes have been carried out and the service of area police inspectors has been organized, according to international experience, as the status of "area sheriff." In organizing this work, the experiences of numerous developed countries were taken into account. Also, the OSCE's Baku office had an active participation in the process. This innovation, which had been strongly supported by the president of the Republic of Azerbaijan, resulted in changes and amendments to legislation in May 2009.

For the sake of information I would like to note that the area sheriff is a police officer deployed to an area with a population of up to 10,000 who has three or four area police inspectors, an inspector of works with minors, and postpatrol service employees under his command. Different public councils act within the jurisdiction of an area sheriff. The members of the council take part in general and individual prevention measures carried out daily and work with formerly convicted persons, families in conflict, people inclined to alcohol and drugs, and people belonging to other risk groups. An area sheriff has the authority to take independent decisions in certain issues and has the right to impose administrative sanctions against accused persons—for example, minor hooliganism, violation of traffic rules, illegal street trade, and other violations. This innovation, along with expanding the possibilities for an area sheriff to react immediately to violations, also serves to strengthen ties with the population and to carry out the execution of social functions more efficiently. Analyses and public surveys indicate that the population praises the activity of this new institution.

*RH:* How did the adoption of the new constitution in 1995 bring about further changes within the national police forces?

*FG:* The new constitution of Azerbaijan adopted in 1995 defined major principles of independence, state building, future development of our country, and priority directions, and also preconditioned the organization of public life, including the activity of law enforcement agencies, on the basis of international standards and norms. We can say with assurance that modern Azerbaijani police seek to be completely apolitical in executing their duties of fighting against criminality and ensuring public security. I feel that the police have managed to establish their place, consistent with their essence, among state structures and completely meet the requirements mandated by society. A major part of police duties is ensuring the rule of human rights and freedoms principle defined in the constitution; the highest objectives of the state are thus imposed upon the police. A strong legislative basis, including a new internal normative basis reworked according to constitutional and new legislative acts, has made the protection of the previously mentioned principles a top priority. Experts from several different international organizations actively took part in this work. Also, the experiences of appropriate state bodies of foreign countries were efficiently applied.

*RH:* What are the impacts of and benefits to the national police force from being a member of the Organization for Security and Cooperation in Europe?

*FG:* The membership of Azerbaijan in OSCE certainly played an important role in the activities of our police. It is with the assistance and mediation of appropriate structures of OSCE that numerous training courses and seminars are organized for the Azerbaijani police. In this regard, lectures and training on ensuring human rights and freedoms in the activities of police and the organization of the fight against transnational organized crime (especially, human trafficking, illegal drug circulation, money laundering, and the fight against terrorism), with the involvement of experts from France, Belgium, Austria, Sweden,

Denmark, Czech Republic, and other states, have been organized. Our numerous employees are involved in practical exchange programs with foreign countries. Along with this, with close assistance from the OSCE School for Training of Ordinary and Junior Management Personnel, the Azerbaijani police organization has been substantially renovated, its material technical base has been strengthened, special subject rooms have been created and equipped with necessary equipment, and the library fund has been expanded. Based on the Czech Republic's experience, the training school's curriculum was reworked and brought into conformity with European standards.

Considerable work has been carried out together with the OSCE's Baku office, including their expert-consultancy services to internal affairs bodies and the organization of numerous seminars and training sessions. Didactic recommendations related to improving the efficiency of service in police and methodological materials of the office were included in our training program. The application of new forms, which serve the strengthening of day-to-day contacts between the police and people, should be noted as a positive step of our mutual work. We appreciate the results achieved and carry out continued work for their further development.

*RH:* I understand that the detachment of Police of Special Purpose was disbanded following unrest in 1993. Are there currently specialized security forces within the Ministry of Internal Affairs?

*FG:* Yes, currently there are professionally trained regular forces with high discipline under the authority of the ministry which carry out tasks and duties defined by law for measures in the areas of the fight against organized crime, rendering harmless armed criminal groups (criminals), and during special operations.

*RH:* Azerbaijan, along with Russia, Kazakhstan, and Turkmenistan, is a participant within the Caspian Border Patrol Force. Is this force under the supervision of the Ministry of Internal Affairs when in Azerbaijan's jurisdictions?

*FG:* No, these forces have no relation to the Ministry of Internal Affairs. Protection of the borders of the country lies within the scope of activity of the State Border Service of Azerbaijan Republic.

*RH:* Are there other police forces within Azerbaijan? If so, what is their relationship with the National Police?

*FG:* According to legislation, the Republic of Azerbaijan police are a centralized law enforcement body within the executive branch. From this perspective, there is no other state entity carrying out the functions defined directly for the police.

*RH:* What is the relationship of the national police with the judiciary?

*FG:* According to article 7 of the constitution of the Azerbaijan Republic, state power in the Azerbaijan Republic is based on a principle of division of powers. The Milli Majlis (legislative assembly) of the Azerbaijan Republic exercises legislative power. Executive power belongs to the president of the Azerbaijan Republic. Law courts of the Azerbaijan Republic exercise judicial power. According to provisions of the present constitution, legislative, executive, and judicial power interact and are independent within the limits of their authority. Taking this norm as a guide, the police work with the judiciary mainly on the following directives: bringing the persons who committed crimes before courts for the administration of justice; carrying out several operational-investigative measures based on court decisions according to rules determined by legislation of the Azerbaijan Republic; carrying out procedural coercion measures; ensuring the enforcement of the decrees of courts on administrative arrest, including decisions on the obligatory sending foreigners and persons without citizenship out of the country according to Code of Administrative Penalties; and others.

Also, I would like to bring to your attention that according to article 12 of "Law on Police," control over implementation of laws in police bodies is carried out by courts within the scope of their authority as defined by law.

*RH:* What special challenges has your organization had in enforcing the law within the Nakhchivan Autonomous Republic?

*FG:* The Ministry of Internal Affairs of the Nakchivan Autonomous Republic carries out tasks defined for police in the area of ensuring law and order in the Nakchivan Autonomous Republic. This ministry is the part of the structural bodies forming a unique system within the Ministry of Internal Affairs of the Republic of Azerbaijan. The results achieved and difficulties encountered in the process of organizing the Azerbaijani police have determined the police structures within the autonomous republic.

In general, there is no problem in ensuring the order of law within the Nakchivan Autonomous Republic. For a long time, public order, welfare of people, and internal security have been highly emphasized within the autonomous republic. It goes without saying that diversity of operational conditions necessitates the application of different measures, methods, and ways for solution of different issues, but all these are carried out within the framework of legislative acts and internal norms.

*RH:* Do you have difficulty recruiting qualified candidates for the police force?

*FG:* That is a very interesting question. Because of the stream of life, changes in personnel, and, ultimately, replacement of generations, this issue is always on the agenda. It is not by coincidence that, upon gaining independence, one of the very first measures was the establishment of a police academy on the basis of MIA's secondary specialized militia school in 1992. Our employees and civil youth, which formerly had to leave for higher police education institutions in different cities of Russia, obtained the opportunity to have this in their own land. The police academy captured its deserved place among higher education institutions and has acquired a huge reputation during the past 17 years; it receives about 300 students annually, which meets the demand of police for lawyers.

Nowadays, the share of lawyers serving in junior and senior managerial positions has increased twice in comparison with 1994 and reached 73% at the beginning of the current year. Another part of personnel recruited for service in police are the citizens graduated from other higher education institutions of our country. In this regard, first place is taken by the oldest educational institution of our country, Baku State University's Law Faculty. Along with these, currently, 85 employees of internal service bodies continue their education in reputable universities and academies of Turkey, Russian Federation, People's Republic of China, and United Kingdom.

*RH:* Please describe the recruitment of police officers. Are there training requirements for officers?

*FG:* According to "Statute on Service in Internal Affairs Bodies of the Republic of Azerbaijan," recruitment to police is carried out based on competition and transparency. Competition for officers is composed of three stages. A first announcement is made in the media on available vacant positions, terms and conditions of holding them, and on rules of competition. As a rule, competition is carried out for those with higher legal education. The first stage is the receipt of applications from citizens with the aim of determining whether they have necessary qualities and skills for service in internal affairs bodies and gathering (with their consent) information concerning their lifestyle, family, health, convictions, etc. Along with other measures, candidates also go through the special medical commission of the MIA and must pass examinations on physical training defined by physical training norms.

Candidates meeting the parameters defined for the first stage of the competition are passed to the second stage. The second stage is carried out by the State Commission on Student Admission based on defined testing programs. The purpose of the stage is to define whether a candidate has the theoretical knowledge and, in general, intellectual level necessary for service in police bodies. This test is composed of 100 questions: 80 questions cover the issues of the state's constitution, criminal and administrative violations codes, normative legal basis of internal affairs bodies, and international documents regulating issues related to human rights and freedoms, and 20 questions are related to public political life, history, literature, culture, and other areas. Candidates providing correct answers to 65 questions are passed into the third stage of competition. This stage is carried out by a special commission chaired directly by the minister of internal affairs and composed of professional specialists. This examination is in the form of an interview in order to determine general intellectual level, behavior, psychological strength, and ability to communicate with others and take right decisions in complex situations. Preparation of the candidate to service is evaluated based on a 10-point system.

Scores of the candidates obtained in two stages are summed up and candidates scoring more according to number of scores defined for positions are approved as winners of the competition and sent to a preliminary preparation course to the police academy by being recruited to service. At the preliminary training course, within a month period, they study internal normative acts related to police activity, get acquainted with the specificities of the service and obtain rules for carrying special forms and internal orders and disciplines; only after that are they sent to service locations. There is every condition for young employees to adapt into service, get practical skills of application of theoretical knowledge, and master minute details of service in police bodies. Each young employee is assigned a mentor from among experienced personnel when he first arrives to a service location.

*RH:* If a person is continuing to serve as a police officer and is intent on continuing his or her education, what opportunities are available to him or her?

*FG:* Getting an education is the constitutional right of every citizen in our country. It is natural that a police officer have the same right, and currently our numerous colleagues are studying on a part-time basis at the police academy and other higher educational institutions of our country, including postgraduate institutions. For this purpose, all conditions according to our legislation are provided for them, including provision of paid extra leaves.

*RH:* What is the status of women within the Azerbaijani National Police?

*FG:* Implementation of requirements concerning the provision of women's rights and freedoms are defined in the constitution of the Republic of Azerbaijan law on provision of gender [men and women] equality. Provisions of international documents and preventing discrimination from social perspectives are the issues always kept in the center of attention. By special decree of MIA, a responsible person for implementation of gender policy within the ministry's system was appointed and an appropriate post was created for this purpose within the structure of the Department of Personnel.

Currently, the share of women among internal affairs bodies' middle and senior management and regular and junior management, including civil personnel, is about 10% and this number tends to increase year by year. But it also must be taken into account that the comparatively low number of women compared to men is natural due to major directions of activities of internal affairs bodies (which is to prevent crimes and other forms of violations, reveal committed crimes and criminals, protect public order, ensure public safety and other difficult and severe tasks) and due to the nature of work requiring uninterrupted execution of duties during the day.

*RH:* What is the relationship between the police and visible and cultural minority groups? Has that changed over the years and have there been specific initiatives designed to address concerns?

*FG:* It has historically been the case that national minorities living in Azerbaijan consider themselves entirely part of the Azerbaijani nation while keeping both their national identity and ethnic traditions. Therefore, there have never been any incidents among ethnic Azerbaijanis and Russians, Jews, Tatars, Tats, Lezgies, Avars, Ingiloys, and other minority groups. Friendly, kind, brotherhood relations have existed and that continues today. The Azerbaijani government approaches this issue with sensibleness. Representatives of national minorities are represented in all state bodies. This is the case with police bodies as well. National composition of our personnel reflects the composition of the entire Azerbaijani population. For the sake of information, I would like to note that hundreds of Russians, Jews, Tatars, Lezgies, Avars, Talishs, etc., serve in different posts in internal affairs bodies and national identity doesn't play any role in this regard. Among them, there are senior officials such as chiefs of head departments of the Central Office of the Ministry and heads of city, district, and regional police departments.

*RH:* You have seen many positive changes as well as some difficult challenges during your police career. What have been the biggest challenges for you?

*FG:* First of all I must note that by its essence being in the police organization is generally a difficult profession. Only those who have true passion for their profession comprehend its necessity for society and—I would not be afraid to use this expression even if it sounds exaggerated—"take it as their mission" to accept all these difficulties and serve in the police up to the end. Those who join the police by accident are revealed very fast and are obliged to take other professions that are not as difficult. Therefore, for me, there is little concept of physical difficulty; it is the moral difficulties that are experienced by every person.

*RH:* How do you see the role of policing in citizens' security in Azerbaijan?

*FG:* The task of police in Azerbaijan is to protect life, health, rights, and freedoms of humans, state, legal, and physical persons' legal interests and property from illegal activities. The role and place of police within society, which at first place are defined as creation of a secure environment and welfare for human life and living, prevention of violation of their rights, and restoration of violated rights, are determined by legislative acts and internal normative documents based on these legislative acts. These documents define the basis of its activities. Nowadays it is not possible to imagine police activity in the area of ensuring public safety as being isolated from public life. From this perspective, special attention is given to strengthening of cooperative ties within civil society institutions. At the same time, all necessary measures are carried out for strengthening cooperation with media representatives.

102 Service–Call Central System serves to build the activity of police on high principle, which is a human factor. This service is created from the perspective of exact registering of crimes and executing immediate operational measures against illegal offenses affecting citizens' daily life. The system is principally a new form of strengthening the direct contact with the populace in our country and enables immediate response from Ministry of Internal Affairs on committed or planned crimes and incidents that have taken place and accelerates the process of reaching the incident location of investigative operational groups by defining the location of postpatrol service with means of special navigation. It considerably increased the centralized control over quick reaction to signals incoming to area police bodies. Immediate control over submitted appeals and their operational solution was achieved by the functioning of a "hot line" electronic e-mail address in the ministry.

All these measures, which are under direct attention of the head of our state, are aimed at strengthening of legality, execution of functions of police more efficiently, and involvement of humans more actively into the democratization process and into the work of ensuring public security.

*RH:* How important is crime prevention? What do you think should be the priority areas for preventing crime?

*FG:* Prevention of crimes, along with being one of the very important and actual issues, at first serves the protection of rights and freedoms of humans. The conditions conducive to commitment of more severe crimes can be established if no preventive character measures are carried out. Expansion of criminality in its turn might create threats to security of state and society. Therefore, one of the reforms in police bodies is timely prevention of crimes, elimination of causes creating them, resolving of problems existing in this area, including keeping under attention at all times and conflicting families, drug users, persons inclined to alcohol, and persons falling under the category of criminally risky in society but not limiting their freedoms and rights. One of the most effective of prevention measures is the close contact of police with the public and in assisting citizens with purposeful and systematic public awareness measures.

*RH:* What crimes do you see as being most challenging for the Azerbaijan National Police to deal with?

*FG:* Although the disclosing of very complicated crimes might be very difficult, I believe there is not any undetected crime and, even if such crimes exist, their number is very minor. In this case, the decisive role here depends on approach and professionalism of the police. Therefore, increasing the level of professionalism of police personnel is one of the priority objectives to which MIA pays special attention.

*RH:* Regarding the recent developments in policing, what are your expectations for the future? What is required to improve police performance?

*FG:* Looking back to the path of development of police I dare say that, despite passing through extremely complicated and difficult service experiences, the Azerbaijani police managed to stand all these tests with honor and successfully implemented all tasks and objectives put before them. During recent years the material and technical bases of police were expanded and strengthened and its structural organization was brought into conformity with current conditions and defined requirements. It is significant to note that on the basis of the state program, "On Improvement of Police Bodies' Activities" for the 2004–2008 years initiated and approved by President Ilham Alyev, reforms were carried out in the areas of perfection of the structure of the ministry, improving the material technical base, social protection of personnel, and increasing the public awareness measures on the role of police in society. New information and analytic entities carrying out the fight against dangerous types of crimes and also having an important role in adoption of appropriate governance decisions were established.

The measures on the application of new information technologies in the MIA system are carried out successfully with close support of state and government in order to improve the governance mechanism, increase the prompt reaction of forces and means, optimize proactive activities in changing conditions, strengthen operational positions, and enhance control over criminogenic situations. Currently, there are 12 information resources acting in the areas of prevention, detection, investigation of crimes, search for criminals, ensuring of public order and public security and organization of traffic security, and other areas.

*RH:* How would you describe relations between police and criminologists, the relationship between theory and practice, and your organization's management's attitude toward research conducted in this area.

*FG:* There is one famous saying that "practice is blind without theory, theory is dead without practice." We consider the issues related to the study of criminalistics problems and their research, generalization, and application in practice to be very important. While there is not a separate body which has the primary function to carry out scientific research, training is provided in the police academy to prepare police and sheriff's personnel to conduct organizational and criminological analysis.

Engagement of separate employees in scientific activity along with service is positively appraised and all conditions are created for them. Currently taking into account both educational and medical entities, three doctors of sciences, 27 doctors of philosophies, and 36 candidates of doctoral studies are serving within police personnel structures. Certain research, analyses, and investigations on the activities of police are carried out also by structural units under my supervision. However, these inquiries are absolutely related to the practical side of this activity. The results of our research find their reflection not in scientific lectures, articles, or dissertations but in development of numerous practical measures, methodological recommendations, and resources.

*RH:* Are there areas of police practice that are currently under-researched?

*FG:* Police activity is an area that develops together with society and public relations. In this regard, I think there are lots of measures standing before us. Their termination is not expected as time passes; on the contrary, the necessity for deeper and wider research is emerging.

*RH:* What do you feel have been your greatest accomplishments?

*FG:* I have encountered numerous difficulties and hardships in 26 years of service but must note that there were also many moments of success and happiness during the execution of my duties. It is very difficult to select the most significant among them. My conclusion is that my most significant achievement during my service period is my service itself and having the opportunity to be engaged in my favorite profession.

*RH:* You have more than 25 years in policing. Have you developed a personal policing philosophy? Has that philosophy changed over time?

*FG:* Of course. The differences in approaches to the professional activity of young people aged 25 and police personnel with considerable service experience are inescapable. In 1983, when I started service, I was a product of the period. I carried communist ideas and in certain meanings considered them as fundamental principles. But as time elapsed and my work experience increased, I understood that it was not the case at all. The highest blessings in the lives of human beings are their rights to safe and secure lives. This is the essence of the changes in my police philosophy, and my approach and my service activity are justly related to this. Certainly, these changes have not happened in one day. They are results of my mediation over different problems and topics during my many years of service. My current police philosophy is to serve the Azerbaijan Republic and Azerbaijani nation with dignity and conscience.

*RH:* When you go to police conferences, like the one you recently attended in Ohrid, do you find that many of the issues are the same for police leaders?

*FG:* Each time during my participating in international events and being in contact with police officials of different countries I come to the conclusion that, despite different conditions in societal developments, historical traditions, and national features, there are lots of similarities in the problems faced by police bodies in all countries. This is natural, as all problems by their fundamental nature come from our duties of ensuring public security and order. Along with this, there are huge similarities in regard to the solution of these problems despite the existence of differing conditions of police service.

*RH:* Finally, General, do you have any additional comments regarding policing?

*FG:* I think your questions were sufficiently broad and comprehensive; therefore, there is no need for comments. Let me express my gratitude to IPES and personally to you for your interest in Azerbaijan and activity of its police bodies and for enabling me to share my thoughts concerning this with a broad number of readers. I hope this will not be your last article concerning Azerbaijan.

*RH:* Thank you very much for sharing your experiences, observations, and insights into policing with us. It has been a pleasure.

# 4

# Interview With Muhidin Alić, Minister of Internal Affairs of Federation of Bosnia and Herzegovina

INTERVIEWED BY JASMIN AHIĆ
AND NEDŽAD KORAJLIĆ

**Contents**



## Background

This interview offers us the views of Muhidin Alić, current minister of internal affairs of Federation of Bosnia and Herzegovina, on several aspects of police work and police enforcement in Bosnia and Herzegovina.

Coming from the Ministry of Internal Affairs of Federation of Bosnia and Herzegovina, Mr. Alić analyzes the transition and restructuring of the police sector after the war in Bosnia and Herzegovina. He emphasizes the problems that occurred in police structures and agencies due to the dysfunctional organization of the police set up through the Dayton Peace Accord. He provides his thinking about the relationship between academic analysis and police practices, his professional experience, and his visions of the principal issues and of the results obtained, as well as his opinions on possible future developments and improving police work in Bosnia and Herzegovina.

The interview took place on October, 20, 2008, in Minister Alić's office in Sarajevo.

### Introduction

Minister of Interior of Federation of Bosnia and Herzegovina Muhidin Alić was born on September 14, 1960, in the town of Tesanj in Central Bosnia and Herzegovina. Minister Alić graduated from the Law Faculty in 1986 at the University of Sarajevo in Bosnia and Herzegovina. His professional engagement in police started in 1987, where he was appointed as chief inspector for economic crime in Ministry of Interior of Socialist Republic of Bosnia and Herzegovina. In 1991 he became chief of the Department for Classic Crimes in the same institution.

After the breakdown of Socialist Federal Republic of Yugoslavia in 1991, war started in Bosnia and Herzegovina. After the war (1992–1995), he was deployed to the newly formed and decentralized Ministry of Zenicko–Dobojski Canton, where he worked as chief of Department for Blood and Sexual Felonies. He is currently federal minister of internal affairs of Federation of Bosnia and Herzegovina.

### The Interview

*JA & NK:* Minister Alić, for the beginning of the interview, can you please describe your professional experience?

*MA:* I joined the former Socialist Republic Police department for economic crime through a competitive examination process and, in 1987, I worked as a senior police officer in Zenica City in Central Bosnia. Since then I have been always engaged in developing activities related to various police work. I have worked in almost all departments of our ministries from the work and specialization in "classic" or general crime to blood and sexual felonies or even organized crime. After the horrible war and devastation of our country, a restructured police system based on total decentralization of police agencies guided my activities in the newly formed Ministry of Interior, first at Zenica–Doboj Canton and then at the federal level.

*JA & NK:* Minister, do the Dayton Peace Accords offer good ground for an efficient fight against criminality in Bosnia and Herzegovina—mainly at an organizational level?

*MA:* Well, since the Dayton Peace Accords were signed in December 1995, Bosnia and Herzegovina's (BiH) multiple police forces have been a major obstacle to their implementation and consequently the country's progress toward a normal democratic state and its integration into the European Union (EU). It is my sense that Dayton doesn't provide a good framework for an efficient fight against crime, especially organized crime.

I will try to explain. Like Dayton, Bosnia itself (the country's police forces) is divided. We have two entities (the Federation of Bosnia and Herzegovina and Republika Srpska [Republic of Serbia, RS]) and maintain our own police forces under the control of our respective interior ministers. Authority over the police is further decentralized in the Federation, with each of the 10 cantons also possessing a ministry of the interior or MUP (Ministarstvo unutrasnjih poslova).[1] While the RS police are merely subdivided geographically into regional public security centers and local police stations, the chiefs of which remain directly accountable to the RS interior minister, the cantonal ministers of interior have significant autonomy vis-à-vis the Federation ministry. The limited power of my Federation interior ministry is indicated by the short list of policing tasks that fall within its purview: coordinating interentity and intercantonal cooperation, especially in regard to terrorism and other serious and organized crimes; protecting VIPs; and guarding diplomatic premises. The 10 cantonal interior ministries are responsible for all other aspects of law enforcement, with each municipality having a police administration.

The RS ministry of the interior, by contrast, is responsible for all crime prevention and enforcement in the entity.[2] Under the Ministry of the Interior, there are five public security centers that match the areas covered by district courts. Also, Brcko District has its own autonomous police force and structure. The director of police in Brcko reports to the mayor and provides monthly reports to the district assembly. The assembly, in turn, convenes a police supervisory committee.[3]

*JA & NK:* I would like to start with questions related to the police profession. What have been the most important changes in the profession? By this, I mean changes in the pure philosophy of police work. Based on your experience, which changes have been the most important to the police in terms of philosophies, organizational structure, specializations, politics and programs, equipment, and personnel? I have in mind the crossover from a socialist or Communist police work philosophy to a democratic one.

*MA:* The first and the most significant change that happened is that, in socialism, law enforcement agencies had the prior goal of securing the state or state institutions from external and internal ideological enemies; citizens as a category were somewhere at the end of securing objects. In democracy, the first and most important goal is securing its citizens. That is, in my modest thinking, the biggest conceptual switch, especially taking in mind that we didn't have a tradition of democratic policing. The main organizational change was that our police had to reform from a highly militarized concept to a democratic civilian system. Separate items are processes of renovation in the specialization, politics and programs, equipment, and personnel.

*JA & NK:* When you say "renovation process," what do you mean—taking into account the fact that the small country of Bosnia, with only 4 million inhabitants, already has 16 law enforcement agencies on different levels from municipality levels to state level?

*MA:* I think that we badly need reform. A small and divided security area and the organization that we have now is a haven for criminals and a hell for the police and citizens. Today in Bosnia and Herzegovina we have very unorganized and inefficient police solutions, thinking in an organizational sense.[4]

*JA & NK:* Taking into consideration this postwar period and this transitional switch from socialism to "capitalism," I would like to ask if, in the work of your organization, you have been affected—and if so, how—by developments outside the country (human rights demands, universal codes of ethics, practical

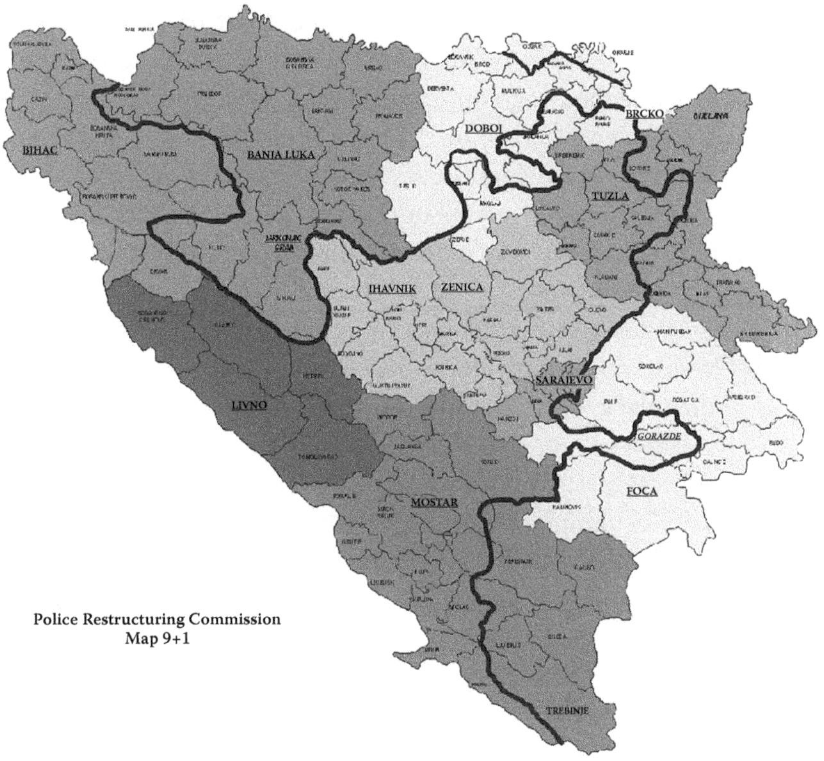


**Figure 4.1** Administrative police division in BiH. From the Police Restructuring Commission, www.ohr.int/ohr-info/maps/images/prc-map.gif

interactions with police from other countries, personal experiences outside the country, new crime threats, etc.)?

*MA:* From the aspects and experiences that we have in Bosnia, I would say that we have good developments in the field of practical interactions with the local community, citizens, and also policies from the neighborhood, but we haven't met standards of EU policies yet. We are still in a transitional phase. But the important thing that is characteristic of this region is that our police organs don't have resistance toward changes. I had the opportunity to be a part of some of those processes, and I think that we have accepted and implemented very qualitative and proposed changes—for example, from the EUPM [European Union Police Mission][5] in Bosnia and Herzegovina.

I think that the police are willing to speed up the processes of reform but, unfortunately, our postwar political situation is very complex and difficult, and most of this process is blocked because of that. I think that police should be faster in implementing approaches to citizens, especially through the project, "Work of Police in Community." I worked on this project in Zenica City for 4 years and I can say that we had remarkable results in this work with community.

*JA & NK:* Is it harder to be a police officer now or was it harder in the time of socialism?

*MA:* If we are comparing this system with our old socialist system, I would say that it is much harder to be a police officer in this postwar system. In the old system, police officers had special status—social, institutional, economic, and so on—but the control of the police work was not the priority. Nowadays, we have emphasis on control and the protection of human rights, and the police are a little bit afraid in implementing those concepts (when to use authority and force or not to overcome resistance), while the social and institutional status—that is, the protection of police officers at their work—is in the second stage of the plan. I think that the optimal solution would be the balance between both courses.

*JA & NK:* How should policing in Bosnia and Herzegovina be performed? What should be the preferred priorities and strategies in Bosnia: hard-edged crime control, prevention, services, order maintenance work; what mix for which types of problems: proactive–reactive; community policing–law enforcement, or maybe full repression or some other framework?

*MA:* I am a supporter of the combined strategy, both prevention and repression. I am at that standpoint because I have the experience of both: repression in socialism and the "only prevention concept" now in the postwar period. We could evaluate the success of both, but in my personal thinking neither one gave us expected results. A combined approach is the solution for Bosnia.

*JA & NK:* Except for this project, can you point out some others that, in your thinking, are the crucial ones for Bosnia? Do you have some unsuccessful projects?

*MA:* A very important and very sensitive project is the project of protecting refugees and displaced persons and returnees. For example, we have the Serbian associations that want to be able to "stay" in the Federation of Bosnia and Herzegovina, who wrote to the international agencies that ethnic Serbs in Zenica City (a city with a majority of ethnic Bosniacs) were slaughtered because one Serb committed suicide with a bomb. They have used this death to say that Serbs are not protected in Zenica just because the man was ethnically a Serb. We have organized one council of the returnees in which they, the people that have returned to Zenica City, will report every 15 days to the domestic and international agencies how the security situation is and not depend on some politically oriented association from another entity. Because of its success, this project spread throughout all of Bosnia and Herzegovina in the places where people returned to their homes after the war.

Overall, in this postwar political situation in Bosnia, it is very hard to convince domestic and international agencies, in our case the EUPM or the Office of High Representative,[6] that you are doing a good job when you have political lies that politicians from one or the other association use for their political goals in everyday life.

*JA & NK:* Are these political problems which are affecting the police work possibly the biggest threat to the internal security of Bosnia?

*MA:* They are a threat, but in the general rate of criminality in Bosnia they are not a high percentage. The biggest problem is in traffic felonies and road accidents. Bosnia is a country with the highest percentage of road deaths per inhabitants in Europe. We don't have quality roads or highways and the traffic accidents have become a big problem. Jurisdiction over traffic is in the hands of cantonal policies and the efforts to coordinate joint operations in preventive measures don't yield expected results. The Federal Ministry of Internal Affairs has a coordinative role only. I have tried to harmonize all cantonal strategies and my ministry paid 1.5 million

Euros to buy the needed technical equipment (radar, tests, and all other instruments needed for traffic accident prevention and control), and the expectation is that we will have a decrease in traffic felonies of 5% each year, so we could a have reasonable percentage by 2012 when we are expecting to enter the European Union. And, as I said, it is not in the jurisdiction of the Federal Ministry.

*JA & NK:* In this beginning of transitional times, did the events after September 11, 2001, have an effect on police work in Bosnia?

*MA:* Bosnia was faced with some highly sensitive questions, keeping in mind that the majority of the population of Bosnia is Bosnian Muslims, and there was a problem of some foreign fighters [Mujahedeen] who didn't come to help in the fatherland war of the Bosnian people. The legal revision of a naturalized Bosnian citizenship gained after the war gave a good result. Together with our international friends, we have resolved some international criminal cases. In this sense the presence of international actors and international community in Bosnia is very significant.

*JA & NK:* How would you evaluate the pay of police officers in Bosnia? Are they at some acceptable level and what about your efforts in your professional career in the financial area? Can underpaid police officers do their role in action against terrorist acts, for example? Is the police job in Bosnia a job worth fighting for?

*MA:* Well, if I have to evaluate the pay of the police (especially in my Federal Ministry for Internal Affairs), I will try to be objective, taking into consideration that I am a representative of the government now working in police department. The pay is at some acceptable level, maybe not totally acceptable, but in the last year we had two increases of salaries for the police, in the field and in administration. I, personally, think that if I would compare some colleagues of mine in other branches and their careers, I would say that the police job in the Balkans is not some "reward," but, as you also know, that it is a job that the person needs to love.

*JA & NK:* Is there a relation between academic society and practice in Bosnia, or what should be the relationship between theory and practice? What can practitioners learn from theory, and what can theory builders learn from practitioners?

*MA:* Undoubtedly, science and practice need to work together; there are some different standpoints from both sides, but in my thinking, only working together can produce good relations and good results. Two months ago I signed an agreement with the University of Sarajevo about improvement of relations in the sphere of education and the employment of finished students. On the question of what we can learn, numerous things are at stake. We can see that maybe the models of work that we conduct cannot be implemented in this multiethnic destroyed community; maybe we cannot fight the new threats such as organized crime without really open cooperation with our neighbors (yesterday, our enemies in war). Many things can be learned, but the competition needs to be on a healthy basis.

*JA & NK:* Where do you find theory-based information? Where do you look: journals, professional magazines, books, publications, reports? Does the Federal Ministry conduct its own research projects?

*MA:* As I mentioned before, we are, in Bosnia, in the process of police reform and I have been one of the participants in the commission for the reconstruction of police in Bosnia. In that process, I had the opportunity to review many models of the work of the police of EU countries. We have tried to find the best solution for Bosnia knowing and comparing the experiences of international police officials involved in reform. So, the theory-based information is domestically and internationally grounded. When the research is in question, I have to say that we have good cooperation with the University of Sarajevo—and, especially, with the Faculty of Criminal Justice Sciences—in conducting really needed research projects. But because of our limited financial and academic capabilities and our structural position in these turbulent times, we do not conduct our own research projects.

*JA & NK:* In this context I would like to finish our conversation. At the current time—that is, a postwar, transitional, reform-oriented, and politically incorrect situation—is there an opportunity for the police to do effective work?

*MA:* If the politicians don't find a good solution and reach consensus, then even very good and quality reform of police will not produce the changes which could lead Bosnia to be a secure European country.

*JA & NK:* Thank you, Minister, and all the best in your future projects.

## Endnotes

1. In addition to its regular police forces, the Federation also has a separate Court Police (under the authority of the Federation Supreme Court) and Finance Police (under the Ministry of Finance and, effectively, the OHR Anti-Fraud Department). The Federation Court Police are responsible for protecting trials, court buildings, and witnesses; transporting prisoners; enforcing court-ordered evictions and carrying out court-ordered arrests; and (somewhat oddly) dealing with cases of child abduction. The Court Police are also mandated to assist the Federation Ombudsman, but have thus far lacked the resources to do so. The RS has neither court police nor finance police.
2. The unified RS command structure means that the EUPM (European Union Police Mission) and OHR (Office of the High Representative) can reasonably hold the RS interior minister responsible for policing failures throughout the entity.
3. The committee is required to meet at least twice a year, but convenes more frequently should the need arise. The committee has proved a useful means of scrutinizing the police and their attainment of established targets.
4. See map in Figure 4.1 for the proposed reform solution.
5. The EUPM, in coordination with and under the local political guidance of the European Union Special Representative (EUSR) in BiH, and as part of the broader rule of law approach in BiH and in the region, is aiming, through mentoring, monitoring and inspecting, to establish in BiH a sustainable, professional, and multiethnic police service operating in accordance with European and international standards. EUPM operates in line with the general objectives of Annex 11 of the General Framework Agreement for Peace in Bosnia and Herzegovina.
6. For more information about the engagement and the mandate of International Community in Bosnia, see www.ohr.int.

# 5

# Interviews With Uros Pena, Director of Police, Republic of Srpska, and Goran Lujic, Director of Police, Brcko District, Bosnia-Herzegovina

INTERVIEWS AND TRANSCRIPTIONS BY LAURENCE ARMAND FRENCH AND ELDAN MUJANOVIĆ

**Contents**

**The Interviews**

The location of the interview with Uros Pena was the premises of the Ministry of Internal Affairs of Republic of Srpska, Banja Luka. The interview took place on December 3, 2009, from 10:20 to 11:40 a.m. The location of the interview with Goran Lujic took place at the premises of the Faculty of Criminal Justice, Criminology and Security Studies, University of Sarajevo on December 1, 2009, from 3:15 to 4:30 p.m. The interviews were conducted in the local Slavic language and translated into American English.

**Interview With Uros Pena**

*Career*

*LF & EM:* Tell us a little bit about your career: length, organizations worked in, movements, specializations, etc. Basically standard stuff.

*UP:* I was born in 1959 in Mrkonjic Grad, BiH, where I finished primary and secondary school. I received my university degree in 1982. After I finished my graduate education in law, I started working in the economic sector with the Energoinvest company. I did this for about 4 years.

I started my police career in 1988 as a duty head of the police station in Mrkonjic Grad, where I worked until the war began in 1991. At this time I transferred to a state security unit, where I spent some time as head of the legal department. Starting in 1996, I became head of the criminal police in the Center of Public Security in Mrkonjic Grad. Then, in 2000, I became mayor of Center, which later transformed into a sector of the RS [Republic of Srpska] entity. In 2002, I became deputy minister of interior affairs of RS and later the associate mayor for human resources and, in 2004, mayor of the Department for Police Training and

Education. Then, in 2006, I was appointed to my current position as director of police for the Republic of Srpska. So, as you can see, I have worked in various aspects of policing. My scientific training? As I mentioned earlier, I am legally trained and passed the juridical exam in 1988. I remembered clearly when I took that exam. There were some 300 auditors there, and being so young at the time, I must admit that I was nervous taking the exam under these circumstances.

Four years ago, I earned my MS degree and last year earned my PhD in criminal law, in Kragujevac, Serbia. My PhD is in criminal justice and I specialized in the field of criminology, although I continue to have a strong interest in the legal process.

*LF & EM:* What motivated you to enter police work?

*UP:* A man does not always get to work in the area he initially desires. I believe that if I had started as a legal practitioner in 1988, such as an attorney or a judge—positions which were short of personnel at that time—I certainly would have earned more money. But life chances brought me into police work. Working as a policeman, for at least 2 to 3 years, gets you hooked; it gets into your blood. As the saying goes: Once a police officer, always a police officer. Motivation is not always based on fame or money. There is an intrinsic challenge in doing a good job every day. It feels good when a police officer does something important like preserving the peace and individual freedoms and working with your colleagues in preventing criminal acts.

Policing is a challenging profession. I also believe it is important to work in a variety of positions within the field of law enforcement. I changed workstations and duties within various police agencies every 2 to 3 years in order to gain new experiences from working with new colleagues and maintain the stimulation and challenges associated with police work.

When looking at police officers in general, it is obvious that they do not all hold the same view of police issues. The experience differs for police officers on street patrol from those involved in criminal investigations or those in administrative positions. Your beat schedule and place of assignment as well as your discretionary authority have a lot to do with job satisfaction in the police profession. These factors have a lot to do with your perception of your job and your actual job performance. You feel most secure when you are doing the job you feel you are trained to do and under circumstances that are favorable to you.

*LF & EM:* What did you find different from your expectations regarding police work? What changes have you experienced?

*UP:* Man exists to change his mind. It is a common fact of life that man is often initially enthusiastic about his life circumstances only to become disappointed later. This is a common phenomenon, but I think motivation is a critical factor here. Motivation is the most important element in job satisfaction. Yet, disappointments are part of policing. You feel disappointed when you cannot finish a job. You feel that you have let down the citizens you serve. You feel caught between doing a through job, protecting society from crime and fear, and the political constraints and countless litigations that interfere with this process.

But, on the other hand, you are dealing with people who are accustomed to the old system, where there was not always a lot of trust for the police.

*Changes Experienced in Policing*

*LF & EM:* What do you see as the most important changes which have happened in policing over the course of your career (philosophies, organizational arrangements, specializations, policies and programs, equipment, personnel, diversity, etc.)?

*UP:* First of all, the old system, the batch system, was one where decisions were made by the political powers. The police were strictly subordinate to this authority. This was more like a military hierarchy, where the orders came down from above with little discretionary authority allowed for the rank-and-file police officer. Police were subordinate to the central powers and the public came to associate the police with the central government. Oftentimes, the public saw this as a "life or death" situation where they had little power over these decisions.

The police today represent a separate part of the legal system and are not used merely as a control mechanism for the central government. The police today operate according to their legal mandate and not on arbitrary orders from political officials.

In the past, the public was alienated from the police; they feared them because they knew that law enforcement represented repressive political measures and was not based on statutory laws as it is now. In the past, the public did not know what the rules were from day to day. The police were seen more as a military force than a public safety agency.

New technology and training have also changed dramatically. New equipment and cooperation with other agencies have really enhanced the role of policing. New investigative techniques and training have helped greatly in curtailing cross-border drug and human trafficking.

The European Union funded our new police academy, where police are now better educated and trained than in the past. Police today are trained to serve the public and not be political bosses. Yet, more changes are necessary to improve the role of the police in RS.

*LF & EM:* What differences do you see between before and now, especially in BiH?

*UP:* There have been dramatic changes. As I stated earlier, in the past the police were greatly influenced by the political structure, especially at the central level of government. There were police officers who were selected merely based on their political loyalty to the government or party. Now, you are selected based on your academic and physical abilities. Even then, some police officers still adhere to their political, ethnic, or sectarian upbringing, sometimes placing this above their legal mandate when performing their duties.

*LF & EM:* What changes in external conditions (support from communities, legal powers, judicial relations, relations with minority communities, resource provision, political influence, etc.) have had a significant impact on policing?

*UP:* In the past, public support was not a consideration. The orders came down from the central government. The police did not need to please the public—only control them. The public was torn because some of their neighbors were police informants. Essentially, the police held considerable power—even that of "life or death" for citizens who they felt were not supportive of the central government.

Today this is no longer the case. Police are now better trained and operate according to promulgated laws that the public is aware of and can change through the legislative process.

*LF & EM:* What is the relationship of the police with politics?

*UP:* For BiH it is hard to say because the situation since 1995 has been very political. The country is divided along ethnic, sectarian, and political lines. In this sense, politics is hard to define. Everything is political: monetary investments, building construction, road construction—you name it.

Nevertheless, the most important element today that separates the current political environment from the past is the developing body of laws designed to provide constancy and direction to the public regardless of which entity they reside in or what their sectarian/political affiliation is. I know that politics will always be a factor, but laws limit the manner in which it operates today in BiH.

For example, it has been over 3 years since someone politically attempted to influence me. Much of this is because they know that I do play by the rules. But I cannot speak for all police officers and officials in BiH. And I would not say that police corruption is any greater in BiH than it is in any other neighboring European county.

*LF & EM:* How has the authority of the police changed?

*UP:* In the past the police had greater authority to control the public. Now, orders are made at the director's level and not at the political level. One example is that in the past police could hold someone without charges for days. Now you have to charge someone within 24 hours.

*LF & EM:* Relations between juridical organs and police, formerly and now? How have things changed?

*UP:* Since 2003, new criminal law procedures have been in place, including new and improved investigative measures and police training in these procedures. Moreover, criminal and civil investigations are now the role of prosecutors and not left merely to the discretion of police officers as they were in the past. Now every police action is reviewed by a prosecutor. This is an important check on the abuse of police powers and authority. Police make the arrest but the prosecutor determines probable cause for continued adjudication.

The police still represent a powerful force in every country. But now prosecutors mediate that authority by determining which cases merit continued adjudication throughout the legal system. Today, the police and prosecutors work cooperatively in ensuring that the legal system operates in a fair manner.

*LF & EM:* Compare society support and resources formerly and today.

*UP:* The public is the same. Police have to have good relations with the public to function properly. Police have to demonstrate to the public that they service them and not themselves. Police need to have the public's trust and cooperation to do their job properly.

And we must do this within a legal framework, one that operates in every municipality, providing public safety and security for everyone. All public officials, heads of police departments, mayors, courts, and the public, including minorities, need to participate in the process of safeguarding society. Everyone needs to assist in identifying problems and help prioritize the seriousness of these problems. Essentially, this process is now known as community policing. Here, policing is geared to the security issues that exist within the community and are identified as such by the community.

*LF & EM:* Overall, has the quality of policing improved or declined (street work, specialized units, managerial capacity, self-evaluation, interagency cooperation, etc.)?

*UP:* As director of police in RS, I do my best. But remember that there are external pressures that influence the role of the police, including parliament and other aspects of government.

If one element of this mix is not working well, then it affects the police as well. Sometimes our hands are tied by the political process. But improvements have been made. In the past there were no laws regulating drug and human trafficking or even prostitution. Now we are trained in addressing these social issues. We have police officers that specialize in these criminal matters. Today, we are more specialized and better trained to address the criminal elements plaguing society.

*LF & EM:* In general, is it more or less difficult to be a police officer (street, manager) now than in the past?

*UP:* Absolutely [more difficult]. Yes. Today we need to accept the public's perception of police and gain their support while this was not a major concern in the past when the police had nearly absolute authority over the citizens. Today, the police have to maintain a new image, that of public servant. The police in RS today are more diverse, with more females on the force, representing all the various groups comprising our society.

*Personal Policing Philosophy*

*LF & EM:* What do you think should be the role of the police in society? What should be their job, functions, and roles? What should be left to other people or organizations?

*UP:* The police are but one component of society. They should not be allowed to possess unchecked power and authority because, if so, then you will have a police state, you will have militarism.

If the other government institutions function adequately, then the police will be able to function adequately as well. By this I mean that the ministry of justice, departments of health and education, and all other segments of government need to function properly for the police to do theirs job in providing public safety and security.

It is necessary to better educate the public on the problem of drug abuse. And the Ministry of Health has to do more to better control the availability of sedatives and other medicines that lend themselves to abuse. Once this occurs, policing the drug problem will be easier. But, today, Banja Luka has tens of thousands of unresolved drug cases. And this problem impacts not only the police but the prosecutors as well. The courts are overwhelmed with this social problem.

*LF & EM:* Which organizational arrangements work and which do not?

*UP:* There is no particular system that I know of that is totally good or bad. We can look to France, for example, with its highly centralized system, which seems to do well, but this is not always the case. There are examples of countries where the police are decentralized with equal success. It depends on the society and country. So, it is hard to say what is the best organizational structure for BiH, but I strongly believe that effective public security must be at the local level.

*LF & EM:* What policies on relations with the community, with political groups, and with other criminal justice organizations work well?

*UP:* The number of agencies is not necessarily a handicap, as we can see from examples in some European countries. The European Council offers examples of best practice and it shares these with us. What counts are positive results. These results are best when policing is done at the community level with public input about local needs.

Two months ago I conducted some research on the theme of police officers working within multiethnic environments with police officers representative of the different nationalities comprising these neighborhoods. This is an important aspect of policing in RS because we want the public to see the police as being a service agency and not just an agency that favors any particular political or ethnic group. Again, I state my belief that the police should not be held hostage to any political group and instead must work within a formal legal framework.

*LF & EM:* What hampers cooperation with other agencies and groups?

*UP:* Everybody has to appreciate the mandate associated with their job and its purpose. With the police, this is public safety. And public safety necessitates inter- and intra-agency cooperation and coordination of the various agencies mandated to protect the public. The current organizational structure, along with improvements in the selection and training of police personnel, is a great improvement from the past, but there still remain areas that need improvement, notably the exchange of data and information between agencies. This is still a problem within the current system.

*LF & EM:* How should policing be performed? What should be the preferred priorities and strategies: hard-edged crime control, prevention, services, order maintenance work; which mix for which types of problems: proactive–reactive, community policing–law enforcement, etc.?

*UP:* Priorities are difficult to establish given that everything that challenges public safety is an important goal for the police. First of all, the police need to gain the public's trust. The public has to see the police as having integrity and being fair and honest. Of importance, here, is the police being proactive and being seen as being cooperative with other public agencies and institutions.

Germany is a good example of good police/public relations. There, citizens are often willing to assist the police by calling in potential infractions. We are beginning to see similar kinds of things here as well. An ideal situation is where the community helps define law enforcement priorities.

On the other hand, we have to realize that the police tend to protect themselves whenever they come under fire. Personally, I feel that the police should not interfere in the investigative process once they have performed their duty in reporting a crime or arresting suspects. Why? Because this way the police appear to be neutral and not taking sides in the adjudication process. In the past many felt that the police would lie to aid in the prosecution of a suspect. This image has to change if the public is to come to trust and respect the police.

Fortunately, we have few major crimes to police, but when they occur we want the police to remain neutral during the adjudication process. The police have to be seen as being sensitive to the law and acting with integrity and honesty.

*Problems and Successes Experienced*

*LF & EM:* In your experience, which policies or programs have worked well and which have not? And can you speculate for what reasons?

*UP:* Community policing has been a goal during my tenure. This is a major departure from the old system whereby the police were seen as a control mechanism for the central government.

*LF & EM:* What would you consider to be the greatest problem facing the police at this time?

*UP:* This depends upon to whom you are presenting the questions. It has different meanings for different people because the problems are rarely the same.

It is important to see how the public sees things. Even then, people perceive things differently. What is a problem to one is not necessarily a problem to someone else. Public safety falls within this dilemma of differential perception. However, we can all agree that some offenses are more serious than others and need to be addressed. Our police apparatus is now equipped with a sophisticated lab that is capable of DNA analysis and we also have an AFIS [Automated Fingerprint Identification System] system, so we can better analyze evidence.

*LF & EM:* What problems in policing do you find are the most difficult to deal with?

*UP:* For the police of RS, every problem cannot be resolved. I am realistic. There are criminal offenses that will never be resolved. It is impossible to make society free of crime and criminals but what we strive for is an attempt to minimize the rate of crime while improving our investigative skills in solving crimes. This process has shown improvements over the past 4 years: Crimes have decreased by nearly 5% while public order violations have decreased by nearly 8%, as have the number of traffic offenses. At the same time, our ability to solve crimes has increased by 66%. These efforts have met with approval from the European Council. Obviously, we still have room to improve, but our response time and investigative skills have greatly improved from those in the past.

Yet, we have our limitations. We cannot buy new, safer cars for the public, nor can we build safer highways or improve the quality of public education. These are things that could improve public security but they are out of our hands. And the current economic recession does not help matters.

*LF & EM:* What kinds of internal problems (culture of the organization, managerial deficiencies, allegations of corruption or gender-related problems, etc.) or externally generated problems (resources, community support, etc.) do you have to deal with?

*UP:* The police in RS are pretty much decentralized and they have a certain level of discretionary authority. We are constantly looking at ways to improve our organizational structure, looking for ways to improve our police. Yet, we still have problems finding adequate personnel to join the police force. It is estimated that there are some 22 million people within the former Yugoslavia, many dispersed away from their former homes due to the Balkan war. From that, I have to look for qualified people who are honest and willing to do a good job. Many of the former police and security personnel do not meet the current qualifications, so this is a problem when recruiting new members of the force.

*Theory and Practice*

*LF & EM:* What should be the relationship between theory and practice? What can practitioners learn from theory, and what can theory builders learn from practitioners?

*UP:* Theory and practice do not always correlate. Theory without life experience is not always a suitable solution within the police profession. While I understand the need for a scientific education this must be balanced with quality training. In my mind, 70% of the police training should be in the realm of training and practice so that we can better measure their effectiveness in the field.

In the Republic of Srpska, we have attempted to provide both classroom and practical training at our new police academy following the advice of the European Council and our American trainers. Here, there is primary police training for police officers, with advanced training for those aspiring to become inspectors. Our faculty is drawn from the police force itself. So someone who enters the academy with only a theoretical background, someone who has little or no experience with firearms or investigative procedures, needs to receive the practical training to become an effective police officer. I have encouraged potential recruits to visit my office and the academy so they can see the realities of police training and what is involved in a career in law enforcement.

*LF & EM:* What suppresses cooperation and interactions between theory and practice?

*UP:* It usually is the human factor. Educators and practitioners often compete for the same audience and each wants to flaunt the advantages of her or his perspective over the other. This is a reality of professional life.

*LF & EM:* Which research would be useful for a practice, in which form, and which questions should be elaborated in research to have importance for practice?

*UP:* All research is important, even bad research, because we can learn from mistakes and learn what not to do in similar situations. We conduct our own research. Recently, I initiated a research project consisting of only five questions in order to gain some insight into the public perception of police corruption. Our findings show that the public at large does not see the police organization as being corrupt but instead attributes this phenomenon to corrupt individuals within the police force.

We were also part of a larger study on policing, one that resulted in an 800-page report. This study is now part of our training at the police academy. And in a recent study of the perceived effectiveness of public agencies in RS, the police had a 78% positive response, placing it in the same category as the Orthodox Church. This result surprised even me.

However, I still think more has to be done to address the persistent issue of police corruption—a problem facing all our neighboring countries as well. Corruption, at all levels, appears to be pervasive through the Balkans. It seems to be part of the public mentality. Obviously, this aspect of our culture needs to change. Even for me, it is natural to bring a bottle of scotch to a colleague when requesting a favor. It's a normal practice here. But forcing someone to pay you to get out of a police matter is a more serious matter.

*LF & EM:* Where do you find theory-based information? Where do you look: journals, professional magazines, books, publications, reports?

*UP:* My private library is bigger than most public libraries. Unfortunately, a lot of material was destroyed in the war. In Mrkojic, for example, I graduated in 1995 and while the library resources were not burned, many of them were stolen. But we maintain a good police library with contemporary journals and magazines. The main problem we have is having the leisure to read the material due to the demands of our job.

*Transnational Relations*

*LF & EM:* In the work of your organization, have you been affected—and, if so, how—by developments outside the country (human rights demands, universal codes of ethics, practical interactions with police from other countries, personal experiences outside the country, new crime threats, etc.)? Have those interactions been beneficial or harmful? Which kinds of external international influences are beneficial and which ones less so?

*UP:* The problem within BiH is the mentality that cooperation is only required at the national level and does not need to be applied at the lower levels or in the private sector. Corruption within the private sector is rampant.

At the beginning of 2007, "Mission Triangle" was established, resulting in Europol breaking up the biggest forgery ring involving eight countries, along with the largest illegal printing press. We continue to be an active partner with the European Union and the United States in investigating organized crime, which has run rampant in the region since 1990. As well, our police have participated in the largest drug bust (netting 162 kilograms of illegal drugs) in the region, working cooperatively with police departments from Croatia and Greece. This international cooperation is part of the effort to curtail drug trafficking through the Balkans to Western Europe. I am constantly receiving requests from other countries to have our police partner with them in some aspect of fighting organized criminal activities.

I have had two cases of murders in Banja Luka 2 years ago, including the murder of Ankica Luzajic, who had 27 stabs wounds. Our investigation led us to the suspect, who was hiding in Croatia. However, in this case we were not able to bring the suspect back to RS or to get the Croatian police to prosecute the individual. So, while I strongly believe in cooperating with other police agencies, it is necessary that they reciprocate when we need their assistance. This was not the case in the murder investigation.

*LF & EM:* How have developments after September 11 affected your work?

*UP:* This is a global question. I did not draw my conclusions about this event from the mass media. Instead, I contacted the FBI [U.S. Federal Bureau of Investigation] and the CIA [U.S. Central Intelligence Agency]. We discussed different topics and in the end I got to visit a number of agencies in the United States, where I saw what they have accomplished. I learned a lot from this experience, especially how a large agency like the FBI, with some 17,000 personnel, rapidly instituted the changes necessary for a more effective response to international terrorism. I was then better prepared for our response to any potential terrorist threat.

*Democratic Policing*

*LF & EM:* How would you define democratic policing?

*UP:* I talked about this earlier when I mentioned the need for better cooperation between the police and the public, especially at the community level. The community needs to help identify the problems while at the same time providing support for the police. There needs to be a trust relationship between the community and the police. Everyone realizes that the police are armed with weapons and substantial authority, but they must be trusted to use this power in the right way—to enhance public safety and security. The police cannot be seen as an abusive power.

In some situations the police will have to respond to a larger social crisis, but they must still be seen as being responsive to the community and must not get involved in a larger political struggle. The police lose all credibility when they are seen as representing one political faction over another. This is not democratic policing.

*LF & EM:* What practices would bring democratic policing to life?

*UP:* There is no particular formula I know of that works in all situations. Police agencies need to be receptive to changes in society and the public needs to make improvements to assist the police in doing their job effectively.

*LF & EM:* Can democratic policing be achieved in your country or not, and what obstacles stand in the way?

*UP:* The only way for effective democratic policing is for the police to serve the public's interest at the local level and not be used as a controlling military force, as was the case in the past.

*LF & EM:* Should democratic policing be the goal of reforms?

*UP:* Reform is an ongoing process and, yes, we should be working toward making changes that would better facilitate our job performance. We should not be afraid of making structural and organizational changes that would improve our policing role. But this cannot be done overnight.

### *General Assessments*

*LF & EM:* Are you basically satisfied or dissatisfied with developments in policing?

*UP:* Who can be satisfied with only a temporary political solution and divided country as now exists in BiH? Until there is some permanent solution, I will not be satisfied. Do not get me wrong. I feel that I have achieved a lot during my tenure. I am satisfied with my position, especially in an organizational sense. Improved education and training as well as new technical advances have served to greatly improve our police system. We are dealing with an increasingly satisfied public with statistical support for this supposition. Nonetheless, I feel that there is a lot more to do yet. I have a vision, and if I lose this vision for the future, then I should not be in this position.

*LF & EM:* What is most needed now to improve policing?

*UP:* We need to address new aspects of criminality, such as car theft, organized crime, and drug rings. And while there is some improvement in reducing economic crimes, there are still segments of our society where corruption is a serious problem. It is not enough to merely focus on improving the police, you need to see progress in all aspects of society. I cannot speak for the other parts of the country since I am the director of just one entity, the police force.

In progressive countries, the police find areas for improvement. But this is difficult in a country where corruption is a serious factor. For example, everybody talks about university corruption [exchanging grades for money and/or sex] but the police can do little as long as the deans of faculty allow this process to continue. The police cannot prevent crime by themselves.

*LF & EM:* How do you see the future of police in BiH?

*UP:* Policing should be guided within a constitutional legal framework—one that clearly defines the organizational structure of all the justice agencies. Today, there is no universally agreed upon process within our divided nation. Even then, policing should not revert to the way it used to be. The public needs to trust the police and not fear them as their potential executioner. The police, as well as other relevant agencies, need to work under the constraints of law with avenues for public input available at all levels of operation.

Police officers, as well as other employees, need to have discretional authority under certain circumstances—a degree of creativity in carrying out their daily tasks. Police officers must have certain freedom and professional discretion to do their job well.

*LF & EM:* Thank you for taking the time to talk with us.

**Interview With Goran Lujic**

Mr. Lujic was both receptive and responsive to our inquiry. He was frank and animated in his responses and enthusiastic about the future of policing within his jurisdiction. It is important to realize that Chief Lujic has been a police official only since the Dayton Accord. Absent from his perspective is a direct prewar involvement in policing in BiH.

*Career*

*LF & EM:* Tell us a little bit about your career: length, organizations worked in, movements, specializations, etc. Basically standard stuff.

*GL:* My name is Goran Lujic. I was born in 1978 in the Brcko region, where I attended the local elementary school as well as the technical high school. I was a recruiter during the early stages of the war. In 1994 I went to Belgrade and began my studies at the Police Academy. I graduated during 1998 and my professional career began the same year with my return to BiH, where I was employed with the Bijeljina city police within the management and coordination department. I left that position during 2000 and moved back to Brcko for personal reasons (it is my hometown and my family was already there). My new duty here was that of deputy chief of the criminal investigation department. When the Brcko District was established, I took the new position of deputy chief of police, a job I held until 2007. Actually, I was the chief of criminal investigation department from 2005 to 2007. In February of 2007, the supervisor of the Brcko District appointed me to my current position. I currently live in Brcko with my wife and two sons.

During my career I have attended numerous training courses in different fields of police work, including strategic planning, serious crime investigations, etc. I sought out training provided by the FBI, especially those related to hostage negotiation techniques. I also took courses provided by IPFT [International Police Task Force] (so-called "transitional" courses). More recently, I have completed training provided by ICITAP [International Criminal Justice Investigative Training Program]. ICITAP has played a significant role in providing support to the police in BiH. They provide not only financial support, but theoretical insights and training expertise as well. My future goal is to work toward a master's degree at the Law Faculty in Belgrade.

*LF & EM:* What motivated you to enter police work?

*GL:* Family tradition played a crucial role here. My late brother was a police officer and, thanks to him, I have entered into police work.

*LF & EM:* How has your career development surprised you?

*GL:* As a relatively young police officer, I held some idealistic expectations about a police career. But since then, I realize that it is not a perfect profession. I now realize that police work has its bad aspects as well. But, regardless of these negative elements, I still hold a positive view of police work and attempt to carry out my duties with honor and enthusiasm. I like the challenges this work offers.

*LF & EM:* Did your work prove as interesting or rewarding as you thought it would?

*GL:* I have not been disappointed with my police vocation. I consider it as a critical force for peace, order, stability, and public well-being in Bosnia and Herzegovina, now and in the future. While not comfortable with the term "community policing" per se, I do think that the police provide a degree of normalcy in BiH and for that reason I continue to maintain a positive attitude toward the police profession.

### *Changes Experienced*

*LF & EM:* What do you see as the most important changes which have happened in policing over the course of your career (philosophies, organizational arrangements, specializations, policies and programs, equipment, personnel, diversity, etc.)?

*GL:* To begin with, I think that the police have gone through marked changes recently along with the social system itself. I was not personally involved with the police system that existed before the war in BiH but I am aware of some of the rules from that period. The police had much more power during that time. Since then, their authority has been significantly reduced. However, I don't think that major changes are merely the responsibility of the police. This responsibility needs to be shared by others involved in public security. Unfortunately, the vast majority of responsibility is still placed on the police.

To summarize, the previous system was authoritative and this has changed. These changes have affected police as well. In the past, the police were the legal authority. Now, their main role is to enforce statutory laws, not make laws themselves. Citizens now help make the laws through a representative parliament and other institutions. Police now are expected to assist in enforcing the laws, not making them. So the whole philosophy of police work has changed. Even then, *community policing* is not the only element of police practices. Effective policing needs to take into consideration wider social issues.

Even then I feel more needs to be done. We now have better technical developments and police education than in the past. For example, DNA analysis training will be conducted soon in our police laboratory. This delay in accessing modern technologies in police work has placed us behind police forces in surrounding countries like Croatia and Serbia, who already have more sophisticated police laboratories. We had to pay them for these services because we did not have our own laboratory. Situations like this have harmed our investigative effectiveness.

The former police system was established following the end of the Second World War and continued until the middle 70s when the authoritative police system became fully developed and powerful. Currently, we have a situation where our police candidates are better educated. They now attend one of two higher education institutions: the Faculty of Criminal Justice, Criminology and Security Studies at the University of Sarajevo, and the Internal Affairs Police

University [built since the war by the European Union] in Banja Luka. Candidates from these two educational institutions have a priority during police recruitments. This is one way we can improve police professionalism.

Speaking of diversities, I would like to say that today we have a much better situation within the police profession. When I began working within the Brcko police system, it was one of the first multiethnic police forces in BiH. We decided on this route in 2000 even before the status of Brcko was settled by the Arbitration Commission and the establishment of the special Brcko District. We independently established a 4 + 4 + 2 ethnic balance formula (40% of Bosnians, 40% of Serbs, and 20% of Croats) for our police force. So, in my mind, we don't have a problem with diversity within our police force. Similar efforts have been taken in other parts of the state with regard to this problem, but we were the first to establish a workable formula. But, that said, the true nature of police work is such that the same standards should be applied to everyone regardless of ethnic affiliation.

*LF & EM:* What changes in external conditions (support from communities, legal powers, judicial relations, relations with minority communities, resource provision, political influence, etc.) have had a significant impact on policing?

*GL:* Our main efforts today are to get other institutions (inspections, educational and health organizations) to work with us in a joint effort to create a safer environment in the district. Problems with police attitudes still exist and much work still needs to be done in bringing about effective changes within the police. There is also resistance to change within other related public institutions that still want to guard their power and authority. So I must say that there are still many obstacles to comprehensive approach to the security issues. So, for now, most of the public views the police as the only responsible institution working for their general well-being.

For example, there is a serious problem with corruption in our society and the public looks toward the police to curb it. Few people question the role of other agencies that have a greater legal responsibility in this area, such as those that are supposed to conduct internal audits. Why don't people look at the various disciplinary committees that have oversight over specific organizations (from soccer teams to the public institutions). Instead, all eyes seem to focus on the police, the prosecution, and the courts to remedy this and other pervasive social problems.

The Brcko police have some community support but, to me, it's insufficient. Even then, I see police powers as adequate but, obviously, our job would be easier if only the other institutions conducted their business in a similar fashion.

Our relations with the judiciary are based on mutual respect. Interestingly, some of the research on the public perception of corruption—conducted by Transparency International, for instance—is encouraging because the results indicate that this problem within police is seen to exist to a lesser extent than within the prosecution or the courts.

With regard to resources, I must admit that the Brcko police have the support of the community. Our police organization is unique in that we don't have a minister of interior to answer to. We are only responsible to the government—more precisely, to an independent board that is an arm of parliament, with the additional obligation to follow the mayor's security policies. In this sense, there are few financial obstacles to the police in carrying out our mandate. For example, our department was among the first to have AFIS and IBIS [Integrating Business and Information System] in criminal justice, and we have an adequate vehicle fleet, as well. Our main goal now is to bring our facility up to the proper safety standard.

Another influence on police functions is political interference. Politics influences all aspects of our society and the police are not alone in this regard. Still, efforts are being made to better isolate the police from undue political influences. We eliminated one level of political influence since we do not have a minister of interior to answer to. Nonetheless, there still exist harmful, negative political influences interfering with police work.

*LF & EM:* Overall, has the quality of policing improved or declined (street work, specialized units, managerial capacity, self-evaluation, interagency cooperation, etc.)?

*GL:* Taking into account all the previously mentioned obstacles (change of political system, resource issues, etc.) and the general social environment, I feel that the quality of policing in BiH is still impressive. The police are subjected to a set of standards and to oversight that dictate the quality of police work. It is important to stress that these control mechanisms involve national (independent boards) and international (previously the IPFT and now the European Union Police Mission) bodies who are contributing to this level of quality control.

The issue of interagency cooperation is quite complex, but I feel we can still work things out within the existing police organizations in BiH despite the current barriers. There are currently many forms of interagency cooperation in BiH that are supported by different international agencies such as ICITAP (International Criminal Investigative Training Program). With this type of support at the senior management level, progress toward a unified police effort can be eventually established in BiH.

*LF & EM:* In general, is it more or less difficult to be a police officer (street, manager) now than in the past?

*GL:* Police management is a difficult task today, given the current situation in BiH with the challenges it presents for policing. We have to keep in mind that while the war ended 13 years ago with the Dayton Peace Agreement, this situation created a divided state along with a complex security environment. Clearly, our situation differs from our neighbors' throughout Europe, so it is difficult to compare police work in BiH with that in other Western countries. Besides these structural obstacles, there are other problems such as poverty, pervasive institutionalized corruption, and the like.

*Personal Policing Philosophy*

*LF & EM:* What do you think should be the role of the police in society?

*GL:* I think the modern era of police work has to deal with duties such as security issues and maintaining public order and traffic safety using the latest techniques. This should be the police role in society.

*LF & EM:* What should be their job, functions, and roles? What should be left to other people or organizations?

*GL:* On the one hand, administrative matters, such as vehicle registration, personnel matters, and the like, should be delegated to other institutions. We already leave most of these functions to civil authorities, such as the public register. There are still some competencies with regard to vehicle registration that we would like to transfer to civil institutions as well.

*LF & EM:* Which organizational arrangements work and which do not?

*GL:* We have a centralized model of police organization in the Brcko District which I feel is one of the most efficient police models. Within this organizational model, there exists a clear division of authority, as I think there should be. Police officers are identified by their uniform and they need to be true to the standards the public associates with their status. A strict adherence to orders and standards minimizes the potential for corruption and undue influences.

*LF & EM:* What policies on relations with the community, with political groups, and with other criminal justice organizations work well? What hampers cooperation with other agencies and groups?

*GL:* The police need to convey an image of public trust. They need to market themselves in this manner. I think some police are not fully aware of the need to maintain a positive public image, but we are working toward changing that. This is essential if we are to gain the public's trust and cooperation in maintaining public safety. The public needs to be aware of the challenges facing the police just as the police need to be aware of community needs. Essentially, we have to market ourselves in a positive manner to the public we serve.

In relations between police and politics, certain principles should be demonstrated. Police need to fulfill their duties only as prescribed by law. That is the solution for politics [in the police]. I think that police should not have any kinds of relations with political groups.

With regard to cooperation with other agencies, you need a system that facilitates this process. First, you need to identify existing obstacles to cooperation. A unified system is more conducive to cooperation initiatives. For example, cooperation in the area of crime investigation would be a great asset to law enforcement. We could bring together our joint resources during investigations instead of waiting for one agency to pass this information to another system only after they have finished their work. Working together is really the better and more effective model.

*LF & EM:* How should policing be performed? What should be the preferred priorities and strategies: hard-edged crime control, prevention, services, order maintenance work; what mix for which types of problems; proactive–reactive, community policing–law enforcement, etc.?

*GL:* With regard to this question, I would put prevention at the top of the list. Community policing would then follow, again in a proactive fashion. Certain forms of criminal activity, such as organized crime, need to be proactively suppressed. That's why I would use cutting-edge crime investigation and prevention strategies when addressing this problem.

*Problems and Successes Experienced*

*LF & EM:* In your experience, which policies or programs have worked well and which have not? Can you speculate for what reasons? And what would you consider to be the greatest problem facing the police at this time?

*GL:* I would like again to stress that community support is a top priority for a secure environment in the Brcko District. However, this is a complex process given our past history and the war, as well as the ethnic divisions within our society. The police need to be viewed in a positive manner by the public we serve if we are to overcome these historical obstacles. We have a good idea as to how to proceed but we still need more resources and greater community support.

*LF & EM:* What problems in policing do you find are the most difficult to deal with? What would be easy to change? Internal problems (culture of the organization, managerial deficiencies, allegations of corruption or gender-related problems, etc.) or externally generated problems (resources, community support, etc.)? Is anything about policing easy?

*GL:* As I stated earlier, we are subordinate to the laws and the public. We still have some managerial and organizational problems that we have to overcome but we are making headway with our professional training. Even then, we have a heavy burden because too many people see the police as having the capacity to solve all the problems by themselves. If the crime rate increases, we get the blame. Hopefully, things will improve now that there is a new minister of security at the state level.

*Theory and Practice*

*LF & EM:* What should be the relationship between theory and practice? What can practitioners learn from theory and what theory builders from practitioners?

*GL:* As I have already stated, I am part of a new breed of police officers. It is easier for us to promote the scientific approach than for the officers from the old school. We have to model these scientific practices so that the others will follow our example of professionalism. Our leadership is important here.

*LF & EM:* What is the relationship right now? Does it exist? Does it work? What holds collaboration or interactions back?

*GL:* In my opinion we do not have this level of professionalism in BiH today. It doesn't exist. The scientific practitioner approach has little support because of the general social climate and politics. It has little application in practice. There is no direct link between them.

*LF & EM:* What kind of research—in what form and on what questions—would you find most useful for practice? If not very useful, what could or should theory builders do to make their products more useful to you?

*GL:* There are some strategies, like those designed to combat organized crime and corruption, that are based on a scientific approach. But much of this still exists only at the theoretical level and is not yet an integral part of overall police practice throughout BiH.

We could use more research on the efficiency of police organizations, systems, and good practices. We are trying to conduct this research ourselves but need more assistance from higher education institutions, which has been lacking.

*LF & EM:* Where do you find theory-based information? Where do you look: journals, professional magazines, books, publications, reports?

*GL:* I am a member of the International Association of Chiefs of Police, along with Zlatko Miletic, the director of the federal police, due to the assistance of the people at ICITAP, which also provides us with access to professional journals so we can keep up with the latest trends in the field of policing. Moreover, I consider this interview and the forthcoming book as a significant venue for providing current information about modern policing.

*LF & M:* Does the organization do research on its own? If so, on what types of issues or questions?

*GL:* In our organizational structure we have one managerial position for professional development that organizes educational programs for our staff. But there is no overall systematic program throughout BiH for coordinated research endeavors that would benefit all of the police agencies within the state. There have been some joint efforts in the form of roundtable discussions, but more needs to be done.

*Transnational Relations*

*LF & EM:* In the work of your organization, have you been affected—and, if so, how—by developments outside the country (human rights demands, universal codes of ethics, practical interactions with police from other countries, personal experiences outside the country, new crime threats, etc.)?

*GL:* Well, in my experience, I have had the opportunity to be involved in various activities with regard to international police cooperation. These have been held at a regularly basis. And I consider international cooperation to be a permanent activity. On the operational level, the Brcko police have had numerous joint training programs, notably with police from Germany, Croatia, and Slovenia. These training experiences have been very helpful.

Regarding the issue of a universal code of ethics, I would like to say that we have done a lot in this area. On the recommendation of ICITAP, we went ahead and created a code of police ethics for our entire police structure. We have until spring of next year to develop our final version of this document that will then become the standard for all of BiH police agencies.

*LF & EM:* Have those interactions been beneficial or harmful? What kinds of external international influences are beneficial and which ones less so?

*GL:* I consider our experience with international partners very useful. Again, I would like to stress the importance of the ICITAP mission in BiH, as well as our cooperation with the FBI. I feel that we have gained considerable benefits from these relationships. Here we have colleagues with whom we can discuss our work and make use of their experience and their views with regard to police work.

*LF & EM:* How have developments after September 11 affected your work?

*GL:* I wasn't personally involved in the investigation of terrorism but I think that this event [September 11, 2001] served to emphasize the magnitude of this problem worldwide. I think that the United States has made some significant progress in the field of international cooperation improvements. Perhaps, at first we were unable to recognize the real scope of the terrorism problem, but subsequent events showed us that this is an international police matter. The events of 9/11 have contributed to a better understanding of the threat of terrorism. In any case, significant progress has been made in the international effort to fight terrorism. For instance, certain elements of information gathered here have played a role in this effort.

*Democratic Policing*

*LF & EM:* How would you define democratic policing?

*GL:* I would define democratic policing as police serving instead of police commanding. In some cases the police need to take command of the situation but its basic function should be service to the community. The term "democratic policing" contains strict rules and rigorous police powers under one condition: All police practices must be transparent.

*LF & EM:* What practices would bring democratic policing to life? Can democratic policing be achieved in your country or not, and what obstacles stand in the way?

*GL:* The main obstacles to democratic policing in BiH are political influences, corruption, a lack of transparency, and the absence of an established universal professional practice. Effective policing, on the other hand, depends to a great extent on proper training, objective personnel evaluations, and good managerial supervision.

*LF & EM:* Should democratic policing be the goal of reforms?

*GL:* In the spirit of democratic policing, police reform in BiH should be oriented to functionalism rather than to some other principles. That's the essence of the joint agreement on reform: how to define interagency cooperation within the various institutions. Even then, it is a difficult goal to achieve. For this to work, the police need to be motivated to accept change. I think for reform to work in BiH it will be necessary to shut down or consolidate some of the existing police agencies. We need to end the competing jurisdictions that exist today throughout much of the state. The United States has some 17,000 police agencies, but they must be functional and economically cost effective. So police agencies in BiH should only have enough personnel to justify their existence.

*General Assessments*

*LF & EM:* Are you basically satisfied or dissatisfied with developments in policing?

*GL:* Despite all the negative challenges existing within our social environment, I am satisfied with the current situation of policing in BiH. Statistically, we have experienced a trend of crime reduction overall.

*LF & EM:* What are the most likely developments you see happening and which would you like to see happening?

*GL:* I think that problem solving needs to occur at the individual level. A police agency can be empowered with certain authority, but fulfillment of this mandate depends upon the quality of its personnel and to what degree they support the concept of transparency.

*LF & EM:* What is most needed now to improve policing?

*GL:* Qualified personnel need to be selected for the police force: those with vision, experience, and background that will make them good police officers. For instance, I think that every police officer should be of good moral character. Only adequate staff selection can produce success in police work. I would like the opportunity of this interview to strongly suggest to the politicians that they work toward selecting the "right" people for the police.

*LF & EM:* How do you see the future of police in BiH?

*GL:* I think that certain changes still need to occur system wide. I don't think that the existing agencies need to be scrapped per se, but things need to happen so they can become more effective. I am confident that these changes can occur and that the police will rise to the necessary level to provide an adequate level of public security. These changes are currently designed to be part of the new coordinating agencies being created at the state level.

*LF &EM:* Thank you for your time and insights.

**Appendix: The Structure of the Police System of Bosnia and Herzegovina**

In describing the basic organizational structure of the police organizations in Bosnia and Herzegovina, it is necessary first briefly to explain recent historical events, notably the impact of the 1991–1995 Balkan War and the resulting Dayton Accord (December 1995) on the postwar restructuring of the Bosnia-Herzegovina state (BiH).

In May 1992, the parliament of the Socialist Republic of Bosnia and Herzegovina followed the lead of its two northern neighbors, Slovenia and Croatia, in declaring its independence. This action resulted in the Bosnian war involving not only Bosnia and Herzegovina but also Croatia and the Federation of Yugoslavia (now the states of Serbia, Montenegro, and Kosovo). The war ended with the eventual intervention from United Nation forces, whose role as peacekeepers was basically ineffective, notably during the 44-month siege of Sarajevo.

The Dayton Accord resulted from these air attacks on Bosnian Serb positions. Moreover, the Dayton Peace Accord spelled out the conditions for a permanent cessation of hostilities. This document also served as a legal basis for the current political division of BiH into three components: the primarily Muslim (Bosnian)/Catholic (Croat) coalition known as the Federation of Bosnia and Herzegovina (FBiH); the basically Bosnian Serb (Orthodox) Republic of Srpska (RS); and the mixed-ethnic enclave within the RS known as the Brcko District. Essentially, the Dayton Peace Agreement ended the sectarian violence, but at the cost of dividing the state into three political units (FBiH with 51% of the land and RS with 49%, including the Brcko District) with little likelihood of these three factions uniting into a unified whole at any time in the foreseeable future. Obviously, these divisions serve to complicate the role of law enforcement and public safety.

Regarding law enforcement, the Dayton Accord authorized each of the three entities with the responsibility for organizing its own police structure. The Federation of BiH has the more complicated form of police administration, with each of the 10 cantons, as well as the major municipalities, having its own police force. This division of authority is due mainly to the weak coalition of Bosnian Croats (Roman Catholics) and the majority Bosnian (Muslim) population. Cantons are roughly divided along these sectarian divisions (three Croat; seven Bosnian).

At the federal level of the FBiH there is the Federal Ministry of Interior, which is responsible for dealing with (a) intercantonal crime, (b) terrorism, (c) organized crime, (d) trafficking of drugs, and (e) protection of important persons and assets of Federation. At the same time, federal police hold some coordinating authority toward cantonal police but do not have original jurisdiction over criminal and civil matters.

On other hand, the police structure of the Republic of Srpska has a more centralized organizational police structure. Their territory is divided into five regional centers of security (each directed by a central police department).

The Brcko District is an autonomous component of the state of Bosnia and Herzegovina created following the Dayton Peace Agreement by an arbitration commission. Like the other two autonomous entities, the Brcko District has its own police responsible only to the local parliament and partly to the mayor.

There are also some policy and police institutions at the state level of BiH. These agencies have resulted from input and supervision from the European Council, NATO, the UN, and other outside influences. These efforts were mainly designed to curb the use of the police for the purpose of ethnic cleansing and, instead, provide a coordinated effort in fighting international crime and terrorism. Toward this end, BiH established the State Border Service in 2001 as the first state law enforcement agency. Since then, the Ministry of Security was established with policy oversight on the existing state police organizations. The Council of Ministries was created in 2003—a step recommended by the European Commission (EC) as a condition for eventual entry into the European Union (EU). A condition stated by the EC was the establishment of a statewide law enforcement agency designed to tackle the most serious forms of crime (European Commission Report, 2003). Toward this end, the State Investigation and Protection Agency (SIPA), which was originally founded in 2002, became operational in 2004. SIPA's mandate is to address

- Crimes that are proscribed by State Criminal Code (organized crime, war crimes, terrorism, money laundering, trafficking of human beings, etc.)
- Witness protection
- International police cooperation
- Providing investigative expertise
- Protection of important persons, buildings, etc.

The Ministry of Security also cooperates with the National Bureau of Interpol, establishing it as a specialized international police-cooperation body. Finally, the state Service for Foreigners Affairs was founded under the umbrella of the Ministry of Security in order to deal with immigration and asylum issues.

Otherwise, the local (entity, canton, municipal) police organizational structure is seen as being basically uncoordinated and ineffective in nature. Furthermore, some independent analysts have suggested that policing at the regional level continues to be dominated by political influences and local biases, as well as serving as a source of problems arising from internal corruption, inadequate resources, and poor police training (Goold, 2009). Nonetheless, the situation today is no longer characterized by the high levels of crime and political violence that were prevalent initially following the implementation of the Dayton Accord. At the same time, despite 9 years of reform efforts imposed by the international community, the persistence of nationalist attitudes in some areas of the country, indicates that many citizens do not enjoy an adequate sense of security—one free of ethnic biases and prejudices (Celeador, 2005, p. 366).

These issues are currently being debated by the Police Restructuring Commission of Bosnia and Herzegovina.[1] The Commission realizes that BiH police forces need to become more efficient and effective and financially sustainable. Moreover, these police forces should better reflect the ethnic distribution in Bosnia and Herzegovina as well as establishing safeguards that protect the police from improper political interference, thus making them more accountable to the law and the community (Police Restructuring Commission of Bosnia and Herzegovina, 2004, p. 1). Despite the fact that the commission, in its recommendations, suggested that the state establish a single police structure under overall political oversight of the Minister of Interior, with only two levels of police organizations (state and local), there is no political consensus on this and the issue remains stalled in the sectarian politics that continue to divide Bosnia and Herzegovina. Four years following this report, Parliament of BiH adopted laws that introduced two new police agencies with authority of supervision, coordination, and support of existing police organizations.[2] This has not yet occurred.

### Endnotes

1. See Decision of the High Representative (*Bosnia and Herzegovina Official Gazette* 36/04) to Give Police Restructuring Commission Its Mandate.
2. See Law on Directorate for Coordination of Police Bodies and on Agencies for Support and the Law on Independent and Supervisory Bodies of Police Structure in BiH (*Bosnia and Herzegovina Official Gazette* 36/08).

### References

Celeador, G. C. 2005. Police reform: Peacebuilding through "democratic policing"? *International Peacekeeping 12,* 3 (Autumn): 364–376.

Goold, B. 2004. Bosnia and Herzegovina. In *Encyclopedia of law enforcement.* Thousand Oaks, CA: Sage Publications. Retrieved September 2009 from http://sage-reference.com/lawenforcement/Article_n408.html.

European Commission. 2003. Report from the Commission to the Council on the preparedness of Bosnia and Herzegovina to negotiate a stabilization and association agreement with the European Union. Document no. COM (2003) 692 final, p. 26. Retrieved from www.delbih.cec.eu.int/en/index.htm.

Police Restructuring Commission of Bosnia and Herzegovina. 2004. Final report.

# 6

# Interview With Raymond Kendall, Honorary Secretary General of Interpol and Chairman of the Center of Excellence on Public Security's Senior Advisory Board

## Policing Activity and Human Rights

**INTERVIEWED BY ANDRÉ MATHEUS E SOUZA AND GEORGE HOWELL**

**Contents**



**Introduction**

An international expert on crime and security, Raymond Kendall served three terms as secretary general of Interpol from 1985 to 2000. Prior to his work with Interpol, Mr. Kendall spent much of his career at New Scotland Yard Special Branch, rising to the rank of deputy assistant commissioner of the London Metropolitan Police. In 1971, he became assistant director of drugs at the International Criminal Police Organization (ICPO)-Interpol, and was promoted to director 4 years later. More recently, Mr. Kendall has also served as chairman of the Supervisory Committee of the European Anti-Fraud Office, OLAF (Office Européen de Lutte Anti-Fraude).

During his career, Mr. Kendall has been awarded many honors, including Chevalier de la Légion d'Honneur (France), the Queen's

Police Medal for Distinguished Police Service (United Kingdom), and Bearer of the Saint Martyr Triphon Order—First Class (Russia).

### The Interview

*AS & GH:* Mr. Kendall, you have recently presented a paper on public security and human rights.[1] How have you seen a human rights discourse incorporated into police policy and practice over the span of your career?

*RK:* In 1956 when I first joined the British Colonial Police in East Africa and later in 1962 when I entered the Metropolitan Police in London, I received initial training in which there was no mention of human rights as such. We were told that there was a legal requirement to inform a person who was arrested of the reason for his arrest and his right to remain silent. The link was not made between the legal requirement and the human rights aspect. I believe that this is important because it tends to establish why a police officer acts in the way that he does—that is to say, in application of the law rather than in consideration of human rights—and I shall return to this later. In 1948, the Universal Declarations of Human Rights was established as the primary global expression of rights to which all human beings are inherently entitled, asserting the recognition of human dignity of all people as the foundation of justice and peace in the world.

It was the first time in history that the international community embraced a document considered to have universal value—"a common standard of achievement for all peoples and all nations." Its preamble acknowledges the importance of a human rights legal framework to maintaining international peace and security, stating that recognition of the inherent dignity and equal and inalienable rights of all individuals is the foundation of freedom, justice, and peace in the world.

Specifically relating to the police is the 1979 UN code of conduct for law enforcement officials, which states that police officers will respect and protect human dignity and maintain and uphold the human rights of all persons, and that the use of force should be used only when strictly necessary and to the extent required for the performance of their duty.

The Council of Europe within its human rights division has greatly contributed to the establishment and recognition of human rights in general and particularly to the role of police as a pivotal point in the judicial system of a state which aspires or claims to be a democracy. In 1997 it launched a program, "Police and Human Rights 1997–2000." Because the police conduct inquiries into suspected crimes and, in certain circumstances, execute judicial sanctions which bring them into constant contact with the citizens of its country, police behavior should symbolize the respect of human rights and their protection on its territory. The way in which police organizations carry out their duties represents an infallible indicator of the level of quality of a democratic society and the way in which the state of law is respected.

The continuity of the program was assured by the creation of a new program, "Police and Human Rights Beyond 2000,"[2] whose aim was to train police officers in standards of human rights and instill in them the knowledge which would permit them to apply the standards in their daily work.

*AS & GH:* How important is it for police forces to incorporate a rights-based approach to policing?

*RK:* It is of paramount importance to foster a culture in police organizations for protecting and respecting human rights. The organizational culture has to be grounded on human rights standards as fundamental value. Human rights components have to be an integral part of police training, both theoretical and practical.

Human rights matter for policing as noted in a number of regional and universal declarations, such as the Code of Police Ethics adopted by the European Committee of Ministers in September 2001. Such initiatives—and there are many others, often inspired by the action of nongovernmental organizations [NGOs]—show that the issue of human rights has now become an inevitable part of our societal way of life and that we have a responsibility to ensure that the Universal Declaration of Human Rights is truly universal.

I am told that the recent space shuttle carried onboard a copy of the Universal Declaration and that one member onboard cynically said to another, "Perhaps before we take this, we should ensure that it is applied as it should be on Earth."

*AS & GH:* Internationally, what sorts of projects has been developed to promote a rights-based approach to policing?

*RK:* The police are only one aspect of a broader public security context. Focusing on the police and human rights may blinker the human rights discourse from wider human rights abuses which arise from a lack of security.

For this purpose I should like to use as a basis recent experience I have had in working on a benevolent basis for a nongovernmental organization, the International Council on Security and Development (formerly known as the Senlis Council). The council has worked on drug, policy issues, opium cultivation in Afghanistan, and public security policy in Brazil.

When it comes to both Afghanistan and Brazil, I think Europe has an important role to play in sharing the expertise and knowledge it has built up over the past decades in terms of the best practices of policing and how they relate to public security and human rights.

Within the framework of the European Union we are already implementing programs that try to tackle the problem of public security in Afghanistan and Brazil through collaborative projects focusing on technical assistance and sharing of best practices.

In Afghanistan, as you probably know, the European Union has launched an EU police mission (EUPOL) in Afghanistan in June 2007, which combines the knowledge of a great number of European countries in terms of policing. This EUPOL mission aims to help Afghanistan establish sustainable and effective civilian policing arrangements under Afghan ownership and in accordance with the best international policing practices and international human rights standards. The project builds on experiences elsewhere, such as the European Union police missions in the Palestinian territories and in Congo. Progress, of course, takes time, but in Afghanistan there is already more attention for human rights within the work of the police.

A small concrete example is the way the Afghan police are stopping cars. They are more friendly toward drivers when talking to them and asking them about searching the car and seeing their driving license. However, at the institutional level, a lot remains to be done, as there are a lot of uncertainties about the lack of control the Karzai administration has over the police force. In addition, corruption is rife because of the relatively low salaries the police officers receive. Sometimes, the uniformed police themselves commit crimes.

As a result, now and again local communities have chosen to support the Taliban as an alternative to the corrupt police force, which continues to carry out arbitrary arrests and demand bribes. It shows that training the police on human rights and best international policing practices can become an empty shell if the security and development parameters of the country are highly problematic.

The same holds for Brazil, although the security and development parameters are, of course, rather different. Rio de Janeiro is a salient example—famous for summary executions, police corruption, and ruthless drug trafficking gangs—as a way to explore the subject of human rights and policing, a subject which is of a somewhat different perception than here in the North, compared to conditions where our notion of democracy seems difficult in its application.

*AS & GH:* Tell us more about the situation in Rio de Janeiro. How does the human rights discourse influence the daily activities of the police?

*RK:* In Rio, the police have developed a certain animosity toward the human rights discourse. During a police protest in 2008, officers were photographed holding baseball bats with "direitos humanos" [human rights] scrawled down the side of them, for example. The police simplistically associate the concept of human rights with the action of antagonistic NGOs, which are seen to protect criminals, giving them impunity to commit criminal acts, while punishing hard-working police officers who put their lives on the line for society.

At the same time, human rights NGOs and the UN Human Rights Commission denounce the police of Rio de Janeiro for committing human rights abuses en masse to the urban poor through its belligerent public safety policies. Executions and corruption are rife, and the police contribute significantly to the city's high murder rate. How can we understand this antagonism between the police and human rights?

*AS & GH:* What are the root causes of this situation in Rio?

*RK:* This resistance to and political polarization of the human rights is a result of the way the discourse has been employed historically in Rio over the last 30 years as a political instrument which strongly influenced public security policies.

Toward the end of the period of military rule in 1978, prodemocracy groups employed an antagonistic human rights agenda as a central component of the prodemocracy reform platform.

In the immediate post-military-regime period of the early 1980s, the police, stigmatized as oppressive remnants of the dictatorship, were given restrictions in what they were allowed to do in carrying out their normal duties. It is clear that this was a reaction to the brutality of the police during the period of military rule. Newspaper reports from the time openly admit the use of torture as an investigative technique. For example, in one article, a policeman explained with pride that he had already extracted 15 confessions from one suspect and thought that he could get at least five more confessions with another hour or two of beating. He compared the suspect to a squeezed orange, that there is always a last drop to be squeezed out if one works hard enough.

Also, the police form of operating in the poor urban areas was of a complete lack of respect for individual rights. A "foot in the door" policy was employed in poor areas, with police kicking down doors and demanding work registration documents.

In this situation, the police were fully associated with the most repressive aspects of military rule, and the new democracy felt it a priority to curb the actions of the police force. During the eighties, public security policy was marginalized in favor of human rights-based measures. New rules were brought in which forbade the police to enter into the *favelas* [slums], ostensibly as a way of preventing the police from committing human rights abuses on the urban poor.

However, this lack of police presence created a vacuum and allowed criminality and alternative power structures to develop within these areas, contributing to the territorial dominance of criminal groups, instead of the state. This was a result of policy makers' lack of attention to public security policy, but a political rather than functional understanding of the police. It is also a fact that the democratization in Brazil in 1978 was accompanied by a rise in criminality, especially of homicides among young men.

In interviews with both Rio's police and public security experts, there is a consensus of opinion that this historical turning point is one of the main reasons for the entrenchment of drug trafficking gangs in Rio's favelas. This history also goes some way to situating Rio police's disparaging attitude toward human rights. They perceive that the human rights arguments give criminals impunity and enable them to dominate wide areas of the city.

*AS & GH:* How would you describe the public security context in Rio?

*RK:* I will briefly explain some of the security dynamics at play in Rio in order to give some context to contemporary public security issues in Rio de Janeiro.

Drug retailing gangs are locked into a brutal market competition with each other for control of strategic locations from which to sell drugs. Factional competition led to the necessity for weapons with which to defend and acquire strategic locations from rivals and state authorities. Guns easily find their way into the city, given Brazil's porous border with Paraguay, for example, where guns can be bought and sold in illegal street markets.

This situation has led to a virtual territorial stalemate in the city, where entrenched drug trafficking gangs have full domination over almost all of the 700 favelas in the region, and public security forces do not have the resources to reclaim this territory. State forces conduct sporadic military style mega-operations designed to capture specific individuals or operations to reduce drug trafficking organizations' arsenals of drugs and guns within favelas. However, these operations are incursions into foreign territory and do not have the aim of bringing this area under state jurisdiction, as this would require resources that are not available. It has been argued that the high level of killing by the police is in fact symptomatic of a state that never achieved a full monopoly of violence.

Police relationships with drug factions are characterized by extreme violence. Police and drug factions confront each other using war-grade weaponry, employing calibers such as 7.62, 556, or bigger, as well as grenades and mounted machine guns. The police also use armored cars in operations, so as to transport police safely from one area to another, and helicopters to provide covering fire. These operations often result in the deaths or arrests of faction members and police deaths, as well as the apprehension of weapons and drugs.

These confrontations take place in Rio's favelas, areas of high population densities and weak housing structure and a history of the criminalization of the poor. Often, innocent people get caught in the cross fire, as high-caliber bullets easily pass through the thin walls of favela residences.

*AS & GH:* How does the criminal justice system in Rio influence the modus operandi of the police?

*RK:* The criminal justice system is an important factor to understanding human rights and the police in Rio. Inefficiencies in the criminal justice system have a perverse effect on the ways the police and criminal factions operate. Both the gangs and the police operate brutally because of certain aspects of the way the justice system functions. They are frustrated and have the feeling that they are not part of a structured judicial system and, in fact, have the impression that they are the only force of intervention which can protect the citizens.

The shortcomings of the criminal justice system act as perverse incentives for members of criminal gangs toward brutality, and ruthlessness. Given the prevalence of corruption and loopholes in the law, the more the individual demonstrates his worth to the faction, the more likely the organization is to, upon arrest, pay the bribe to arresting officers to let the captured individual go free or, at trial, employ a good lawyer to defend the individual. Loopholes in the criminal justice system mean that the individual has a relatively high chance of acquittal with the defense of an experienced lawyer.

The prosecution system is also very inefficient and fosters a climate of impunity and incentive to commit crime. For example, one study showed that in the mid-90s in Rio de Janeiro, of 4,227 records of homicide occurrences registered with the civil police, only 4.6% of them had the perpetrator and motive established. Another study found that 92% of homicide cases presented by the police were dismissed for lack of sufficient proof to go to trial.

In addition, the Statute of the Child and the Adolescent states that people younger than 18 years old cannot be tried for adult crimes and must be sent to juvenile rehabilitation centers. This means that even for a crime such as murder, minors will only serve until age 18, and then be released and have their criminal records erased. The perverse effect of this legislation is that criminal factions are encouraged to recruit minors, as they can act with a higher level of impunity.

The weakness of the justice system thus encourages impunity, the recruitment of children in criminal factions, and a culture of brutality within criminal factions.

Mirroring the brutalizing effect of the justice system on criminal factions, weaknesses in the criminal justice system also exercise a perverse effect on the way the police engage with drug trafficking gangs. Police officers do not have confidence in the criminal justice system and are revolted by the apparent impunity which the weakness of the justice system confers to criminal factions.

As mentioned previously, police officers know that, once arrested, in many instances drug faction members can escape the full application of the law. In some cases, arresting officers may let them go in return for a bribe; in others, lawyers exploit loopholes in the law, leading to a short sentence or acquittal. Once in prison, early release could be petitioned by lawyers. And, as mentioned before, homicides are rarely investigated thoroughly or rarely reach trial. Finally, arrested minors will serve up to the age of 18 only.

Police are almost given the incentive to kill drug faction combatants because they are aware of the slim chance that the justice system will yield justice. This is a matter of brutal pragmatism for the police engaged in guerrilla warfare with the drug factions. From a militaristic perspective, they know that if they do not kill the individual when they have the opportunity, they face the risk of being shot at by the individual at a later date.

From these brief examples, we can conclude that overhauling the justice system would have the effect of reducing human rights violations. As the police lack faith in the system, they take matters into their own hands. And criminal factions are encouraged in their activity as the justice system seems to allow them to act with impunity.

Under these conditions, it is difficult to know where to begin in our exercise to establish and control the application of human rights principles.

*AS & GH:* How does the international community evaluate this situation?

*RK:* 2007 saw the visit to Brazil and the compiling of a report by UN human rights *rapporteur* Philip Anston.[3] His report concluded that Rio state frequently violates human rights in the incursions to favelas designed to combat narco-trafficking. In his report, Anston noted that Rio's police on average kill three people per day and are responsible for 18% of the state's murder rate.

In his report, Anston cites the example of a police "mega-operation," which took place in June 2007 in which more than 1,000 police officers participated, as an example of Rio police's human rights abuses. The operation, designed to reduce the faction's arsenal, took place at Complexo Alemao, a huge conjunct of 16 favelas and headquarters of Rio's largest drug faction, Commando Vermelho. Anston criticized the operation for putting innocent people's lives at risk and stopping thousands of local children from going to school. He was also very critical of reported summary executions by the police, presenting data from coroners' reports which show that of the 26 people killed, 14 were shot in the back, and six had point-blank entry wounds to the face. Anston concluded:

> It appears that if someone is a drug trafficker, then killing him is justifiable, when there is no justification for killing anyone. If a person sells drugs the procedure should be to arrest him … If there is the policeman's life or somebody close to him at risk, this justifies the use of force, but not killing.

From a human rights perspective, there is no doubt that the police are guilty of human rights abuses as well as criminal offenses. We encounter a "Dirty Harry" syndrome reality, where "dirty" means (i.e., executions) are employed toward a "clean" end: the ending of the drug faction's tyranny over a community. In effect, the police have taken the law into their own hands.

However, if we amplify our understanding of the rights discourse, then we can also conclude that the state allowing criminal factions to dominate state territory is also an abuse of a citizen's fundamental human rights.

*AS & GH:* What are the consequences of this scenario to a democratic environment?

*RK:* Security is essential for the successful democratic development of society—a prerequisite for democratic engagement, economic development, and social cohesion. For example: in the absence of security, there are no conditions for civil society engagement. Without it, civil society organizations cannot flourish, civil leaders do not emerge, and only crime flourishes. Furthermore, security is a prerequisite for the establishment of economic networks. Without security, businesses cannot grow. Security is also essential for social cohesion and the teaching of solidarity with society. Without security, teachers have to mediate their messages or put their lives in danger.

From this example, it is clear that without security, human rights are also inhibited. If we revisit the previous example of Complexo do Alemão, we can see that the lack of security inhibits the human rights of local residents.

In a confidential report from Rio's Disque Denúncia (Brazil's Crime Stoppers organization) for the month prior to the operation in Complexo do Alemão, we can observe many human rights abuses. Faction members in the area obliged residents to give them food, turn their houses into drug-selling points or artillery positions, and hide weapons, or face expulsion. They have also shot residents so as to incriminate the police. Local community leaders have already delivered false denouncements of human rights abuses and executions by the police to human rights lawyers. Residents are beaten by faction members angry with police presence in the area; sometimes, the residents have their water supply cut off as an incentive for them to protest against police presence in the area.

From these few examples it is clear that drug-dealing factions commit many human rights abuses, and their removal from territorial control of territories is essential for the guaranteeing of human rights of local residents. It is the state's lack of control over its territory that allows nonstate actors to perpetuate human rights abuses and denies local residents the fundamental right to security.

Therefore, the state must reclaim this territory; however, the state must demonstrate a permanent presence in these areas and not rely on periodic guerilla-like incursions. Also, the positive dimension of the state must be demonstrated through social policies, bringing health, education, and opportunity to marginalized areas.

*AS & GH:* Which, in your opinion, is the preferable course of action toward a solution of this problem in Rio?

*RK:* The impasse between an antagonistic, antipolice human rights discourse and repressive police actions needs to be readdressed. In the case of Rio, the basic principles of human rights need to be reestablished as a constructive bridge-building discourse between the police and society.

The police's only notion of human rights is in a negative context, where they are the enemy. This leads to a reactive attitude of disparagement of human rights among the police. For them, the human rights discourse only serves to give impunity to bandits and indict zealous policemen defending society.

The police aim to be rights providers, risking their lives trying to provide the fundamental right of security for society. The importance of human rights for the police must be understood from a strategic perspective, in that demonstrating respect for human rights is strategically advantageous. The police must understand that persistent cases of violence and corruption and the perceived impunity of the police to commit human rights abuses contribute to a lack of confidence in the police. This distances the population from the police, resulting in low levels of public–police collaboration and the growth of private security initiatives.

The human rights and the police discourse must be amplified to include human rights abuses that are perpetuated because of a lack of police presence. Human rights advocates must forge alliances with the police in order to encourage them to become human rights defenders.

Regarding summary executions, the environment of the justice system must be focused for intervention. Legal loopholes, inefficiencies, and corruption must be addressed from the principle of providing justice, reducing the incentive for police officers to resort to their own interpretations of "Dirty Harry" style justice.

If I chose the Rio example it is simply because I am now familiar with the situation there, despite its complexities, but also because it illustrates the difficulties that exist between establishing principles on the one hand and applying them on the other.

My experience tells me that if there is not a strong political will to achieve an objective, nothing will be achieved. Fortunately, in Brazil, the political will seems to have been established and a 5-year plan of action has been embarked upon with a multifaceted approach and with appropriate financial resources. So, hopefully, the future will be optimistic.

In conclusion I should like to stress the aspect of political will in the sense that it is at the level of government that law is established and that it is impossible not to look at this aspect when one is considering the subject of human rights and the police. The police act in accordance with the law and it is the law which establishes the conditions in which they operate.

*AS & GH:* Could you please mention some of the international experiences and debates on the topic of human rights and public security?

*RK:* For some time I have been associated with efforts and initiatives which are being made to bring a peaceful solution to the conflictual situation in the Basque country. It is not my intention to enter into the substance of the issue but simply to look at the question of human rights. Those of you who have some knowledge of the situation will be aware that a major issue of contention is that of nonrespect of basic human rights insofar as the treatment of suspected persons and prisoners is concerned.

We are fortunate in our democracies and particularly in Europe that we have established internationally applicable principles in relation to human rights but also a control mechanism to enable us to establish that these principles are being applied. In the European context, regular visits are made, with the consent of state governments, by representatives of the European Commission on human rights, as well as other professional bodies, who produce reports and recommendations on human rights issues. These recommendations are designed to ensure that the right conditions are created for human rights to be as fully respected as possible. This is important in establishing the conditions in which police are to operate, bearing in mind what I said in the beginning of my remarks about police operating within the respect of the law.

The International Commission of Jurists in a report in October 2008 found, for example, that incommunicado detention, even where judicially supervised, cannot adequately protect the safety of detainees.[4] Further, in order to reliably protect rights, the principle of immediate access to a lawyer to consult in confidence is indispensable. Likewise, access to information to help in preparing a defense should not be restricted. These are just examples of issues which could easily be resolved by simple changes in legislation and which would go a long way to creating conditions of transparency and clarifying and justifying police action. I repeat that police take action within the limits which are placed upon them by law and, as far as the public is concerned, justice must be done but also be seen to be done.

It was added in conclusion that it is hoped that the act will help to create a society in which the rights and responsibilities of individuals are properly balanced.

We have come a long way since I joined the police service in 1956 but there is still a long way to go before we can assume that the Universal Declaration of Human Rights is universally applied. We must also remember that this is essentially a question of human behavior which cannot be resolved by legislation alone.

*AS & GH:* Thank you for doing the interview with us.

## Endnotes

1. This interview incorporates points originally presented by Mr. Kendall on the occasion of the Commemoration Conference for the 60th Anniversary of the Universal Declaration of Human Rights, at the

Institute for Public Safety of the University of Catalonia (Barcelona, November 27, 2008).

2. I [RK] should like to recommend to your attention six principles established by the Association of Chief Police Officers of the United Kingdom, of which I am a member, after the adoption of the Human Rights Act in October 2000. These principles are applicable to each area of policing to reach compliance with Human Rights: (1) *Legality*—is there a legal basis for police actions? Is that legal basis in statute, regulations, and case law and is it available to a member of the public? (2) *Proportionality*—can the police demonstrate that actions taken were "proportionate" to the threat or problem they sought to prevent? (3) *Relevance/necessity*—was the police action strictly relevant to the particular threat/problem? (4) *Subsidiarity*—was the police action the best "force/intrusive" available? (5) *Equality of arms*—in any trial process, did the defendant have the same information and access to information as the police/prosecution? (6) *Remedy*—is there an independent public remedy available to the citizen?
3. Anston, P. Report of the special *rapporteur* on extrajudicial, summary or arbitrary executions, Philip Anston, on his mission to Brazil (4–14 November 2007). United Nations Human Rights Council. www2.ohchr.org/english/issues/executions/docs/A_HRC_11_2_Add_2_English.pdf
4. ICJ (International Commission of Jurists). Submission to the Human Rights Committee regarding the consideration of the 5th periodic report submitted by Spain, October 10, 2008. www2.ohchr.org/english/bodies/hrc/docs/ngos ICJ_Spain_94.pdf

# 7

# Interview With Dr. Rodrigo Oliveira, Director, General Department of Specialized Police, Civil Police, Rio de Janeiro, Brazil

## Interviewed by André Matheus e Souza and George Howell

**Contents**



## The Interview

### *Career*

*AS & GH:* Please tell me about your career.

*RO:* I joined the civil police in the state of Rio de Janeiro in 1994 as police notary (nowadays, notary police officer). My first 3 years of duty were at the Day Supervising Division, which is a kind of superior rank in every other police station of the state. In 1997 I moved to the Anti-kidnapping Division where I was until 1999, when I got promoted, by examination, to chief of police. After my specialization assignment as chief of police,

I resumed working in the Anti-kidnapping Division, now as chief of operations. In 2002, I was assigned as coordinator at CORE (the Department for the Coordination of Special Resources). In 2005, I was assigned chief of the Narcotics Enforcement Division. I returned to CORE (Coordenadoria de Recursos Especiais) in 2007 and, in 2009, I was assigned chief of the Specialized Police Departments.

*AS & GH:* What motivated you to enter the police force?

*RO:* I believe it was my attraction to the activities, besides a passion for police work. In my family, I am the only policeman. Since childhood, I always had shown an interest for that career. So, I got myself prepared for the examination and ended up entering in 1994.

*AS & GH:* Did the way your career progressed surprise you in any way?

*RO:* I was always focused in my actions. I always tried to get qualified, whether on the administrative aspect or, mainly, on the operational side. But of course, to be at the CORE coordinator position for so long and having been the chief of the Anti-kidnapping Division are events that bring me gladness and satisfaction, both professionally and personally.

*AS & GH:* Did you find your work to be as interesting or fulfilling as you thought it would be?

*RO:* If you think solely about police actions, I can affirm that it definitely was and is very interesting and fulfilling. Each day is a different reality. The countless successful actions shown in Rio's newspapers speak for themselves. However, a few sacrifices have to be undertaken. The time spent at work is often longer than the time with the family. This is not good, but it is part of the job.

### *Changes Experienced*

*AS & GH:* In your opinion, what were the most important changes which occurred to policing during your career?

*RO:* In terms of the civil police, I believe that the provision of computer systems to the police units gave a big boost to the quality of service. In addition, these updated police units do not take prisoners under custody; the custody is attributed [credited] to another department. Besides technological and physical improvements, the training of professionals is better today and is done more frequently and intensely. Definitely, today's policemen in Rio are better prepared and educated than before.

*AS & GH:* What changes have you seen in external conditions which have impacted policing?

*RO:* The provision of computer systems to police stations resulted in a better service environment. Investigations became quicker and crime-solving processes accelerated. In many police stations, individuals involved in criminal activity actions leave the police station already assigned to trial. Doubtlessly, this is a huge achievement for the civil police, the Justice Department, and the people.

*AS & GH:* Do you believe the policing got better or worse in recent years?

*RO:* The civil police are undergoing a process of complete restructuring of their methods and processes of operations, whether administrative or investigative. Through simple management processes, several investigations and/or patrolling works are relocated or adjusted. That enables the police presence to be where there is criminal activity, diminishing crime and increasing the people's sense of security.

*AS & GH:* Do you believe that now it is easier or harder to be a policeman than it was in the past?

*RO:* On one hand, in terms of material, technological, and intellectual resources, today's policeman is certainly better equipped. On the other hand, in some places in Rio de Janeiro criminals are very well armed. Drug dealers in Rio de Janeiro have great fire power and engage in constant and intense confrontations. For this reason, I would say it is more dangerous to be a policeman today than it was in the past.

### *Personal Philosophy of Policing*

*AS & GH:* What role should the police play in society?

*RO:* The police should be the last institution to intervene in society, instead of being the first one, as has been happening from time to time. Theoretically speaking, the police are only required when all of the other social institutions, whether public or private, have been unable to succeed. The police are meant to serve and protect society, never to be used as a tool for "social control" by the state.

*AS & GH:* Which current police responsibilities should be assigned to other people and organizations?

*RO:* Until very recently (2 or 3 years ago), I believed that preventing drug abuse should not be assigned to the police. Now, I changed my mind completely. The police must in fact fight and prevent drug abuse (80% of the state of Rio de Janeiro's criminality is somehow connected to drug dealing). The police have to be in contact with society, schools, and associations, offering their practical knowledge about drugs and drug-related consequences. But the police should not perform a welfarist role. It is not the police role and that is not what police are trained for.

*AS & GH:* What policies regarding the community, the political groups, and other criminal justice organizations do work?

*RO:* The police cannot be and must not be seen as the "state's armed wing." As I mentioned, the police exist to serve and protect society. In this context, I welcome all the actions developed jointly by police with the communities (mainly poor ones)—not by force, but as a safety agreement. There are countless governmental and private programs like this and the results have been quite satisfactory.

*AS & GH:* What impairs the cooperation with other divisions and agencies?

*RO:* In Brazil we have three governmental levels—federal, state, and municipal—each of which possesses different agencies that are, in some way, responsible for public security. In all of them there are highly qualified professionals, committed to the delivered service. The problem arises when political interferences become manifested in an eminently technical area such as public security. Then the difficulties arise. To supersede these obstacles, we must understand "security policies" as "state policies" and never as "government politics." Security policies must be part of the state's long-term strategies and should not be treated as a political tool by politicians in the government.

*AS & GH:* How should policing be done?

*RO:* Always in accord with the area's needs, in a communitarian way, and be allocated according to changes in crimes which have been defined and identified. In other words, common policing must stay together with the population and follow the "crime stains" which may arise.

*AS & GH:* What should be the main priorities and strategies?

*RO:* Each society establishes its priorities, concepts, and standards in terms of security. In a country with continental dimensions such as Brazil, these criteria frequently differ from state to state, or even from municipality to municipality. In my particular understanding, each and every kind of crime that becomes qualified as "crime against the person" must take priority and deserve special attention from the police.

*AS & GH:* Tough crime confrontation, prevention, social services: Which combinations for which types of problems are best?

*RO:* All these actions complement each other. They are part of a system in which one will hardly "survive" without the other. It is logical that the so-called social cost of prevention is infinitely lower than that of repression. But that does not always prevent the police acting with the necessary strictness and under legality. The problem is that many of these strict actions produce distinctive results. The medicine is bitter, but it is necessary.

### *Experienced Problems and Successes*

*AS & GH:* According to your experience, which policies or programs worked well and which did not?

*RO:* All programs addressed to the improvement of the life of society are always welcome, among them those addressed to public security. It sometimes occurs that their advocates conceive them in an eminently theoretical form, disrespecting the practical possibility of their implementation. It is logical that any well-intentioned person would like to live in a society where violence would not exist. But in the end, we need to know if these ideas have a practical viability. Unfortunately, the police are seldom invited to join these initiatives. This way the population ends up seeing only the repressive part of the police action. That has to be changed. All these programs must have, from their conception, public security professionals, who know the practical reality of each case, taking the lead in assessing the implementation viability or nonviability of these actions. No matter what the policies are, they will only succeed if realized in a continuous and long-lasting way.

*AS & GH:* Can you infer why?

*RO:* Many of the results do not become apparent in a short period. Independently of this, demands for services also rise. When, in some cases, expected results still don't happen, certain initiatives remain unfinished. It is again a matter of government politics suppressing state policies.

*AS & GH:* In your opinion, what is the major police problem nowadays?

*RO:* I have no doubt about it. The street felon in Rio de Janeiro is the same as in any other part of the country or the world. What distinguishes them from the rest is the devastating fire power they possess. Weapons used by the most powerful armies in the world are found in possession of the drug dealers from Rio de Janeiro. Our main objective today is to disarm these criminals, by apprehending the weapons already in their possession or by preventing them reaching our territory. Actions with this objective can be demonstrated from the financial point of view. About 3 years ago, the price tag of an assault gun for a Rio de Janeiro criminal was about R$10,000 (10,000 reais) [about US$5,400]. Today, this same assault gun is estimated at about R$40,000. It shows we are on the right path.

*AS & GH:* Which police problems do you consider the most difficult to deal with?

*RO:* As in any profession, "corporativism" is one of the main infirmities to be taken care of inside the institution. In Brazil, the members of each police institution protect usually themselves and conceal corruption and other crimes—as if protecting their corporate body were their priority. Internal Affairs officers are part of the police institution, and that has been a serious problem in terms of investigating police actions. The Corregedoria (Internal Affairs) is developing very important work regarding this situation, but there is still a lot to be done about policemen who commit misconduct.

*AS & GH:* Is anything easy in police work?

*RO:* The word "easy," unfortunately, is not part of our "police dictionary."

*Theory and Practice*

*AS & GH:* What would be the relationship between theory and practice?

*RO:* Complementary. I am convinced that many theories are not viable in practice. In the opposite sense, many practical procedures still are not based on specific theoretical foundations. Theory and practice must walk together to a common objective. They must never be seen as independent. It impairs, or at last strongly hampers, success for any process.

*AS & GH:* What would the operational team learn from theory and how does theory benefit practice?

*RO:* I believe that, if by operational teams we mean special tactical groups, almost every theoretical knowledge is derived from practice, from day-by-day experience. This knowledge surely can and must be improved through suitable methodologies. Thus, as I mentioned earlier, practice and theory walk together. They are complementary.

*AS & GH:* What is this relationship for practice and theory now? Does it exist? Does it work? What keeps this interaction and collaboration going?

*RO:* Until 2009 I felt honored to head [Special Operations], where this practice and theory relationship occurred every day. Before every high-risk operation, we conduct a briefing meeting to establish procedures and conduct. At the end of these operations, another debriefing meeting is conducted to identify and evaluate rights and wrongs. It permits us to keep fit to the new realities on a daily basis.

*AS & GH:* What kind of research do you think would be interesting to the operational crew or to the practice?

*RO:* Society sometimes sees policemen as if they weren't members of the same society. Research (and publishing) from an eminently personal perspective would really help the society to better understand the needs and desires of the police class. It would probably bring police and society close together.

*AS & GH:* If not very useful already, what would be done by the theoretical team to make their work more useful to you and to the operational team?

*RO:* The so-called "lab ideas"—advocated by some alleged specialists who have never left their study rooms, who do not know life as it is, who do not even know the nature of an armed confrontation—are not well accepted by the police class in general. They are what we call "policeologists." When the day happens that these specialists gain some practical knowledge of a high-risk police action, many of them will probably change their points of view. To do so, the policeologists are invited, together with my team, to join a real "combat" situation to draw their own conclusions "in loco." Without that experience, the ideas are marvelous, but have no practical viability.

*AS & GH:* Where do you find theory-based information? Where do you look: newspapers, periodicals, professional magazines, books, publications, reports?

*RO:* With the advance of information technology, searches are made using the various communication media available. However, we look for national and international exchanges to improve the operational skills of our team. At the moment, eight policemen are attending courses abroad and another six are attending operational courses in other agencies.

*AS & GH:* Does the CORE conduct its own research? If so, about what kinds of issues or subjects?

*RO:* Yes we do. We conduct systematic evaluations every 3 months regarding physical and mental aspects as well as technical/operational aspects. We are also submitted, normally every 6 months, to evaluations under the civil police operational system. These evaluations are made through the computer network of the institution and are intended basically for the actualization of process, concepts, and laws.

*International Relations*

*AS & GH:* Was your work in the organization affected by events from outside the country (demands for human rights, universal ethics codes, interaction with foreign police forces, personal experiences abroad, new crime threats)?

*RO:* Not directly. But sometimes we are questioned about the types of weapons we use in police actions. It is important to make clear that the decision to use assault guns was made by the police. These weapons came first into the possession of drug dealers and the police had to adapt themselves to the reality of confrontations. Recently, the same questions arose about the acquisition of an armored helicopter similar to those used in the Vietnam War and now operating in Iraq. We mean the Huey II. This work tool, similar to the armored vehicles, is intended to protect the policemen by its armor. Certainly many policemen were saved by these work instruments, which are very much criticized by human rights organizations.

*AS & GH:* Were these interactions positive or negative?

*RO:* Some people try to understand our work, our needs. They reach out to us to make us, if possible, better prepared in our operating mode or simply our thinking. Unfortunately, the great majority is limited to criticizing us in a manner that doesn't seem to be constructive. On the opposite side, the feeling among police is that, for these organizations, "the worse the police, the better for us" is a way to justify their existence.

*AS & GH:* Which kinds of international interactions do you consider beneficial and which do you consider harmful?

*RO:* Every constructive criticism, be it international or not, is welcome. We are not and we don't intend to be the owners of the truth. Dialogue and learning are fundamental in order to be more prepared every day to fulfill our needs and the needs of the society, always remembering each one's peculiarities.

*AS & GH:* Did the events after 9/11 affect your work somehow?

*RO:* Not directly. We haven't had yet strong enough reports of terrorist activities in Brazil, especially in Rio de Janeiro. The fact is that in 2007 we had in our town the Pan American Games. Due to this, new concepts and training were incorporated into our day-by-day work. Certainly, a great part of this knowledge came from international police agencies.

*Democratic Policing (Citizen Police)*

*AS & GH:* What democratic policing means and how it can be achieved have been widely discussed. How would you define democratic policing?

*RO:* The police acting in favor of the society, detached from political interference, treating everyone equally, regardless of their social position, acquisitive power, ethnic origin, belief, age, or sexual orientation. In other words, a police exempt of prejudice and acting mainly in a preventive manner.

*AS & GH:* Which practices do you consider able to create democratic policing?

*RO:* A deep concept change of what the police are and whom and what they serve. Only the education of the society added to the professional qualification and a valuing of police knowledge will permit this to occur.

*AS & GH:* Do you believe that democratic policing will be achieved in Brazil? What obstacles do you foresee in the way?

*RO:* The first initiatives were already taken. Especially in some destitute communities, the police are already a presence among the community. This work is related to the military police, to which I do not belong. But I have no doubt we are on the right path. Nevertheless, the journey is long.

*AS & GH:* Do you believe democratic policing will be the objective of the reforms?

*RO:* I do believe that. The closer the population is to the police, the safer it will feel and the more recognition the police forces will have. We need to break some paradigms among which (and maybe the main one) is that the police forces are enemies of the population and act solely for the public powers. I repeat: There is much work to be done and those who believe that these actions can be carried out in a short time are wrong. No, we need a change in the cultural mentality of an entire society and certainly that is not achieved in a short time.

*General Questions*

*AS & GH:* Are you basically satisfied or unsatisfied about the developments that the police have undergone?

*RO:* I believe that since I entered the police it has evolved a lot through more material or human resources. As I said, today's civil police in Rio de Janeiro state are undergoing a huge process of change related to all operations and their management. Every change brings some resistance from within. The resistances are being overcome and soon the society will count on a police force that is more humanized and at the same time more efficient.

*AS & GH:* What are the developments you foresee happening to policing and which would you like to see?

*RO:* I believe it is unavoidable and vital that the police and the population become more connected in order to have a fairer and more democratic society. A relationship of mutual confidence needs to be established.

*AS & GH:* Which developments do you consider most necessary to improve police activities?

*RO:* Greater professional qualifications and recognition of their value. Professional qualifications of the police are made through better work conditions—training, equipment, wages, and welfare. Recognition by society through the excellence of service we intend to deliver. What comes first? For sure we must show our value, our competence, and mainly our commitment to the society. Recognition will come naturally and I have no doubt that society itself will demand from the public power the existence and the presence of the police it wants to have.

# 8

# A Conversation With Colonel Jean-Etienne Elion, Congo National Police

**INTERVIEWED BY CHANTAL PERRAS AND DOMINIQUE WISLER**

**Contents**



## Background

Located in the heart of the African continent, the Republic of the Congo shares borders with Central Africa, Cameroon, Angola, the Democratic Republic of Congo, and Gabon. Its territory is about 342,000 km$^2$, with an oceanfront 179 km long. Brazzaville is its capital city.

The historical territory of today's Republic of the Congo consisted of several kingdoms and chiefdoms. First reached by the Portuguese sailor Diego Cao in 1492, this territory would be placed under France's tutelage on October 3, 1880, with a treaty signed between Makoko, then king of the Anzico kingdom, and Pierre Savorgnan de Brazza, a French explorer of Italian descent. The Colony of the Congo was officially established in 1881. It became autonomous in 1903, under the name of Moyen Congo (Middle Congo) with Pointe-Noire for its capital. Moyen Congo belonged to the Fédération de l'Afrique Équatoriale Française (French Equatorial Africa Federation, AEF), along with Gabon, Oubangui-Chari (Central Africa), and Chad.

Brazzaville has been the capital of the AEF since 1910. Following the German occupation of France in 1939, Brazzaville became the capital of Congo. Congo obtained its independence on August 15, 1960, 2 years after a referendum on self-rule organized by the French government on November 28, 1958.

Congo is one of the most urbanized countries of Black Africa, with about 60% of its population living in cities. French is the official language of Congo, and Lingala is the local language. After years of civil war that ended in 1999, the economy, which had suffered greatly, is now being rebuilt. Growth and development efforts are on the economic agenda. With the new constitution of 2002, the Republic of Congo now operates under a presidential regime characterized by a balance of powers (executive, legislative, and judicial).

In relation to justice, it is evident that there is a scarcity of staff and logistical support. Further, there are still military courts in Brazzaville and Pointe-Noire, with extended authorities over the territory, but they were not functional because the military code of justice had not yet been established. The repressive civil justice system was inherited from French colonization in the second half of the nineteenth century. It was originally characterized by treatment based on race. On the one hand, the colonial government dispensed French justice to French nationals (and *evolues*) in Equatorial Africa and, on the other hand, repressive justice was dispensed to indigenous people in Moyen Congo. These two forms of justice were unified in 1947 and lasted until independence in 1960. The democratic period, which began in May 1990 after a period dominated by a Communist regime between 1960 and 1990, did not bring any significant changes. The penal code and the penal proceedings code remain in use. Consequently, the repressive judicial system in Congo remains antiquated and not adapted to modern times.

The history of Congolese police is that of a colonial police force bound to ancestral identities and feuds. It grew in parallel with societal evolution in Congo. Some landmarks should be mentioned here. In 1972, the National Police was dissolved and integrated into the National Popular Army (the latter formally constituted as "Popular Army" in 1966 under the single-party Communist regime). In June 1990, following the Conférence Nationale Souveraine (National Sovereign Conference), it was the turn of the National Popular Army to be dissolved. The democratic transition instituted a new Force Publique Nationale (National Public Force) made up of the Congolese Army, the Gendarmerie (military police force), and the

Police Nationale (National Police), a civil force with paramilitary characteristics and the autonomy to manage its personnel.

Breaking with the Communist past, the National Public Force became an apolitical administrative body. In 1991, the Police Nationale organized its first États Généraux (General Estate) to define the principles on which the new democratic police would operate. Between 1997 and 1999, the country was plunged into a civil war which destroyed much of the police infrastructure. Following the peace accord, the Police Nationale underwent a profound reorganization sanctioned by the publication of an ordinance in June 1999. Following the adoption by referendum of the new constitution the year before, the government published in 2003 the description of the organization of the police, now integrated into the Ministry of Security and Police.

The Ministry of Security and Police has two civilian administrative organs, a General Inspection of the Police Services and a General Secretariat, the latter being mainly responsible for so-called support services, including human resources and financial and equipment management for the entire police service. As executive agencies, the ministry has three general directions (divisions): the National Police, the Surveillance of the Territory (mainly an intelligence agency), and Civil Disaster Management. In addition to these general directions, the ministry has a number of "units" such as special units, criminal investigation units, intervention units, and logistical support units.

In 2003, the Gendarmerie was not attached to the ministry but remained affiliated to the Ministry of Defense. Decree No. 2001-195 of April 11, 2001, regulates the missions, organization, and functioning of the Gendarmerie. Not unlike the French original design, the division of labor between the National Police and the Gendarmerie is mainly territorial: The National Police operate in urban environments and the Gendarmerie in the rural areas. However, the Gendarmerie can operate in urban areas when public disorders occur and, legally, the competency of the Gendarmerie is national. The necessary coordination between the two policing agencies is secured by two interministerial committees.

There are no municipal police in Congo. However, a legislative draft currently discussed in parliamentary committees envisions the creation of municipal police forces in the two main cities of the country, Brazzaville and Pointe-Noire. In addition, it should be underlined that so-called "tribal police forces," which were in operation during the colonial period and known under the appellation "Mboulou-Mboulou," no longer exist—formally or informally—in the Republic of Congo in contrast to what is the case in the neighboring Democratic Republic of Congo.

In matters of international cooperation, it should be said that the Republic of Congo has signed and ratified the Geneva Convention (1949) and its additional protocols (1977). Congo's main economic and security partner countries in the African continent are Angola, Egypt, and Algeria. There are also cooperation agreements with Europe (France) and Asia (China). There is no known cooperation with the United States. Police cooperation focuses mainly on two sectors: training and the furnishing of equipment. The National Police also belongs to, and exchanges information with, Interpol.

### The Interview

This interview was conducted through a series of conversations during IPES (International Police Executive Symposium) meetings in Cincinnati, Ohio (in 2008), and in Ohrid, Macedonia (2009). It was also pursued through e-mail and information exchanges and finalized in the first quarter of 2010. This interview was conducted entirely in French because the interviewee and the interviewers are primarily French speaking. In fact, the interviewee utilized French as a working language, even though his mother tongue is Lingala, the local language most spoken in Congo. The translation was undertaken by the interviewers.

The interview is a unique opportunity for readers to immerse themselves in the little known reality of policing in Congo and to access the views of Colonel Jean-Etienne Elion, who spent his entire career with the National Police. The interview will begin with some autobiographical notes about Colonel Jean-Etienne Elion. Colonel Elion was born in Brazzaville on January 1, 1959. He went to primary school in the Grande Ecole de la Mosquée-Brazzaville (the Great School of the Mosque), which was a laic school located in the Mosque neighborhood, from 1964 to 1966, then to the Grande Ecole de Ouenzé from

1967 to 1970. Before formally starting the interview, let us also clarify for the readers that the Republic of Congo—often known as Congo-Brazzaville—is not to be confused with its large southern neighbor, the Democratic Republic of Congo or Congo-Kinshasa, formerly known as Zaire.

*CP & DW:* Colonel Elion, to start this interview and allow our readers to get to know you, please describe your education and professional experience.

*CJEE:* My enlistment in the National Police, in parallel to my incorporation in the security services, is the natural outcome of decisions taken much earlier. By completing my study at Général Leclerc, a preparatory military high school, I was fated indeed to undertake either a military career or to follow a police curriculum. The vocation of the Leclerc school is twofold: (1) to provide the fundament of an education to young people coming from civil life, and (2) to educate "enfants de troupe" (so-called "troop children," an appellation reserved to designated young people receiving an education in this school) in anticipation of a future military career or (but less often) a police career.

As I was passionate about the principles of the rule of law and justice and order, I decided to join the National Police after completing elementary and high schools. I then took my first steps in the new and complex universe of the police organization.

*CP & DW:* Can you talk a little bit more in detail about your formal education and career?

*CJEE:* I entered the Général Leclerc High School in 1970 and obtained a baccalauréat littéraire [high school certificate in humanities] in 1977. From 1977 to 1979, I went to École Nationale de Securité [National School of Security] in Romania. Then, in 1979, I studied at the state-funded Marien Ngouabi University in Brazzaville and obtained a licence de droit public [degree in public law] in 1981. I completed my police education in 1981 at the Service de Coopération Technique Internationale de Police [Office of International Technical Cooperation of the Police], in France, and at the École Supérieure des Techniques S. M [Technical Superior School] in 1986 in Algeria.

Let me clarify a point for the readers. Obviously, this mix of military and policing training is the result of the setting that dominated political life in Congo in the 80s. The National Police was part of one single overall institution constituted by the Armed Forces, the Gendarmerie (a military force), and the National Police. It should also be underlined that the military academy, Marien Ngouabi, located in Brazzaville, was and still is a prestigious institution with a long tradition of excellence. But in matters of higher education, the National Police lags behind. A new national police academy [Ecole Nationale Supérieure de la Police] has begun to professionalize policing, but, according to observers, it will need time to be able to adequately fulfill its mission.

A word on my military and policing diplomas. I received the Certificat d'Aptitude Technique no. 1 in 1973; the Certificat d'Aptitude Technique no. 2 in 1974; the Brevet de Parachutiste in 1975; the Diplôme de fin de stage de Sécurité in Romania, a law degree, in 1979; the Certificat de fin de stage de Sûreté de l'État in 1981 in France; and, finally, the Certificat des Études Fondamentales ès Sciences Militaires in 1986 in Algeria.

My ranks were obtained in this chronological order: in 1973 I was promoted to the rank of chief corporal; then, in 1975, I became sergeant; I rose to sous [under]-lieutenant in 1979 and lieutenant in 1981; I was promoted to captain in 1984, lieutenant-colonel in 1992, and, finally, colonel in 1996. I was nominated for the Chevalier de l'Ordre de Mérite Congolais Titre Normal [an honorific title bestowed by the president] in 1986.

*CP & DW:* And what about your employment?

*CJEE:* In 1979, I began my first job as chief of the training section of the Political Division of the Regional Direction of the Security of the State. From 1979 until 1982, I was also chief of cabinet of the director of the Services Centraux

Techniques [Central Technical Services] and assistant director of the General Direction for State Security.

From 1982 until 1985, I was chief of the Diplomatic Division in the Regional Direction of the State Security in Kouilou. I occupied the same position in Brazzaville from 1985 to 1988. From 1988 until 1991, I was advisor of the Sécurité Populaire [Popular Security] of the governmental political party, the Parti Congolais du Travail [Congolese Labor Party]. Under the Communist regime, this department of the party was responsible for all issues related to people security and the contact point in the Congolese Labor Party to discuss security issues with the State Security Services.

After the first wave of democratization of 1991 and 1992, I became regional director of territory surveillance in Niari-Lékoumou and I occupied a similar position from 1992 to 1995 for Niari. In 1995 and 1996, I became the central director of the intelligence services [Directeur Central des Renseignements Généraux] of the General Directorate of the National Police [La Direction Générale de la Police Nationale]. From 2000 to 2002, I was special police superintendent [Commissaire Spécial de Police] at Maya-Maya International Airport. From 2002 to 2009, I occupied the position of director of documentation in the Division of Special Police Units.

Finally, I should mention my involvement at the international level. In October 2003, I became the Congo delegate for IPES and soon after, in September 2004, I was nominated director of IPES for French-speaking Africa.

*CP & DW:* Can you tell us something that has been surprising to you in your career?

*CJEE:* Of course, it would be a wrong assumption to believe that you are in control of what happens to you in a policing career. Surprises, if you want, are inherent to the job! But perhaps I could mention a few things in particular. I had always thought that legislators were omniscient and that they had planned for all the contingencies in case of a crime, an infraction, or a simple offense. It is this erroneous understanding of the articulation of the fundamental principles of the state juridical-institutional architecture that was my first illusion. Second, I was surprised by the fact that as a police officer you are constantly absorbed by action; there is no relief, no break, from the action. Deviant behaviors are omnipresent in the society. Similarly, individual and collectives liberties are often threatened.

*CP & DW:* What are the advantages that you have found the most interesting in your career?

*CJEE:* The advantages of the police function are certainly of two orders: (1) a social aspect and (2) an intellectual aspect. Being a senior police officer in my country brings prestige and social recognition, and this is an aspect of the advantages you get from the profession. My personal dynamism, curiosity, clear-sightedness, aspiration for excellence, if you want, have helped me a lot to leave my country, meet professionals around the world, and explore my profession side by side with bright specialists of criminal justice and the police. I had the privilege to work with distinguished International Police Executive Symposium members and Interpol staff.

*CP & DW:* OK, which changes did you feel were the most important in policing in Congo during your career?

*CJEE:* Two elements, corresponding to two important sequences of history of my country deserve, in my own opinion, to be mentioned here.

A first important moment of the history of the police in Congo has been the multidimensional change in the national political landscape associated with the perestroika movement in the former USSR. In fact, after the vast reforms toward democratic pluralism in the East European bloc, and because Congo was considered an Africa satellite Communist state, my country had to adopt the new configuration inspired by this new type of political system. In fact, perestroika was the real turning point. Congo started to look in other directions, especially in the direction of the Western democracies and the early trend of modernization and professionalization of policing can be traced back to the perestroika period. We wanted to "get back in the concert of nations," so to speak, and stop being considered as a world apart and confined to isolation. It became clear that it was up to us to rebuild a network of collaboration and cooperation with foreign police forces. This was important as our needs in terms of internal security and public tranquility were important.

We arrived at the critical date of 1991. The first États Généraux [General Estates] of our National Police were convoked in April 1991 and took place in the Congress Palace. It was an important moment. Senior police officers sat at the table for four consecutive days and thought about the future and the new foundations of the police in Congo. For me, it was the starting point for the rewriting of our police history. One of the key decisions of this assembly was the depolitization of the police. Imagine that during the Communist time a simple chief corporal who had risen to senior positions in the party could request to review the army and give orders to a colonel and to his troops. This was highly damaging for all institutions of the Public Forces that were by definition strongly bureaucratic, vertical organizations. The former Security Services was also dissolved at that time. Motions, recommendations, and resolutions for change were taken by consent during these Etats Généraux.

Consequently, the Congolese police started to regularly engage in international collaboration and the cooperation agreements that were signed impacted the professionalization of policing in the country. As I mentioned earlier, we obtained training and equipment that helped us to develop new programs and become better.

Seven years after that historical moment, while Congo was making progress on the road of political pluralism and while freedom of opinion was becoming a reality, all achievements were undermined by another wave of conflicts and civil war. The police were one of the victims to fall during these events and were highly vulnerable to the partisan interests and circumstances that had given rise to the general civil conflict. This was the second moment in the contemporary history of the national police that prompted a new wave of debates over the police, its practices, and its organizations. We needed a new beginning. This was a real challenge as it took place at a moment when the entire national administration had disintegrated. Between 1997 and 1999, violence of all kinds caused tragic loss in human lives and destroyed administrative buildings in the towns and in the hinterland.

The physical reconstruction and institution-building started after this last wave of violence is still going on today. All departments in connection to security and police were revisited to improve the very foundations of policing and to respond more effectively to social demands.

Today, no sector of policing is spared from the necessity to adapt itself continuously to reality. This is true for the patrols or the criminal investigation teams down to all management practices.

Today, more than before, crime is becoming internationalized. Organized crime knows no frontiers. It is at our door. Worse, criminals have invested in the high-tech world and improved their criminal capacity by using cybernetics, new technologies of information and communication. They do not hesitate to use heavy or small arms.

The inventory of new trends in criminality in the twenty-first century calls for appropriate responses that require high-quality training and equipment, which are vital for the efficiency of patrol officers as well as of managers.

*CP & DW:* What is the role of police in society?

*CJEE:* Traditionally and in the doctrine, the role of the organization of the police is to be the guardian and protector of fundamental liberties in the country. The Congolese police are in fact in charge of protecting people and properties as well as securing the Republic's state institutions, which also is of benefit for the community. Finally, they are also in charge of protecting the inviolability of the national frontiers. The functions of police are, then, multiple, diversified, and complex.

The services the police provide night and day to the population seek to prevent in all places and in all circumstances the occurrence of all hazards and unpredictable contingences. In our understanding, police have to inspire confidence and security rather than fear, except in the case of delinquents, offenders, and other antisocial individuals. The police are for the community, obviously—a resource available at any time.

To be able to reach those objectives and to be also more efficient, the police should stress prevention rather than curative responses and prefer proaction to reaction. But the core business remains the enforcement of the law without exceptions.

Let me talk a little bit on the subject of the governance of the police. We have made considerable progress in this matter. First of all, the General Inspection of the Police Services is "external" to the policing general directions and responds directly to the minister. The police do not self-inspect, if you want, and are accountable to the civilian authority. We have also an additional institution of the general controller of the police services and, of course, disciplinary councils to handle disciplinary cases. Administrative courts address policy issues while normal criminal courts address issues of penal cases involving police officers of the National Police.

The judiciary and civil society have set up a joint "alert mechanism" that rests on regular inspections of detention places to ensure that human rights are enforced, that preventive detention rules are complied with, and that sanitary conditions of detention places conform to regulations. We also innovated with the multiplication of letter boxes allowing citizens to complain, criticize, and suggest ideas of improvement of policing services directly to the general prosecutor of the Republic of Congo. This initiative allows keeping police forces and individual abuses under control.

*CP & DW:* From your experience, which policies and programs did work well? When did they not work well and why?

*CJEE:* To be short and not necessarily systematic, we can mention training programs and various programs of acquisition of police equipment, in particular crowd control equipments. These programs took place within the highly dynamic police cooperation with countries such as France, Algeria, Angola, and Cameroon.

The ILEA (International Law Enforcement Academy) experience in Gaborone in Botswana, under U.S. aegis and with the assistance of the FBI and the Pentagon, is also an example to capitalize on, particularly because it illustrates the positive climate and current openness of the United States to relations with Africa, which has a history of having been neglected for too many years. These are very positive developments.

We should not forget the positive experience of the Congo's contribution to the missions of the United Nations and African Union in Darfur.

More anecdotal but still relevant as best practice, let me mention the brilliant results obtained by high-profile police operations of the past 20 years or so. The "Pacific" Operation in 1990, the "Espoir" [Hope] Operation in 2000 and, more recently, the "Tranquility 2009 Operation" are cases in point. Depending on the situation, these are joint operations conducted with the Armed Forces, the Gendarmerie, and the National Police. The Operation Tranquility 2009 was conducted by the National Police alone between December 12, 2009, and January 12, 2010, and resulted in the impressive number of 445 arrests for various allegations ranging from selling/consumption of drugs and robbery to public disturbances. The collaboration between the army and police might be compared to the well-known VigiPirate operations conducted from time to time in France when terrorism threatens the security of the country.

Globally, it is important to stress once again that much of the underperformance of the Congolese police and the failures that can be spotted from time to time are the result of recurrent civil war and conflicts. Cyclically, Congo is confronted with the immense challenge of having to start almost from scratch and rebuild a damaged social cohesion.

The main obstacles to the progress of the police are essentially twofold: the lack of training accompanied by its corollary, corruption, as well as the critical lack of logistic and material means capable of helping police fight often heavily armed outlaws.

But the country is far from remaining passive when confronted with corruption. There is good news to be reported. First of all, a recent anticorruption law (law no. 5-2009) was promulgated on September 22, 2009. Second, a strategic plan to curb corruption has been approved. Third, a national commission and an observatory have been established to tackle the issue of corruption in Congo. Fourth, a large public campaign has just been conducted in public administrations, territories, and neighborhoods that targets in particular the public forces as well as the public through the neighborhood headmen or their representatives.

Many war weapons are still available in big or small towns, and the reintegration of ex-combatants is difficult to achieve (currently there are 3,000 ex-combatants waiting to be reintegrated either into the armed forces or into their communities, with the assistance of cofinancing of Congo and the United Nations). The collection of weapons has yet to prove successful despite the program offering money in exchange for illegal weapons.

Reflecting the challenges of the national reconciliation, the relations between the police and the population remains a matter of daily concern and the improvement of this relationship would certainly contribute to peace, concord, and reconstruction. Nothing should be assumed as "given" to the police and the police are confronted daily with the challenges of rebuilding a nation.

*CP & DW:* In your opinion, what should be the relations between theory and practice, learning and field work?

*CJEE:* Ideally, theory and practice must share a common understanding of different types of facts and events in the society and this common ground is the key to allowing transfers of analyses inspired by a good theory to successful practice on the ground.

In total symbiosis, theory and practice should be complementary, so practice will confirm the accuracy of the hypotheses, and theory will be useful to understand the rationality of practice. A wise old adage is that everything that is well conceived can be formulated clearly and can be put in practice without particular difficulties. The intimate relationship between theory and practice is then a "marriage de raison" (an allusion to a marriage between two persons for economic reasons rather than passion).

Practitioners who are equipped with a sound theoretical background will have more confidence in executing their mission. In general, when this rule is applied systematically, then problems vanish in the execution of policing tasks.

Obviously, we have to accept that external contingencies open some room to maneuver in the execution of tasks. These contingencies are often unexpected by the theoreticians or by the legislator. No one can be totally exhaustive in envisioning the vagaries of the future.

A judicious exploitation of the problems that occurred in the application of a theory is to stimulate the builders of the theory to reformulate the fundamentals of their approach. Nowadays, we should not hesitate to affirm the existence of a relation between theory and practice. A little incoherence between theory and practice will induce bad consequences in one or both, which then can destroy their natural and common link, their consubstantial existence.

Like a sword of Damocles, the deontological code (code of ethics) of the police profession is instrumental in reducing to a large extent the mistakes, abuses, and other deviant behavior of the police. These abuses are recurrent in the exercise of the profession. Bearing this idea in mind, we must honestly stress that police officers are not necessarily what we call in French "des enfants de chœur" (children who volunteer to serve in church).

In my opinion, research focusing on improving policing practice should be done with a broad vision. It should not focus exclusively on issues such as justice and human rights because, in the end, practice is at the confluence of numerous experiences and perspectives that jointly contribute to shape it in a particular way.

*CP & DW:* Let us ask you one question. For the past 30 years or so, police forces around the globe have adopted the principles of community policing. We can think of Cameroon or Senegal in francophone Africa. What is your opinion regarding these ideas and, perhaps in the introduction, can you tell us what community policing is, in your opinion?

*CJEE:* The experiments conducted in Great Britain, New York, France, Senegal, or the Republic of Congo to develop the "proximity" relations, as it is called in France, between the police and the population encourage me to define the "police de proximité" [proximity police or, rather, community policing] as a modality of managing public security. The originality of this modality is that it does not equate policing with coercion and repression. I would describe it as a new posture or positioning of the police within a social field. This positioning is characterized by a readiness to institute partnerships with various other social actors capable of contributing to public security. Police are no longer alone but work in networks. This new posture produces major gains in terms of legitimacy of policing.

The methods used by the proximity police are proactive, soft, and obviously less brutal. This new approach of policing seems to be based on a communitarian understanding of policing. It rests mainly on the ideas of a strong acceptance by local communities, a decentralized organization, and, above all, an extended interpretation of the police mission as problem solving through the collective search for social factors generating public disorders and deviance. This requires that there be permanent adjustments of police priorities to the social expectations and demand. This obviously requires a systematic and standing evaluation of police services. Such an evaluation presupposes the necessary data collection and the identification of social issues that can be "sensitive."

I am personally inclined to believe that this idea and vision of an integrative police work or action conform to the pluralist ideology.

To sum up, one can assert that the notion of a proximity police has managed to enter into the professional and institutional vocabulary of the police, into journalistic discourse, and even into the opinion of the local population. One of the great advantages of the approach is that it cuts across the dividing lines of repression and prevention. Here I should not omit to mention the Gendarmerie, which is polyvalent and has multiple competencies. I sincerely think that the Gendarmerie uses, by tradition, a model of proximity police in the rural regions. We should not forget that this proximity is indeed at the very foundation of the Gendarmerie.

Now coming to Congo. A model of proximity police has its place in the Republic of Congo. It should be implemented by both forces, the National Police and the National Gendarmerie—the former operating in urban areas and the latter in rural areas. The policing agencies in Congo have already adopted some of the modalities of this type of policing. Let me mention "sector policing" [îlotage]; foot patrols or mobile patrols during the day and the night; units in charge of fighting delinquency; surveillance in proximity of schools, public parks, commercial zones, and main roads; and the use of letter boxes for complaints and suggestions for the improvement of services.

*CP & DW:* Can we come back to the subject of international relations? You started to talk about it in relation to your career, and it was really interesting.

*CJEE:* OK. The tremendous progress of science and technology, the universally imposed respect for human rights, the ethical charter of the police, the profitable exchanges with the police service around the world through numerous cooperation programs, training courses, seminars, and conferences—all this is encouraging and contribute to knowledge and learning. They impact positively on the productivity of the police in Congo and raise the standards of a police force in reconstruction. Those collaborations are beneficial and also salutary. We should capitalize on them.

Now, I want to talk about September 11, 2001. We will never forget this day. First of all because it was a sinister blow to peace in the world and, second, because it was really a big bang in changing the mind-set of professionals dealing with security. The means, methods, and policies to ensure security have been fine-tuned and, indeed, radicalized. In the domains of aeronautic and airport security, for example, the new technology of information and communication, security devices, and systems have become much more sophisticated and are also more reliable.

*CP & DW:* What about the democratic policies in your country?

*CJEE:* My country, Congo, is a country in the postconflict phase. Since the end of the fratricidal hostilities, my country has started to rebuild a police institution based on republican values. On the political side, we advocate a firm anchorage to democracy in all aspects of life of the nation. In this respect, the Republic of Congo ultimately needs, for its police, the assistance of advisors who have the necessary expertise and experience. These people are needed to help in restoring order and assuring the enforcement of the law and respect for human rights.

Shaping policing with democratic values means concretely—in my understanding and, as a matter of fact, in the view of the public—that a culture of justice and equity grows internally within the policing agencies. In the end, it is necessary to promote and stimulate the marvelous tendency of the democratization of the public life.

In my opinion, reforms make sense and have authority only if they take into account the values of democracy and justice, principles at the core of the protection of fundamental liberties.

*CP & DW:* Finally, can you give us your general assessment?

*CJEE:* The modest administrative and operational positions that I successively occupied in the policing world allow me to strongly affirm that the recent successes of the police are due to the rapid progress made in increasing access to information and intelligence in a timely manner. Successes obtained by delicate police interventions taking place mostly in hostile environments are an illustration of these positive developments in my country. We are satisfied with the level of performance reached by police units in the execution of their noble mission to preserve peace and to maintain public order in the community.

Similarly, each day brings its small contribution of unexpected successes in the field of scientific policing. All this is highly encouraging, brings joy in the profession, and clearly brings standing for the police in the context of often complex judicial proceedings.

It is urgent to upgrade our methods to respond adequately to often technically astute and imaginative criminals engaged in complex transactions of organized crime internationally.

I am one of those who believe that a broad and encompassing training matching today's technological advancements will improve dramatically our service capacity. Acting in a modernized working environment and with an adequate salary, police officers in any country will give the best of themselves to achieve the highest standards of the profession and, in doing so, win the hearts and minds of the population.

### Conclusion

Colonel Elion is clearly more experienced than most of us. He has held senior positions in a police force that underwent multiple transitions: from Communism to democracy, from war to peace, from a "militarized" policing system to a more civilian policing system and even the introduction of elements of community policing. He masters diverse understanding or ideologies of policing: Communist popular security, military policing (Gendarmerie), new democratic governance theories, and community policing. He is clearly at ease with a variety of systems of ideas, has a passion for theoretical discussions, and understands the positions of the police in various ideological constructions. He is a man who belongs to the salons of luxury hotels hosting conferences of global experts in policing. That, in itself, appears a paradox and we are sure comes as a surprise to many readers. Is not Brazzaville the capital city of a "satellite country" that lived for decades in isolation under Communist rule and an African country that was ravaged by waves of civil wars until very recently?

At the same time, for these very reasons, Colonel Elion is who he is. He is someone who was educated in another satellite or friendly community country; someone who was handpicked by his hierarchy to move up to higher ranks and to participate in international training; someone who was selected by international cooperation agencies in Congo to be trained abroad. But still he is rare bird, we think.

Colonel Elion is an enthusiastic proponent of the reforms of his country and quite proud of the successes of the National Police. Still, scratching under the surface of his rhetoric seems necessary to identify issues that seem unresolved. Many of the substantive responses of Colonel Elion are limited to "his" National Police and give little understanding of what happens in the second half of the country—namely, the countryside where the military police (the Gendarmerie) operate alone. We understand that many developments have put the National Police on track with democratization but are left with little clue as to what really happens with the Gendarmerie.

While, at first sight, a French model is simply followed in Congo, this is not really the case. The Gendarmerie is entirely run by the Ministry of Defense, while this is no longer the case for France. For quite some time, the Ministry of Interior in France was the regulating authority of the French Gendarmerie. In another country with a similar model—Turkey—again, the Gendarmerie is entirely regulated, financed, and controlled by the Ministry of Interior. This is not the case in Congo.

Regarding police misconduct, we should remain cautious with the arsenal of measures that is proudly displayed by Colonel Elion. In fact, there is no independent police complaint commission to investigate cases of police abuses—contrarily to what is the case in South Africa, one of the first countries worldwide to establish such a commission. But Congo has other impressive institutions to valorize such as the external General Inspectorate for the Police Services. Here, we agree. This appears to be a state-of-the-art external inspection allowing the civilian authority to inspect its police.

In general, what we missed in the interview was a vision of the reform that is necessary for Congo to achieve more democracy. We found the focus on training and equipment a bit limited. Colonel Elion reminded us that police officers are no "enfant de choeur." What seems to be the message from Colonel Elion is that democratization is nice but as long as the police lack capacity to do the job, more layers of external control will not help much. What we understood and could agree with is that the road to democracy has to be pursued, at the same speed, within and outside the police.

## Reference

Elion, J-E. (2005). Republic of the Congo. In Das, D. K. and Palmiotto, M. J. (Eds.), *World police encyclopedia.* New York: Routledge.

# 9

# Interview With Leading Police Director Werner Heinrich Schumm (Ret.), Former Deputy Chief of Staff of the Federal Border Police of the Federal Republic of Germany

## INTERVIEWED BY ROBERT F. J. HARNISCHMACHER

**Contents**



**Background**

For more than 20 years, the interviewer and Mr. Schumm have been very good friends. They have worked together on many prior occasions on the topics of policing and on actual police problems as these influence the education and training of the Federal Police, civil society, and the state. Helpful in maintaining the working relationship have been lectures delivered to the police in the legal sciences, criminology, and police affairs by the interviewer, as well as his background in the German military and Japanese martial arts, and his international contacts around the globe. These activities have always been the primary basis for good and successful teamwork and a cordial and engaged friendship.

*The Federal Border Police*

Ever since its formation on March 16, 1951, the Federal Border Guard (Bundesgrenzschutz) has been a multifunctional police force of the federation far beyond its assignment as a border police force. The Federal Border Guard was reorganized in 1998 and on July 1, 2005, was renamed the Federal Police. The Federal Police Central Office has its seat in Potsdam (since March 1, 2008), the capital of the land of Brandenburg. President of the Federal Police is Matthias Seeger (since March 1, 2008). The Federal Police organization is subordinate to the Federal Ministry of the Interior. It is administered by its own federal police section within the ministry, carries out special police duties in the security system of the Federal Republic of Germany, and extensive and manifold federal police duties on the basis of a modern police law (Federal Police Act) and numerous other laws.

In the Federal Republic of Germany, the principal duty of the police forces of the individual federal states, together with other authorities, is to maintain public safety and order. They must protect the individual citizen and the general public from danger, enforce law and order in general, and control any disturbances. The focal point of the duties set down by law is the protection of the liberal-democratic order of the state in Germany and ensuring the basic rights that are guaranteed in the constitutional law of the Federal Republic of Germany.

The constitutional law as well as federal laws charges the federal government with police duties in important areas of public security and order. These duties are carried out by the Federal Police (Bundespolizei) and the Federal Criminal Police Office (Bundeskriminalamt [BKA]). In addition, authorities within the sphere of other federal ministries have police duties—for example, Customs at the Federal Ministry of Finances and the Water and Shipping Directorates at the Federal Ministry of Transport.

Due to its prior special duties, particularly at the external borders, the Federal Police organization today already has multiple experiences in international collaboration, a collaboration that has gained more and more significance for the internal security of Europe. The Federal Police force collaborates closely with the existing security networks through security cooperation and security partnerships with the police forces of the German federal states and other security authorities of the government and the federal states, as well as with foreign border control authorities.

The extensive duties of the Federal Police are mainly regulated in the law on the Federal Police (Federal Police Act) as well as in numerous other legal regulations (e.g., the Alien Act, the Asylum Procedure Act, and the Act on Aviation Security. According to these laws, the Federal Police have the following specific duties:

- border protection of the federal territory
- railway-police duties
- averting threats to the security of air traffic
- the maintenance or restoration of security and public order aboard German aircraft
- the protection of the constitutional institutions of the federal government and the federal ministries
- maritime duties on the North Sea and the Baltic Sea
- police duties in states of emergency and in national defense
- involvement in police duties abroad under the responsibility of the United Nations, the European Union, or any other international organizations
- support of the police at the German Parliament
- support of the Ministry of Foreign Affairs to protect German diplomatic and consular missions abroad
- support of the Federal Criminal Police Office in protection and escort services (protection of persons)
- support of the Federal Office for the Protection of the Constitution in the field of radio communication
- support of the police forces of the federal states, particularly with large-scale operations
- assistance in cases of catastrophes or particular accidents, including airborne rescue services

The Federal Police has about 40,000 employees, including about 30,000 male and female police officers. Of these officers, about 21,000 deal with tasks concerning border protections and railway aviation security; about 6,000 serve in special standby police units, and around 3,000 officers work in the other functional units (Aviation Service, GSG 9, Central Office for Information and Communication) and other organizations.

Police officers are supported by about 2,000 salaried employees, mainly in border-police matters and flight passenger checks. About 6,800 civil servants are available for administration and service matters.

### The Interview

*RFJH:* Can you tell me a little about your childhood and adolescence? What influenced and convinced you to join the Federal Border Guard, now the Federal Police?

*WHS:* I was born in Nuremberg on April 6, 1939. My unmarried mother did not want to take me home from the hospital because she was ashamed. So I landed in a home for children managed by a state organization. This was not a very good start of my life, indeed. One year later one of the nurses took me home to present me to her parents with consent of the home's management. She convinced them to keep me as their foster child. It was the first year of the Second World War with all its threats and sufferings. I shall always be grateful to my foster parents that they had the good will and the courage to take such a decision in those difficult times.

Although my foster parents were rather poor, they cared for me in a perfect manner. They even sent me to a secondary school; however, after 6 years they could no longer afford the expenses. So, despite quite good marks, I had to quit school and to start earning money, first in the wage department of a factory, later in a county commissioner's office. There I heard of a unique opportunity for me to continue secondary school and take the final examination qualifying (the Abitur) for university admission (an objective that I had never given up). It was the Federal Border Guard that offered this possibility. Although I knew next to nothing about this organization, I sent my application form without delay, passed a physical and written and oral examinations, and joined the BGS [Bundesgrenzschutz] at the age of 18 in July 1957.

*RFJH:* Can you tell us something about your training and education in the BGS? What was your personal development in the years of 1957 until 1971? Please be so kind to characterize your professional experiences.

*WHS:* When I joined the Federal Border Guard in Coburg, Northern Bavaria, in July 1957, I found myself in a paramilitary force. As far as legal and practical aspects are concerned, it took two decades until the BGS was transformed into a real police formation as it is today, now called Bundespolizei (Federal Police).

Dr. Konrad Adenauer, elected as the first chancellor of the Federal Republic of Germany after World War II in 1949, was of the opinion that Germany would never regain sovereignty unless the Germans guaranteed, on their own, their national security by military forces. The victorious powers had verbally forbidden this. So Dr. Adenauer regarded the BGS as a first and preliminary element of armed forces.

The Western Allies agreed to set up the German Federal Armed Forces in 1955. Only BGS officers got an option to join the new army. A considerable number of them did so. The future of BGS was uncertain for a while. Later, the BGS recovered from the dramatic loss of manpower. Its strength even increased from 10,000 to 20,000 officers due to political developments in Eastern Germany in the course of the cold war.

The BGS appeared as a force of public security similar to a National Guard, subordinate to the secretary of the interior and ready to support local police forces in case of major internal conflicts like riots. On the other hand, the BGS was supposed to defend the young Federal Republic against minor military or subversive attacks below the level of war from beyond the East German border. We were regarded as a buffer between the military forces in the Eastern and the Western world and we were well aware of this task. Our equipment comprised armored cars, machine guns, grenade launchers, and hand grenades.

From legal aspects, we were policemen and military combatants according to international regulations. Most of our commanding officers at company level and higher came from the former German army with little or no police background. Our basic training was tough, almost completely military, with many hours of field exercises, parades, sports, rifle and pistol shooting, and regular running, interrupted only by a few lessons in legal issues of police intervention. Order and obedience were the main principles of our education; complaints were not normal as we were told that thousands of young men would be glad to join the service in our place. This was a matter of fact in 1957. Somehow, I learned to live under these conditions. Having finished basic training, I passed a squad leader's course successfully in 1958.

After that, life was much better. I was the leader and trainer of a squad then and frequently served as a patrol leader at the demarcation line.

As more and more East German citizens escaped from East to West in the early 1950s, the authorities in the German Democratic Republic—the previous Eastern (Russian) zone of occupation—had started fortifying the demarcation line (which ran for a length of about 1,000 kilometers) by fences, antivehicle trenches, minefields, watchtowers, and bunkers. East Germany developed more and more into a prison. The East German border services (at the beginning called "National People's Army, Border Command" and later "Border Troops of the German Democratic Republic") behaved in a hostile manner toward citizens in the border area, refugees, and our official services. They had an order to shoot to prevent escapes.

We often tried to contact Eastern border patrols across the line, thinking that they were Germans like us; however, they were not allowed to talk to us. And usually they did not.

Later, the East Germans used specific reconnaissance officers, who operated directly at the demarcation line, on our side of the fences. Those officers, who were considered 100% reliable to the political system from the point of view of their superiors, addressed us, asking questions or trying to work political influence on us. We were free to talk, but of course we reported contacts of the kind regularly.

In one of those meetings, my East German "colleague" said to me, "We know that you don't have more private cars in the West than we have. Your propaganda plays dirty tricks. Whenever a West German citizen buys a new car, he is forced to drive it to our border at least one time to give us a wrong impression!" He obviously believed this nonsense.

I shall never forget my first border patrol in the fall of 1957. With my patrol leader, an older first sergeant, I was standing behind a road barrier in the middle of a forest when, suddenly, two East German border guards emerged from the area in front of us at a distance of about 20 yards. They said nothing while they were aiming at us with their Kalashnikovs. My more experienced patrol leader realized that I was about to automatically tear my rifle from the shoulder, as I had learned in training. In a calm voice, he said to me, "Leave your rifle where it is. We turn around and leave now. Don't look back!" While we were walking away for about 200 yards, I kept feeling a weapon pointing at my back—an unpleasant situation, indeed.

In 1959 we had an exciting event in our border section of Coburg. It describes how critical the situation was at that time. East German engineers had crossed the demarcation line and cut off the only access road to a hotel situated on our territory. Our battalion commander sent out one of our companies and three armored cars with mounted machine guns. He went up to the border himself and requested a senior officer of the East Germans to come to negotiate. When, after a while, a major appeared, our CO shouted at him, "You have an hour's time to put away all this stuff or else we shall start shooting!" As there was no reaction for a while, the colonel put the company into a firing position and ordered the men to load the machine guns. A few minutes later, the East German engineers started dismantling the blockade and withdrawing with all of their equipment.

The year 1960 brought a decisive change in my professional life. I was lucky to join the secondary school program in Lübeck. It was only then that I became aware of the fact that only 20 out of 20,000 officers of BGS got this opportunity every year after selections at battalion, division, and national levels.

For 3 years I was in the wonderful position of a police sergeant of the BGS (wearing uniform) and a pupil of the minisecondary school of BGS, staffed by professors of local Lübeck [a town in northern Germany] secondary schools. In 1963 I received the Abitur certificate. A 1-year officer's training course in Lübeck followed. After that I was transferred to a border battalion in Örlenbach near Bad Kissingen (in Northern Bavaria) and promoted to the rank of second lieutenant in 1964.

I served there from 1964 to 1971, starting as a platoon leader. Later I was a deputy company commander, S 2 officer, and liaison officer with the United States Armed Forces in Bad Kissingen and Schweinfurt as well as with a military intelligence unit in Bad Neustadt. With the U.S. Forces, we carried out joint border patrols, many field exercises, and a marvelous parade in Bad Kissingen during the German–American friendship week every year. Several times I participated in common training with the Green Berets (U.S. Special Forces stationed at Bad Tölz) and British Special Forces.

In order to improve my language abilities in English and French, I served as a guide of border tours with official international guests or tourists. Learning languages turned out to be a key element in my career. Thanks to my contacts in this period, I was invited to the United States twice, along with my wife. We met good comrades and their parents, saw 13 states, and developed lasting friendships.

*RFJH:* During your career from 1971 until 1985 you conducted many missions and duties at various ranks. What kinds of missions did you participate in during your progress at the BGS?

*WHS:* From 1971 to 1976 I was a company commander in Bonn, the capital of the Federal Republic of Germany. A reinforced battalion of the Federal Border Guard, the BGS Guard Battalion, was responsible for protecting the sites of constitutional authorities of the Federal Republic. I became the commander of the 2nd Company, responsible for Villa Hammerschmidt—the Federal president's office and residence; the Ministry of Interior; the Ministry of Justice; and the residence of Federal Chancellor Willi Brandt. In addition, my unit had to provide security for the guest house of the Federal Republic, the Castle Gymnich near Cologne, with a large park around it (later the Hotel Petersberg on top of a hill near Bonn).

The mission was pretty exciting for my family and me. We were always prepared for the worst in the years to come. A small story may illustrate the situation. One Sunday morning (I had started my task in Bonn only a couple of days before), I got a phone call at my home near Bonn. A platoon leader reported that a man was walking up and down in front of the Foreign Office, undoubtedly wearing a gun in a holster. I ordered preparation of fire protection for myself and raced to the site in civilian clothes in my private car. When I approached the gentleman and asked him what he was doing in front of the official building, he answered, "This is not your business." In order to identify myself, I made a move to present to him my service card. When I reached for it in my jacket, the man simultaneously put his hand into his jacket, obviously holding his gun at this moment. The situation seemed to run out of control. I advised the man to be very careful now, saying truthfully that two submachine guns were directed at him from behind. He slowly looked around and noticed two of my guards lying in a firing position. He slowly raised his hands and disclosed that he was one of the bodyguards of the Israeli ambassador, who was praying in the synagogue nearby.

The period of 1971–1975 was the most active time of the Bader-Meinhoff Gang and the RAF (Red Army Faction)—groups of leftist terrorists who were involved in several assassinations in Germany, killing representatives of the government, banks, and big industry. In addition to many German targets, they also attacked the V U.S. Army Corps in Frankfurt/Main on May 11, 1972 (one person was killed and 13 people injured), and the U.S. headquarters in Europe in Heidelberg on May 24, 1972 (three persons killed and five injured).

Under the permanent threat of terrorist assaults and massive demonstrations in the city of Bonn, official state visits were a special challenge for my staff and me. We had to provide exceptional security measures for the visits of Indira Gandhi from India; Emperor Hirohito from Japan; President Ceaucescu from Romania, in 1971; Idi Amin from Uganda; Queen Elizabeth from Great Britain, in 1972; Leonid Brezhnew, Soviet Union, in 1973; Marshal Tito from Yugoslavia, in 1974; and U.S. President Gerald R. Ford, in 1975. Despite the tension I was always aware of, I would not have liked to miss this time in Bonn. I received a close look at famous personalities of the time. And I often got exciting insights into political events which did not appear even in newspapers.

In 1976 I went back to the BGS training center in Lübeck, this time as a lecturer. I had asked my superiors to transfer me. Meanwhile, the BGS had become a regular police force with extended jurisdiction. Professional knowledge had changed and increased considerably. And my very specific mission in Bonn did not leave me enough time to keep up to date in all areas of BGS responsibilities. So, as a lecturer, I was teaching and learning at the same time. Step by step my knowledge in various areas grew. In 1979 I had the privilege of teaching all subjects relevant at the BGS training center and I was well prepared to pass the selection for the senior officers training.

In 1981 I passed the final examination at the police academy in Münster, together with police officers of the federal states (Länder). The training of the Federal Border Police and the federal states had been harmonized at all levels in the meantime. Our common training produced mutual trust, which was important in joint operations, as I experienced very often in the future.

Promoted to the rank of major, I was transferred to Bonn again. I became the head of a special unit subordinate to the Ministry of Interior. With this unit I drafted and negotiated manuals for all tactical and technical fields of police work with police experts of the federal states. The meetings were decentralized. So I traveled all over Germany, saw many unknown beauties of our country, and met excellent professionals in police management, tactics, crime prevention, riot control, prosecution of crime, and other specific police issues. In every meeting, I learned something new and my vocational expertise grew further.

In July 1983 our German secretary of the interior traveled to Turkey for political negotiations, and I was selected to accompany him in a small delegation due to my knowledge of English and French. The head of the police department examined me and several colleagues. I got the job and was very proud. Turkey was then governed by a military dictator, President Evren. Turkish society was dominated by military thinking. Therefore, the secretary wanted me to wear my uniform.

After landing in Ankara, we were taken to our hotel in a convoy. There, the secretary complained about the Turkish Border Police, who had taken away his passport. When I shook my head, the Secretary said, "Don't tell me that you have kept yours! How did they treat you?" Truthfully, I answered, "They saluted me, sir." As a major wearing a uniform, I was respected more than the secretary on a state visit! Still in the hotel hallway, I said to the secretary's head of cabinet that I had a bar in my apartment. Although his rank was much higher than mine, he had none. So I offered to change the rooms, and I tried to find out the reason of this obvious mistake. I found it on the name tags at the doors of our rooms. My rank was spelled correctly—"Maj."—while he was a "Mr." on the tag (instead of MR for the German title Ministerialrat). We had a big laugh when I explained to him that, in Turkey, as a major, I was more important than he was as a mister, of course.

In evening receptions I could make use of my knowledge of French. Representatives of higher education spoke French in Turkey at that time, as I learned. Probably this has changed, like many other things in Turkey since then. During the visit I participated in all political talks. And, of course, I enjoyed the tourist part of the journey in Ankara and Istanbul.

Later in 1983 I returned to the BGS guard battalion in Bonn as deputy commander. The activities of RAF terrorists had reached their peak in 1977. But they had not yet given up. In 1984 a bomb attack against the NATO training center in Oberammergau failed only because of a technical defect, and in 1985 during an assault at the U.S. Rhine main airbase in Frankfurt, two persons were killed and 11 injured. We had to keep on the alert!

I think it was in this time when you, dear Robert, came to Bonn and saw me pretty often. You were invited by Colonel Wegener, the commander of Group 9 Special (GSG 9), and the hero of Mogadishu who had freed the hostages from a Lufthansa plane with his unit. Later, General Wegener was my immediate superior as commanding officer of BGS Commando West in Bonn.

In 1984 contacts between the police of the Arab Emirate Abu Dhabi and the GSG 9 led to the plan to establish an antiterror police force in the emirate. In May 1985 a group of experts from GSG 9 flew to Abu Dhabi to explore the conditions in the country. Again, for language reasons I was invited to accompany the group. We flew Lufthansa first class—the sheiks had paid the fare in advance.

For 2 weeks we studied the organizations and equipment of the Abu Dhabi police. On a helicopter we flew to offshore oil-well derricks and saw the famous town of Al Ayn in the desert. I will never forget the impressions of a culture and a professional world so different from ours. Fortunately, I had gone to the department for the Arab Emirates in our Foreign Office to get some useful information on what we might expect. This made sense in fact. Without a minimum of knowledge of the culture, we might have been ill-behaved at the first welcome ceremony, which in Arab countries still reflects habits of Bedouins in the desert. It starts with coffee in tiny cups, served to the guests only. They are expected to have it without looking at the hosts. The hosts shall be given a chance to watch the foreigners. The cups are refilled without cleaning and brought to the hosts—the same way tea is served. After the ceremony, it is the hosts who start a conversation; polite guests wait for their moment to speak. During our stay we realized several times how important mutual respect of our cultures was for successful negotiations.

*RFJH:* The years 1985–1991 had great personal importance in your life when you worked as commander of the Border Battalion in Goslar (inter-German border). I had been a guest for lectures about juridical, criminological, and sociological topics. Furthermore, I remember that the citizens of Goslar wanted to vote for you to be the lord mayor of Goslar! With only a few votes, your way of life would have been changed. Do you have fond memories of your time in Goslar? What do you think today about having lost, at that time, the chance for a political career?

*WHS:* During my time as commanding officer in Goslar I was elected to the City Council, indeed. By the way, our federal secretary for the environment, Sigmar Gabriel, was a colleague of mine there. The campaign for lord mayor of Goslar took place much later. I may come back to this point.

During his birthday party in 1985, General Wegener surprised me with the news that I should become commanding officer of the Border Battalion in Goslar—a little town at the former inter-German border in Lower Saxony—at the rank lieutenant colonel. By the way, in the barracks used by the BGS then, famous Field Marshal Rommel, the "Desert Fox," had served as a young major in 1933.

Goslar is a beautiful, historical town of 50,000 inhabitants. There was a large post by the German Air Force, and also a French radio unit was located there. Opposite our border section, on top of the Brocken Mountain, was one of the most powerful radar stations of the Soviet Army in Germany. There were also installations for intercepting Western telephone systems on the Brocken.

Our sector of the border was about 80 km long. The system of fortifications set up by the East Germans was effective, although they had started to remove the mine fields completely. The system included high double fences, electronic alarm systems, dogs, antivehicle trenches, watch towers, and many more guards than on our side operating in the border area. Only a few refugees managed to cross from East to West every year. Sometimes border guards escaped to us. One of those told me during an investigation,

"Sir, I know you well. Your picture is hanging in all our watch towers!" I did not like this idea very much.

A very special experience for me was a tour at the border with the leader of the Communist youth organization Sputnik in Kazakhstan. As an official guest of the state of Lower Saxony, he had asked to see the border during his stay in Goslar. While we were riding along the fences in my official car, he suddenly asked me, "Where are your fortifications?" When I told him that we had none, he obviously did not believe me. Later he said to me, "Sorry, I could not believe you. This is my first stay in a free country!" An amazing statement of a Communist leader, isn't it?

Due to the effect of the East German fortifications, border duty did not keep us extremely busy. Two or three border patrols in my section of the border were enough to know the situation. Therefore, the BGS battalions were deployed in operations all over Germany, supporting local police forces in all kinds of operations. There was a lot of political opposition against the use of nuclear power in this time. The protests were often violent, taking on aspects of riots. In Frankfurt/Main, demonstrators against the construction of a new landing field used firearms against police forces for the first time. More and more violence also occurred during soccer games.

Our tasks required high flexibility by the leaders. We had to prepare our officers for these sometimes warlike situations. We developed our own tactical methods, improved our equipment, and did a lot of training, and Robert Harnischmacher came to Goslar for lectures to support us in his way. Thank you again, dear Robert, for your help. You remember that my staff and I were very grateful then.

As of November 1989, the East German border vanished step by step. It would be a story of its own to tell all the details of this historical event. The main mission of BGS disappeared. It started with one passage in the middle of my section. Without any prior warning, hundreds of East German citizens overran the border guards one day and cut open the fences. Similar events at the Berlin Wall had encouraged them to do so. We were completely surprised but happy that without any violence or even shooting our fellow citizens in East Germany had reached freedom.

The BGS was not closed down. Soon our jurisdiction was extended. We started operations in East Germany—keeping violent hooligans in Leipzig and Dresden under control, for example. And for a couple of weeks my complete battalion was deployed to the Oder River, our new external border with Poland. During a helicopter patrol at the border, I was advised to hand over my battalion to a colleague and to go to Bonn in order to work at the Ministry of the Interior.

*RFJH:* What were your duties during 1991–1995?

*WHS:* I started as a member of staff of the inspector general of the Riot Police of the Federal States (Länder), whose office is a section in the Federal Ministry of the Interior. Only 3 months later, I was promoted to deputy inspector general.

The Riot Police in Germany are subordinate to the governments of the federal states. They had a manpower of about 30,000. Because the federal government provides a great part of the equipment, it has the right of inspecting the units spread out all over Germany. The inspector general reports to the federal secretary of the interior; evaluates quality, quantity, and readiness of the Riot Police units; and negotiates the federal budgets for them.

The Riot Police often cooperate with units of the Federal Border Guard in joint operations of larger scale—another reason for permanent exchange of information with the Ministries of the Interior of the federal states and the commander-in-chief of the Federal Border Guard. In addition, the inspector general of the Riot Police represents all German police agencies in the police working group at the EU Commission in Brussels. There he speaks for the federal government and the federal states. Extensive consultations are necessary to reach mutual understanding prior to meetings. I was involved in all those activities.

A funny situation occurred during one of those meetings, in Brussels, when Germany held the rotating presidency of the European Union. In this case my inspector general had to act as the president of all European police working groups. I was in the role of head of the German delegation. In a pretty delicate issue, my German superior took me by surprise, asking me, "What does Germany think about this issue?"

My knowledge of English and French helped us a great deal during the EU sessions. Official negotiations were translated by professional interpreters, of course. But we learned that sometimes in breaks we were able to solve difficult issues by addressing members of other delegations in their own languages. Agreements were found in no time after tiring discussions during sessions.

As part of our police cooperation in Europe, I focused my work on methods of fighting hooliganism. First, I was involved in working groups of various federal ministries in Germany (sports, justice, health, family, construction) and external partners such as the German Soccer League. We discussed a national information center, which exists in North Rhine–Westphalia today and successfully receives and provides information on expected violence at sports events for the police management at state and federation levels. In seminars at EU level, I had the privilege to present our German experience in this field of police work—in Ireland and Mallorca, for instance.

In May 1992 the deputy secretary of the interior of Zimbabwe, Mr. Dumiso Dabengwa, came to our ministry in Bonn for a visit. He was highly interested in human rights issues and police work in democratic states. I got the task to deliver a lecture for the gentleman about police structures and police tasks in Germany in the English language. It was astonishing how eager this politician was to learn every detail of legal regulations, training of police officers, and their daily practice. He kept making notes and asking questions. In August 1993 the phone rang in my office. His Excellency, the German ambassador in Harare, Zimbabwe, invited me to hold seminars for the top management of the police in Zimbabwe. Mr. Dabengwa, who had meanwhile become secretary of the interior, had persuaded President Mugabe to invite me to his country. In December 1993 I spent 2 weeks in Harare and Bulawayu with the police chiefs of the Zimbabwe provinces. The weekend in between my hosts took me to the Zambezi River and Victoria Falls, another unforgettable experience of my professional life.

In theory, the police chiefs were very knowledgeable. On the other hand, the local newspapers reported violations of human rights by the police every day. Trying to find out the reason, I asked my hosts to show me a police station. There I saw children standing in the bright sun, tied to a wall like horses. The shift leader told me that little thieves were kept like this for 3 days, normally. In the evenings I walked through the city behind police patrols at a distance, observing how they acted. Whenever they saw a reason to intervene, they simply walked away. Very soon I found out that their training did not meet the needs of police work in a civil society. They simply did not know what to do, as they were trained like soldiers, not like policemen.

So the further contents of my seminars concentrated on the issues of vocational training, selection and qualification of staff, development of personality, and individual decision making instead of waiting for and obeying orders. My proposals were to cut down the number of policemen in the country by 30% and to extend the basic training from 6 months to 2 years. I had the impression that the police chiefs were willing to accept my proposals. Unfortunately, I have to say that, later, the political development in Zimbabwe destroyed all efforts to introduce human rights into police work and to convert the police into an integrated element of a civil society.

*RFJH:* For the period 1995 and 1996, you mention a lot of activities in your résumé. Could you talk about these activities?

*WHS:* In 1995 the head of the situation center of our Ministry of the Interior retired. This was a full colonel's post, and I was happy to get it. This unit worked in shifts 24 hours a day throughout the year. We had to collect information of importance for the secretary and the departments of the ministry. Our sources were the Ministries of the Interior of the federal states, but also the news agencies—national and international. Again, languages were extremely important for my team and me. Soon I introduced the direct exchange of information with situation centers of the Ministries of Interior of EU member states. This improved our work by firsthand information.

We had to decide which pieces of information had to be delivered to the secretary and the undersecretary immediately, out of duty hours, to their homes or wherever they were traveling. Every morning at 8:15 o'clock, we had to provide the management of the ministry with a presentation of relevant events and news reported in the past 24 hours, within 15 or 20 minutes. This required high concentration and careful selection.

*RFJH:* From December 1996 to February 1998 you had been abroad in Bosnia and Herzegovina as deputy commissioner in charge of operations. Are you able to tell me about your duties, tasks, activities, and, moreover, your experiences?

*WHS:* This task came by surprise again. One morning in early December 1996 the commander-in-chief of the Federal Border Guard came to my office and this was quite unusual. He told me that he urgently needed a commanding officer in the peace mission of UN-IPTF in Bosnia and Herzegovina for half a year. The Dayton Peace Accord aimed at transforming the country into a peaceful society, against the will of local leaders who had caused the war and who had committed terrible crimes. They wanted to stay in power by all means.

I agreed on the spot. As I had expected, my wife, Lydia, did not object, although it was not easy for her and our two children to let me go. Bosnia was a nonfamily mission. Everybody knew it was dangerous. But she had always supported me in professional issues. This was an important element of success in my career.

In little more than 2 weeks I passed health checks, attended a mine-awareness course with the German Army, and handed over my local duties. And I studied the situation in the Balkans as well as the structures and tasks of the UN International Police Task Force (IPTF) and its cooperation with NATO Stabilization Forces (SFORs) in Bosnia and Herzegovina. I flew to Zagreb a few days before Christmas. By car I proceeded to Sarajevo.

The first impressions of the country were terrible. The devastations of the war were visible in every little village I came through. The war had produced hatred between the ethnic groups of Serbs, Croats, and Bosnians. The country was divided into ethnically cleansed areas. Mines hidden in the open fields and in buildings were a permanent threat for us and the local population. In the beginning, there were about 50 mine accidents in the country every month, often caused by children whose fathers had stored the mines in the basements of their houses or in barns and sheds.

In Sarajevo I started as regional commander of IPTF. Three months later, the American commissioner promoted me to his deputy for operations on condition that I extended my service to 1 year. Finally, I stayed 14 months. I was responsible for UN-IPTF operations in the whole country. UN-IPTF consisted of about 2,000 unarmed police officers from 40 nations. Thirteen nations were represented in our headquarters in Sarajevo. The official language was English. I had to learn to understand English in American, British, French, Italian, Indian, African, and even Russian pronunciations. Like all my officers, I lived in a private house with a Bosnian family, unarmed and without bodyguards. The heating system did not work at all in the first winter and water supply was often interrupted unexpectedly.

Military SFOR troops were to protect us in cases of risk; we needed them very often and could generally rely on them. However, they could not be present everywhere. Cooperation with SFOR was excellent at all levels.

Together with the high representative of the UN, SFOR, and nongovernmental organizations, we started developing various strategies to reach the objectives of the Dayton Accord. We began reorganizing the police—the task of colleagues of mine. Their principles were selection, reduction, training, and providing modern equipment. Mark Kroeker, from the Los Angeles Police, has done an outstanding job in this field. I admired him for that.

My operational work started with a checkpoint policy. We counted more than 300 checkpoints throughout the country, where "policemen" regularly stopped cars, checked documents, and searched for goods. The license plates disclosed from the distance, where the cars were registered.[1]

Passengers of other ethnic groups were often physically attacked; goods were stolen from their cars. Against resistance from many sides in the country, we managed to introduce uniform license plates. Supported by SFOR, we even confiscated patrol cars of the Mostar police when they refused to remove their Croat state symbols.[1]

The next step was a weapons policy. In many private houses, military weapons of all kinds were hidden; people wanted to be prepared in case of new hostilities. They did not believe that peace would last at that time. By decree of the UN high representative, the citizens were ordered to deliver military weaponry to their local police stations. They brought machine guns, grenade launchers, antitank mines, rifles, and hand grenades. Together with SFOR, we collected thousands of tons in order to destroy them.

Prisons were a specific problem. During the war, many citizens had been imprisoned for months without any legal procedures. Now they simply stayed in prison. Political opponents were secretly kept as prisoners of war. Their families did not know why or where they were. We regularly searched prisons and police stations and set people free or took care of legal procedures.

The Dayton Peace Accord had foreseen that refugees could return to their homes after the war. When they came back, they were often threatened by hostile neighbors or people who had unlawfully occupied their property in the meantime. Very often, the police were unwilling to help them, refusing to implement the peace regulations. In this situation our legal position was weak in the beginning. We were advisors without authority. By a UN conference in

London in 1997, UN IPTF received the right of independent investigations—a very strong remedy against police officers unwilling to cooperate.

I mentioned earlier that this mission was dangerous for all of us. Two exciting events I would like to mention here. In Mostar, the Muslim population had been displaced from parts of their city during the war. In 1997 their religious leader, the Mufti, officially addressed the city administration, SFOR, and IPTF, asking permission for a visit to their cemetery (which was on the other side of the river) for a mourning celebration. The Croat Mostar Police said no in the beginning. Later, they officially agreed. So did SFOR and IPTF, of course, as visits to graves are a human right. When the Muslims approached the cemetery, a group of young plainclothes Croat policemen appeared and started beating the Muslim visitors with rubber batons. When they were running away, three Croat policemen started shooting at them from behind with handguns, killing one man on the spot and injuring 20. I organized an independent IPTF investigation and took the lead. You may imagine that we were not welcome while we were talking to the perpetrators in their offices in Mostar. We were dealing with murderers in their terrain and we did not feel very safe. As a result of our investigations, we provided excellent evidence to the local court. The Croat police delivered nothing of the kind.

In Serbian-controlled Gayevi, a large number of houses had been restored or newly built for Muslim returnees, financed by the international community. The day before they arrived, their homes were burned down. An independent IPTF investigation revealed that the local police were involved in this crime.

As in other places and as a result of similar events, police officers were dismissed or received relevant punishment. Professionalism of the police grew. The situation in the country improved slowly—very slowly. At least, war did not come back. In February 1998 I went back to Bonn after 14 months, very glad to have survived many dangerous situations and to have made new friends from many countries.

*RFJH:* From March 1998 until April 2000 you served in the Ministry of the Interior in Germany. What were your tasks, duties, and activities till your retirement?

*WHS:* During the months until I retired in April 1999, I served as section leader at the Federal Border Guard headquarters within the Ministry of the Interior. This was a "right-hand position" to the commander-in-chief of the Federal Border Guard, a force of 40,000 officers. Opening of borders in Europe caused a lot of reorganization work. Large sections of the ministry, including the Border Guard headquarters, were moved to Berlin.

In 1998 the Soccer World Championship took place in France. Together with representatives of German federal states, I traveled to Paris twice to negotiate cross-border cooperation of police and border police to be prepared for violence from hooligans. Despite intense preparations, a French policeman was seriously injured by German hooligans in Lens.

Operations of riot control, hooliganism, and border control, as well as cross-border cooperation, kept me busy for the rest of my duty.

My time of a possible political career that you mentioned before seemed to come then. In the very last weeks of my service in Bonn I got a call from the former lady mayor of Goslar. On behalf of her political party she asked me to campaign for mayor in her town. I agreed and after my retirement I immediately moved to Goslar with my wife. We started a fierce election race and after less than 2 months of campaigning against the mayor in office, I received 47.3% of votes. Having in mind that I had not been a resident of the city for 5 years, the result was not bad, but not sufficient. The incumbent mayor remained in office and I was free of responsibilities.

*RFJH:* But after your retirement you were active as an advisor from December 2000 until March 2004 in Poland. What did you do there? Can you report something about your activities?

*WHS:* A few days after the election in Goslar, the commander-in-chief of the Federal Border Guard persuaded me to go to

Poland. The Polish government had applied for membership in the European Union. As a consequence, the whole border control system of the country had to be reorganized. The militia type of border forces had to be molded into a professional border police according to European Union standards. Most of the technical equipment had to be exchanged; staff had to be trained both in Poland and in other Western European countries. I formally applied as long-term advisor, and in a competition with other nationalities I won. Together with my wife I moved to Warsaw and stayed there for 3½ years. My office was situated in the Ministry of the Interior. As soon as I knew I would go to Warsaw, I started learning Polish together with my wife. Despite the mistakes I made, Polish people always reacted with gratefulness that I tried to communicate in their difficult language. Today I can read newspapers in Polish and understand Polish TV pretty well. Small talk is no problem anyway.

The most exhausting task was to organize hundreds of courses in all types of border police and general police work: management; structures; law; tactics; human rights; technical issues like radio communication, vehicles, and weapons; investigations; and construction of new border-crossing stations at the level of EU member states. Lecturers came from various countries like Great Britain, Spain, Austria, and, foremost, Germany. Most of the courses were delivered in Poland. The best qualified officers from most of the courses earned an opportunity to see the practical part of their studies in other EU member states.

Step by step, I developed a network of permanent communication, which included, among others, the border and police administration within the Polish Ministry of the Interior, the headquarters of the Polish Border Guard and the Police in Warsaw, the EU Delegation in Warsaw, embassies involved in EU police cooperation, the training centers of the Polish Border Guard, long-term advisors from different countries dealing with border- and customs-related issues, and others. My very good personal connections with the management of the Federal Border

Guard helped me a lot. I have to thank my colleagues for their support. Whenever needed, I got specialists from our training centers or from operational units as lecturers or short-term advisors, so I could act in a very profound and flexible way. Regular checks by the EU Commission approved the result of our work. Because the Polish management at the ministry and border guard levels wanted the changes, my work was easy. Mutual respect was a good basis for fruitful cooperation. Now Poland is an EU member state.

Today the Polish Border Guard is able to cooperate with its Western neighbors as far as professionalism is concerned. Their cross-border cooperation with neighboring EU member states is excellent. Controls at the external borders of the European Union with Russia-Kaliningrad, Belarus, and Ukraine are well organized and effective.

In the last few months of our stay in Warsaw, my wife and I had decided to live in Bamberg after my final retirement. It was my wife's place of birth and familiar to us. Everything was prepared to move there after more than 3 years in Poland. When we were about to leave in April 2004, I got a phone call from the Ministry for Foreign Affairs in Berlin. A section leader had heard that I was leaving Poland. He knew about the jobs I had done in Germany and abroad so far and he invited me for another task.

The general secretary of the Organization for Security and Cooperation in Europe (OSCE) was about to establish a Department for Border Issues in its headquarters in Vienna. I knew this organization from my operations in Bosnia and Herzegovina. Work should start without delay, so my wife prepared our home in Germany and I flew from Warsaw to Vienna directly. There I did my best to set up a working unit for border issues and, together with colleagues, organized and carried out seminars with the commanders-in-chief of the border guards of the Balkan states: Albania, Bosnia and Herzegovina, Bulgaria Croatia, Macedonia, Montenegro, Serbia, and Romania. This was the last exciting task of my professional life, with many interesting contacts in the

Balkan countries and within the international society in Vienna.

Today my life in the beautiful city of Bamberg is not boring at all. The center of Bamberg is world cultural heritage of UNESCO. I am active in clubs like Lions International and the International Police Association. Still, I continue improving my knowledge in foreign languages and stay in contact with many people around the world by mail or Skype. With my wife I travel a lot— from China and Russia to the United States. And I look back to an inspiring and exciting life, hoping that the Lord gives me some more years to enjoy and to be thankful.

*RFJH:* During your professional life you have always been a "workaholic," always on the top of expectation at every moment. Evidence are your language skills in English, French, and Polish; your key national and international qualifications (please give some examples); and your specific country experiences. Would you again enter the BGS/Federal Police of today to start a career with such national and international "air and flair"?

*WHS:* Yes, absolutely. I could not know how things would develop. And of course I could not know that I would climb the career ladder to the top management of the German Border Guard. It is true that I always worked hard following my principle: Whatever you do, do it well! And a great part of professional work was learning. Everything changes so quickly today. You are never perfect. As soon as you give up improving, you get worse.

But I always liked my work. I respected the colleagues who worked for me. You can only be strong in a good team. Mutual respect is a precondition for good cooperation. And I never lost my good humor. There was always time for a break and a good joke, even in most difficult situations. So the answer is clearly yes. I would join the BGS—today called the Federal Police—again.

*RFJH:* From your treasure of experience, what can you say to young people interested in the tasks of the Federal Police for their professional future? What should they do? Would you perhaps change some or many points of view when considering your personal professional life as police officer of the Federal Police of the Federal Republic of Germany? Do you have some proposals?

*WHS:* As I said to my children: First of all, learn languages. By speaking foreign languages you open hearts, cross barriers, and learn much more about other people. Languages were a condition for my work in different countries of the world; they considerably extended my opportunities.

Look around what you would like to do and make proposals to your superiors. And be flexible: Go where you are needed. Don't wait for jobs to come to you. Accept any offer of vocational courses to improve your skills. You never know which specific skills you may need one day. The more you know, the more opportunities you get.

Today work of border police does not end at the boundaries of the country. Cross-border crime has to be prosecuted at a global level. In this profession, the world is open to you. Be prepared!

*RFJH:* Thank you. It was a pleasure.

## Endnote

1. License plates in BiH, before the introduction of uniform plates by the international administration, identified where the plate was issued using a combination of letters. Because areas coincide with the distribution of ethnic groups, police manning roadblocks could and did think that drivers of cars belonged to a specific ethnic group and (mis)treated them accordingly.

# 10

# Interview With Lawrence Cauchi, Assistant Commissioner (Administration), Malta Police Force

INTERVIEWED BY C. M. JESSICA LI

**Contents**

## Introduction

It is my impression, based on this interview, which lasted longer than 1 hour, that Mr. Cauchi is a smart, observant, and alert person. In the course of the interview, he provided straightforward answers to my many questions. He is very good at listening to others and, in fact, this is very essential for effective leadership: A good leader must be a good listener as well. In my contact with him, he always mentioned "teamwork." It indicates he treasures a harmonious relationship with his boss and subordinates—an attitude I believe is the cornerstone of success in his career.

## Career

### *A Little Island*

Malta, officially named the Republic of Malta, is a small island country located in the Mediterranean Sea in Southern Europe. It gained independence from the United Kingdom in 1964 and become a republic in 1974 and a member of the European Union (EU) in 2004. According to the National Statistics Office of Malta (2008), the whole country covers a total area of 316 square kilometers with around 410,000 habitants, and its population density was 1,298 persons per square kilometer in 2007.

Mr. Cauchi provided me with a brief introduction to the police force of Malta at the beginning of the interview. The Malta Police Force is the principal law enforcement agency on the island with the strength of 1,400 police officers, including one commissioner, one deputy commissioner, and eight assistant commissioners. Mr. Cauchi is one of the eight assistant commissioners, mainly responsible for administrative and strategic planning matters such as, for example, human resources of the police force, community relations, investigating complaints, dealing with the EU relations office, and IT (information technology)-related offenses in cooperation with the cybercrime unit.

*Career Development and Lifelong Learning*

Mr. Cauchi started his career as a police constable February 21, 1976, soon after he finished his schooling. At that moment, due to good salaries, many people were eager to get employed in the police force in Malta. Coupled with the situation of a job freeze (imposed by the government), it was rather competitive to get into the police force; only around 200 people would be selected among 2,000 applicants. Mr. Cauchi managed to succeed in the examination and was finally selected by the force. After joining the police force, he kept pursuing his studies in such subjects as criminal laws, forensic psychology, etc. One possible thing that assisted him in climbing the career ladder is his commitment to lifelong learning.

*LC:* I continued my studying as I enjoyed it. I needed to keep on studying because I did not want to remain a police constable forever.

*JL:* May I say you are ambitious?

*LC:* Yes. I am not going to stop studying.

The statement "knowledge can change our destiny" is particular true in the case of Mr. Cauchi. His continuous efforts enabled him to have a smooth career path. On January 3, 1980, he was promoted to inspectorate grade after passing the internal examination. Since then he has been posted in different districts and exposed to different kinds of jobs, including doing investigation of various crimes such as homicide, robbery, or fraud cases. Nominated by his senior supervisor, he became a superintendent in 1988 and assistant commissioner (criminal investigation department) in 1995. Mr. Cauchi enjoys his work a lot and he is finding his career very rewarding and interesting. He has no reservations in sharing his knowledge and wisdom related to policing with others. He has also served as a lecturer at and a board member of the police academy.

*Key to Success*

Mr. Cauchi pointed out to me that personality, leadership, and academic qualification are perceived as significant for career advancement in the police department, at least in his country. In addition to work competence, knowing how to manage interpersonal relationship is crucial. He said:

> If you are a high-ranking officer, you are supposed to lead the team and you have to work with people; I do not intend to make a distinction between constable and inspector, just treat them equally as a human being. And also my father always insisted on my continuation of my study and asked me not to remain in one position.

In short, his case shows us that one's ability, efforts, and commitment to the police profession are indispensable. Police officers nowadays do not act like watchmen or soldiers, but rather as teachers and analysts who are required to have knowledge and intelligence (Roberg & Kuykendall, 1990).

### Changes Experienced

#### *New Policy and New Challenges*

The country underwent major changes in 1996, 1999, and 2004. In 1996, a new government took up the reigns. Based on a proposal of the prime minister, the police were reformed. At that time, Mr. Cauchi was assigned by the commissioner to take up the role as a "change manager" overseeing strategic planning for policing. At the same time, the prime minister appointed a group of people to form a "management unit" independent of the police. This group of people did not belong to the police and had no experience in policing. They were responsible for looking into police infrastructure. Mr. Cauchi gave this account of the changes in the police force in 1996:

> In 1996, there was a new government and the new government decided to make a general reform of the police force. And the commissioner said to me that he wanted me to become the change manager for the police overlooking the new reform. The prime minister wanted to introduce a strategic plan—something which we had never had before. The prime minister assigned a management group who were not from the police force. The prime minister's office looked into the police organization, structure, policy, and legislations. And it finally came up with 97 recommendations. So my responsibility was to ensure whether the 97 recommendations could come be done. I was chosen to take up this job

> (as change manager) because I had just finished my diploma course in management and business study. I had passed with distinction.

Without doubt, Mr. Cauchi would go through a challenging period. He subsequently had to work with a group of people who may not have shared his views and understood the work culture of his department easily. Doubtless to say, it was a tough job for him.

According to him, the course in learning about management definitely enabled him to put what he had learned from this course into practice. The reform would achieve some degree of positive changes. Nevertheless, there are always two sides of a coin. Mr. Cauchi believed resistance of police officers to changes was unavoidable. He said:

> Changes always are resisted by people, even in the force. I can tell you, police officers, like inspectors worked on split duty from 8 a.m. to 12 noon and again from 4 p.m. to 8 p.m. However, every officer in Europe starts their duty at night and finishes in the morning. Why didn't we try the same? But here the officers were resistant [to this practice]. They finished their duty at 5 p.m. and stopped working even though they had an investigation at 6 p.m. This still is the norm.

Police officers normally would not continue their work even though they had not finished it. This system was in fact totally deviant from other European countries. Facing the demand for longer or more flexible working hours, the police officers, who had become used to the old system, showed great reluctance to follow the new policy. This offered another challenge for Mr. Cauchi's efforts to reform management policies in the police force.

### *Service Charters*

According to Mr. Cauchi, the introduction of service charters helped to uphold the service quality of the police force. In 1999, an independent unit handling complaints against police officers was established. Citizens now can easily convey their ideas, for example, through a newly designed form. He said:

> In the face of other changes, we always need to do some improvement of the existing quality of the police. The positive results include that more

people from the general public believe in the police force. We got an 80% positive response. For the rest—the 20%—they had some minor complaints. To support their need, we designed a complaint form for collecting their grievances. I am the regular trainer for the police. I offer trainings on customer care, ethnics, and report writing.

In his description, the changes mandated that the police force pay attention to the expressed needs of citizens to become more customer oriented. Regarding the reason for the introduction of the new complaint form, he offered a further explanation:

> We made sure that the public receives a fair investigation. Before this new initiative, they just went to the police station and reported the complaints to his [the officer being complained against] senior police officer, and the senior police officer may not have conducted a good investigation. And the public may say that the police officer [being complained against] always goes out to drink with the senior police officer. We would like to ensure that investigation be fair and transparent.

Reforms can get rid of some existing malpractices by staff in the workplace, and the police department in Malta is no exception. The general public in Malta can voice their opinions, needs, and grievance toward the police through a proper channel. This contributes to maintaining harmonious police–public relations.

### *Becoming a Member of the European Union*

Another major change happened in 2004 when Malta joined the European Union. On joining the EU, the Malta government had to become involved in numerous activities with the CEPOL (European Police College). The Malta police force had to invest manpower in assisting international training and exchange events. In Mr. Cauchi's perception, there are always positive and negative aspects to any changes. He said:

> Everything has its advantages and disadvantages. The fact is that when we joined the EU, there were a lot of advantages for the police force. Lots of cooperation with the other states, lots of exchange with other countries, and lots of opportunities for training for our police officers, a

> lot of opportunities for attending meetings and conferences; regularly, we attend the working group meetings of the European Council and Commission. However, like other police forces, the main problem concerns resources—both financial and human resources. For instance, we were not given an extra financial subsidy but we still had to go to council meetings. Our officers had to attend a lot of Interpol meetings, the Europe Commission meetings, and the training organized by the European Police College. We had to stop attending these meetings because of a lack of money. I was a committee member of CEPOL and helped in training. And I am a member of the Financial Institution Analysis Unit (FIAU). My government has to contribute to those organizations financially.

Involvement in international collaboration and cooperation is indeed beneficial to police officers who look for more exposure to the outside world. Through these international interactions, officers' vision can be broadened. Truly, there is no "free lunch": The government has to pay the expense in money and manpower. It is likely a burden to the police department.

*Police Officers in the Past and Present*

Having served in the police force for over 30 years, Mr. Cauchi witnessed the changes experienced by police officers. In response to the question whether it is more or less difficult to be a police officer, Mr. Cauchi offered this answer:

> It is easier today. Why? I tell you that 30 years ago when I was a police constable, I did not have much training. Today officers have a lot of training, opportunities to work with other countries, exchange experiences, brand-new tactics, and learning about trends in crime. These never happened, even 15 years ago. I can conclude police officers nowadays can have more self-confidence to do their jobs. Besides, we have a brochure for introducing our service to the public. And our police officers can get closer to the community than before. In return, our community is respectful to our officers, which is helping our work.

Support to police officers seems to have increased over the decades. Nowadays, police officers are better equipped and given more chances to training. In addition, the attitude of the general public toward police officers has become more friendly and cooperative, making policing work easier than before. Nevertheless, with increasing demand on manpower but having no extra resource, police officers have to deal with a much greater workload than in the past. Resistance from some officers was anticipated. On the other hand, the increasing crime rate makes the life of police officers more difficult and complicated. Mr. Cauchi concluded that, over the years, in some aspects policing was improved, but there is always "room for improvement."

### Personal Policing Philosophy

#### *Core and Noncore Policing*

The role of police officers is clearly laid down by the Criminal Code. Mr. Cauchi described the roles of a police officer as follows:

> It is to uphold the law and order, to prosecute offenders, but some police officers are now doing noncore policing duties. We have to be on the street and we have to get in touch with the public. One advantage that we have is we (Malta) are small. We are doing community policing as well.

In his view, more manpower should be devoted to core policing: arrest suspects and control crimes. Regarding the work priority for a police officer, he asserted that crime prevention should be at the top of the list and some other noncore work should be reduced. He put it in this way:

> Our main responsibility is crime prevention, making people feel secure. For instance, one particular issue comes to my mind with which I do not particularly agree. The police can do more core policing work. Such work as delivering the notes and citations of the magistrate should be eliminated. Why should the police waste their time in doing this job? We have police officers who can be described as clerks.

In Mr. Cauchi's eyes, it is not a suitable arrangement for police officers to engage themselves too much in clerical work. It appears that few in the police force are willing to take up office work; rather, the assignments consistent with the "crime fighter" image are admired in the police force, not only in Malta but worldwide.

*Working for and Working With the Community*

In Mr. Cauchi's eyes, good communication exists between the police and community. The 67 police stations have frequent contacts with the 67 local council offices. Contacts with the general public help to create a sense of safety. As he said: "We are close to the public. The community feels safe because we are here with them."

In fact, according to the police code, meetings between police and the community happen at least once a month. Police officers, together with the council office, handle complaints from citizens. As Mr. Cauchi put it:

> The community would not like or be afraid to go to the police and give information. They don't want to be involved; they don't want to be an eyewitness; but they go to the local council and tell them (the council staff) their problems. We are aware of this problem, which we need to tackle. If we deal with the problem in a right way, it will not persist.

However, he believes problems expressed by the public have to be dealt with as soon as possible. Otherwise, problems may worsen. In fact, efforts and programs are in place to maintain a close relation with the community. Liaison police officers from every specialized unit (e.g., CID and Drug Force) constantly work closely with the local council and carry out some crime prevention work—for example, delivering lectures to the elderly, nongovernmental organizations, and schools conveying the message of crime prevention and maintaining communication with community. Other than this, the police force has close contacts with the Customs Department for combating crime issues related to drugs and smuggled cigarettes. Contacts also happen with probation officers for handling the juvenile offenders. He admitted the community policing concept helps officers better understand the community, which can help to prevent juvenile delinquency at early stages. He said:

> As you know, the criminals are always more advanced than the police; they are always finding new trends and new equipment which sometimes the police cannot afford. But criminals can afford these because they are getting a lot of money. But having contacts with the community, we can say it helps to reduce crime by about 20%. The police are getting close to the community and the community is assisting us by giving information.

It is no doubt that Mr. Cauchi keeps a close eye on offenders and realizes that crime fighting relies heavily on citizen support. Obviously, the Malta police are doing their job in actualizing the philosophy of "community policing"; it stresses policing with and for the community rather than policing of the community (Tilly, 2008). It emphasizes a collaborative effort with the community to solve the problems voiced by citizens.

*Issues of Diversity and Human Rights*

All in all, the roles and functions of a police officer in Malta, as perceived by Mr. Cauchi, tend to be richer and more diversified than before. He said:

> You know there are different aspects of policing, so you have police officers on beat patrol and their main role is to ensure the safety of community, and obtaining information and collecting intelligence may be passed to the detectives … therefore the roles of our police officers are being enriched. In fact, we are speaking about diversity. We are receiving a lot of North Africans, Nigerians, and people from many other places. They are mixing our community. Diversity does not only refer to race, it refers to different cultures, different sexes, different religions, handicapped people, gays, etc. … We are serving people with different backgrounds. Diversity is one of the main subjects that we teach our police officers.

In meeting the increasing diversity in society, the Malta police officers have to pay attention to their skills and knowledge in dealing with people from a rich variety of backgrounds. It appears to be a tough job to perform their duty with adequate cultural sensitivity and be ready to mediate the possible conflicts among people from different backgrounds.

**Problems and Success Experienced**

*Fulfilling the Principle of Equal Opportunity*

Once Mr. Cauchi's country joined the EU, some changes happened in police internal management. For instance, the police force has to follow the principle of preserving human rights. Under this principle, every citizen is offered the equal chance to be recruited into the police force. He admits that it is good in principle but not feasible in practice. He said:

> We are speaking about in general about human rights. That is the EU direction that we cannot discriminate against anyone. We have never discriminated. But for a number of reasons, we cannot employ an obviously disabled person in our police force; we cannot engage a person at the age of 50 as a member of staff. But with the EU's directive, we cannot discriminate. If a person at 50 wants to apply for the job, we have to let him/her apply. This is the directive that we have to follow. For instance, we have to remove the age limit on the advertisement. In the past, a police officer had to be at least 5 feet 4 inches tall. But nowadays, we cannot say that anymore [the requirement on age and height] ... You cannot refuse an application from a handicapped person ... And diversity is another difficulty; for instance, a team of police can be composed of people coming from different backgrounds and you have to respect each of them. You have to allow a police officer who needs to pray because of his/her religion [to pray]. However, it is a team.

Catering to the needs of a disadvantaged group involves extra manpower and has resource implications. In his observation, it is a waste of resources due to the fact that the physically disabled applicants are unlikely to pass the physical test. It creates a dilemma for the Malta police force—keeping the international standards on actualizing "equal opportunity" for everyone in society, on the one hand, and fitting the situation of reality on the other hand.

*Diversity in the Workplace*

In line with United Nations code of practice, the police department has made efforts to deal with issues like human rights and diversity. For example, one should ensure no discrimination arising from color, sex, religion and culture in the process of job recruitment. Also, mixed minorities in the organization emphasize the culture of harmony and professionalism in the workplace.

> We find having such kinds of transnational relations beneficial. Our officers are more and more motivated and know more about how the

> officers work in other countries. Sending the police officers to receive training and be a trainer abroad is beneficial to our organization. These exchange experiences are beneficial ... they learn about organized crimes, they are becoming more experienced and professional.

The department indeed benefited from joining the United Nations as the police officers can have more exposure, better exchange of experiences, and gain assistance, particularly in investigating organized and transnational crimes. On the other side of the coin, when accommodating the demand of the United Nations for preserving human rights and diversity in the workplace, the police force has to deal with complicated recruitment procedures, which Mr. Cauchi regards as unnecessary.

*Extra Workload Brought by Terrorism*

Until now, Mr. Cauchi's country has not been under the threat of terrorism. However, the police department has to put more manpower to handling the possible conflicts of different embassies. He emphasized:

> So far we do not have any terrorist incidents happening in our country. But we have different embassies here. There were conflicts between some embassies. We have to provide security, especially the security in the airport and harbor. We have the CCTV system to ensure everything is under control. It has increased our manpower.

*The Rise of Tourist Activities*

Over the years, the police force has come across a number of difficulties. A lack of resources in terms of manpower and finance is ranked at the top. As a result of the increasing chances of participating in overseas exchange and training, a certain number of working hours in direct services has to be sacrificed. Some scholars have pointed out that staying visible is one of the core tasks of police officers (Roberg & Kuykendall, 1990); however, from Mr. Cauchi's point of view, intensive engagement of police officers in the overseas exchange and training sessions may reduce their visibility in public. In addition, in line with the flourishing of tourism in the country, more and more manpower went into providing service for the tourists. This has further accelerated the manpower problem.

> We have a lack of human resources. I find that visibility of police is lacking. This is the great problem in our country. ... We have 400,000 people in our country but we have a million and a half tourists every year, so the problem is that the tourists may bring along crimes—more available victims. It occurs seriously during summertime. The manpower demand is increasing. We cannot just "throw in the towel" or surrender. We have to fight in spite of limited manpower.

It is undeniable that some police officers under such circumstances may feel "burnout" and they can have little job satisfaction. Morale in the force will go down unquestionably. It is really a headache for police management.

*Money Alone Cannot Solve the Problem*

Due to the economic situation of Malta, it is less likely to hire more police officers at the moment. A shortage of police officers is a problem. To deal with this problem, money is not the best solution. Mr. Cauchi has his own ideas:

> To get police officers, motivation is the most important. He will be proud and won't mind working for extra hours and giving more. He may get what he wants. "Want" does not mean money; it is a kind of satisfaction of job. For example, if involved in investigating a crime, they could successfully get the work done. That is satisfaction and they will get motivated.

To increase the police officers' work incentive, the department introduced the special-duty allowance. Those police officers working in the specialized units like CID, the anti-money-laundering team, security branch, and special-assignment unit can get a special duty allowance. However, he pointed out the possible drawbacks:

> Regarding the special duty allowance, the lower rank officers [the constable or the sergeant] can get 120 Euros a month for working in a specialized branch or plainclothes. They have to buy clothes, you know.

> The officers from inspector above can get about 200 Euros a month. Then, the uniformed officers do not get the benefit, so they may say, "Let him work because he gets the money." Otherwise, they want to transfer there. What is happening is that all of them just want to go there. Thus, the police officers on the street are reducing and the staff for specialized units is increasing. ... In the past, I was proud of being a CID, but not because of money; you have to be chosen.

In Mr. Cauchi's explanation, using monetary incentive to motivate officers not only arouses the grievance of the police officers who do not benefit from the allowance but also undermines the police professional value—serving the community on their own will. Under the new system, the general public may believe that police officers work hard because of tangible reward rather than their mission.

## Theory and Practice

### *Theory and Practice Are Interrelated*

As Mr. Cauchi mentioned, a theory is formulated following several research studies and analysis of a particular situation, and hence it is reviewed extensively and set up. This may then very easily be put in practice. It also seems possible to him that practitioners may prove the theory wrong. If it happens, further amendment on theory is needed. He said:

> That's nice; in the conference [IPES] we have researchers and practitioners. When you put it into practice, you know whether it is a good theory or not. ... The theory comes first. It is because if I am going to practice something, to introduce a new system in the police, I need to know something exists which is likely a theory. Therefore, the practitioners can get it easily with the reference of theory.

Thus, in his eyes, theory and practice in policing are not exclusive; rather, they are interdependent. This thought is quite consistent with the philosophy of "problem-oriented policing," which "is concerned with achieving the purpose of policing by systematically addressing relevant problems in the community. Identified problems should be thoroughly researched and understood" (Tilly, 2008, p. 318).

*Research and Strategic Planning*

The police department of Malta has no research department. But there is a unit responsible for strategic planning. Being in charge of this unit, Mr. Cauchi needs to have reviews of different journals, books, publications, and reports of the particular topics. He believes those research findings help the department to set goals for its policy and practice. He said:

> We do research work regularly. When we started strategic planning, there was research for it and theory for it. With the Internet nowadays, we can search for different sources of information, but when adopting the theory, you have to make sure what fits your organization, and what is going to be implemented in your organization … and find what works. … You know, when doing the strategic planning, it needs to involve all stakeholders of your organization—staff and government. In doing so, you have to make it a priority … in making this priority, you need to research.

It is tough work to make every stakeholder happy. Mr. Cauchi recognizes the power of research. He always looks for empirical support to assist him in making decisions for management and planning, and this may be more convincing to decision makers of his government.

*Staff Training and Knowledge Building*

The police officers can locate some useful information in the police academy library and the Internet resource center. Each police officer can go to the library to do his own research and get access to the Internet to read the journals and books, whatever they like. According to Mr. Cauchi, as part of the 1996 reform, one of the recommendations is sponsorship of the officers' studying. He said:

> As part of the 1996 reform, one of the recommendations is sponsorship. And we did offer the sponsorship to police officers to study laws and psychology. … All sponsored police officers are supposed to stay in the force at least for 5 years. The department has to pay 6,000 Euro throughout the 5 years for each officer.

The sponsorship system did not seem helpful to keep the manpower strength in the police force. According to Mr. Cauchi, many police officers change their career to become lawyers and psychologists after they have accomplished their studying. Under the new policy, police officers generally can only be supported for part-time study, and they pay their own tuition fees.

### General Assessments

*More Autonomy and Less Intrusion*

All in all, Mr. Cauchi is satisfied with the developments of policing in his country. However, he would like to see less political intrusion in policing. As he put it:

> Personally, I would like to see less political intrusion to the police; I cannot understand how the newly appointed members of parliament become immediately the expert … they should tell us what they wish but not tell us what to do. Because we [the police] are the expert [in policing]. You would see the [police] chief changed all the time. You have to start again the work relationship. Because you have started a good relationship with a particular person, but you will find he/she is no longer there. This is not beneficial to us. The new person in charge may not have the same opinion as you. And you have to start [the relationship] again. It is not healthy for our organization, it is not healthy for our community, and it is not healthy for our country. It is a waste of money and manpower.

Obviously, in his eyes, the turnover of police chiefs is not a good thing and is a waste of money and manpower. It is particularly true that a police department should be given a substantial degree of work autonomy. Otherwise, the police administrators may easily get frustrated with the political changes.

### References

Financial Intelligence Analysis Unit (2007). *Annual report of the Financial Intelligence Analysis Unit, 2007.* Valletta, Malta: Author. Data retrieved on June 20, 2009, from www.fiumalta.org/pdfs/annual_report_2007.pdf.

National Statistics Office (2008). *Malta in figures 2008.* Malta: Author. Data retrieved on June 20, 2009, from www.nso.gov.mt.

Roberg, R. R., and Kuykendall, J. (1990). *Police organization and management.* Pacific Grove, CA: Brooks/Cole.

Tilly, N. (2008). Modern approaches to policing: Community, problem oriented and intelligence led (pp. 373–403), in T. Newburn (Ed.), *Handbook of policing.* Cullompton, Devon: Willan.

# 11

# Interview With General Enrique Pérez Casas, Preventive Police, Mexico City, Mexico

INTERVIEWED BY ELENA AZAOLA

**Contents**



**The Interview**

The interview was carried out at the Ministry of Public Security of Mexico City (Secretaría de Seguridad Pública del Distrito Federal) in two 2-hour sessions, on March 6 and 10, 2009.

*EA:* Please tell us about your career: How many years have you been in service? In which institutions? What posts did you have? Do you have a specialty?

*EPC:* I was in the military for 47 years. In the army I reached the rank of general. My first contact with the work of the police forces was when I was part of the Seventh Battalion, in the state of Veracruz, and I was notified that I would be in charge of the police forces of the city of Poza Rica. At that time, in the 60s, I realized that no resources were given to the police; the police had to generate their own resources, which were obtained in an illicit way. The government used to buy patrol cars but police officers had to bribe in order to maintain them. That was probably because at that time we used to live in a society that did not need police. Nowadays, things are different and we criticize the police force because it is corrupted, but that was the way police officers were taught. They were formed in that kind of system.

Later on, I held the office of military attaché in different countries and this allowed me to study their police forces. Police are armed forces under civil control. My first mission was in Canada, where police have such prestige that it is considered an emblem of the nation. Unfortunately, in Mexico the police have lost their prestige and people do not attribute any civic value to it. I was also in New York and in Brazil. Then, I had the fortune to meet the Carabineros from Chile, which are one of the best police forces that I have ever seen. When the time came for my retirement, I was in one of the best commissions I ever had: I was principal of the School for the Army and the Armed Forces (Escuela del Ejército y las Fuerzas Armadas). After 47 years of service, I retired from the army and joined the Ministry of Public Security of Mexico City, where I now have the office of subsecretary of institutional development (subsecretario de desarrollo institucional). My mission here is to develop plans to create a new police unit: the Units for Citizen Protection (Unidades de Protección Ciudadana).

*EA:* Was the way your career unfolded surprising for you?

*EPC:* As a military person, one develops in the field one is ordered to serve in, but as a civilian I decided to study the police forces and that led to the proposal of creating the Units for Citizen Protection.

*EA:* Did your work turn out to be interesting for you? Do you feel it has rewarded you as you expected?

*EPC:* Yes, I feel satisfied, although there is still a lot to do in order to change the police.

*EA:* What are the main changes, from your perspective, that have happened in the police forces during your career (in terms of philosophy, organizational transformations, specializations. policies and programs, equipment, personnel, etc.)?

*EPC:* The police work under the civil law, which is ruled by the philosophy of Machiavelli—that is, "divide and rule." In contrast, the military follows Napoleon, from whose philosophy legal systems were born. I follow the maxim of the principle of the objective.

In 1995, when I joined the Ministry of Public Security, I proposed to the mayor a project named "Transformation 2000" for the Preventive Police. By this, I was trying to implement some things that I have seen among the Carabineros from Chile. The project was working fine but at that time the Mexico City Police had already 70,000 personnel and it was very difficult to promote a change in the whole institution; I was just a small part of the whole and there was pressure coming from everywhere against change. I decided to resign.

Later, in 2003, Marcelo Ebrard, minister of public security at that time and now mayor of Mexico City, invited me again to participate and continue with the project. It was then that I started to structure the Unit for Citizen Protection and that started the process of transformation in the Mexico City Police. These units each comprise 400 police officers who have better training, better work conditions, and better salaries compared to the rest of the police. What we expect from this is that they are able to provide a better service to the citizens. This is one of the few projects that I have been able to continue for the last 5 years, despite the head of the Mexico City Police being changed three times over that period and the fact that, usually, when a new minister takes office, he modifies policies and programs.

We know that it is impossible to transform an institution which includes 80,000 police officers overnight. For that reason, we have stopped the training and graduations of individual police officers from the Technical Institute of Police Training (Instituto Técnico de Formación Policial); only graduations of the integrated Units for Citizen Protection are allowed. These unit are assigned to specific geographical areas of Mexico City. The city has 70 coordinators of areas serving a population of 10 million inhabitants.[1] At this point, we have 40 Units for Citizen Protection—that is, 16,000 police officers, which represent one fifth of the total police forces of the city.

One of the main changes has been to lower the age at which police officers join the institution. At this point, average age is 22 years. This allows us to train police officers in a better way. Another important factor is an improvement of salary and of resources for police officers so they can have better nutrition; we have a problem of obesity due to poor nutrition. I am trying to assign a dining area to each Unit for Citizen Protection.

*EA:* What changes have you noticed that have had a significant impact on the police in regard to external conditions (e.g., the support police receive from society, the legal powers that the police have, relations with the justice system, relations with minorities, resource provision, political influence, etc.)?

*EPC:* Each society and its police are different from others. In Mexico the law allows one to lie, as long as one is not caught. In contrast, in the United States, for instance, one of the worst criminal behaviors is perjury; that is simply unaccepted. Societies are different and we need to adapt police forces to societies. For the Carabineros, subjects related to values, courtesy, and good manners are fundamental. In contrast, our society has forgotten values, and a civil servant who has forgotten that his/her mission is to serve is not a civil servant anymore.

I can't understand a society which assigns more resources to support a criminal in jail than investing in a police officer who provides security; this does not sound right. Police officers are not accepted so far because our education has failed. Our society does not have enough civil consciousness to abide by the law.

*EA:* From a general perspective, would you say that the quality of the work performed by the police has improved or not (in terms of the work done on the street, the special units, the administration capacity, self-evaluation capacity, and cooperativeness among police officers)?

*EPC:* It has improved, although not as much as we wish for, but we know it is not possible to get dramatic changes in a short term. Society demands more, but does not know what to expect from the police because society does not understand what the job of the police is. That makes the performance of the police inadequate. Fortunately, at this time, our mayor and minister of public security know very well the problems the police are facing and have helped us a lot, something that would not have happened if other persons would have been in office. For instance, we have recently turned over 1,200 houses to police officers.

We are still far from fulfilling our project and we have multiple problems, regarding budget, among others, that do not let us provide a different treatment to police officers. We are working under the system of proximity police [community policing]; that is, the main objective is to maintain communication with the citizens. I am convinced that police officers will behave according to the way we treat them and that is why I try to give them a dignified life and humane treatment.

The war that has been declared in Mexico against drug trafficking is, in reality, a war between one side of the police, in alliance to one cartel, against another side of the police related to another cartel. The least this underworld wants is to have the police as an enemy, so they use three powerful tools: money, alcohol, and women—three temptations difficult to resist. Criminals respect their laws; we don't. Besides, they have tighter rules. Capital punishment exists among them.

*EA:* In general terms, is it easier or more difficult to be a police agent nowadays than when you started your career?

*EPC:* In Mexico, activities to provide security have always been difficult. Drug trafficking is not the real problem. Lack of education is the real problem. As long as our society does not have values, police forces will not be accepted. We have rebellious citizens and an educational system that has failed. That is the reason why Mexicans prefer to pay for their children's education instead of letting them go to public schools. But what good does it do to spend millions of pesos in education if, when these children graduate, they are exposed to assault, kidnapping, and violation? Mexicans should cooperate with the security forces in the same way they invest in education, particularly by abiding by the law.

*EA:* What is the role of the police among society? What are its functions and which functions should be carried out by other institutions?

*EPC:* Police officers are the government representatives who have more contact with the citizens on a daily basis. Their mission is to keep order and make the law be respected.

*EA:* In your opinion, which kind of organizational diagram works and which one does not? What kinds of policies regarding society, political groups, and the justice system do you think will work better?

*EPC:* To have only one police organization, as in the case of the Carabineros, is appropriate. In Mexico, since the police were divided, we are following the game of the criminals because we have become weaker. Strong countries have just one national police force.

*EA:* How should the police carry out their work? What should be their priorities and main strategies: crime prevention or repression; proactive or reactive; communal police?

*EPC:* We have adopted the model of proximity; the citizen finds security in being well treated, and in police officers being helpful. Citizens are not concerned with the kind of training or the sophistication of the equipment the police have; they want to be well treated.

*EA:* What kinds of policies or programs have worked better and why? Which ones have not worked and why?

*EPC:* The Units for Citizen Protection work better because in them the work conditions for the officers have been improved.

*EA:* What, in your opinion, is the main problem the police face at this time?

*EPC:* The main problem is that society is not prepared to comply with the law. Security starts with education and in Mexico we have not been able to provide the quality of education we need. Civic and moral values have been lost in education, and that is a lack in our society.

*EA:* Among the problems the police face, which are the more difficult to face and which would be the easier one? From your perspective, are the internal problems (like corruption, and institutional procedures) or the external ones (like support from society and resources) that police face more difficult?

*EPC:* There are some security axioms that must be respected. One of them is that "security has a price." The kind of security provided depends on the budget. You cannot expect to have the kind of security that would require the investment of double the resources invested now; without such investment, corruption is promoted. Lack of security comes from a lot of factors: lack of values, poor education, inadequate laws, regulations that are impossible to fulfill, poor implementation of justice, ineffective penitentiary system, and poor media orientation. The police forces cannot solve all these problems; it is impossible. The police have to act within their limits in the best possible way, but if there is no cooperation from other groups involved, they will not be able to provide security. Even if the police were to have enough budget money, if they do not gain collaboration from society and citizens who acknowledge when they have violated the law, the police will not be able to provide security.

*EA:* What should be the relationship between practice and theory and what is the relationship now? Does it function adequately? What is blocking collaboration or interaction?

*EPC:* I believe theory should be the same everywhere, but the application of theory is different in each society, and success consists in knowing how to adapt theory to reality. When Giuliani came here, for instance, he gave very valuable advice. Nevertheless, in his opinion, Mexico City has too many police officers. What happens is that he does not know our reality. In our city, in contrast to New York City, we have streets with poor lighting and no pavement and also very poor areas. We have citizens who only respect traffic signals when they see a police officer who makes them respect traffic controls; for those reasons, we need many more police officers than we have now.

*EA:* What kind of research, do you think, could be useful for police practice here? How could contributions of theory be of use?

*EPA:* The most valuable contributions would be those acknowledging the specific circumstances of our reality in Mexico City. Contributions from the "strategy of indirect approach" have made me understand that in order to solve a problem and reach an objective, we have to face it when it arises. We should not attack it directly, but take into account its weak points.

*EA:* Where do you think that you can find valuable information that can be useful to you: in books or journals, in the media, in internal reports?

*EPC:* In books. I had military training and studied the universal security principles. Nowadays, people talk a lot about strategy, but strategy can only happen when there is a struggle between human wills. Strategy means thinking, pondering, analyzing, foreseeing all types of circumstances in order to respond in the best way, according to a given situation. When one does not know how to evaluate the decisions made by others, one can make terrible mistakes. I am passionate about Napoleon; although he was from the military, he made the civil law and organized the modern state.

*EA:* In which ministry are they carrying out research about police practice? What are the subjects they study?

*EPC:* We can't work with lack of information. We have a system that allows us to measure the performance of police officers. This measure gives us a clue about the way in which we have to distribute police officers, the way in which we need to carry out operations and prevent crimes or prevent flagrant violations of order. We have an information office and another one for police intelligence. In that office, information obtained by police officers on the streets is filed. Unfortunately, there is lack of respect and the citizens do not collaborate. For instance, many emergency calls that we get are false reports.

*EA:* Has your work ever been affected by foreign circumstances (human rights, ethic codes, new criminal realities)? How?

*EPC:* Security around the world changed after September 11. For a long time, the belief was that if you are strong, you are safe; but September 11 changed this view as it allowed us to see that 20 individuals can put a whole state at risk. With the growth of terrorism, we face another kind of insecurity: psychological insecurity, which the media promote. Twenty or thirty years ago, the news was not what it is now. Ninety percent of the news nowadays has to do with crime, disaster, economic problems; all this causes insecurity.

*EA:* Do you consider those external interventions beneficial or harmful?

*EPC:* Societies are different. Human rights declarations have been developed in countries which are very different from Mexico. From my perspective, human rights should be accompanied by human obligations. There cannot be only rights and no obligations. We will be breaking the foundations of Roman law, where every right presumes an obligation. I am convinced that long ago, the Mexican state abused the citizens, but nowadays I can see society abusing the law. If at that time the state had not used a heavy hand, I don't know what would have happened to this country. Society is like a family: A timely smack can avoid further problems for a child. The parent would probably suffer for repressing the child but that is his/her job. Exaggerating human rights in a society that has no resources is demagogy.

*EA:* Are you satisfied, in general terms, with the performance of the police? What kinds of changes do you foresee in the near future in the police and which ones would you like to see happening?

*EPC:* I would like all the police officers to have the standards of the Units for Citizen Protection. I am convinced that any improvement in the treatment that police officers receive from the institutions will lead to an improvement in the way they treat citizens. We need to treat police officers as human beings. I feel satisfied with the work I have done within the police forces. It is not all I would like to achieve but 16,000 from the 80,000 police have better work conditions and as a result can provide a better service.

*EA:* What do you think needs improvement within the police forces?

*EPC:* The police derive their values from society. In a corrupted society, the police officers will be corrupted; they come from the same society. Nowadays the units are receiving a better salary: US$550 monthly. They do not have a high level of education. They have only finished middle school; nevertheless, I would rather work with dumb people who want to work than with wise people who do not want to work. We complain that the police are corrupt, but I think we should have a campaign asking the citizens not to offer money to police officers and to report them when they ask citizens for it.

*EA:* Thank you for your time and willingness to meet with me.

## Explanatory Note

In order to better contextualize the previous interview, I would like to add some information from a study I conducted between 2001 and 2006 on the preventive police in Mexico City.[2] The key goal of the study was to give voice to police officers so as to understand their views and their understanding of their job and the obstacles they face when doing their work.

The study is based on the testimony of 280 police officers in all ranks of the hierarchy. Of these policemen, 170 were interviewed at police headquarters. Information was taken from an analysis of 110 eight-page long autobiographies, written by police officers of different ranks and career lengths who responded to an invitation from their institution to write the story of their lives as policemen.[3]

The preventive police in Mexico City,[4] with a population of nine million people, has a strength of 76,000 officers, half of whom are considered employees of the Secretariat of Public Security (Secretaría de Seguridad Pública [SSP]) and the other half of whom (auxiliary and bank police) have an irregular status—although they are members of the force, their labor rights are not fully recognized, and they operate autonomously and according to arbitrary and not very transparent criteria. Of the total, including auxiliary forces, 20% are traffic police (policía de vialidad). Belonging to the traffic police is considered a privilege, even though not all officers have access to a patrol car or a motorcycle. This is because these officers are those with the greatest opportunity to extort money from those who have violated the traffic code, and the income they receive from extortion far outstrips their wages.

The preventive police are the most numerous not only in Mexico City but also in the rest of the Mexican Republic, as they also comprise 91% of the national level police force. The different preventive police forces have the commitment to preserve public order, to take care of the demands of citizens, to protect their lives and goods, and to control motor traffic, while judicial or ministerial police, and the Federal Agency of Investigations take care of crime investigation. Nevertheless, preventive police can detain and present to the authorities those who commit a crime and are caught while committing crimes (in flagrant violations).

It is a known fact that there is widespread dissatisfaction with police performance among the inhabitants of Mexico City. It is a perhaps lesser known fact that there is also deep and widespread job dissatisfaction among the police. High levels of uncertainty prevail, as norms are not consistently applied in the contractual relationship between the Public Security Secretariat and the police. There is also widespread vertical (interrank) and horizontal (among peers) lack of trust within the institution, which constitutes a significant obstacle to the adequate performance of police work. Because norms and procedures are not consistently applied, a parallel informal or paralegal regime governs relations within the force. Deplorable working conditions have also generated a sense of abandonment or lack of protection among police officers, leading to their growing loss of interest in properly fulfilling their duties. Another important problem is what the rank and file describe as a continual lack of citizen respect and recognition.

There are some recurring issues that emerge in both the interviews and the autobiographies. First among them are the problems related to deficient working conditions. Second, there is the problem of corruption and the way in which the police address this issue. Other issues that come up frequently are relations with police chiefs, a negative self-image and the image citizens have of the police, problems related with lack of training, the way officers feel they are treated by the institution, and alcohol and drug consumption among officers.

In what follows, I will briefly summarize some of the study's main findings:

*Wages.* There is great dissatisfaction with wages among the rank and file. It is commonplace to hear officers of all ranks say that low wages promote and even justify corruption. They also say that poor police performance is related to low wage levels.

*Equipment and uniforms.* Police officers are almost unanimous in their discontent with lack of equipment and with their uniforms, which are either inadequate or of very bad quality. Regarding equipment, the problem is not just that they are not given the minimum equipment necessary to do their job properly, but also that equipment is distributed discretionally or stolen, or that police officers are forced to pay for it, whether it is access to a weapon, a motorbike, or a patrol car.

*Working hours.* Although working hours appear to be a greater source of discontent among the upper ranks, there are many reasons why it should concern police officers with no leadership positions as well. The main one is probably that the area where they live is not taken into account when assigning them to a sector or group, which often means that the journey to and from work prolongs their working day by up to 3 or 4 hours. Indeed, policemen are not allowed to request reassignment for this reason.

*Unsatisfied basic necessities.* Another issue addressed by many interviewees is the bad quality of the food they are given at police barracks or that they get when they are on the street, as well as the difficulties they face when trying to satisfy their most elementary necessities while at work. Many policemen said their bosses were indifferent or insensitive to their basic necessities, and that the same was true of citizens who make fun of them or censure them for eating in the public space. This is to the point that they feel their humanity is ignored.

*Promotions.* Another main cause of discontent is lack of respect for procedures and norms that regulate careers and promotions. There is a broad consensus about this within the rank and file (not among the top ranks). The testimonies include frequent references to disappointment because promotions are not made even when the requirements stipulated in the regulations have been met. There are also references to the innumerable arbitrary decisions that ignore the requirements and lead to the practice of giving jobs to family members, friends, or people that are recommended, without recognition of the efforts made by officers who have served for years without ever being promoted.[5]

*Lack of the rule of law.* Various testimonies pointed in the same direction: loss of motivation due to repeated attempts to make rules work that are never applied, lack of trust and uncertainty that generate a sense of insecurity when rules exist but are not obeyed, and, finally, a sense of apathy and paralysis caused by these situations.

*Corruption.* The simplest explanation we found is that corruption is caused by low wages paid to the rank and file. Nevertheless, for others, the problem is the lack of institutional support they receive at the onset of their professional careers, which becomes a decisive factor in the corruption of police officers. A common element we found was the ease with which people admit their own and others' participation in corruption, the absence of a framework in which legality is the frame of reference, and the acceptance of a parallel order or paralegal regime that in fact governs the institution. Equally, the lack of questioning corruption and the sense that one is confronted with something inevitable is striking.

*Citizens' participation in corruption.* Another view is that police corruption cannot be explained without taking into account the participation of the citizenry, although in some cases the emphasis on citizens' responsibility appears to be an attempt to exonerate the police. In addition, some policemen cover up corruption, saying that they do not extort citizens, but rather that the latter give them "gifts" to show their gratitude and appreciation for their services.

To finalize this note, I would like to call attention to the many difficulties faced trying to reform an institution with a personnel strength of 76,000 officers. There are significant obstacles to improvement of working conditions and the elaboration of incentive programs for officers. At the same time, constant changes at leadership level undermine serious efforts for stable practices. The design of new policies calls for high-level expertise; indeed, the lack of experts in this area has been a liability. As for corruption, there is a complete collapse of mechanisms and procedures to ensure accountability at all levels of the organization. Equally, there is no strategic plan to combat the culture of corruption and the predominance of the paralegal regime within the organization.

## Endnotes

1. The Federal District has 10 million inhabitants while the metropolitan area of Mexico City has 20 million inhabitants.
2. The study has been published as a book in Mexico. See Azaola, E. (2006). *Imagen y autoimagen de la policía de la Ciudad de México.* México D. F.: Ediciones Coyoacán.
3. When interviews were carried out, police officers were told that interviewers had consent from the authorities, that interviews were done strictly for academic purposes, and that they could not have any impact on their work situation or their professional development as police officers. Interviews lasted for about 2½ hours and were done in groups of eight to ten police officers of the same rank, covering the 10 ranks that integrate the hierarchical structure. Autobiographies were done freely and voluntarily by police officers who agreed to tell their experiences for a contest held by the Secretariat of Public Security.
4. Although the metropolitan area of Mexico City has 20 million inhabitants, the Preventive Police of Mexico City can only act within the perimeter of the Federal District (Distrito Federal), which encompasses 10 million inhabitants.
5. See Reglas para el establecimiento y operación del Sistema de Carrera Policial de la Policía del Distrito Federal, *Gaceta Oficial del Departamento del Distrito Federal,* Febrero 28, 1994: 5–8.

# 12

# Interview With Alvaro Vizcaino, Academic Director of Instituto Nacional de Ciencias Penales (INACIPE), Mexico City

**INTERVIEW AND TRANSLATION BY ANTHONY P. LAROSE, SANTIAGO INIGUEZ FLORES, SEAN MADDAN, AND MORGAN GARETH TANAFON[1]**

**Contents**



## The Interview

The interview was conduction in Mexico City on May 22, 2009.

## Changes in the Law of Mexico—International Policing

It is no exaggeration to say that Mexico is undergoing tumultuous social and political times. Violent crime has risen steadily over the last decade to reach an all-time high, with border violence dominating headlines on both sides of the Rio Grande. In response, the Mexican government has increased the role of the Federal Police and even occasionally has deployed the army to combat the drug cartels, which have become so brazen that they have even assassinated top government and police officials with perceived immunity. The rising tide of violence has recently forced the mayor of Juarez to relocate his family to El Paso for their own safety. Additionally, an increasing number of news reports suggest that the reach of the cartels has spread into the United States.

In order to combat both corruption and citizen mistrust, now Mexico has begun to implement numerous structural reforms throughout the criminal justice system. For example, the federal government of Mexico replaced an entire agency—the Federal Judicial Police (PJF)—which was seen as so corrupt that it could not even be reformed. Additional reform attempts have included creating a national security office, partnering police with universities, greater use of the created Federal Agency of Investigation (AFI) in local jurisdictions, use of the military to combat domestic crimes such as drug-cartel-related violence, and partnering with the United States government and federal agencies.

Perhaps the most compelling changes involve sweeping national reform and restructuring of the police, courts, and corrections system aimed at improving street-level crime control, increasing investigative efficiency, and combating corruption. For police agencies, that includes the unification of the preventive police and the investigative officer, who traditionally have had separated patrol and crime investigation duties with little or no interagency cooperation. Under the new system, police officers will participate in criminal cases from investigation through adjudication. Previously, an arresting officer would turn over the suspect to investigators, who would likely not contact that officer again regarding the case.

In the courts, perhaps the most radical change in the history of Mexico's legal system is taking place with the help of the United States Agency for International Development and federal and state prosecutors' offices from different parts of the United States. The adjudication process in Morelos and Chihuahua (two states where these changes are being tested) will be transitioning from what was formerly a completely paper-driven adjudicative process to an adversarial system based on the U.S. and Chilean models that will include oral arguments as well as direct witness testimony. In addition, defendants will have the presumption of innocence, the right to bail, and greater use of forensic evidence, and the courts will place a greater emphasis on providing defendants with a "speedy trial," although jury trials will be foregone in lieu of three-judge panels.

It is in this current climate of reform that we interviewed Dr. Alvaro Vizcaino, director of academics at the National Institute of Penal Science, Mexico City, Mexico, for a discussion that included not only the current state of policing in Mexico, but also contemporary police reforms and their relation to the larger set of changes being implemented in the Mexican criminal justice system. (A brief overview is provided in the appendix at the end of this chapter.) We sat down with Dr. Vizcaino for over 2 hours at the INACIPE facility and we received a comprehensive tour of the facilities.

*AL, SI, SM:* Can you tell us about the current state of international research in Mexico? Who is currently conducting research on security and police in Mexico?

*AV:* I know of at least five people off the top of my head, but there are plenty of American researchers that write about Mexico as well. George Fletcher is one; also Michael King, a former police officer now with the FBI as profiler; Ana Maria Salazar, a renowned Harvard alumna, who has her own television and radio shows and who has published several works through Harvard University; and Nina Catalano, another Harvard graduate, who is now with INACIPE under the Fulbright/Garcia-Robles scholarship. Her most current writings are about "Plan Merida," and weapon trafficking between the United States and Mexico. Concurrently, several universities in North America are doing research about Mexican law, such as the University of California-Los Angeles and other California universities, as well as Harvard, and the Massachusetts Institute of Technology. INACIPE and I have organized 15 different international conferences with the Canadian Embassy with themes such as "the rule of law."

*AL, SI, SM:* What is the general idea that people (criminology students) in Mexico have about CSI science and techniques compared or related to the popular CSI TV shows in the United States?

*AV:* Well, right now we have 120 students training and developing skills in the criminalist and forensic sciences; we are creating experts in these areas. This training is offered for the attorney general's office (procuraduria general de la republica [PGR]). The major areas we are focusing on right now are chemistry, medicine, and institutional technology engineering and telecommunications. There are also courses in forensic accounting and in copyright and plagiarism. INACIPE has 17,000 students enrolled nationwide; we offer different courses, minors, masters, and PhDs lasting 4 years. INACIPE has students in around 45 cities in the country, and we also have mutual cooperation in these matters with 45 countries.

*AL, SI, SM:* Could you please give us a brief summary of your professional career?

*AV:* I graduated from the Pan-American University (UP) with a degree in law. I spent time working with the attorney general's office from 1990 to 1996, eventually being named chief director of the Crime Prevention Department. In 1997, I worked at the Supreme Court of Justice (SCJ) in Mexico as the information chief director, performing as the official translator of sentences at SCJ for release to the media. I was with the SCJ because at that point the federal judicial counseling office did not have an information office; I left in 2001. That year, I started working with INACIPE; I was named director of the Professionalization and Extension Departments between 2001 and 2005. Since then, I have been working as the director of the Academics Secretary Department. I attended courses in England, France, and Argentina in special programs like the accusatorial penal system and implementations of judicial reforms.

*AL, SI, SM:* What was the trigger for the change from the inquisitorial to the accusatorial system?

*AV:* This is a movement taking place in Latin America and overseas countries such as France. The change was made from a mixed inquisitorial to an accusatorial system early in this year, when the instruction judges [supervising judges who decide on who should be prosecuted, based on the evidence] were decommissioned in France by President Sarkozy. It took a decade for Mexico to decommission all of the instruction judges. INACIPE organized an international conference in

2002 in order to discuss the modalities in procedures and alternative justice. Twenty-one Iberian-American countries sent representatives, such as fiscal prosecutors, vice fiscals, legislators, and other members of the legal system. They made an analysis update for the Iberian-American countries to change into the accusatorial system.

*AL, SI, SM:* Was INACIPE the one who proposed and launched the changes?

*AV:* Not just INACIPE! Mexico has many problems with justice, and talking about change leads to talk about all the past problems in Mexico. If we synthesize the problems, it is clear we had a slow, expensive, and inefficient system. These things triggered the Latin American movement, which took longer to take hold in Mexico. Argentina, in the city of Cordoba, was probably the first to change to the accusatorial system in the 1950s. In the last decade, some reforms were successful, others somewhat successful, and others just haven't worked. Colombia, Chile, and Argentina have been successful, while Bolivia and Guatemala have not. The issue in the latter case was that their system became extremely accusatorial, which resulted in their law warrants losing power and became less aggressive and, in other words, inefficient. Other problems that have occurred with being exclusively an accusatorial system are that there have been budget shortfalls and bad strategic planning.

*AL, SI, SM:* Who is leading this movement?

*AV:* No one institution can be truly said to lead the movement. Many groups are involved, and INACIPE has participated since 2002. I have been in charge of writing several translations of a penal code meant to apply to all Iberian-American countries. All political parties in Mexico agreed on this change, but they haven't been able to agree on methodologies. There were 10 law initiatives that passed, three of which were actually very important. The Institutional Revolutionary Party agrees with legal aspects endorsed by the United States, the National Action Party agrees with President Felipe Calderon's policies and initiatives, and the Party of Democratic Revolution has mingled the views of the other two parties. I was in charge of writing the constitutional reforms and secondary laws and working with the Commission for the Implementation of Penal Criminal Law reforms. However, the government has a limited budget to institute reforms. INACIPE is the largest institute in Latin America in its category: training, promoting diffusion, and spreading the news about new laws of criminal law sciences.

There will be a second national course of penal law in the accusatorial system. The courses will be held in each capital in every state in Mexico. The themes in courses will be determined and led by 3,000 public servants, consisting of PGR personnel, members of the court system, legislators, etc. There will be an introduction course to the constitutional reforms in 2008 and the introduction to the criminal law system in 2009.

The adversarial system is a contradictory system, like in Anglo-Saxon countries. The main point is who prosecutes and how the case will be prosecuted. In the past, the instruction judge would be in charge of the judicial power, the investigation, and, in large part, the prosecution. The first challenge was to create a more powerful attorney general's office for the nation, such as had been done in Brazil, Colombia, and Argentina, among other Latin American countries. However Mexico had a somewhat different challenge because we had already created the AG and fiscal offices since 1917, but they had to be reorganized to take on even more traditional prosecutorial duties than these offices have in an adversarial system.

*AL, SI, SM:* What changes have been made in the system and in the police? What is actually expected from this new accusatorial system?

*AV:* In August 2008, article 21, paragraph 10, of a constitutional reform law established the constitutionality of national public security. Also, a new law was published in the *Federal Journal* on January 2, 2009. This new law establishes the career services [civil service] of police officers and all law enforcement agencies.[2] This means that it covers the three levels: federal, state, and local police, as well as forensic experts and agents of the general and state attorney's offices. This law unifies the procedures for recruitment, income, selection, and promotion of law enforcement officers. The law mandates that every law enforcement officer on the federal, state, and local levels in Mexico be certified and qualified on their level of control and reliability.

These qualifications consist of drug testing, polygraph examination, socioeconomic evaluation, psychological evaluation, and physical assessments. These are evaluated every 3 years in order for law enforcement officers to be admitted to or remain in their agency. Another requirement in this new law is that every state has to have a police academy, with regional offices. There is a 1-year period before every state has to possess a police academy or training center and for every law enforcement officer to be certified. Another law established that the federal police must enact new security measures to fight organized crime.

*AL, SI, SM:* What will happen to the law enforcement officers that do not qualify anymore? How will they be controlled if they go over to the criminal side?

*AV:* Law enforcement officers that do not qualify anymore and decide to get involved in crime will be easy to track down because they have been registered in the criminal justice system; they have had to be introduced into it in order to go through the selection process. Their personal data will be in the system, including address, bank accounts, family members, previous employment history, any prior criminal record, credit history, and any private information. The other thing about law in Mexico is that our criminal justice system's mentality is to punish hard, really hard.

*AL, SI, SM:* What do you think Americans [the U.S. government] mean when they say Mexico is a failed state?

*AV:* Mexico is definitely not a failed state, and it is impossible to believe it could happen; it is actually ranked in the 88th position worldwide.[3] The U.S. government has stereotyped Mexico with this label. One of the main reasons is the high level of patronage—city mayors or delegates of a municipality hiring their friends or relatives, who are absolutely not qualified. These people don't have the training or equipment to be real law enforcement officers. These people probably come from previous jobs related to construction or some other type of labor position. There are 2,500 municipalities in Mexico—both rich and poor due to socioeconomic inequalities. The poor municipalities have inefficient, incompetent police officers, so crime is very high and organized crime can operate easily. The Mexican army has to be involved in the streets because local police in these areas tend to lose control.

The municipalities that are located on the coast and border are the most easily targeted because of the routes of drug trafficking. So there might be failed municipalities, but not states or the entire country. According to the secretary of state, the Mexican army will cease being deployed for law enforcement by 2013, which makes a lot of sense because it matches with the date when the police have finished their certification process. The law enforcement agencies have already been unified and their jurisdictions and assignments given to each. In May 2009, the Constitutional Reform Act, article 73, frac. 22, granted Mexico's congress authority to legislate on matters of organized crime, such as drug trafficking. The federal law, as a result of new initiatives, now has common rules on kidnapping and drug trafficking, which are part of a packet of three reformed laws: the penal code, general health law, and federal criminal procedures.

There are two different competencies: one is drug trafficking, which is federal level, and the other is drug dealing in the streets ("narco-menudeo"), which is on the state level. There was a mixed and unified police program to attend these issues, but no one on the federal, state, or local level knew how or wanted to take the responsibilities of these tasks in drug seizures.

*AL, SI, SM:* Can Mexico change the system by changing the people in it—such as law enforcement, judges, and attorneys—and not just reform the law?

*AV:* Part of changing the law is changing the people. It wouldn't be enough if we just change the laws. The laws order people to change; the actual change requires training and counseling everyone on proper methodology. Seventy percent of the people who operate the legal system change every decade in Latin American countries; this means change won't occur all at once. However, it is possible that Mexico can make this happen. Many people will change and the laws will change; this means it is necessary to improve the people, the institutions, and the methodology or "modus operandi." This change requires strategic planning, training, budget, faculty, and people that know how to make laws: deputies, senators, mayors, legislators, etc. Guatemala tried to implement reforms by changing the law alone, and it didn't work.

*AL, SI, SM:* What are your expectations for the outcomes of the government's changes of laws in the next 10 years?

*AV:* This just started formally with the constitutional reform last year. The Congress and the secretary of state think that the changes can take place in 8 years, and it would be opportune to make an evaluation of results in 1 year. There have been some advances in diverse laws that were necessary so that change could occur. There are necessary structures to operate, yet we still lack other things.

There are 10 states that haven't started anything yet. This is due to an upcoming political change in the administration, as they will be going through elections for governor and other official positions within those states this year. Most of these states don't believe that it's worth it or even feel interested in making the change because they are already stepping out of office. Their mentality is focused on leaving the work to the next people taking the job, delegating responsibilities to the successor—an attitude of "why bother?" The secretary of state created an organism, the technical secretary, which was created as a politically coordinated, operative organism. This organism doesn't have an assigned budget yet, but it will have one next year. INACIPE has always worked with the same budget by relocating and orienting the themes and priorities.

*AL, SI, SM:* Have these changes been reflected in the states of Mexico that border the United States?

*AV:* The state of Chihuahua is one of the most advanced states.

*AL, SI, SM:* Particularly, how is the change reflected in Ciudad Juarez, which is known to be an area of high crime?

*AV:* There are many ways to measure change. In common justice, on the matters of mundane citizen issues related to common crimes, the change is considerable, compared to organized crime. Five percent of all crimes committed in Mexico are violent crimes, of which half (2.5%) are committed by organized crime. Yet that 2.5% will occupy 100% of the information broadcast in the media and in worldwide TV networks. If you focus all the cameras and media on that 2.5%, it becomes 100% of society's concern about and fear of these crimes. However, the statistics used by the media don't match official statistics. It is very radical and traumatizing to find a human head chopped off and just lying there for the public eye, but the head and crime involving that head only represent a small amount of the crime in Mexico. This issue can also be viewed in terms of money, or the number of people involved, but the issue will remain categorized as a big problem. Organized crime might actually represent 50% of the volume of illegal money and involves approximately 400,000 Mexicans.

*AL, SI, SM:* Is there some possibility of changing these problems?

*AV:* In fact, the major problems originate from the United States. Ninety percent of firearms in Mexico come from North America. There are about 7,000 gun shops located in the southern states of the United States along the border with Mexico. Most of these places do not require any identification or background check; as long as you have money to buy, they will proudly sell their merchandise. Any kind of gun can be acquired: handguns, assault rifles, AK47s, grenade launchers, rocket launchers, air assault batteries, and other air combat fire weapons.

After the massacre at Columbine High School in 1999, a federal law was passed in the United States forbidding the sale of assault rifles. Shortly thereafter, there were protests by private associations, the military, advertisers, and other groups supporting gun sales such as the National Rifle Association. One of the companies was owned by U.S. President George W. Bush (2000–2008), and the law was thrown out, making it once again legal to sell and purchase firearms and assault weapons.

Mexico has frequently requested that the United States pass a law of prohibition or at least be more rigorous in controlling access to weapons, but there are too many political interests. As long as our neighbors continue to sell firearms freely, organized crime will always have a higher weapon capacity that can only be fought with the aid of the Mexican army. If Americans keep their free market for guns, Mexico will continue to struggle with cartels and organized crime.

In addition, the United States is the major consumer of drugs worldwide. The population of the United States is 300 million people and approximately 10% are addicted, which means that there are about 30 million Americans that have an addiction problem and use drugs frequently. The main idea here is to cut off the demand and supply using the basic laws of economics.

Now I ask the United States or, to be more precise, this is the question from the Mexican government to North America: What is the United States going to do about the 30 million addicts and the free sale of firearms? Mexico has a death count and suffers the collateral damage; how is the United States going to contribute to solving these problems?

To start with, the United States should shut down firearms sales and establish more aggressive and effective rehab programs for addicts. The United States government response was "Don't ask or criticize, just take this money [US$450 million] destined for Plan Merida."[4]

After the 9/11 incident, all criminal justice systems from around the world became more rigorous. The purpose was to privilege the security guarantees on public or collective security by restricting personal and individual guarantees.

The view of the people was more or less positive about this new application of the justice system and it was viewed somewhat this way: "If I am going to be checked or strip searched, it is OK as long as we fly or travel safely; I am not armed, but maybe someone else is."

Finally, there is a lot of material to research and information to share and contribute and many ideas to work on in collaboration in the future. The main point is to propose concepts to work on and then to cooperate on them.

*AL, SI, SM:* Thank you.

## Conclusion

We are thankful to Dr. Alvaro Vizcaino for providing us such an open and honest interview to discuss not only policing in Mexico but also the criminal justice system at large. His academic position and focus offered very substantive analysis of police reform, as well as how it fit into a larger national effort of criminal justice reforms, including even changes to the constitution. No discussion of contemporary policing in Mexico can be complete without understanding its relation to other, large-scale institutional reforms. We are also appreciative of Dr. Vizcaino's expressed interest in future collaborative efforts with scholars from the United States and elsewhere.

## Appendix: *The ABCs of the New Penal Justice System in Mexico, Second Edition*[5]

1. Utilize alternative mechanisms to resolve the conflicts:
   The justice system should settle minor cases so they do not go to court. For example, sometimes in car accidents, the individuals prefer to come to an agreement as to who should pay for the damages among themselves. This avoids a long, drawn-out court process, which benefits everyone.
2. Establish the authority of public ministry agents:
   A public ministry agent should have the right to initiate or decline an investigation. They might decline a case on the grounds of it being minor or nonviolent. Agents will have

to watch all cases in which the proceeds have been claimed in order to assess and guarantee any damages incurred. Victims should have the right to push the charges in a case to a judge if they are unsatisfied.

3. Solicitation before the judge; the exercise of penal action without intervention by the public ministry:
   In a case in which the law is established, the offended victims can directly go before the judge to enforce penal action without having any previous investigation from a government agency. In civil/family cases, the victims can hire a judge to open up, show, and explain their case. Victims might use reverse psychology to prove the guilt in a perpetrator. The victims can then bring all information/charges to the judge so he can make the decision whether to proceed with the case.
4. Implement verbal or public judgment/trial:
   In this alternate justice system, the majority of criminal cases will be resolved without going to trial. There are certain cases which, depending on the severity of the crime and if the parties do not come to a resolution, need a judge to examine the case. After the reform, the small cases will be open to the public. The public ministry and the defense will be able to equally refute or display any contradictions in evidence. The judge is mostly present for the mediation of everything. The arguments will be presented orally, so the trial can operate fairly, faster, and more clearly. Naturally this will require the development of new skills for advocates in legal arguments and presenting a detailed explanation of the facts to the public. The protagonists of the process must present the facts and rebut the opposing positions by going into great detail at each point. The court will recognize the honesty of the judges, the preparation of fiscal probity of defenders, and the technical proficiency of police and experts.
5. Suspend a case in process:
   Consistent with international practice, the reform provides that criminal proceedings may be suspended prior to sentencing in the manner provided in criminal law. If it is decided that a fair solution can be reached without the

lengthy procedures of a trial, these cases may be suspended. In a crime-related property damage case, for example, the court could use "early departure" if it is in the best interests of victims, and the accused accepts the restrictions and conditions imposed by the judge. Such restrictions may include, among others, not to approach the victim, and not to perform work on behalf of the community such as sweeping streets or painting fences. If the defendant violates the conditions imposed by the judge during the time indicated to him, the trial is resumed and the accused must confront the possibility of being deprived of liberty.

6. Shorten the proceedings by establishing a defendant's participation in the crime:

   Another way to shorten the process is determining if the defendant committed the criminal acts attributed to him, in the presence of the judge and the defendant's counsel. The judge can convene a sentencing hearing and verify that the evidence and witness statements prove the defendant committed the crime, in order to prevent the innocent from claiming their guilt. In this case, the defendant's sentence may be mitigated. However, it should be noted that admitting his participation in a crime is a right of the accused. However, if the defendant wants a trial, which will bring forth evidence and statements from experts and witnesses, he has the opportunity to do so.

7. Expand the rights of the victim or offended:
   a. Can apply directly for reparations for damage, without impairing the Public Ministry's ability to do the same.
   b. Can request an examination by a judge of the action or omissions of a public ministry through a simple procedure, to ensure that the investigation was conducted with punctuality, certainty, and efficiency.
   c. Can ask the judge to take preventive measures that ensure his or her protection and the restoration of his or her rights without waiting until the end of the trial. The law defines the cases where victims or the aggrieved may submit their complaints directly before the judge.

8. Protect the rights of the accused:

Another aspect that will be strengthened by the constitutional reform is increased protection of the rights of defendants. To achieve this purpose, we included:

a. The presumption of innocence is enshrined in the constitution, which means that until the defendant is found guilty, he or she is considered innocent and will be treated as such.
b. Only the judicial authority, at the request of the Public Ministry, may issue search warrants. In any case, the public prosecutor may conduct such searches without a judge's order.
c. The defense may only be made by a law expert. This will prevent people without knowledge of the law from making a poor defense of the suspects and complicating the issue rather than solving it.
d. The court will not allow communications that violate confidentiality, although private communications may be produced as evidence on a voluntary basis by persons who participated in them. The judge will value their importance, provided they contain information related to the crime.

9. Publicly explain the case:

It is common for a judge to impose a sentence of imprisonment on the perpetrator of the crime without explaining his reasons. The next highest court can review the case unit and often reduces the penalty by half. Then, the collegiate court orders the release of the accused, arguing that he or she is innocent. In Mexico, the secrecy of the justice system obscures the appeal procedure and makes many cases gets reviewed. This translates into backlogs and significant costs to the justice system and citizens. The constitutional reform states that when a sentence is handed down, the judge must explain in an open court the reasons he had to acquit or convict a person—for instance, the elements in his decision that the convict be given 5, and not 7 years. Such a measure is implemented in judicially developed countries where only 10% of the cases are appealed because most people are, if not satisfied, at least aware what the judge is considering at the time of sentencing.

10. Strengthen criminal investigation by the police under the Public Ministry:

When determining the powers of each public institution, it is vital to require efficient administrative management. The reform sets corresponding requirements on the police and the public ministry. In the past, the investigation of crimes was in charge of the Public Ministry, which controlled the police. This created problems of coordination between them and led to the prosecutors failing to adequately attend to their primary function of proving the facts of their cases before the courts. The police used to disengage from the investigation because they were not directly responsible for it. This lack of coordination resulted in a lack of authenticity about who was responsible for collecting data, gathering evidence, and converting such data into an effective tool for prosecutors to pursue the crime; in order to secure high sentences for criminals who had damaged the community seriously. The reform will allow the police to have technical and functional autonomy in conducting the investigation of crimes, under the command and legal conduction of the Public Ministry. This will not only allow better communication between the two, but also will make the process more scientific, objective, and professional.

11. Restrict imposing custody on the accused:
    a. Preventive detention is the exception, not the rule. Freedom can only be deprived if a person subject to criminal prosecution organized a serious crime such as homicide, rape, and kidnapping, or committed a crime by violent means such as weapons and explosives, or engineered serious crimes against the security of the nation, free development of personality, or another's health.
    b. In other cases, preventive imprisonment shall be imposed only when other measures are not sufficient to ensure the presence of the accused, the proper development of the investigation, protection of the victim, or in the case of

fraud. The judge will have to decide, at the request of the Public Ministry, where this precautionary measure is appropriate and explain his decision. This may not exceed the time set by law as punishment for the crime for which the accused is being processed.

c. If 2 years have elapsed without the judge pronouncing a sentence, the accused shall be released immediately. The process of investigation may continue without restriction against creating other protective measures.

12. Create a controlling judicial authority:

The judicial power of the federal, superior, and state court judges must possess controlling authority. The function of these courts will not only make sure that the rights of persons involved in criminal cases are not violated (whether victims, witnesses, or defendants), but also verify the legality any actions of all involved in the criminal process, even before the trial. At the request of the Public Ministry, judges may authorize measures that may restrict the rights of the accused in connection with the investigation. There must be reliable record of all requests and communications between prosecutors and the judge. Judges perform the judicial supervision of the conciliation agreement reached between the parties in an alternative justice process and will dictate the sentence in cases of summary procedure.

13. Encourage the establishment of sentencing judges:

The authority for penalty modifications will correspond in all cases to the correct judicial authority. Until now, the law has given authority to the penal administrative bodies to grant early release to those convicted who have fulfilled certain requirements. It meant, in short, that the administrative authorities modified their judgments according to their relationship with the convict. To prevent this, the reform proposes creating sentencing judges, who will review the sentences imposed and can alter them in keeping with a framework of legality about their modification and duration, according to the behavior and degree of readjustment of each offender.

14. Strengthen the ability of the justice system to combat organized crime:

    Attempting to fight organized crime as if it were common delinquency has proved counterproductive. In effect, the constitutional amendment establishes special measures, among which some provide the General Congress exclusive authority to legislate on this phenomenon that so worries Mexicans. If each state of the Republic issues its own regulations to prosecute organized crime, we risk having these rules contradicting and nullifying each other's effects because organized crime finds it easy to plan its actions in one state, operate in another, and flee to a third. The law establishes judgments that provide effective help for the investigation and prosecution of offenses related to organized crime.

15. Special measures to ensure those convicted for organized crime serve their sentence:

    The reform determines that, in a case dealing with organized crime, special detention centers and enforcement will be established to house the convicts. If this is added to the disposition to restrict inmates' communications with people outside and appropriate monitoring is imposed, it will be easier to break up organized gangs.

16. Limit the scope of detainments in organized crime cases:

    While performing investigations on organized crime, the individual who is under investigation may try to escape or endanger the victim. This makes it necessary to detain people presumed to have participated in a criminal action. Notwithstanding, this hold was not regulated by the constitution. This caused a lengthy decision process by the judiciary, as it is a measure affecting personal liberty, and thus was examined to determine whether it was constitutional. To prevent abuses in its application, the reform establishes that the detainment can only be ordered by a judge, as necessary for the success of the investigation, protection of property or persons, or where there was well-founded risk that the accused escape prosecution. The hold, which will only proceed in organized crime cases, cannot exceed 40 days, unless the public prosecutor states that substantial causes that gave rise to the need for an extension. In this case, it may extend up to 80 days. Some associations that protect human rights have argued that this could lend itself to some abuse, but the constitution states that the presiding judge will determine the place and time of the detainment, eliminating the discretion of other authorities.

17. Seize the assets of organized crime for the state:

To effectively combat organized criminals, it is necessary to hit them where it most affects them: in their profits. Previously, a person convicted of possible involvement in organized crime could still enjoy profits through family or accomplices. Even worse, the person could still use it to commit crimes. With the reform, through a new forfeiture proceeding, the judge may rule that economic goods that have been the instrument, object, or product of organized crime or have been used to conceal illicit goods may become state property and will be used to finance the fight against crime, as well as medical and social services. This measure has been used successfully in other countries because the loss of profit inhibits the operation of organized criminals and prevents them from managing the gains made by the commission of a crime through others.

18. Strengthen national public safety:

The reform will strengthen the national public security system by establishing rules for the selection, admission, training, retention, evaluation, and certification of officers employed by public security institutions. This is in an effort to coordinate the various areas of public safety with one another and achieve the objectives for which they were conceived. At the same time, it seeks to professionalize and earn respect for all members of the public security institutions nationwide, with the stance that addressing crime requires a personnel force that is efficient, professional, and committed to the society it serves. As a tool to perform better work, the public security system will form criminological databases with information that will develop programs and policies to combat crime. The police will also establish databases containing personal information about the institutions that shape public safety to minimize the chance that bad elements will become part of the security forces.

19. Strengthen crime prevention:

Developing countries favor prevention over the prosecution of crimes. The constitutional reform addresses the prevention of crime with functions that correspond to the federal, state, and municipal levels, which will be required to generate public policies that ensure the decrease of crime. Crime prevention is everybody's job. Therefore, the participation of society will be crucial, both in reporting the offense as well as in the implementation of community strategies to prevent misbehavior. There will be public evaluations of preventive policies at the municipal, state, and national level, as well as in the performance rating of public security institutions, in order to achieve greater transparency and decrease the crime rates.

20. Check that punishments are proportionate to the criminal act and the affected property:

Today, the Criminal Code covers offenses which differ in their definition and the applicable penalty. For example, so-called express kidnappings (a person is deprived of his liberty for a few hours while the criminals extract the numbers of his or her confidential credit card) are treated differently in the various criminal codes of Mexico; for some, it is an aggravated robbery, while others regard it as extortion and still others as a deprivation of liberty, tempered by a short duration. Therefore, penalties differ from state to state. This provision of the reform prompts a review of which crimes are serious and which are not. For example, criminals that seriously injure a person should be punished similarly to those that make unwanted sexual contact. These crimes will be punished in a manner more commensurate with the seriousness of the acts, through fines or administrative arrest. The principle of proportionality laid down in the constitution details rules for the state legislatures and Congress to review federal criminal codes regarding the penalties that are applicable to each criminal type and the definitions of each crime.

## Endnotes

1. Special thanks to Mellorie Garcia, University of Tampa, for her assistance with this effort.
2. Article 21 of the Mexican constitution was modified and essentially federalized the coordination and oversight of Mexico's criminal justice system. Specifically, the amendment demands that certification be required of all police officers and police agency employees; the establishment of a central, national criminal database; the development of comprehensive crime prevention policies; the promotion of community participation in public order; and federal funding for state and local police agencies. For an English translation of the Mexican constitution, see www.juridicas.unam.mx/infjur/leg/constmex/pdf/consting.pdf (retrieved 12/5/2009). For a discussion of contemporary amendments to the Mexican constitution and how they pertain to the criminal justice system, see http://mexidata.info/id1796.html (retrieved 12/5/2009).
3. Fund for Peace 2009 Failed States Index. Mexico ranks 98 out of 177 countries rated and is listed in the "warning" category. Scores are compiled based on various social, economic, and political indicators of stability. For more detailed information, go to www.fundforpeace.org.
4. More formally known as the Mérida Initiative, this U.S.-designed program of military aid is intended to help Mexico combat the drug cartels and, particularly, stem the flow of drugs into the United States. According to the U.S. State Department Web site:

   > The multi-year Merida Initiative will provide equipment and training to support law enforcement operations and technical assistance for long-term reform and oversight of security agencies. The initiative complements broader efforts by Mexico, the Central American nations, Haiti, and the Dominican Republic to fight criminal organizations and drug trafficking.

   See www.state.gov/p/inl/merida/ (retrieved 12/5/2009).
5. Translation into English is a product of reading the text directly, a lecture presentation by the staff of the INACIPE, and further discussion with Dr. Vizcaino. The original document can be referenced as *ABC del Nuevo systema de justicia penal en México*. 2008. Instituto Nacional de Ciencias Penal, Mexico City.

# 13

# Interview With Francisco J. Bautista, Founder and Former Major Commissioner of the Nicaraguan National Police, Managua, Nicaragua

INTERVIEWED BY BRUNO M. BALTODANO

**Contents**



**Background**

In September 1979, two months after the end of the armed revolution that deposed Anastasio Somoza Debayle, the interim government for the reconstruction of Nicaragua ordered the termination of the Guardia Nacional (National Guard) and the creation of a civil police.[1] This project, officially begun with a symbolic "payment" of 500 córdobas to the group of former guerrillas that became the founders of the new organization, provided the basis for a democratic police, a novel institution in a country where militarized police was the norm.

The concept of a democratic police is relatively new in Nicaragua. A civil police was first organized in 1880 when the constitution called for police to "protect public order, the discipline and proper customs, and the safety and well-being of landowners by means of laws that repress idleness."[2] Following a revolt in 1893, the two political parties

(Conservatives and Liberals) formed irregular armies. These partisan armies replaced the police but served primarily as the tools of the political party (or individual politicians) and provided little civic services outside their local communities. From 1909 to 1933 the U.S. Marines occupied Nicaragua and were the only "legal armed force"[3] in the country. Upon their departure they created the National Guard, appointed Anastasio Somoza García as its commander and charged it with becoming an "indigenous security force."[4] Two years later, Somoza García seized the presidency and the National Guard degenerated into his private army. From 1935 to 1979, this military police force focused on population control, eliminating threats to internal security, and securing the family dictatorship as it continued with the two sons of Somoza García. The Somozas and the National Guard ruled the country until they were overthrown by the Sandinista revolution.

In 1979 the interim government began to separate institutional functions between a civic police and the Ejercito Popular Sandinista (Sandinista Popular Army). They ordered that "the NNP [Nicaraguan National Police] will be subject to special rules that reflect the nature of its civic functions."[5] The police were created via political consensus but La Policía Sandinista (Sandinista Police) did not arise in a political vacuum; the Contra war began within a year. The war against exiled counterrevolutionaries (Contras), headquartered in Honduras and Costa Rica, proved devastating to a Sandinista government overburdened by hyperinflation and a strangulating economic embargo.[6] The war preserved the link between the police and the military, to the extent that all members of the police were subject to military discipline; counterinsurgency was its mission and it functioned under special jurisdiction in order to support the war effort against the Contras. It is notable that high rankings in the Sandinista Police ran concurrent with the military. The end of the Contra war afforded the ability to shift its mission and force the organization "to guarantee internal order, the safety of the citizenry and the prevention and prosecution of crime."[7]

In 1992, 2 years after the election of Violeta Chamorro to the presidency, the government acted to "effectively sever the link between the military and the police"[8] and embarked upon the creation of a "professional, nonpartisan, civil police with a clear goal of public service."[9] Dual rankings at the highest levels of the police/military hierarchy were invalidated; for the first time, Nicaragua had a chief of police and, most importantly, a police academy that did not include military training in its curriculum. At this point, the organization evolved to meet new legal requirements, shifting its focus and resources from counterinsurgency toward civil security. The NNP began the process of institutionalization of its functions within the framework of the judicial system, penal law, and the democratization of its forces. It is important to highlight five major shifts in the development of the Nicaraguan National Police:

It was created in a revolutionary context, with limited social capital, no institutional culture, and a simple goal: being the antithesis of the National Guard.

Its initial effort to demilitarize was encumbered by the escalating Contra war, which forced the Sandinistas to focus on counterinsurgency for almost a decade.

Crime prevention was not legalized as an institutional goal until the constitution of 1987.

Legal demilitarization did not take place until 1992.

Professionalization officially began in 1996 when the police academy was created.[10]

Francisco J. Bautista was one of the individuals originally charged with creating a new police organization at the end of the Sandinista revolution in 1979. He went on to serve as major commissioner of the National Police, as head of the Criminal Investigations Directorate of the National Police, as director of the police academy (a post that he held from the founding of the Academy in 1996 until 2000), and as deputy chief of the Nicaraguan National Police. He has written on the issues of legitimacy, civil security, and human rights in professional articles and received specialized training in Bulgaria, Spain, Taiwan, France, and the United States. More recently, he coordinated the Institutional Evaluation and Modernization Program of the Nicaraguan National Police from 1999 to 2005.

### The Interview

Formal conversations with Mr. Bautista began in October 2008. The interview process took place via electronic conversations and Skype online media beginning in December 2008 and ending in March 2009. Mr. Bautista remained in Managua, Nicaragua, while Bruno M. Baltodano (the interviewer) conducted his work in Pullman, Washington, in the United States. The interview process began on Saturday, February 28, but, due to technical difficulties, had to be finalized via written electronic communications the week of March 21–28, 2009. (Mr. Bautista had to travel outside Nicaragua between the first half of March, making communications difficult.) Exchanges were conducted in Spanish throughout and later transcribed into English by B. M. Baltodano. For the sake of simplicity, Mr. Bautista is identified as FJB and the interviewer as BMB. (Points emphasized by FJB appear in italic.)

*BMB:* Can you tell me a little about yourself and how you became involved in the police?

*FJB:* I was born in Managua, the 31st of May, 1960, and I am the fourth of 10 brothers. With the triumph of the Sandinista revolution I joined, like thousands of young people involved in the armed conflict against the dictator, the diverse projects of national reconstruction. We did this with the goal of marching towards a utopia: a new nation and a new society. The great majority of us had no idea what it was that we had to do but we all held a strong conviction of *what to avoid:* namely, repeating the abuses of the GN [Guardia Nacional]. In the police we wanted an organization that the young people did not have to fear, something one did not have to cross the street in order to avoid, an organization that held *respect* for the people it serves. From a professional perspective, I hold a bachelor's degree in economics and a master's degree in business administration.

*BMB:* Why did you join the police after the revolution?

*FJB:* It was not by choice, I was assigned to the post. At the end of the war people in charge of the reconstruction began to charge us with different functions. Some were sent to the Army, some became social workers and I was sent to the police. We had to do whatever was needed to rebuild the country and that was not a simple step. It was a monumental jump! Without realizing it our little world was changed drastically.

Youths, some not even done with puberty, became the chiefs of police in provinces and municipalities. We did this with a strong sense of duty. In fact, we questioned the payments we received for our "jobs" as *violations of the revolutionary spirit.* I was stationed in Juigalpa and directed the provinces of Chontales, El Rama, and Nueva Guinea.

*BMB:* Did you have a difficult time adjusting to life as a policeman?

*FJB:* My career was dynamic by nature, characterized by change, surprises, joy, and unpleasant situations. In the early years there were few boring moments; we had to balance building a new institution during a time of war, so the difficult part was not doing the same thing that the GN did, which was repression and abuse. For me, the most difficult times were two: The first was the defeat of the Sandinista Party in the popular election of 1990. The police at the time were Sandinista and we were not ready for this result. We had a strong link with the government, so this change forced an identity crisis upon us. We had to reconsider our goals and focus. One can say we had become "orphaned." It was difficult but it also provided us with the chance to create reform, to sever the cord to the Sandinista Party, begin to demilitarize the organization, and professionalize the force. The second difficult adjustment in my life was of a more personal nature. In 2005 I was forced into early retirement by then President Enrique Bolaños from a purely arbitrary decision. At the time I was general subdirector of the NNP.

*BMB:* Did you have an image of how the police should interact with society?

*FLB:* The creation of the NNP was a pilgrimage of trust—in other words, a fearless adventure. For us, in the early years, the challenge was monumental. The world of police was truly unknown to us but what we lacked in knowledge we made up in the youthful, revolutionary enthusiasm of the day. We would work long hours, tirelessly, without a schedule. First, we made it a point to talk to the common people and then critique ourselves and other compañeros(as).[11] This is how we came up with proposals and stayed in touch with the reality of the country.

Interestingly, the relationship between the police and society proved a process of constant reconstruction; in fact, it was a symbiotic relationship: As one evolved, so did the other. Given that the domestic and international contexts were closer than before (in the Contra war) the issue of perception was vital. One can even argue that perception was more vital than the facts. It is for this reason that relations between police and society had to ascribe to the five following aspects: (1) The institution had to be professional toward the service of society, (2) our behavior had to be constrained by law, within the framework of clear rules, (3) the organization had to be able to recognize social demands and, perhaps more importantly, respond within the framework of our lawful duties in an immediate, accessible, effective, and open form, (4) society and, by extension, the local community had to take responsibility for expressing its own issues, priorities, and "areas where the shoes don't fit" in order to demand that the institutions live up to its stated role, and (5) the community could not substitute institutional responsibility or, vice versa, under no circumstances should the local community compete with police in the enforcement of its duty.

*BMB:* How was the transition from the Sandinista Police to the Nicaraguan National Police?

*FLB:* We went through a lot; by 1990 we had made significant strides in establishing technical proficiency in the force and in the struggle against delinquency but we still remained linked to the party. We expected to lose support for our work and this left us uncertain about the future. I remember a friend telling me: "We are going to have to dance with a very homely girl." But the truth is that we had been through a big transition before so it was not very difficult to begin the process of internal adjustments once again. In fact, the transition provided a good amount of high-quality influx into the NNP because a lot of the members of the Ministry of Interior were absorbed into our organization. While these new members came into the police without any experience (a good number came from the Office of National

Security), they brought their own set of rich experiences from the past.

For the police, the two major transitions were (1) 1990 and 1992, when the FSLN [Frente Sandinista de Liberación Nacional] went from the ruling party to an opposition party. The war had just ended and we began the process of dissolving the connection between the police and the FSLN. It was a period of *re-creation* of our identity from a professional, technical and political perspective; (2) 1996, when a new law of police (Law 228), defining a legal framework for the NNP, was born. We were ordered to conduct an internal evaluation and to modernize the force. It was at this point that we began to reorganize the police from the perspective of local, communal demands (in view of common crime), social demands, and the Central American context of democratic security.

To once again reiterate, the biggest concern for us was separating the deeds from the perception of the police in this transition period. We had to balance *long-term institutional planning* with the growing need to provide *short-term solutions* to the pressure of criminal violence.

*BMB:* What was the most important goal in the process of developing the organization?

*FLB:* I would have to say that the most important goal was to maximize professionalism. Within the Central American context, we had to find a way to change the perception of the police as a *military entity.* The acuteness of the armed conflict of the 1980s demanded the inclusion of the police in military actions, so this did not help us at first. But one thing that is important to remember is that the country was living in an internal state of general mobilization for the armed forces. Within the legal framework of the time, both the EPS [Ejército Popular Sandinista] and the SP [Policía Sandinista] were parts of the "armed forces." In those days, the central threat was national security, so the counterinsurgency campaign was principal over the prevention of crime.

The combination of the end of the *Contra war* and the creation of a new legal framework for the police allowed us to make the most visible reforms in the work of the organization. Given that the police function within a strictly civil nature, the political consensus achieved in the 1990s allowed both the EP and the NNP to focus their work according to their separate mandates. This transition preserved the principal organizational and technical goals of both entities. From my perspective, this was the most productive and accurate political decision. Additionally, we had to find a way to demand that the forces earn a healthy amount of respect for the "rules of the game" and for the "law of the land," something that never existed with Somoza's GN. This also addressed the issue of professional stability because it prevented individuals from modifying the rules of the game anytime that it was convenient or whenever a new regime came into power. This consistency is fundamental to preserving the organizational culture and establishing a concrete system of promotion (within the organization) based on efficacy, professionalization, and production. The final product—namely, professional police—makes it difficult for any regime to then modify the laws according to its own needs.

*BMB:* In general, how has the quality of policing changed in Nicaragua?

*FLB:* I would have to say that we have made great advances at the organizational and technical level. Without a doubt, even in the face of imperfections and critiques that are born out of the imprecise mixture of deeds and perception, we have been able to demilitarize the police and refocus policing toward public safety. This simple separation, born from the triumph of the revolution, strengthened the mechanisms of the organization and those of its individual operatives and of its leadership to the extent that it provided the basis for a professional institution. Even though the NNP is, according to constitutional law, "an instrument of the institutional political power" (Law 228, 1996), this is not Somoza's GN. The organization is expected to act in a responsible manner, given that it is no longer a "belligerent group." The NNP is no longer exempt from the consequences of its deeds and omissions.

The problem is that, in reality, the social demand (the threat of organized crime and a growing feeling of insecurity from the part of the citizens) has overwhelmed institutional capabilities. In Nicaragua, the criminal element is multifocal; it obeys socioeconomic and cultural conditions, as well as domestic and international factors. The geographic location of the nation places it in the very center of the isthmus; we are a prime route for the transit of illicit drugs that travel from the south to the north and for the illegal traffic of weapons and money that moves from north to south. The amount of resources enjoyed by organized, international crime is many times higher than that of the country itself. This, in light of our meager local infrastructure, the fragility of the institutions, and the poor socioeconomic reality of the country, presents a grave and growing risk. This situation forces a parochial calculus upon the public institutions, even in the case of the most stable countries in the region. In my view, this regional strategy hinders the quality of policing in Nicaragua.

*BMB:* Do you think the daily routine of the police became easier after demilitarization?

*FLB:* In general, the work is not easier. The conditions are still very risky in the field and the criminal element is no more compliant. Within a context of civil rights and ample warranties, our job is harder, especially at the level of the individual operative. It requires greater preparation and a smart and effective organization. Nonetheless, the current condition in Nicaragua has the benefit of strengthening relationships between the police and the community. In the long run, this will also improve the condition for the police and the nature of the organization.

*BMB:* What is the principal role of the police in Nicaragua?

*FLB:* The principal role of police is to contribute to the resolution of daily conflicts that arise in the normal routine of the common citizen. Our goal has always been to do this in an expedient and peaceful manner. In the communities we serve, we strive to work closely with the population, to remain accessible and work from a simplified model. To this point, we instituted the program of "community policing" based on a direct link of (1) the demand for service on the part of the community, (2) the quality of service provided by the NNP, and (3) the perception that our customers have of the services we provide. In reality, the NNP provides two types of services to our population (1) administrative services—processing driver's licenses, vehicle registration, etc., and (2) operational services: patrolling, investigation of domestic violence and crime, emergency policing, traffic accidents, sexual assaults, and care for victims.

Annually, the NNP sees a daily average of 250 individuals accused of criminal activity and 910 for administrative services; this is among all delegations in the country. Surveys from 2002 and 2004 show that the major complaints from the population center on the administrative services provided. This highlights the value of a professional organization—one that facilitates participation, transparency, and rationality in its mode of action toward the community.

*BMB:* Are there any functions that the NNP must share with other institutions?

*FLB:* Those that are not directly related to the resolution of conflicts, as previously explained, and within the framework of the two primary services provided by the NNP. I think that some of the administrative functions can be assumed by other state or municipal entities—for example, the regulation of traffic, the furnishing of permits, licenses, etc. It is best for the NNP to avoid spreading itself so much that we lose sight of our priority.

*BMB:* What is the biggest difference in the work of the NNP?

*FLB:* The work of the police is now carried out in a decentralized and attenuated manner, close to the population, accessible and simplified. We are closely linked to the community where we provide our services and we adapt ourselves to the demands and social culture. We cannot afford to be alien to the sociocultural reality of the citizens. We work directly under a legal framework and no longer depend on "personal discretion" as a viable means of action. The policing entity draws its payroll from the state and not individuals and we demand periodic evaluations and mechanisms of social control.

We must remember that, as an institution, we started from "scratch." The entire state apparatus was ineffective at the end of the revolution. All of the members of the police came from the guerrilla or from popular sympathizers. That generation, even after legal edicts proclaiming the institution as a civil organization, *considered itself 100% as part of the military* (of course, this occurs within the context of the *Contra war*). Their motivation to join was politicorevolutionary. That generation is now a very small minority in the NNP; it represents less than 4% of the total membership and will continue to retire a little bit at a time. The new generations joined the NNP via different means. The new generation comes from the people, trains via a regular curriculum, and is career minded and professionally motivated.

*BMB:* From that perspective, what is the biggest challenge for the police in Nicaragua?

*FLB:* I think that the major problem facing the NNP right now is linked to the growth in the rate of common crime as well as the growing threat of organized crime. This is especially troubling given the discrepancy in resources, even in light of the strengths of the institution. From the perspective of the composition of the organization, "human rights" and a "focus on gender" are relatively new concepts, which the NNP is incorporating as part of its modernization program.

In Latin America, the police forces are not alien to these issues given that, historically, they have focused on coercive models, as opposed to prevention of crime, and centered their efforts on procuring national security instead of public safety. The direct consequence of this is a deep erosion of the social legitimacy of the role of the police force. Additionally, the participation of women has been traditionally limited to low percentages and to nonsubstantive roles or lower hierarchical posts. The absence of women in the administration of public services, particularly in active policing, may be one of the biggest challenges and/or factors leading to discrimination.

Another challenge is the fact that the NNP is a single entity. It is structured nationally in the same manner in each province of the country. At times this prevents the organization from adapting in a successful manner toward some regional idiosyncrasies. The NNP is working in this but we must understand this is a problem that affects not only the NNP but also the nation-state. We must understand the multiethnic and linguistic differences and apply effective models at the level of the organization and national politics. But in the end, the biggest challenge to the integrity of the NNP is the perception, from the part of the community, of low credibility and inefficiency of the organization. This can directly affect the concept of civil security.

*BMB:* What should be the relationship between the theory and practice of policing?

*FLB:* There are some aspects that are more important than others in relation to the connection between theory and practice. In the experience of the NNP, the most important to highlight has been the relation between the organization and the professional framework from which it draws the capacity to function as a career. Historically, there was no bridge connecting the GN and any educational institution—other than purely military. This *had to change* in Nicaragua; it was our first goal. We saw, firsthand, that the lack of an academic background created a shameful incapacity to respond to the needs of the citizenry and left the organization susceptible to changes in the political environment. During the SP years, we had to react to the daily problems, which proved to be very different in the different provinces. Honestly, we were not always ready to correctly anticipate these problems. So we faced the challenge of constantly having to modify our methodology, our operations, and even our organizational hierarchy in order to adapt to the changing social demand and the fast-growing criminal elements.

To do this in an informal manner requires keen observation and constant analysis in order to assimilate new tendencies. It was very difficult having to learn from our mistakes. The creation of a police academy reduced these problems and affords us the freedom to plan our future as an organization. Nonetheless, while we now have a better relationship between theory and practice in Nicaragua, it is (from my point of view) very limited. Currently, we provide training in becoming a police officer with a focus as career development. But we still have room to grow in regard to the study of political and social phenomena, as well as the analysis of the institutional process that contributes to the improvement of the policing entity. Additionally, in Nicaragua, there are only a few of us who write systematically about policing from an academic focus. An increase in this contribution will be useful for the education of our members and for the formulation of public policies.

*BMB:* How have international developments affected the NNP?

*FLB:* Without doubt, the development of international crime places strong demands on the NNP, especially in regard to information, education, and the development of new procedural manuals. Since the early 1990s, the NNP has been paying attention to the increase in youth and gang-related violence, a problem related to the migration of young people in the region. Some Central American countries applied "zero-tolerance" policies that carried heavy costs, both monetary and to the image of the police. From the beginning, we looked at it instead from a different angle and applied rehabilitation polices. Moreover, the Code of Childhood and Adolescence[12] implies a pioneering shift of vision from the police in relation to children and youths. This impacted the role of police in the investigative process as well as the penal process. Later on, regional compromises, like the suspension of visas for some types of citizens from the northern countries of Central America, showed the type of control needed to strengthen international cooperation.

*BMB:* What would be your ideal model for a democratic police?

*FLB:* The police force provides service to the community and receives legitimacy from the people. Historically and sadly, it has been manipulated by those in power to selfish ends that stand in sharp contrast to the common good. The policing model that strengthens democracy is one focused on crime prevention, one that facilitates the social and communal participation and identifies strongly with the social demand. This model demands that the priorities of the police match those of the community it serves. This requires the existence of an educational system that yields a dedicated group of professionals along with clear mechanism of control of the civic power that is given to the institution. But, most importantly, we must be able to avoid *external political interference and control* in order to protect the democratic functions of the police. The GN was the perfect example of an undemocratic institution: They used brutal, coercive methods of control, the indiscriminate detention of "subversive suspects," the criminalization of individuals or groups based solely on their appearance, and the practice of making "deputies" of persons to whom were given dangerous powers to become vigilantes, armed patrols, etc.

*BMB:* Are you happy with the progress of the NNP?

*FLB:* In general, I am happy with our progress. Our development has been dynamic and constantly evolving and adaptive to the social realities we face. The most important aspect is to create and maintain the process of modernization of the institution. I believe that, in general, the NNP has been successful in doing this. Nonetheless, the biggest challenge to our institution is to maintain public trust. In order to do this, we must continue to act in a professional manner. This is not always easy, especially when different political, social, and economic actors pull you one way or another in accordance to the political dynamic of Nicaragua.

*BMB:* What changes does the NNP need to institute at the present time?

*FLB:* The biggest changes have already been instituted. But, to be specific, I must highlight two different points: the long-term and the immediate problems. I basically must insist that the most important challenge still continues to be the need to reform police law in order to protect the everyday functions of the NNP and to find a way to simplify the organizational structure (which, in my point of view, is already far too broad and complex). This requires new public policies and for the central government to concentrate its focus on the development of citizen security. In the immediate level, we need to improve the working conditions of the average police officer. We need to provide better benefits to the lower ranked members and the enlisted as they are the ones who face the biggest risk and (currently) enjoy the least protection.

**Conclusion**

The interactions with Mr. Bautista provide a window into a very complex situation. The NNP, born from a revolutionary context, is a relatively young organization with limited social capital and an emergent institutional culture. The major themes presented throughout the interview reflect those highlighted in the literature on policing in Nicaragua. First is the significant obstacle of overcoming the noxious legacy of the GN and the counterinsurgency *modus operandi* of the SP. The formative years of the institution were spent in preparation to fight an insurgency; thus, security continued to be defined in military terms. The end result is that legitimacy remains a major concern. Nicaraguans over the age of 40 remember the GN acting as an instrument of repression against political opposition (a charge that, during the Contra war, was equally leveled against the SP), so it is easy to see how trust is a big impediment to institutional development.

Second, after the NNP shifted its vision from counterinsurgency toward citizen security, the question became how the police officers defined themselves. This is another major theme developed by Mr. Bautista and he accurately points out that the percentage of those members of the NNP that self-define as *military* is relatively low but the highest positions in the NNP are still held by approximately 40 former Sandinista guerrillas.[13] He points out that the NNP has not yet fully divested its military legacy. According to the last survey (conducted in 2001), when *high-ranking members* of the NP were asked whether they considered themselves to be members of the military or a civilian organization, 45% self-identified as a military force.[14] This generational legacy may explain considerable setbacks in addressing gender inequality and resolving attachments to coercive models of interaction (at the individual level). From the perspective of the populace, this self-identification also affects the perception held by the NNP.

Finally, another major theme in looking at the NNP concerns the matter of "regional idiosyncrasies" (as Mr. Bautista calls the relations between the police and remote communities). This is no small matter, especially in the two autonomous regions of the Caribbean Coast of Nicaragua where six *ethnic communities and indigenous populations*[15] must balance political autonomy and (in the case of the indigenous peoples) tribal law while granting judicial powers to the NNP and the Nicaraguan central government.

In the final analysis, it is important to highlight that, at this point, regardless of marked deficiencies, the NNP has been successful in the most important of its necessary changes: The police academy has effectively removed military training from its curriculum and replaced it with a focus on citizen security. More importantly, it has created a viable career in law enforcement open to the populace—a necessary step toward building confidence in its institution.

## Glossary

**Contras:** Counterrevolutionary insurgents fighting against the Sandinista government. Their armed attacks began in 1980; initially, the group consisted of former Guardias but their ranks would eventually include expatriates, peasants from the northern provinces and former Sandinistas as well as a coalition of ethnic minorities and indigenous groups from the Caribbean Coast. The group depended on hard funding from the U.S. government (see Iran–Contra affair for more details) but was never successful in forging cooperation among its myriad of insurgent groups.

**EP (popular army)**

Created by Executive Order in 1992 to the extent that, legally, it no longer was connected to the Sandinista Party.

**EPS (Sandinista popular army)**

Created in 1979, closely connected to the Sandinista Party. In this regard, it differed only in size from the partisan armies of the late 1800s. High rankings in the EPS ran concurrent with high rankings in the Sandinista police.

**FSLN**

**Sandinista National Liberation Front:** Armed insurgency against the Somoza family. It began as a student-led organization in opposition to the Somoza dictatorship and grew to include multiple insurgency groups that eventually cooperated in bringing an end to the Somoza rule.

**GN**

Somoza's National Guard. Created in 1933 by U.S. Marines and controlled by the Somozas.

**Junta**

Interim Government of National Reconstruction. Officially ruled Nicaragua from 1979 to 1985. This was a coalition made up of five members: one of the leaders of the FSLN directorate, two left-wing activists, and two right-wing representatives.

**NNP**

Nicaraguan National Police. Created as a separate entity by executive order in 1992.

**SP**

Sandinista Police. Created in 1979 immediately after the end of the Sandinista revolution and directly linked in function and leadership to the Sandinista Popular Army.

### Endnotes

1. Article 23 of the Fundamental Statutes of the Republic of Nicaragua, Sept. 5, 1979.
2. Executive Order of the 25th of October 1880. "Idleness" is further defined in the document to include those "that own no property, job, or property rental from which to draw an income, those with no profession or legal job with which to provide for themselves, or those with profession or job that do not so practice it on a daily basis."
3. Cuadra-Delgado, Adán. *Leyes, Decretos y Reglamentos en Materia Policial* (1880–1993). Editorial BITECSA; Managua, 1993.
4. Ibid.

5. Article 27 of the Fundamental Statutes of the Republic of Nicaragua, Sept. 5, 1979.
6. Adolfo Calero, interviewed in Managua, Nicaragua, 2008.
7. Article 97 of the Political Constitution of the Republic of Nicaragua, January 1987.
8. Article 144 of Law of Functions of the NNP in regard to judicial aid.
9. Executive Order 45-92 called "an armed institution of civil nature, nonpartisan, apolitical and nonbelligerent."
10. Executive Order 228, Article 142 October 25, 1996.
11. This type of peer critique was the norm for the Sandinista guerrillas; during field interviews conducted with former guerrillas in the summer of 2008, they all refer to this process as a daily routine.
12. Law no. 287, May 12, 1998.
13. Rocha-Gómez, J. (2007). Mapping the labyrinth for within: The political economy of Nicaraguan youth policy concerning violence. *Bulletin of Latin American Research 26* (4), 549–553.
14. Montealegre, F. (2001). *La Policía Nacional: Su Papel Actual, Fortalezas, Debilidades y retos*. General Director, Policía Nacional.
15. This is the legal definition used in the political constitution of Nicaragua (adopted January 9, 1987). The indigenous populations include the Miskíto, Sumu, and Rama, while the ethnic communities include the Garífuna, Creole, and Mestizo.

# 14

# Interview With Chief of Police Ragnar L. Auglend, Hordaland Police District, Norway

INTERVIEWED BY RUNE GLOMSETH

**Contents**



The interview took place at the Norwegian Police University College on November 30, 2007.

## Career

Ragnar L. Auglend was born in 1949. He finished his law degree in 1975 and has since added to his educational capital by taking various courses on specific aspects of policing, as well as on organizational development and management (for instance, courses offered by the Norwegian Armed Forces and the Norwegian National Defense College).

Ragnar Auglend has had a very long and varied career. While studying law, he worked as an auxiliary (unskilled) constable. In 1975, after having finished his law degree, he became a junior police prosecutor in Hønefoss, after which he became a junior police prosecutor in

Bergen. He then worked for a period as an assistant judge in Bergen while on leave of absence from the police. Subsequently, he was posted for service at the Police Department of the Ministry of Justice. Afterward, he was an assistant police prosecutor in Bergen until he was appointed assistant chief of police and head of the education section at the Police Academy. In 1983, he was appointed assistant chief of police and head of criminal investigation in Bergen. He held this post until 1986, when he became a district court judge in Oslo.

In 1998, he became head of the Police Department at the Ministry of Justice, and he held this post until he became a judge in Sarpsborg in 1991. In 1988 he was appointed district chief of police in Sarpsborg, and he held this post until 2002, when he became chief justice of Sarpsborg. That same year (2002), he became director of the Norwegian Police University College, a post he retained until 2005, when he was appointed district chief of police in Hordaland Police District.

Ever since he took his law degree, Ragnar Auglend has been involved in various capacities at the University of Bergen's law faculty. He has taught criminal law, criminal procedure, and road traffic law. He has also served as an external examiner for students sitting exams for their law degree. Since the end of 1980, he has taken part in developing and teaching the subject of police law.

He drafted the Police Instructions (submitted in February 1988). He also drafted part of the Immigration Regulations. He prepared a draft for the new Police Act (submitted in December 1990). Finally, he took part in a study about police collaboration across the internal borders of the European Union, in connection with the Schengen collaboration. He is coauthor of the book *Politirett* [*Police Law*] and has also written about legal aspects of road traffic issues.

He was appointed colonel 2 in the armed forces in connection with his functions as a military court judge. In this field, he has dealt with aspects of international law in times of war and military criminal law.

He has been a member of several panels, among them:

- A panel about community service as a penal sanction; he headed the panel, which prepared legislation and examined developments

- The panel about the Police Reform of 2000, Report to the Parliament no. 22 (2000–2001); he participated in the reference group as a representative of the district chiefs of police
- A steering group in connection with Report to the Parliament no. 42 (2004–2005); he participated as a member of this group

He does not consider himself a careerist. From year to year, he has shouldered tasks and faced challenges within fields of work that interested him, and the pieces of his career all fell into place more or less by themselves without his having any preconceived plan or goal. Throughout, his career has at all times been in some way or another linked to various phases of criminal proceedings. He became a judge at the age of 37. His career choices have been based on professional interest, notably his interest in public law and criminal proceedings. However, he has taken pains to maintain a certain level of expertise. Leaving his post as judge and returning to that of district chief of police in 1998 was a move that deflected him from the typical course of most legal careers. His decision to do so was ethically motivated: He was interested in being involved at an early stage in the process of criminal proceedings, so as to be able to contribute more directly to crime prevention.

### How Police Work Has Changed

The most notable changes mentioned by Ragnar Auglend are the following:

- *Law and order policing and prevention* are now defined as distinct disciplines. This is a result of the fact that a proactive perspective is being embraced, something that is reflected in the textbooks used at the Norwegian Police University College and by the establishment of departments devoted to these policies.
  - The first textbook on general policing was published in 1976.
  - The first textbook on public order policing was published in 1978.

- Preventive work was established as a separate function within the police in 1981 and 1982.
- These disciplines have been described and given greater priority in police legislation of 1990 and 1995.

- *Analytic and knowledge-based policing* has come to be defined as a distinct field. As a result, we have witnessed a growing emphasis on intelligence and analysis. Work has become more professional, and key words such as "structure," "system," and "analysis" stand out. The fact that this has been put into practice has "opened the door" for problem-oriented approaches to police assignments.
- At the structural level, *systematic collaboration with external parties* has become an integral part of policing. In modern society, such collaboration is important and useful. Collaboration creates synergy. Society is faced with various problems that the police, among others, are expected to solve or prevent. This cannot be achieved without interagency and interdisciplinary collaboration. In collaborations of this kind, the police may be considered standard bearers of society's values and goals.
- Growing attention is being devoted to *organized crime and terrorism*. This is not least due to new legislation that provides for special judicial measures targeting these particular types of crime and to developments within policing disciplines such as analysis, intelligence, directed surveillance, etc. International collaboration is indispensable if we are to deal with these issues in a satisfactory manner. Continuous upgrading and development of skills are also required.
- *Networking, professional, transnational crime* has gained ground and presents new challenges for the police. It is no longer limited to the trafficking of drugs and human beings or to financial crime, but encompasses theft of cars, car parts, white goods, mobile phones, etc. Again, the upgrading of skills and collaboration at an international level are essential if the police are to be able to deal adequately with the issues at hand.
- There has been a marked *increase in the number of women* in the Norwegian police force. Until recently, the proportion of female police officers was very low. But, in the spring of 2008,

women constituted approximately 20% of the officers in the Norwegian police force. The proportion of women studying at the Police University College has in recent years grown to somewhere between 35 and 40%. This is an important development.

- *The legal basis for policing has been added to.* The Police Act of 1995 upgraded and formalized the powers and duties of the police and the principles of policing.
- In organizational terms, the police have become far more modern and streamlined. *Management and direction* of police districts and specialist agencies have clearly improved after the introduction of management by objectives and performance management.
- Society has changed in many ways. Norway has turned into a country with cultural diversity. *Understanding cultural differences* is therefore a prerequisite for good policing.
- The *education and training* of police officers have undergone substantial changes. The police education program, the duration of which has increased from 2 to 3 years, now culminates in a bachelor's degree. The standards and number of further education programs and supplementary courses at the Police University College have risen noticeably. Generally speaking, the education of police officers in Norway holds a very high standard. Both basic training and further education have to be in step with developments in society at large and keep abreast of crime. In this respect, additional resources are needed.
- With regard to *police investigation,* we have seen an encouraging trend. Approaches and methods have improved and they have been documented. An analytic and thoughtful approach is the ideological and professional cornerstone of policing. Good and relevant training programs have been designed to cover important fields of investigation. The majority of Norwegian police investigators have taken these programs. Instructional technology-based tools and databases have been introduced both locally and at a national level. We have seen an increase of transnational collaboration. All in all, the degree of professionalism has risen markedly at every level.

- *Resources allocated to the police:* we are told that society gets the police it deserves, in that it allocates resources and determines the scope of police duties and powers. In recent years, allocation of resources to the police districts has been "criteria based" (i.e., based on a predetermined set of factors designed to calculate crime-generating social mechanisms and other mechanisms that affect the police workload). Criteria-based allocation promotes proactive policing.
- There has been a shift of emphasis in *criminal proceedings.* We have witnessed a growing awareness with regard to the effect of criminal proceedings and now see them as one continuous process. This means that we acknowledge and take into account the need to act in a synchronized manner throughout the entire process.

To summarize, Ragnar Auglend points out that, in many ways, being a police officer is easier now than in the past. On the other hand, the police face greater challenges now, with regard both to the operational aspects of their work and to investigation. Tasks are more complex and intricate; crime has increased, and criminals are far more professional and cynical now than in the past. Meanwhile, the police have better tools with which to work and improved skills. Working methods, equipment, organization, and the system's logistics have been enhanced. Management of human resources has improved considerably. Resources allocated to the police are acceptable. International police collaboration has come a long way.

All in all, Ragnar Auglend believes that holding a leading position in the police is easier now than in the past.

## Policing Philosophy

Ragnar Auglend is anything but enthusiastic about the word "role," which he considers vague and inappropriate in the context of our conversation. He prefers the term "function." He suggests we discuss what functions the police will have to fill in modern society. As he sees it, the following summarizes the functions held by the police in Norway:

- They maintain public order, peace, and security.
- They prevent and combat crime.
- They assist and serve the public, when this is called for.
- They assist other public authorities that need assistance or protection.
- They also have other tasks that, strictly speaking, are not police tasks, but fall within their range of responsibilities because they enhance the police's civil profile and are, moreover, closely related to the police's primary functions.

Ragnar Auglend also refers to the latest report about the role of the police, "Report to the Parliament no. 42" (2004–2005), in which the 10 main principles of the Norwegian police are clarified.

He refers, moreover, to the Police Act, which emphasizes some values with which he easily identifies and that he believes guide him in his function as a leading police officer. Section 1 lays out the general standards the Norwegian police should strive to uphold:

- Due process protection of individual rights
- Safety
- General welfare

Section 2 lists the tasks of the police. Section 3 describes the powers of the police. In addition, he refers to Sections 4, 5, and 6 as important and valuable guidelines for the police in their work.

As has already been touched upon, Ragnar Auglend stresses proactive policing, a policy he supports and advocates. A proactive approach should be the backbone of the police's civil functions. Naturally, the police must also continue to crack down on illegal activity and crime. He also emphasizes collaboration between the police and other public authorities.

As a leader, he emphasizes performance management and appropriate management processes. As far as human resources are concerned, he believes it is important to stress systematic development of employees—for instance, by planning skills-building schemes. Key concepts for management could be "goal orientation," "good processes," and "confidence in and delegation of responsibilities to subordinates."

### Successes and Failures

When asked what factors contribute to success, he prefers to approach the question from a generalized perspective, discussing the Norwegian police as a whole. He mentions three factors that he believes have been important for the Norwegian police:

- The *Police Act* of 1995 has been very important. It can be understood as an amplification of police duties and powers, and it gives important guidelines. In this context, the new police instructions from 1990 should also be mentioned.
- The *analytic, thoughtful, and methodical approach to policing*, which is reflected, for instance, in intelligence and analysis, has brought the Norwegian police a long way. It has allowed them to gain greater understanding of their duties and challenges and, by the same token, to be at the cutting edge.
- Newer forms of *organization and management,* arrived at gradually, and clearly reflected in the police reform of 2001, lead to a greater degree of professionalism, in addition to being better suited to the purposes. They also reflect that the police have become more aware of their goals and their performance.

Ragnar Auglend believes that, in the course of his career, the police have become more goal oriented and professional. The police force now has a wider perspective in its work than it did in the past. All things taken into consideration, he believes that, thanks to these factors, the police now serve Norwegian society better than they did.

### New Challenges

Nevertheless, the police are facing a number of challenges, which probably will continue to exist for quite some time. Ragnar Auglend stresses three factors:

1. We will have to deal with the *balance between common crime and organized crime.* Common crime need not be particularly serious, seen from a police perspective. It affects, however, individuals and the property of individuals. It causes financial

and personal losses and is perceived as painful, irritating and offensive by those who are affected. All in all, the extent and cost of common crime is relatively large. Organized crime is often more sophisticated and involves a greater degree of organization and skill. Each criminal act involves several perpetrators, gives a high yield, and requires a demanding investigation. Balancing between these two types of crime will be a challenge nationally and locally.

2. *We will need to educate* police officers who are sufficiently skilled to deal with all their tasks in a way that is acceptable to a democratic welfare society. At the same time, we need the capacity to face the range of crime we find in Norway nowadays, particularly sophisticated organized crime.
3. *Recruitment:* see the next section.

### Greatest Difficulties

In Ragnar Auglend's opinion, the greatest difficulties for a leading police officer are as follow:

*Recruitment* is a problem. There are too few police officers in Norway. Too few are being trained. In the near future, the number of people retiring from the police force will be relatively high. Recruitment to certain kinds of leading positions within the police also seems to have declined.

*Personnel management:* working for the police force should be an attractive option. Career and educational opportunities and good wages attract and retain personnel and generate motivation, initiative, quality, and efficiency. Policing skills are appreciated by the private sector, and police officers receive tempting offers with regard to working conditions, advancement, and, not least, considerably higher wages than they receive in the police force. This has unfortunately led to an erosion of the number of specialized police officers. In the long run, this may cause setbacks for efforts to keep ahead and also with regard to our organizations and the spirit that permeates them.

### Remedial Measures

It would be unrealistic to expect the police corps to match the wages offered to police officers working in the private sector. One needs to find a suitable balance between the various kinds of incentives that can be deployed in the context of personnel management. The scaling of wages could, for instance, be more flexible. It is also important to stress the need in every district for continuously upgraded skills, to a greater extent than is currently the case. This applies to policing and management skills alike. Policing has developed into skills-based activity, something that is reflected not least by the fact that training now takes place in a university college. Newly recruited officers have other professional opportunities and expectations than those who were trained at a vocational training institute. The third option is to lengthen the active service of elderly police officers, who, apart from their relative number, hold skills that are important for the police.

To summarize, Ragnar Auglend stresses that wages and an emphasis on skills building will be decisive if we are to solve our future tasks.

### Theory and Practice

The Police University College is responsible for research, the extent of which has grown in terms of numbers as well as scope. This is a tendency that will presumably continue. The research department publishes its work, so it is available to police personnel.

Here, too, one sees signs of globalization in the sense that empirically obtained knowledge about the police, police methods, and the resources spent by the police on various duties in various countries, are far more accessible than in the past. Sufficient knowledge and well-founded experience can thus be shared for the betterment of the Norwegian police. National and international studies are made known.

Theoretical advances have, among other things, led to a lengthening of the basic police education program that, as has already been mentioned, culminates in a bachelor's degree. What is now a university college was once a vocational training institute. This has naturally also had an effect on general policing skills. A police officer's education is more profound and at the same time of greater amplitude now than in the past. The theoretical perspective has won the day, as it were. As a result, policing is generally more thoughtful, systematic, and analytic than it was.

### General Assessment

On the whole, Ragnar Auglend is very satisfied with the Norwegian police. Much has happened in many important respects since the 1970s. Legislation, organization and methods have been upgraded, and will have to be continuously upgraded also in the future if Norway wants to keep its high standards. Staffing has to be in step with the needs of our society, and recruitment has to be ensured. This can be achieved with good wages and ample opportunities for personal and professional advancement.

In many ways, Ragnar Auglend considers the Norwegian Police University College to be the "jewel in the crown." Education, added knowledge, and the ability to use this knowledge in practical work are decisive for how the police will handle duties in years to come.

# 15

# A Conversation With Police Chief Superintendent Leocadio St. Cruz Santiago, Jr., Director of the Special Action Force of the Philippine National Police

INTERVIEWED BY MELCHOR C. DE GUZMAN

**Contents**



**Introduction**

Chief Superintendent Leocadio Santiago is the director of the Special Action Force (SAF) in Philippine National Police (PNP). SAF is a national operational unit directly under the PNP National Headquarters (NHQ). Director Santiago is a graduate of the Philippine Military Academy (PMA) class of 1979. The PMA is the premier military academy of the Philippines whose graduates are normally appointed to the highest positions in the military and the police. Chief Superintendent Santiago has been in the service for 30 years and has 4 more years before he reaches the mandatory retirement age of 56. However, since he has a so-called one-star rank, he is eligible to become the chief of the Philippine National Police anytime the vacancy occurs. The author addressed Director Santiago during the interview as General Santiago because he holds a rank equivalent to a brigadier general in the armed forces.

The succeeding interview will show his love for the service and his principled belief about discipline and detachment of the police from politics. Being a former military man, he relishes his days as a Philippine constabulary (PC) officer. Therefore, he exhibits love for the elite combat unit that he now heads. He also believes that a two-tier system is necessary to isolate the national police from the local politicians and improve the image of the police service.

He believes as well that theory and practice could go hand in hand. However, he believes that those theories should be implemented within the context of a specific police environment, taking into consideration support and cultural acceptance. He also thinks that researchers play an important role in the development of police practices. He advocates for a more realistic cooperation between the academicians and the police. He believes that unless the police are involved or consulted in the development of specific research, it would not be reflective of the realities in the field. He thinks that international police cooperative endeavors are beneficial to all the parties. He sees a need to change the image of the police from being perceived as oppressors to being looked upon as honest public servants.

### The Interview

*Melchor C. de Guzman (MCdG):* Please tell me the career path that you took to get to your present rank and position.

*Gen. Santiago (GS):* I started my career in 1979 when I graduated from the Philippine Military Academy. I used to be with the Armed Forces of the Philippines (AFP). I was in the infantry school in the United States when I became a policeman by being integrated in the Philippine Constabulary–Integrated National Police organization. I was not asked formally whether I wanted to become a policeman or not. I remained in the armed forces by being a Philippine constabulary officer. I have worked in several units. I have worked with the Presidential Security Group.[1] I have worked with the first antiterrorism unit of the PNP, called the Task Force Sanlahi. I have worked as a deputy chief for the PNP's chief of administration during that time, now PNP Chief Director General Oscar Calderon. Before that I was the provincial director of the province of Rizal.

I am also a former provincial director of Camarines Sur. I have long been a regional intelligence and investigation chief of CALABARZON (Reg. 4A).[2] There have been a lot of small assignments. For instance, I have been assigned in the Visayas as company commander in the 1980s. I have been an intelligence and operational officer of Samar and Bicol during PC/INP days.[3] So, those are basically the different highlights of my career.

*MCdG:* What is your specialization as a police officer?

*GS:* I am essentially involved in special operations and special tactics. So the majority of my career was spent basically with intelligence and operations in the field. But categorically, on specialization, I worked on special operations which are very much connected with intelligence operations. I spent most of my career as intelligence officer and special projects officer.

*MCdG:* Did you have special training that prepared you for this work or did the experiences on the job help you more?

*GS:* I will tell you. I was first utilized involving projects in intelligence operations; then, eventually, I was given an opportunity to formalize my field experience in intelligence when I went through intelligence operations training for officers. Then I went to a strategic intelligence training, which deals with foreign intelligence when you are to be posted abroad. It involved relationships with other foreign services. So basically those are my training areas plus other training.

*MCdG:* In the long stretch of your career, what is it that surprised you along the way or what do you think are the surprises that you have encountered?

*GS:* The really big one was when we organized the PNP-SAF back in 1983. I realized then that in the whole organization not everybody is fit for the service, either physically or professionally, even though they know that it is the need of the service. Normally, people will join the service when they raise their hand and pledge and say, "for God and country." In reality, it's just a career for them. There are very few who enter the service because of God and country. The alleged ideal of service is just on the surface, not completely focused on God and country.

*MCdG:* What I heard you say is that the sworn officers that you encountered in the initial reorganization of the PNP were not willing to lay down their lives.

*GS:* You know, people get into the service for many reasons, but very few enter the service because they love the service. From the very start, they really want to leave. However, this is not surprising. Even abroad—the United States, for example—people applied to the service not primarily because they wanted it from the start. Some of them entered it because they had limited options. This is why I have some bias, I might say, in the service for those coming from the PMA and against those coming from the police academy or those coming from line commission. There are always biases or differences on how they treat the service. I love the service I'm in. I would say that those who enter the service, I would say only 10 to 15% really want to serve. Sometimes, some of the 85% realize what the service is all about; they start to love the service. But initially, it is an opening for them for a new career when they first start. So, you find people not so focused on service. That 10 to 15% is those that entered the service because they really wanted to serve. It is an ideal option in their life. Now, there is a big difference between SAF and all the other police units. With the SAF, we enforce a higher level of discipline. The SAF is really devoid of political pressures.

*MCdG:* In what way are you devoid of political pressures?

*GS:* To give you a description of PNP-SAF: We are deployed only as required by the NHQ. So, my chain of command is the CPNP [chief of the PNP] and above him are secretary of interior and local government followed by the president. Those are the only three superiors that I have. The other units have to secure some approval from the local government executives for them to operate.

*MCdG:* What are the most important changes that have happened in the police service in the course of your career?

*GS:* The biggest change was that, before, we had a two-tier police system. Previously, we had the Philippine constabulary (PC) and the local police forces. The PC used to oversee and overshadow the local police. You should understand that the local police have to get approval from the local executives to get positioned. In the same manner, the ordinary police officer has to cater to, at one time or another, the local executives. With nationalization, even the national police assigned in the local areas need to have approval from the local executives. That was the biggest thing that I saw happening in the police system. The local executive interference is really an obstacle. However, there is an initiative program by the secretary of interior and local government (SILG) to overcome this handicap. We are working on initiating a Magna Carta for the police. We also requested that, if the politicians want control over the local police, we institute a two-tiered policing system: one that is really national and one that is local.

*MCdG:* Given the choice, would you like to go back to the two-tiered police system?

*GS:* I think that is the best option that the PNP should have in the long run. That is something that is usually good but the problem is whether we will be allowed to have one. For example, we had the Marcos period and people look at it as if Marcos utilized the police and the military as his personal guards for protection purposes. We do not like to have that task inserted in the new law. We want the police to really serve the community where their work will lead to doing a lot of good.

So, if we centralize the police, it will be again dependent on the executive. If we have a wrong executive sitting, then we will again have the same problem. This is the peculiarity with federal countries where they have a very mature public service. Civil service is really strong and the public administration is really strong, so even if there is no head executive or whether or not there is a leader, the system functions until a suitable public leader is found. For us, it is still personality based. Surprisingly with the SILG, he was able to push a lot of these changes to make the police really function with lesser interference from the local politicians.

*MCdG:* What were the major interventions that he did to insulate you from local politics?

*GS:* When one chief of police is functioning badly, he is invoking his power as the National Police Commission's (NAPOLCOM) ex-officio head and asks the chief of the PNP to relieve the chief of police. The chief of police is now aware that somebody is looking at his back and it makes him function. The CPNP has the choice to place whom the people really want. Before, the CPNP did not have that much leeway. So, if a politician said, "No, I want this officer," the CPNP could not impose his order on the officer to be reassigned. Now the CPNP can invoke his orders and can even say to the politician, "Please confer with the SILG." So he does not have to receive all the political flak.

Today, the decision of the PNP stays. For example, before I came to SAF, a lot of my people were being utilized as bodyguards. So, when I came to SAF, we recalled them and politicians had a problem with it and wanted them back. I told the politicians, "No, please communicate with SILG. If he approves, we have no problem of returning them to you. If he does not approve, then I am sorry." This is the big change and it applies even to the regional offices. As a result, we have more arrests now of scalawags in the service. Unlike before, when you did not know what happens if a policeman is involved in a crime or not, now you know that the full acts of the law will be applied to them. They will not hide behind the service or the politician. It is not a perfect organization, but the prospective for better service in the future is really there.

*MCdG:* So that is a good development, then, when a local government is isolating the police from political interference. I just want to ask you about the level of support that you get from different sectors. How much support do you think you get? Maybe you can give me a number if you want.

*GS:* I cannot give you a number. The majority now of the PNP has better support from the public.

*MCdG:* Perhaps we can go through these different sectors one by one. Let us start with the community in general. Does the community give support to the PNP?

*GS:* The community gives us a lot of support. Before, we did not get the same level of support that we have now. Of course we still have organizations that say that all police officers are bad. It's a culture that has to be changed. When I was a kid, my mother used to tell me, "Be quiet or I will ask the Bombay[4] to get you." Now it is different; parents say, "Be quiet or I will ask the police to get you." So at a very young stage, the parents are already corrupting the image of the police.

*MCdG:* You think perception has gotten better now?

*GS:* It is a lot better now. People come to the police much more often. They have come to understand us more. In the past, before and during the martial law, they looked at the police as private bodyguards of the politicians. These are the impressions that we have to overcome. There are areas like provinces far from metro Manila that have really interested and civic-minded public servants. But unlawful use of the police by politicians still exists in some areas. So it really depends on the head executive how the police are utilized and that also influences how the police are visualized (i.e., perceived) by the community.

*MCdG:* So you think the local head is the critical link or are you talking about the local executives?

*GS:* The local executive is the critical link.

*MCdG:* What happens if the police officer who has political backing clings to the position?

*GS:* A police officer who does not obey the leadership command will have a case filed against him/her for insubordination or he/she will be thrown out to a far-flung assignment and be dislocated from his/her family. Those are the pressures sometimes that I told you about. This means that when you are in the service, you are in the service to the people. You do not get married or you do not have a normal family. But then some time or another, we start a family. We come into situations in which we do not want to be separated from the family. Now I will throw you away to a far away place.

*MCdG:* One of the complaints by the police in general is that sometimes they are not supported by the legal community. I am talking about judges, prosecutors, attorneys. Do you think they are getting enough support from these legal personalities?

*GS:* The police investigators sometimes do not take law seriously. Not all prosecutors take the time to check the case. The prosecutors are unlike the federal prosecutors from the United States, where they sit down and prepare the case with the police, especially when the person being prosecuted is influential. That is seldom done in the Philippines.

*MCdG:* Do you think there is a lack of communication among them?

*GS:* Yes, but also probably because of the burden of the work of the public prosecutors, police interests are not seriously considered.

*MCdG:* Overall, do you think the quality of police service has improved?

*GS:* Yes, it did. In the streets, you see more police. You see them as more disciplined. We cannot compare it with London, where you see police officers walking on every street corner. Here, we still lack police officers. The ratio is still 1:1,000 or more. The ideal is 1:300.

*MCdG:* What about in terms of management? Has it improved or declined? Please exclude the unit that you are heading and speak in generalities.

*GS:* We now have the police management office, which implements or systematizes the system of management. It is a UN-sponsored program. It is making headway. More or less, the police administrators now follow a system of management in their offices. Before you can become a director, you should undergo this particular training and background. So people in position now know their jobs and they are evaluated on a periodic basis.

*MCdG:* So do you think it has lessened the "bata-bata"[5] system in the PNP?

*GS:* Yes! Like myself, I am not close to the president or SILG. They only looked at my background and classification and they appointed me to this position.

*MCdG:* But how many people are like you, who get appointed based on merit and not on political connection?

*GA:* A lot! Even at the regional director level there are a lot of people who know management. They become regional directors because of their qualifications and not because of their political backing because, if in the evaluation of higher officials, they turn out to be the most suitable, they were appointed to the position.

*MCdG:* How would you describe your level of cooperation with other law enforcement agencies such as Philippine Drug Enforcement Agency (PDEA) or the National Bureau of Investigation (NBI)?

*GS:* We conduct joint operations. They have their own charter focusing on specific problems. So there are no conflicts at all.

*MCdG:* The following questions are personal matters and if you want me not to include them in the transcript let me know and then your answers will be off the record. What do you think should be the role of police in society?

*GS:* The police should be partners of the community. The police should have multiple roles and they should be approachable. In Philippine society, they should be role models; they should be active in the community. They should be very visible. Then, as big brothers/sisters, they should be someone to lean on in times of crises. These should be the motivations for the police. They should be connected to the community.

*MCdG:* If you were the CPNP, what organizational arrangements would you remove or enhance?

*GS:* Probably not organizational reengineering but only increasing the discipline in the police system. The disciplinary system in the PNP now is complex but, in effect, if someone files a case against the police, he/she does not know which agency he/she should be attending. For instance, there is the People's Law Enforcement Board, which is in the local municipality, the Metropolitan Trial Court, Regional Trial Court, National Police Commission, or the Internal Affairs Service.

*MCdG:* Is there an overlap?

*GS:* The pressure is so high that if somebody files a case against you, it is not handled in a professional manner. So you can throw the officer off track in his career. Before you can clear him/her, you have already paralyzed her/him for several years.

I think that should not be the case. The absolute discipline should be that the chiefs must have the power to fire. It should be direct. If I see an officer committing an offense (for instance, if I conducted a random drug test and it turned out positive), right then and there I should have the authority to dismiss him/her.

*MCdG:* But they also say that they should be given due process and access to administrative remedy.

*GS:* Yes, but in the meantime he/she should be issued a presumptive case and he/she should prove his/her innocence. Police service as compared to civilian employees has a very wide difference. The police have authority to coerce—unlike civilians, who do not have any authority to coerce witnesses. Since we are in the uniformed and armed service, immediately we should be removed from the authority because of the possibility that if you are really corrupt, you will coerce all the witnesses. If you are good, then everything will speed up for you.

*MCdG:* So discipline is the key?

*GS:* Yes. For example, in this unit if you lack discipline, I will put you in an assignment that is like a janitor or something. So you have a choice. You stay with us or get out. If you get out, a case will be filed against you. SAF officers have a contract to serve. If they do not do any part of that contract, I prosecute them. But immediately after the investigation is finished, I can sign for their dismissal from the rolls or separation from the service.

*MCdG:* Going unit by unit, what would you change?

*GS:* What I am doing here cannot be done outside or in other units. We have a legal document here that the personnel will undertake several activities—unlike other units, which do not have that.

*MCdG:* If you were the CPNP, is there any unit that you would remove?

*GS:* No, not remove but integrate into one group.

*MCdG:* What are those units that you think should be integrated?

*GS:* For example, the service components—all the strategic and tactical levels at which we operate. I can integrate aviation security groups with the maritime and traffic management group.

*MCdG:* What about goals or functions? Do you think the police should be doing counterinsurgency work? That's always a question that comes up—that it should be with the AFP and not the police.

*GS:* No, the only reason why I think it is with the AFP is because they have the manpower and the fire power. But the police can focus on anything and they can do military functions. But some necessarily do not see that. The handicap with the police is the social ties with the local government system. In some areas, if the insurgency is strong or the terrorists are strong, the local executives tend to think that they need to have a special election [to protect themselves]. So the problem really is the executive and not the police. If we remove the local government influence over the local police, counterinsurgency is very possible. The police officer in the area knows the community or knows almost everybody. So, she/he knows who's connected with whom, how he/she is connected, and the thing is, you address insurgency in a manner that is people to people. And you can do that by benefaction [doing good work]. You can fight the insurgents by making the community support the government more than the insurgents.

*MCdG:* So what specific difference do you see between the police and the military in counterinsurgency work?

*GS:* The military only clean up and everything. Later, they move on. The police will stay there and stay there and stay there, and probably some of the military will come by there too. Staying in the area permanently will be a great help because people will tend to support their own more than the people that you know will be leaving you afterward. Besides, it's a police action. It is just so often that the military have stronger firepower. There are different levels of conflict. At the height of the conflict, the insurgency is stronger than the police; then we need maximum firepower. The military clean the place. Afterward, it should be turned over to the police.

*MCdG:* This is a little bit controversial, but when I was in the Philippine senate, there was a proposal to remove the enforcement [prevention] of illegal gambling from the police. Do you think that was a good proposal? Why or why not?

*GS:* Gambling, especially local gambling, will only prevail in a place if the local executives wanted it to exist. It's not because the police wanted it. It is not because the police cannot stop it. It's because the pressure is so high that your choice is leaving your station or being bogged down in one corner of your career rather than progressing in it.

*MCdG:* What do you mean by that?

*GS:* In the United States, they were not able to stop gambling, so they created Las Vegas. It's the same thing here. There is a social collision; we did not see the collision. The best thing is to provide avenues for the people to earn a living. As I said, it's not a police problem; it's a social problem, and you cannot address that by saying, "Remove me from the position." Now, it's the local executive who has responsibility over gambling. So why tell the police that you have a problem there? The local executive is the lead person against gambling. So why do you blame the police? They keep blaming it on the police.

*MCdG:* What do you think, then, is the biggest problem facing the police organization?

*GS:* It's more on image projection. We carry the image of the pre-martial-law days. The image portrays the police as the private or local armies of the politicians. That's the image they have of us.

*MCdG:* Is the image accurate?

*GS:* No! We're no longer the same police organization as before. Whatever they say about the SILG now, he has done significant things to bring up the image of the police. Whatever they say about the president, she supported improving the image of the police. It would be nicer if they say not PNP, but PC. It would have been perceived differently by the public.

*MCdG:* Why would the name change matter?

*GS:* People relate to the local police based on what happened before.

*MCdG:* Oh, I see. Meaning incompetent and corrupt?

*GS:* People look at the PC as having more discipline because they are more military in nature and everything. But, of course, it is just a name. But we would be described by the saying, "Oy, constabulary, hindi naman police yan eh." [Hey, it is the constabulary. They are not police officers.] Those are the aspects that should have influenced them. It is more psychological.

*MCdG:* Let me now ask your perspectives about police education, training, and research. What can practitioners learn from theory? Do you think theories help you in any way?

*GS:* Theory with some practical exercises helped me a lot, especially when I underwent training for a senior investigation supervisory course. Theories give you an idea when you are faced with scenarios or incidents. Theory provides you additional courses of action. An example is the management of rallies. Why is a medical team on site during rallies and available to the protestors? In theory, we have emotionally charged people. In theory, rally groups think they cannot go to the police when someone gets hurts. However, when injury occurs, a police medic is giving you aid. The result is that you develop a positive attitude toward the police. This aid will change people's perspective.

*MCdG:* Is there any theory that is very popular but does not work in the Philippines?

*GS:* The concept of using emergency response similar to a 911 system is very popular. In the United States, a call you make to 911 is charged to you. [But that is not correct.] In the Philippines, people wanted it to be free. How do you maintain that state of readiness without taking it from the coffers of the government? The people who are recipients of the service do not want to pay for it. They do not want to see it in their bill.

Another example is the *koban* in Japan. We implemented a block system. In the koban system, just like in Japan and in the United States, the government and the police organization make sure that the police officer has a decent standard of living to properly adjust to the community. In the Philippines, even if you are dislocated from your family, you have to go to your assignment. How can you survive if you have to support your family and do your work there? That is why if you want police officers to work in any locale, they should not have family ties.

However, that is impossible to impose. In the United States, the whole family moves. The government provides them with housing and moving support. [That depends on the level of government.] The result is that when you move to a new assignment, you do not know anybody in the community. You cannot even show that you are a good family man because you do not have decent family quarters in some areas. Family is not a hindrance to service but the government should give the opportunity for the police officer to be a good family provider. Every time there are novel ideas abroad, we try to imitate them, but we do not provide enough support to implement them and make the programs successful.

*MCdG:* There are some researchers and research institutions in the Philippines. Do you have linkages with them?

*GS:* We have our own. Right now we have the Police Transformation Program that is supported by the United States and some nongovernmental organizations. However, we have no linkages with other institutions.

*MCdG:* Do you think the PNP is open to researchers coming in and doing research about the PNP?

*GS:* The police will be happy about that. However, it all depends on the preferences of the leadership in the field if they allow that to happen. Similar to any public agency in the Philippines, the organization is personality focused, not organization focused. The personality overshadows that performance of the organization. If the director of the unit is open minded, then he or she would welcome researchers.

*MCdG:* Is there any specific research topic that you want to do right now? The Philippine Public Safety College has some doctrine development research. Do you make use of that research?

*GS:* Lots of research is of good academic quality. However, it is merely for academic exercises. It does not respond to the needs of the times. In the first place, the PPSC is not even under the PNP. It will be very difficult for academics to improve the service if they are not part of it. The context by which the studies are conducted might be different from the need of the service. There is detachment from the academic exercise to the realities in the field. The researchers did not even confer with the hierarchy of the PNP. They also have different ways of doing things depending on the professor or adviser. Also, they have a very limited budget. The instructors are not part of the service and they may not have the same performance evaluation that we use in the service. Therefore, the doctrine developed in the PPSC is unacceptable because they cannot even connect with the junior officers in the field. Research conducted in the college is done just to pass the course.

*MCdG:* Isn't the dean of the college a police officer?

*GS:* He was assigned there because he could not find a position in the hierarchy. The college is not a "dumping" ground, but the officers assigned there become detached from the realities in the field. In the Philippine Military Academy, cadets are trained by specialists of that field. In some other academies, officers and cadets go there on their own sweet time. If it becomes inconvenient, they stop training. The PNP should control the training in order for the needs of the service to be addressed. Once the police organization is in control of the education and training of the officers, that will be the only time that those doctrines developed will be accepted by the organization.

*MCdG:* Have you been affected by the developments outside the country such as the September 11 attacks on the United States?

*GS:* Personally, I was affected. I had to cut short my tour as a provincial director in order to be the deputy director for the antiterrorism unit of the PNP. We have also increased our interaction with other countries.

*MCdG:* Has the international trend toward gender sensitivity and awareness affected you?

*GS:* It did. I applied those concepts here in SAF. There is no discrimination in terms of assignment and position because of gender. The only thing that differentiates the female from the male is the weight that they carry. The weight has to be differentiated because women's physiological composition cannot handle the same weight that men carry. They undergo the same training. The commando force is similar to the ranger training in the military. We also have a policy that 15% of our unit should be females. Thus, they need to do what men do because I need more manpower.

*MCdG:* Is there greater awareness about human rights now in the PNP?

*GS:* We do a lot of training where University of the Philippines professors and the Philippine Commission on Human Rights come and provide education and training to our personnel. We make sure that police personnel follow strictly operational requirements and observe the preservation of human rights.

*MCdG:* I often visit human rights Web sites. They do not seem to differentiate military abuses from police abuses.

*GS:* The problem is they take their information from the newspapers. They do not investigate. I can also say that the human rights violations among the police have been greatly reduced. However, their image is still similar to that of the martial law period. I admit we need to improve on our image.

*MCdG:* What improvements would you like to see in the PNP? Is a fingerprint database something that you want and need?

*GS:* Yeah. However, some people do not want that. The police would want that. If you have fingerprint data, then every time there is a crime, the perpetrator can be identified immediately. The people should be made aware of the benefits of having that. Take, for example, the national ID system. The police want that but human rights activists do not want that. They say that it is a violation of their human rights, intervention in their personal rights, privacy rights.

*MCdG:* What are your perspectives on international cooperation? Do you think it is beneficial?

*GS:* Yes, we have those. I think they are beneficial.

*MCdG:* In what way?

*GS:* They have technologies that they share with us that we don't have. Whether you like it or not and say that RP is a violent community, New York is more violent than us. Unfortunately, those that say that the Philippines is very violent do not give the data and show them here. The murder rate in New York is much higher than the murder rate here with Manila and Cebu combined.

*MCdG:* But how do international bodies benefit from the cooperation that they get from you?

*GS:* You know, we cannot offer actually anything to them as far as practices are concerned. But they have expatriates here. And if we have a better standard of policing system, they know that what is true here is evidently also going to hold in their home country. So, what we can prosecute here will also be prosecuted in their place. As long as we have foreign nationals here, they have the advantage of better policing. Now, as to the Philippines, as long as developments and practices are proven right and more efficient here, they can benefit from it also.

*MCdG:* Thank you for taking the time to talk with us.

## Endnotes

1. The Presidential Security Group is an elite group that looks after the security of the president of the Republic of the Philippines.
2. CALABARZON is a composite police regional command also called Region 4. The acronym stands for the provinces of Calamba, Laguan, Batangas, Rizal, and Quezon.
3. PC-INP days refer to the time when a national police force was created by President Marcos when he declared martial law. He integrated the police into the military unit called the Philippine Constabulary. The local executives lost command, control, and supervision of the local police forces.
4. Bombay refers to any person of Indian nationality.
5. "Bata-bata" is a colloquial term for favoritism where the politicians' or superiors' favorites are assigned the most lucrative position in the service. Personality loyalty is emphasized rather than merit.

# 16

# Interview With Ivan Djorovic, Head of Police, Kragujevac, Serbia

## INTERVIEWED BY BRANISLAV SIMONOVIC

Contents



### The Interview

This interview took place over the course of a couple conversations in June 2008 at the Faculty of Law offices in Kragujevac, Serbia.[1]

*BS:* Would you briefly say something about yourself and your education?

*ID:* I was born in 1968 in Priština, the Republic of Serbia, where I finished primary school. I started secondary school in Priština and finished it in Kragujevac, where I had moved with my family in 1984. I started at the Faculty of Law and graduated in Kragujevac at the beginning of 1992.

*BS:* How did you imagine the policeman's job before you got the job in police?

*ID:* I didn't think a lot about that. For me it was important to graduate from my faculty on time. I respected the police profession because I had a few relatives who worked in police. The crime inspector's job seemed to me very elevated even though I didn't know a lot about that. Crucial influences for me were subjects taught in the Crime Department at the Faculty of Law where I was studying, where I had found myself. The whole procedure in documenting crime—from the committing of crime, police actions, and finding the perpetrator of a crime to pronouncing a final verdict and the uncertainty of the whole procedure of determining somebody's guilt—was a magnet for me and had a big influence on me to get to like that field of studies. The fact is that nothing is the same in police, proceeding from contacts with suspects, analyzing their behavior and ways of determining who committed the crime. The fact that a police inspector always has to be faster and wiser in order to solve a crime has been always what impressed me. The circumstance that it is always necessary to take care about the frame of authorization in crime investigating is contrary to the fact that everything is allowed to the suspected person, and that has also impressed me.

*BS:* When did you notice your interest in criminal materials and police work?

*ID:* I showed the interest for criminal sciences during my studies as I organized, for my school generation, visits to jails, court hearings, the institute for forensic sciences, and lectures by well-known experts in the sphere of criminal process law.

*BS:* Would you like to say something about the beginnings of your police career?

*ID:* My first job was in the Serbian Ministry of Internal Affairs. I started to work in August in 1993 in the Kragujevac Police, in the criminal department and the section for stamping out economic crimes. After about 2 years, I was the head of one of the three units in the section for stamping out economic crimes.

*BS:* What kinds of memories do you have of the first 2 years of your professional career in the police?

*ID:* Ever since I started to work, my chief of that time (and also the current chief) assigned me to the hardest cases along with experienced operational personnel. I accepted that work with enthusiasm. In my first year of work, as a beginning employee, I independently solved a number of crimes, just like an operational person who had a license. I remember that I asked to enter my password in the system in order to add crimes under my name because, as a beginning employee, I didn't have the license.

In the first period I was engaged just as a part of a team that worked on cases, and later I became the head of an operational team. In this way I saw that an operational person had to work strenuously in order to solve crime the right way. For example, any police activity related to solving the crime of accepting a bribe is not organized without my permission.

I happily remember my work in police in that period, especially my assignment by the Ministry of Internal Affairs in investigating crimes throughout Serbia. It happened that during one year I had to spend 5 to 6 months outside Kragujevac. I thought this reflected an excellent evaluation of my work from my superiors in Kragujevac and from the Ministry of Internal Affairs office in Belgrade.

*BS:* What kinds of jobs were you working on when away from the police office where you originally were stationed?

*ID:* That police unit was authorized by the minister to investigate heavy economic crime. It was a very complicated job for many reasons: difficulties in providing evidence, suspects who were very powerful directors of the largest business companies in the country, suspects who had support of political parties, some suspects who had influence on the media, police investigations that induced a large number of media stories, etc. At that time I was a very young police inspector. I was between 28 and 34 years old and it was a big professional challenge for me.

*BS:* Was it a special unit of the Ministry of Internal Affairs that was engaged on the territory of the whole country?

*ID:* In that period it wasn't a separate unit, but leaders of the Ministry of Internal Affairs were choosing several persons from the police throughout Serbia for the hardest cases of organized and economic crimes that local police could not deal with on their own. That ad hoc team quickly became a separate operational group, and then it became the UBOPK (Administrative Office for the Struggle Against Organized Criminals). The only reason why I didn't stay in Belgrade and work in that office, in the founding of which I had participated, was my personal wish to come back to Kragujevac, where I had a family, a defined life, friends, etc.

*BS:* What would you like to say about your professional career development?

*ID:* After I had worked as an operational person, I became a head of the line of work in the field of economic crimes. Essentially, nothing was changed in my work. I still worked some cases like before and, in the case of need, I was taking the place of the chief of department.

After 10 years of work in the police I was appointed as chief of the Ministry of Internal Affairs in Kragujevac, one of the four biggest cities in Serbia. And I still work in that place.

At 35 years old, I became the youngest police chief in the Ministry of Internal Affairs in Serbia. Now I am leading a police office which covers seven municipalities (Kragujevac and six additional municipalities), around 350,000 citizens (central Serbia region). When I was appointed as chief, I knew what was waiting for me and how strenuous a job it was.

*BS:* What was the biggest challenge at the beginning of performing the function of the top policeman in region?

*ID:* At that time, my main impressions, which I hold even today, were assumptions of the service, which were given by the minister of that time, and they were related to the complete police depolitization, professionalization, and demilitarization. It is something I, as a policeman, was craving in the period before. These were main prerequisites for one structure, which the police are, to function normally and with quality.

I think we started, for the first time, with struggling against criminals essentially, not just declaratively, at the beginning of 2004. It was necessary for 4 years to pass since big political changes had happened in the country to feel their real influence on police work.

*BS:* What was your opinion, as a young chief of the police head office, about strengthening the ideas of police depolitization in public?

*ID:* I applied literally principles of depolitization and professionalization of the service. I said in public that politics could come to the entrance of police, but not further.

*BS:* Was something similar told explicitly on the level of Ministry of Internal Affairs?

*ID:* I think it was the assumption of the whole Ministry of Internal Affairs from that period because I was supported for implementing that policy in Kragujevac. I have never had problems with the implementation of ideas about depolitization and professionalization in police work. I have implemented that strategy today. Soon after beginning with that way of work, we showed that there was no unreachable person and nobody was more powerful than the country. We were processing all cases, especially economic crime cases, in the most professional way.

*BS:* In which way did you realize the idea about police depolitization with local authorities and centers of political power?

*ID:* Police in Kragujevac, at the end of 2004, on our initiative, made an institutional frame and connections with the organs of local authorities. These are reflected through the introduction of usual, once a week, official and direct contacts between the police head office with the mayor and district chief. After that, on our initiative, we organized work of the Kragujevac Security Council. Therefore, relations between police management and political leadership of the city weren't built, like before, in informal circles (for example, in bars) but in public places, in the frame of work of the security council, actually in the institution in which work is accessible for the inspection of every single citizen. I think we restored, by the way of work, our image, which was burdened with the happenings in past. All these brought the police of Kragujevac on the top of the ranking list, which included police from other cities by all criteria in which police work could be evaluated.

*BS:* How was the implementation of principles of police depolitization and professionalization reflected in everyday work?

*ID:* We touched the things which were "pushed under the carpet" for many years and decades. For example, there was a problem with drug addiction. In the first year we took away more narcotics than in the decades before and we brought to the court all serious narcotics sellers from the territory covered by our police office.

*BS:* How did public opinion react on the changed attitude of police management, which was showed in the media, through founding the security council and changed relations with local carriers of political and executive power?

*ID:* Maybe our biggest recognition is reflected in the results of public opinion research, which was organized by the city of Kragujevac at the end of 2007. Confidence in police work was shown by 71% citizens of Kragujevac. Compared to the 18% in the same public opinion research done in the second part of 2004, it was a big success.

*BS:* What were the other challenges you faced at the beginning of your career as a chief of the head office?

*ID:* I have to remark that personnel policies are the most important assumptions. Since I have become a chief, I have been fighting and have won for personnel policies to be under my control and to be based on my criteria, which are exclusively professional. I have to mention that I have never imputed just to myself everything in which I succeed. The success can be made only by the team, and the leading person is there just to give one nice note to the managing of the whole office, which is followed by others. And the biggest results we reached are merit of operative persons and policemen of Kragujevac. I also think that interpersonal relationships are very important. This is something I was working and I am working on even today.

*BS:* The last period in police work was characterized as closed and distanced for the media. But changes have happened in the last few years. What do you think about that?

*ID:* Our work is characterized as completely open for media and public, and I have been insisting on it since I have become a chief of the police head office. There is no information which one journalist, of any media house, couldn't get from the police of Kragujevac, except some operative information or the information which could hurt the honor and reputation or any other citizen's right. I was supported on all these by the superiors in Ministry of Internal Affairs of Serbia. On the other side, there were a lot of obstacles in work created by some interest groups in the city which weren't accustomed to that way of working. But it was overcome with persistence in implementing these principles. At the same time, the police organize regular press conferences for journalists where media representatives are informed about results and activities. In those press conferences for journalists, there is no question on any aspect of police work which won't be answered.

*BS:* You explained how the depolitization process passed on the local level. Could you explain the process of depolitization on the state level?

*ID:* In the law related to police work, which was passed 2 years ago, police depolitization and professionalization are quoted as the basic principles. The new laws made big changes on the top of police organization. The main police office was separated from the other structures and independent in its work. The police director was chosen by the government of the Republic of Serbia, not by the police minister. Assembly boards for security have complete insight into police work and they get reports. Those boards are consisted the representatives of all political parties and I think it is good solution.

*BS:* Women in police, especially in its uniformed sector, are also one of the new solutions in the Serbian police. What do you think about it?

*ID:* Women's presence in the police is also an innovation. Women became a part of the uniformed sector around 2002. I make efforts, whenever I can, to suggest and choose a woman for the leading position because there are a lot of women in the police of Kragujevac who work their job professionally and have good organizing skills.

*BS:* When we are talking about women, what can you say about maternity leave? Are there any problems on the level of men–women relations, and what is the opinion of citizens about introducing women into uniformed police sector?

*ID:* Maternity leave is a matter that is accounted for in advance. In our police head office, we really take care about women's rights and we make efforts not to disturb them. That area is also defined by law. I think that our friendly relations and men–women relations are on the highest level. We don't have any problem based on it in Kragujevac. Citizens with sympathies look on the women's roll in the police. It is a relatively new practice. Also, as a chief, I can say I am very satisfied with their engagement and professional way of working. I have never caught myself thinking that something was wrong just because it was done by a woman.

*BS:* Women in patrol? Women in shift work?

*ID:* Because of health reasons, we usually get requests that women work just in the first shift. All these requests are answered. Those are circumstances related with long stays in the cold, gynecology problems, pregnancy. All the chiefs take care about that and usually those things don't come to me because we defined the philosophy of leadership in that way.

*BS:* What do you think about processes of intensifying international police cooperation in Serbia, although it had a traditionally closed police system?

*ID:* The international police cooperation has invaluable importance. Exchange of experiences from different parts of world has great importance. It is an ideal opportunity for every good idea, which was implemented in some other environment and had a positive effect, to be used in other police systems. The fact is that all police in the world face problems—more or less similar or the same problems. It is very valuable to hear how every police force in the world faces those problems.

The second aspect of international police cooperation is the fact that a criminal doesn't know borders and that usually it is necessary to follow one criminal group through more countries. It obligates all of us to cooperate. The best examples for that are human trafficking, narcotics trade, financial and computer crime. Those are cases where the police have no choice then but to connect and cooperate. I think that the Serbian police in the past made a great quality improvement in that area, and international relations in the sphere of police cooperation will be improved further.

*BS:* How do you evaluate intensive international cooperation in the area of police education?

*ID:* A lot of opportunities for police education in all fields of police work, in the country and abroad, improved service further. Large numbers of policemen attended seminars and courses in many countries of Europe and in the United States. It is a very valuable experience. It enabled good contacts between our policemen and their colleagues from all around Europe and the world. First of all, I think, in many seminars and examples from many areas: money laundering, human trafficking, community policing, implementing of special police operative techniques, etc., were discussed. All of these things had a big influence on development of the quality level of police work. I was surprised, for example, by the fact that, through direct contact with colleagues from Sweden, I heard that they had been impressed with the knowledge and work of forensic scientists that they had met in Kragujevac. Also, colleagues from Norway, chiefs of the Oslo district, were very enthusiastic about everything we did in community policing development in Kragujevac.

*BS:* What is your attitude about the permanent process of police education?

*ID:* A policeman or woman always has to improve and educate himself or herself. We organize internal education during the whole year and after that they have to pass the exam in which they show acquired knowledge. It is a practice which is implemented on the level of the entire country's police. But education of our policemen, which is delivered by foreign police experts, is essentially a new quality and makes our horizons and views on our profession wider and opens new possibilities in its realization.

*BS:* What can you say about your experiences in police work with minorities?

*ID:* Recently I have had a meeting with all representatives of Gypsy associations in the city. There are 12 of them. All of them were talking in the media, actually in public, about their satisfaction with our relations. Just 5 or 6 years ago, it was very risky for police patrols to go in the Gypsy area in the city. Today, in the same area, we organize sports activities and parties for the Gypsy holidays, where large numbers of policemen are present, but as guests. Twice a year we play a football [soccer] game, once in their area and once in the city sports hall. We organize visiting of the police station for Gypsy children (open-door days) where we invite them to come and to communicate informally.

Also, the national minority of Gorans lives in Kragujevac. They are originally from Kosovo. They are neither Serbian nor Albanian. They have their customs and language, which is a mixture of Serbian and Macedonian languages. They have been living for several decades in Kragujevac and they usually work as bakers and make cookies. We maintain direct contact with them in order to be informed about all security problems which they have. We solve those problems together. And they gladly show their satisfaction by their cooperation with police.

The Muslim population in Kragujevac consists of just 50 members. For the first time, 3 years ago, we established direct contact. We showed them ways and possibilities of cooperation in solving security problems which they have.

We present in the media all of these activities with minorities and vulnerable groups because we want to show to all citizens that we are here, in the real meaning of the word, in their interest. And we are very honest. We don't do that just because of advertising. Those contacts have their purpose and yield extremely positive result.

We were glad because we were marked "excellent" by the OEBS representatives on relations between police of Kragujevac and media, as between local police and socially vulnerable groups, especially about relations with Gypsies and homosexuals (lesbian association).

*BS:* Is it easier or harder to be a policeman today than it was before?

*ID:* I think it is harder to be policeman today, but because of reasons that are, in my conviction, good for police. Today it is impossible for a policeman to use means of force without someone noticing it, to exceed the authorities and get forgiveness, or act indecently and think that nobody can do anything just because he is a policeman.

Three years ago, for the first time in the history of the Serbian police, I had to say that the patrol exceeded their authority in one intervention. Policemen were suspended because of that. In that case, one person survived hard physical injuries in the form of a nose fracture. I organized a visit to the citizen in hospital because I wanted to alleviate that situation and publicly admit our guilt. Policemen were punished properly, as I promised. That kind of attitude provoked wonder in public because citizens weren't used to that kind of police speech. And I told the truth. That is the point of the service's professionalization. And today every policeman knows what the limits of his authority are and he has to act in the frame of these limits.

*BS:* Would you say something about your experience in police management?

*ID:* Relations in the police are the question before all other questions. Those relations are stratified and they are reflected through many aspects. Personnel policies are the first and basic principle that leadership positions take people because of their professional success. It means that every form of corruption is eliminated. After that, there is a clearly defined system of responsibilities and clearly defined group of problems for every management level. In the system set up this way, a leader can't allow himself, by giving the orders, to skip anyone in the chain of management. We succeed when everybody works his own job and everybody takes responsibility in accordance with his managerial level. After that, a leader should be interested in interpersonal relations in police. I think there is no success in the service if interpersonal relations aren't good. When things are set up like this, professionalism is set up in first place, which means that the police are immune to all pressures and it reaches the highest level of depolitization. Without that, there is no professionalism in the right meaning of that word.

*BS:* How do you understand relations between police and citizens?

*ID:* Only when we define internal relations in the police organization like that can we be in position to build quality and partnership relations with citizens and other institutions in the environment where we work. The essence of the police success is in mutual relations between police and society. There is no success in police work without that essential quality of mutual relations. On one side, there are relations between police and citizens and, on the other side, relations between police and other institutions and local authorities.

*BS:* Could you say something about crime prevention?

*ID:* Generally, we support partnership relations with the citizens. I think that citizens recognize it in Kragujevac. It is basic for preventive police work, which is a much harder way of crime prevention, but the last result is a real challenge for us. In Kragujevac, from year to year, we have achieved a reduction of the crime rate. Actually, the number of crimes is decreasing in absolute amounts. With those relations with citizens, we show that we are sincere in the aim to protect their interests, and we are "awarded" by the mobilization of everybody to introduce solutions to security problems.

We persistently try to fight for the attitude that a security problem is a problem of all of us, not just the police's problem. Everybody has to take care about security in the measure to which it belongs to him—not just about his own secruity but also the security of the people around him. It is a two-way and very sensitive relation. It has to be approached very carefully because success depends on that.

I am not a person who should talk a lot about results, but the indisputable fact is that, from year to year, we are noticing reduced numbers of crimes done by unknown perpetrators and committed violations. It brought us to the situation to be declared, by the UN agency Habitat, as the safest city in Serbia. Those marks are the greatest award for police. Of course, we are aware that the things aren't ideal and we don't want to idealize them, but when we define a problem, we don't leave it, but we face the problem trying to solve it. That kind of approach needs a lot of efforts, but a positive result is something that compensates all those efforts.

*BS:* What kinds of institutional frames of cooperation does your police head office have with society?

*ID:* The strategic idea was to "convince" citizens to recognize quality in police and our sincere wish to be at their service. Institutional frames, which should be built with local authorities and other institutions, are very important things.

In Kragujevac we achieved it by creating a security council with members that are representatives from police, local authorities, governmental institutions, other institutions, and formal and informal citizen groups. In the council, everybody can give his opinion about every security aspect and ask the police every question which seems important to him. Council work is public and every citizen can inspect its work.

Besides that, we also take care about direct contacts with citizens. We achieve it in an institutionalized way through police presence in the meetings of different groups of citizens. For example, police participate in meetings of local communities and meetings of parent associations in schools. We organize public meetings about different security aspects. We also receive citizens in the police through activities of the counseling office. We organize "police open-door days." And, of course, we affirm police work in neighborhoods and policemen by, without any special reason, visiting citizens and having an opportunity to hear everything that citizens think about their personal security.

We present all of this to the public in press conferences or in the media. As a result of all these activities, citizens' feelings of safety become stronger. Increasing citizen confidence in police is connected with that feeling of safety. In that way, we closed the circle of activities, and achieved good community relations and results. Every point and every aspect in that circle is important and we have to pay equal attention to everything. Interrupting that chain will not give the wished-for result, which is citizens' confidence.

These are long-term activities of implementing preventive methods in communication in one territory. The first results of this way of working appear after a couple of years. And as the time passes, that effect of citizens' confidence and feeling of safety is growing. If we neglect anything I was talking about, we risk destroying the whole system and making impossible to achieve the main goal. The biggest gain for police of using this method reflects in reducing the number of crimes which endanger personal and property safety. It is the goal we wanted at the beginning and it is our award that we got results without using repressive methods. So we reduced repression levels and strengthened preventive work, although it didn't give the results at the beginning of implementing those methods. This could have swayed us and introduced the position of thinking we were implementing the wrong thing. That trap has to be overcome by the persistence in implementing those methods and a strong belief that the goal will be achieved.

*BS:* Last year's new work methods were implemented in the work of uniformed police in the community. For example, police in the neighborhood, community policing, and other methods are being implemented. Would you give your impressions about that?

*ID:* The sector way of uniformed police work has a tradition in Serbia. The policeman's obligations in the sector are to investigate crimes that happened in his sector, in his jurisdiction. Usually it is investigation of easy crimes. Besides that, sector policemen have tasks to implement the court orders, for example, delivering court summons, collecting the information about crime perpetrators who live in their sectors, taking care about public law and order in objects in their sectors—for example, in restaurants, etc. Communication with citizens is insufficient because the sector policeman doesn't have time for positive contacts with citizens.

The neighborhood policeman idea is a developed sector way of work. To achieve that, we divided the city into neighborhoods and we connected policemen's responsibility in a neighborhood with the security situation in the territory that he covers. Neighborhoods, by the territory size and shape, are not in accordance with sectors. The main task of the policeman is to develop positive relations with the citizens, to meet citizens, to meet their problems, and to do everything to solve those problems if they are of a security nature. The policeman has an obligation to introduce himself to the citizens, to explain his tasks, to give them his mobile phone number and give them a possibility for direct contact in every moment. The whole project was gladly accepted by the citizens. My friend told me that a very rare thing happened to him: A policeman knocked on his door, introduced himself, and asked to come in with the goal to meet the citizen and make positive contact with him. These are actions which strengthen citizen confidence in police. I have to mention that the neighborhood police concept is being developed just in Kragujevac, not in the other parts of the country.

The role of "school policeman" has great importance as the continuation of that story. With persistent affirmation of the school policeman role, this concept gained great parent and pupil confidence and was popular. It should be mentioned that the school policeman project developed in the territory of the whole country. First the policeman was in the school in civil clothes. Later it was noticed that his role had been reduced a lot. We realized he had to be in the uniform and to cover the school environment, to check the ways children usually go to and come from school, to notice who came to wait for the child, to be in the school if the school manager or other authorized persons asked him. We achieved much better results and allowed the young people to see the police uniform as something positive. In this way, we formed the attitudes which young people will have for the uniform and police when they grow up. I think it is an ideal preventive moment, but for its effects we need a longer time period. The idea we suggested was accepted by the colleagues in the Ministry of Internal Affairs.

I think that a very important role in creating confidence between citizens and police is the counseling office for citizens which we founded around 3 years ago. The goal is that every citizen can come, any time he wants, into a police station and tell the problem he has—any kind of problem. Police will suggest a solution of the problem or send him to the address where he can solve his problem. The interesting thing is that more than 90% of people who asked for help in the counseling office came because of problems that weren't related to police work. Most often, problems are unsolved neighborhood relations, problems with borders, problems with getting documents which are being issued by the other governmental offices, problems with workers in the institutions (paying electricity debts, water debts, etc.).

My general impression is that everything we have been using in developing police projects in the community (community policing) for the last 4 years didn't have any negative effect, just positive effects. There is no negative effect, but all of them are positive. The good side is that every idea created is applicable and aimed at creating positive relations with citizens and developing partnership relations.

*BS:* What are the biggest problems which policemen of your head office are facing and how do you solve them?

*ID:* We notice a lot of problems in police work. Problems that we have in our police organization we located in cooperation with a small circle of collaborators, and we mostly solved them. I think that the main problem in police organization is motivation. Motivation is related to badly paid, difficult, and risky police jobs. Our policemen, especially faculty graduated policemen, can see people in other institutions with the same profile of education who have easier, but better paid jobs. I think I am very badly paid. But as a chief I don't have an opportunity to show that kind of discontent, while everybody else can do that. From the first day when I became a manager in police, I was dealing with this fact through relations with operational personnel and uniformed policemen. I was working all the more serious jobs, no matter what period of day or night it was. I knew it had been very important to every man to see his chief on the job for hours before or after midnight. My presence is very important while they are working on the case. I know it because it was important to see one of the chiefs being with me when I was an operative person. So I know that my presence, as a chief of the police head office, gives them self-confidence and shows that we share the same destiny. In that case, a successful conclusion of a case mitigates other complaints, including those about salary.

The second very important thing is work conditions. Policemen want to see that we take care of them in correct ways. Since I have become a chief of the police head office, I have been trying to improve work conditions. It could be the simplest thing, like toilet cleanliness, which looked like the worst public toilets in the city. Every office has a computer now and we had one computer per sector before. We didn't have air conditioners, and now every office in the criminal sector and criminal police has air-conditioning. We connected all SIM cards for mobile telephones and we talk inexpensively; in the past we had to use our private telephones and cards. I've tried to improve simple things in the offices like work desks and carpets, which usually were from the 1960s. Today we have these things mostly renovated.

Those are the things which couldn't be unnoticed especially if we keep in mind the fact that I provided most of these, and the ministry didn't give us that. Positive relations we develop with the citizens usually make people ready to help. Then, we take care about the motives for giving presents and carefully judge if somebody could ask for something in the future; we have to escape falling in the trap of corruption. Until now, we didn't have any unpleasant situations and it shows that we made good choices. And we refused many people because we knew that their motives hadn't been sincere. Simply, it is our reality and the reality of the moment. I think policemen see it and I have full moral right to require maximum engagement in addition to small salaries. I think that with my behavior, as a leader, I serve as good example to the others.

Also, it hasn't happened that some worker in the police office has come to me for a conversation, no matter the problem he had, and has been turned away by me. I think that I show respect for the people and it is additional reason to require only best results. I think that, beside the material situation of most employees in our police head office (small salaries, unsolved housing problems, marital partner unemployment), with these relations we reach the maximum of morale.

*BS:* What is your impression about the relation between theory and practice?

*ID:* An institutional relationship between science and practice doesn't exist. The existing level of the theory is reduced in the education processes at the criminalistic-police academy and theoretical activities are downgraded. The articles in the Serbian police magazine *Bezbednost,* published by the Ministry of Internal Affairs, are very useful, but there is no habit to analyze them by the practitioners. In practice, "hostility" for the theoreticians is implanted. There is an opinion that they don't know how policing functions on the terrain (in the reality). My experience says it doesn't have to be always like that. I know faculty professors who care about the contacts with practice. The fact is that it is not a rule, it is exception.

I think that everybody who aspires to be a good expert in any police science field has to have constant contact with the practitioners and to check sustainability of his attitudes in practice, like the policeman trying to find a connection of his attitudes toward theory. For example, criminal procedure uncertainty, changes that happen in the proving procedure, and behavior of the suspected person, are hard to predict things and it's hard to compress them into the book.

I think that theoretical attitudes shouldn't be refused. They are good because a practitioner has an opportunity to check actions he made constantly. It should be great support to the people from the practice and an opportunity for constant building of the attitudes. I think the situation is different now. There is one more hindering fact. The average policeman has a lot of regular obligations and, after he finishes all those obligations, he has neither wish nor will, except rare individuals, to check his professional actions through the theoretical attitudes.

*BS:* In the police practice, are the better people those who graduated Faculty of Law or students who graduated from the police academy as police officers?

*ID:* The difference between those who graduated from the police academy and the Faculty of Law exists. I think that the answer lies in the police education transformation in Serbia. In new the system of police education, many military things were thrown out, although they had been a part of the curriculum in the past. Now attention is more focused on real operative-police activities. Results should be expected. A man who graduated from Faculty of Law can, by the level of the knowledge he gained, adapt to all police aspects without connection with the uniformed sector. He has the advantage. Positive effects from the changes in police education should be expected, so I can't talk about that now. I can give one example. A much better approach to the police activities, work, and results of work is achieved by a graduated lawyer in the economic criminal department than the graduated police officer who is working in that field.

*BS:* Could you, for the end of the interview, give your general impressions about police work, what was well done, and what is waiting for police in the near future?

*ID:* In general, I am satisfied with police work in Serbia. Besides, I think it is important that I like police and police work. I think that a policeman who doesn't have that approach can't be a good policeman. Therefore, the police job has to be liked to be successfully done. In my opinion the most important change is police transformation from the repressive organ into service in the function of citizens. That circumstance impresses me. I think we have traveled a long way for a short time from the closed and untouchable service to the service which works the job because of what it is. I think it is a special quality.

In my opinion, the thing we should work more in the future is police equipment. First of all, I think of criminalistic techniques (actually, of forensics). As much as we develop it, efficiency will be higher. As the quality of processing the crime scene improves, a positive result in crime investigating is more certain. I think it is very important.

In Kragujevac, we proved that a safe community project is totally sustainable. Preventive police actions through different forms of contacts with citizens and the local community, all institutions, and citizen associations have led to many benefits for the police. We completely changed the picture of police in a positive sense and that is something we will work on further.

*BS:* Thank you for taking the time to talk to us.

## Endnote

1. Kragujevac is a city in central Serbia with a population of about 200,000 residents. It is a large, regional, industrial, and university center. It has big economic problems and a large number of unemployed. Kragujevac is remote from Belgrade, capital of Serbia—about 1.5 hours by car.

# 17

# Interview With Edward Sikua, Assistant Police Commissioner, Solomon Islands Police Force[1]

**INTERVIEWED BY OTWIN MARENIN**

**Contents**



**Background**

The interview was conducted at the office of the special representative to the Solomon Islands[2] government of the Regional Assistance Mission to the Solomon Islands (RAMSI)[3] in Honiara, August 5, 2009. The office of the special representative provided the facility and equipment to record and then transfered the interview to my computer. I wish to thank the office for the assistance rendered.

**The Interview**

*OM:* At the beginning, we always say that the interview took place in whatever situation it was, so I'll add that later on. First of all, let me ask you how you got interested in policing. What attracted you to policing? When did you join the force? What kinds of different jobs and roles did you have and carry out as you moved up through the ranks?

*ES:* Thank you. I left school early in my teens. During that time there was a change in the education system. We had what we called in those days provincial secondary schools. I was one of those who went to study at one of these secondary schools and finished what we call form two, the A level.

That is equivalent, I think, to the Australian level. I was attracted to the police because of one thing: discipline and the uniform worn in those days.

*OM:* This was still during the colonial days?

*ES:* No, this was after Solomon Islands' independence, in 1978. And then I joined the Royal Solomon Islands Police Force. The main thing, I was attracted to the discipline of the organization: how police officers behaved—well dressed—they kept themselves looking good. I mean that was what attracted me very much to join the police force.

*OM:* So you entered at the constable level?

*ES:* I joined at the constable level. I had my recruit training then. At that time recruit training was for a period of 6 months. So I enrolled in March and completed the course 6 months later.

*OM:* And what was your first assignment when you graduated from recruit training?

*ES:* After graduation I was assigned to what they called a focal training center, a training center which accommodates newly passed recruits. In that training center you go through all of the core policing roles. You do traffic, you do general duties, investigations, and you do prosecutions.

At this training, the aim is getting the newly recruited police practicing what is learned in the academy, to put theory and learning from the academy into practice. You have supervisors who are directly responsible for, I think, about four or five people. But in addition to the supervisors you have senior members mentoring you on a one-to-one basis.

*OM:* Was this classroom training or did you actually do the work?

*ES:* No, they send you out into the field with your counterpart.

*OM:* How long was that training?

*ES:* We were at the training center for 18 months. It is a 2-year probation period. But if your supervisor sees that you are adapting quickly and you can work independently they confer and then you move on. My first assignment was traffic control in Honiara.

*OM:* How difficult was it controlling traffic at that time?

*ES:* We only had one bridge in Honiara. There was a stand on the bridge and we would get there before 7 the morning and as soon as the traffic became light we came down, and we went up there again before 12 o'clock and again before 1 o'clock.

*OM:* Was this a one-way bridge?

*ES:* It was a single-lane bridge, so we had to control the inflow of traffic.

*OM:* At that time you were still a constable. But some time later you moved up?

*ES:* It took me 13 years to leave being a constable. I moved around in various areas in the police. From traffic I went to the prosecution branch. After that I spent 6 months in general frontline duties. Then I was sent to what we called the police field force. It is a response group within the police force. Within the police force we have the explosive ordnance disposal unit and I was moved there and I spent about 8 years in the explosive ordnance group.

*OM:* These were explosives left because Guadalcanal was a battle zone during the Second World War?

*ES:* Yes, because we have numerous types of ordnance that were from the Second World War. We have a specialized group to try and attend to reports when people find things which are dangerous.

*OM:* So after 13 years, then you moved up the ranks?

*ES:* Yes. After 13 years I was promoted to sergeant. I was still in the field force as a sergeant. I was able to lead a group of five to 10 people on field patrol. During that time we had an issue with the border of Bougainville.

From sergeant I was promoted straight to inspector—sort of an accelerated promotion. We have sergeant and the senior sergeant and then inspector ranks. I was fortunate to be accelerated straight to inspector. I was then moved from being in the field up to administration and more managerial duties. That was a real change for me, moving from the field to the office. It was a challenge and I had to learn quickly; I had to adapt quickly to moving from being a sergeant to an officer. And it's not easy adapting quickly to being an officer, being saluted by colleague sergeants and all that kind of thing. So, for me, it was both a challenge and an achievement.

*OM:* You are currently the assistant commissioner. You are now the highest ranking officer who is from the Solomon Islands.

*ES:* I am the assistant commissioner and am also acting deputy commissioner for administration. There is only one position left for me to reach: commissioner. Certainly, I could move up. I am looking at moving up to that position.

*OM:* Looking at your career, you have seen a lot of changes.

*ES:* Yes.

*OM:* Basically what started off as a colonial force, when you were trying to regain independence, changed to a force which now deals with very different kinds of situations. Looking at those changes, how have these complicated police work? Are the challenges of policing very much different from when you started out?

*ES:* Certainly. I think one very simple example I can give in terms of changes is the number of people in the streets. When I joined the police force as a constable, by 10 o'clock at night we hardly saw anybody in the streets. Vehicles? Probably one vehicle in 2 hours during the night. That has changed very, very dramatically these days.

*OM:* You're talking about Honiara?

*ES:* I'm talking about Honiara because it's the major city in the Solomons. When you go around to the other stations [outside Honiara], it's the same. Back when I joined the police force, by 10 o'clock, people were asleep. Now, these days even in the urban centers you still see people moving around late at night. When you go around to the other substations of the urban centers, it is the same.

*OM:* Are these mostly young people, or all ages?

*ES:* I think the majority are young people, but there are several ages within Honiara moving around and doing business. It is more populated now. And not only people. Businesses operate 24 hours, shops operate 24 hours. Back then shops closed at 8. In the evening people went home. So the environment has changed for policing. We need to change from the style of policing back then to a style of policing that will suit current situations.

*OM:* Would it be fair to say the style of policing back then was more order oriented compared to now, and that it has changed to a more crime-related or crime-focused style of policing?

*ES:* I think, yes. We did change from a style of policing back then to a style of policing capable of dealing with crimes and disorder. I mean, back then you had order. People were orderly and lived a quiet and, what do I say, an orderly life because the population had not yet grown. These days, I think, certainly, policing is more focused on crime. What I can say is that we are now very sensitive of what crimes occur or what may come up next.

*OM:* What crimes occupy your attention now? As the administrator and manager, what would you say to your police in terms of "I need you to focus on this or this or this kind of behavior"? What kinds of crimes are the ones which the police should focus on?

*ES:* Well, at the moment we are focusing on antisocial behavior. I think this antisocial behavior is not simply drug related in essence, not simply disorderly behavior, but rather disorders can create bigger problems. Because if you remember back in April 2007, we did not predict the riots which occurred in Honiara.[4] But there were antisocial behaviors and all of the disorderly behavior that we see around the place, but they, these small situations, contain a big, big issue and, I think, for us violence can happen very quickly like that. So, we do not anticipate a major riot, but any small incident can spark major events.

*OM:* What sparked the riots in 2007?

*ES:* It's certain there is a political aim to it. But I think it is people who are trapped. They took advantage of the situation to capitalize on the situation and that is politics.

*OM:* Looking at the history of riots and major disturbances; at that time the police were faced with a problem that is not a typical police problem. Were the police prepared at that time to deal with that kind of violence?

*ES:* I think, in 2000 and in the April riots in 2007, we ignored the possibility; the RSIP [Royal Solomon Islands Police Force], in particular I think, were not prepared for the riots. We did not see it coming; we were certainly not prepared for that kind of riot.

*OM:* Looking at the history of the Solomon Islands Police, has the quality of policing followed something like a U-shaped curve, first declining and then coming back up? Is that the way you see it?

*ES:* I think, certainly, there was a decline. When I joined the police force, we had a British commissioner, and then we changed over, and the position was localized around 1984 or 1985. We had a local commissioner for about 10 years. And during the majority of the period, I think general duty policing became less focused for the organization. The focus was directed to border policing because we had this problem with the Bougainville border. Therefore, all the efforts, I believe, were directed to the protection of the border and less were directed to policing elsewhere in the country. Therefore, you see the deterioration of police housing, you see less fuel and supplies going to policing elsewhere in the country and the morale of people doing general policing went down, while the morale of people doing policing at the border went up. That is still a big issue between groups of police officers.

*OM:* Even right now?

*ES:* Um, I don't think that it still happens right now because the change of the focus is more on general duties.

*OM:* Just to explain. You talked of the Solomons, which does not have a military, so the police have to do the normal work of the military. When you were talking about the border police, that sort of work could be done by military in other countries.

*ES:* Certainly the Solomons don't have a military to provide protection. The RSIPF is the force that had to be deployed by the government in situations of major internal—how do I say—crises or incidences of disorder and violence.

*OM:* This is a special force?

*ES:* Yes, it is within the police, utilizing resources and personnel in the police.

*OM:* Now, to get to the issue of having foreign interventions helping the local police in terms of capacity and training and so forth. Just looking at the local police, looking at the situation in the country, what sort of policing would you prefer to see done in different parts of the country, in rural and urban areas? Most of the people here in the Solomons live in fairly isolated villages; it is difficult to get to them. What kind of policing is appropriate in rural areas and how is that different from policing that should be done in urban areas or smaller urban areas?

*ES:* Well, I look at it this way: Most people live in the rural areas, the villages. I think the most important thing for them is their gardens, their fruits, and what they do to live in the villages. The priority for people in the urban areas is probably their jobs, their properties, and probably their homes and their shops. Policing in both areas: they want police presence; they want police to be there.

*OM:* On what basis do the police enter and come out of different areas?

*ES:* I think, in the urban areas, they want police to be there. In rural areas, they don't necessarily want police to be there. They want it to be visited; they want to be spoken to and updated and all that, but when they have incidents, they want quick response, they want something to be done, and they probably hope that justice takes place. So, policing for these two areas, certainly, is different and something that, as police management, we need to manage properly and understand how we could provide the services that are required. But, at this stage, now, for the Royal Solomon Islands Police Force, we are still going to be a long way from achieving both situations.

*OM:* What are the constraints—resources? Is it that there are not enough police (which is probably true) and people will themselves take care of a lot of things? And the police (this also happens in other countries) need to deal with local communities. So one of the issues that comes up is the handling of local issues by the police. What should be the relationship of the police with local groups and who should be in charge? How much authority should local people have and how much the police?

*ES:* We are currently working on this and this has been a problem here for a long time. The colonial era used the concept (and it sort of headed away postindependence) of utilizing area constables. This is a concept that, I think, has been used by the British in England before. They have a constable in the village who has some power to deal with issues with the chiefs who are in the village, so that police do not go down there and do everything. We are looking at that again and are working with my police subordinates to see if we can trial this in certain areas and expand it into other areas if found useful.

*OM:* That would be a sort of semi-officer, semi-police?

*ES:* Yes, we are thinking about a name at the moment to suit this position. Certainly, they are not fully sworn officers. They are appointed and they have certain powers, but not as much as, probably, regular police. But they will be working, and alone, on big issues and other issues in the villages.

*OM:* An issue that does come up is coordination with local leaders.

*ES:* Yes, the local leaders, and we would also work with this person who could be a liaison in terms of courts, local courts, and the magistrates. And that way, we bring down justice to a local level and for people to deal with their issues; they may be minor issues, but some of them are important to them.

*OM:* How confident are you that this will actually be done?

*ES:* I believe it will take time. It will take other agencies—not necessarily only the police, but also the courts, the local villagers, and, certainly, some government departments that need to enforce it.

*OM:* Or integrate it?

*ES:* Yes, integrate the approach. Rather than a single approach by the police, it must be an integrated approach.

*OM:* Have you talked, as the police commissioner, with the government agencies you think should be involved with this new concept?

*ES:* Yes. We have been meeting vigorously with the courts, the minister of justice, and the legal people. We have spoken with some elderly statesmen who would like to see not a return to the concept but rather a review of the concept of the village constable. There are things to be added on and there are things that can probably be taken away.

*OM:* A modernized version of the idea?

*ES:* Yes. Yes.

*OM:* Can I ask some question about the RSIPF? That takes a long time to say. Right now, what is the size of the organization?

*ES:* We have an establishment list of 1,070. I think we are now 1,100 strong; we are in 37 locations all throughout the country. There is a master management team that runs the organization and then we have a commissioner and two deputies, four assistant commissioners and several chief superintendents, superintendents, inspectors, and constables. We have nine levels in the rank system.

*OM:* And this is for 2009?

*ES:* Yes.

*OM:* And this is for a population of about half a million people. When you recruit people, what minimal standards do they have to meet to be eligible? First of all, do you recruit only at the constable level and everyone has to work up or do you recruit at the inspector level also?

*ES:* We only have one stream of recruitment through the constable level.

*OM:* In terms of formal education, what are the criteria?

*ES:* In terms of education we take in applicants people who have public reached Form 5, which is around year 13, yes, about 13 years of school. It's really a high school, secondary level.

*OM:* And do you have other qualifications, such as criminal record?

*ES:* Yes, we do criminal checks. We do physical checks, medical checks, and the recruits have to pass, during training, physical fitness tests.

*OM:* Such as?

*ES:* Well, at a minimum, you have to do 50 sit-ups in—I can't remember the precise time—but I think it's about 3 minutes or so. And they have to run a 2 km run in around 10 minutes.

*OM:* That's not too difficult.

*ES:* I think it's not for young people.

*OM:* How hard is it to recruit police?

*ES:* I don't think it is hard. One of our classes just started yesterday. We had 31 people in the course. In our campaign prior to this course, we had 600 applicants, but we only managed to get about 100 people ready for recruitment.

*OM:* They didn't have the qualifications that you wanted?

*ES:* Yes. Some of them have them; some could not make it in terms of the tests taken prior to the selection.

*OM:* Are these written tests?

*ES:* We have a written test and we have an English comprehension test.

*OM:* Do you make an effort to recruit from all the provinces or do you recruit mainly from the bigger islands?

*ES:* Certainly. We have a target for each of the provinces. And we also, for every recruiting class, have a goal of 10 places for females and 20 places for males.

*OM:* So that's a new class. What's the current ratio of police in terms of gender?

*ES:* I am not quite sure of the figures, but I think our female numbers have risen from about 20 prior to the tensions[5] to now more than 100 women—a little more than 10% of the organization.

*OM:* Are women, after they are recruited, given the same jobs as males?

*ES:* Yes, we do try as much as possible to give them all the jobs that male police people do. We don't want to carry women and if they want to join the police they have to go on the beats, they have to do night shifts, they have to do all the rest of the work.

*OM:* Once you are recruited, how long is the training?

*ES:* At the moment, the recruit training is 17 weeks and then you are on probation, which includes the 17 weeks, for 2 years. Yes, the probationary system is still there. And once you are recruited, during the probationary system, you come in for your quarterly retraining, just a refresher process and then after 2 years you are posted out. The ones who are posted out work alone in stations and in posts for about 2 years. For us, that is good enough for a person to become familiar with the work.

*OM:* When you look at training itself, is it mostly classroom instruction? Physical training? What kind of topics are covered in training?

*ES:* In the training we cover most of the core policing subjects in a classroom setting, yes. During the 17 weeks they have the opportunity to visit all policing areas and during probation they are rotated through various areas to get a feel for and to know what's happening in these areas.

*OM:* It sounds like you have a lot of young people in the force. So is the quality of the kind of people that you get improving? Does the future look bright?

*ES:* Yes, there are a lot of young and talented officers coming through. However, I think after the probationary period we have lost quite a number of experienced people because a lot of senior officers have left through dismissal or resubmission and natural retirement. So there is new blood coming into the organization. It will take a couple more years for us to regain the experience and the maturity that we had back then, before the troubles. I'm confident that it will happen.

*OM:* You mentioned the tensions. Can we shift topics and look at the implications for the government and the police? Right now, you have many foreigners, foreign police officers here. Were you involved in the request made by the government to the Pacific Island Forum to come in and assist the local police? Were you part of that discussion or was it just a political decision?

*ES:* Certainly, I was involved in the discussion with the team before that came to a sort of outline of the mission before they actually arrived. I had a not very long discussion, a 1-hour discussion with the chief of the mission. I was part of the group that spoke with them.

*OM:* The obvious question now is this: What have been the relations between the foreign police forces and the local police? Are these cordial? Do the outside police forces respect the local police? In general, what is the atmosphere?

*ES:* Generally for me, certainly in the initial stages, there were misunderstandings. There were issues that probably foreign police officers do not understand like local police officers. Or they don't understand how the local police operate.

*OM:* Do you have a specific incident that comes to mind about misunderstandings? Or is this just a general sense?

*ES:* There are some specific instances. One specific problem is officers walking out of the jobs. There is one incident I can remember back when I was a police commander for Honiara. My staff just walked away from a work situation because they thought they could not work with the foreign officer—a clash of personalities. So we had to deal with the situation.

In terms of the organization, I think the organizations work together cordially and properly and professionally. There are small incidents where personality comes in and this is where we as managers must get in and try to stop the situation right away.

*OM:* Do you work with the managers of the international police contingent?

*ES:* Yes, yes.

*OM:* The current goal that the international police focus on is capacity building. In what areas do you think have the international police been most successful in building capacity and what areas have they been less successful?

*ES:* That's right. I think in terms of one of the areas that I believe the PPF (Participating Police Force) have succeeded very well in capacity building is training. I think, training for the RSIP has come up to a very high level, especially in the training of leadership. I think that was not there before.

*OM:* Is leadership training a special course?

*ES:* Yes. The leadership program is conducted, through RAMSI, by the Australian Institute of Police Management, who is conducting training for us. We have five levels. The first level is operational leadership training at level 1. Then you have levels 2, 3 . . . 5. From 2 to 5, we run assessment services for people on those levels—not to take away anything but just to gauge people to be certain at what level people are. When they're placed at level 2, they go through an assessment center again to go to levels 3, 4, and 5.

*OM:* So your leadership qualities are determined systematically?

*ES:* Yes, yes. I think that's one of the success areas: Training is happening and we intend to keep it going, continue to breed, to grow leaders within the organization.

*OM:* So training leadership development is one success area. In what other areas has the international team been very successful?

*ES:* The other area, I believe, is providing support for the RSIP in terms of, not necessarily material support, but rather how to manage and utilize material resources. I like the way they do it because we need to be able to manage our own resources. Certainly, they give support where necessary and where it is needed. But in terms of teaching people how to use the limited resources, certainly they're scarce in this part of the world but we need to learn how to use what we have.

*OM:* Just to make sure: Foreign police do not do executive policing.

*ES:* That's right. And that's one of the changes. There was a clear time between 2003 and now when we stayed back, and now we are going to move forward and they will do the advisory role.

*OM:* So, initially, they did what?

*ES:* Initially, in 2003 when there was the intervention, they had to do policing because the situation required the international police force to do the arrests, to patrol in the streets and to do the beat work and all that. Around 2005 we started moving forward and the PPF started moving back as advisors.

*OM:* This reminds me of a photograph: Some people are sitting in the first row on chairs and others are standing behind them. At some point the people in the chairs get up and move back and the people in the back come forward and sit down.

*ES:* Yes. Yes. That's right. And I think the PPF did very well in the initial stages. They had to ask RSIP officers to do the beat with them and then moved back, and from there it sort of came naturally that once a call or a report is received, the RSIP officers take it first and respond.

*OM:* Now, those are areas where RAMSI was helpful. Are there areas where you would like to see more technical training or whatever will help the police be more effective?

*ES:* I'd like to see more work in terms of how to progress cases, do investigations. I think what we have now is a whole lot ... [phone ringing] ... sorry.

*OM:* I am taking too much time away from your job. Your real job.

*ES:* [Laughs] That's all right. Yes. We have a huge number of back-load cases and not necessarily major investigations. I think they are simple drunken or disorderly conduct, simple cases. And there are stations that have 400 probably, maybe 1,000 cases outstanding, large backlogs.

*OM:* And that is because of courts. There are no courts in rural areas?

*ES:* Certainly. There are no courts but there may be some cases which—what can I say?—do not have a defendant for a long time and only when the public police find them—there's nowhere to go, there's nowhere to run.

So, I think, that at the supervisory level, if we can do something, we can try to see if cases can be taken care of at the supervisory level. I think this is an area where we still have some difficulties, some resistance from the supervisory to the middle-management level. If we can put some effort there and tidy up the system's procedures and management practices at that level, I believe there will be a lot more improvement in the organization.

*OM:* Do you think the police should have the power to make administrative decisions about cases so they can be negotiated or dismissed?

*ES:* Yes. I think there is something there. The administrative staff may not have that knowledge, may not have that confidence to say, "I'll write this off," because having gone through this process they are scared to do something that can hit back on them again.

*OM:* Do police prosecute cases?

*ES:* We have a prosecution branch in the police, yes. And we have the director of public prosecution, who does the major cases.

*OM:* Is prosecution capacity something that needs to be improved?

*ES:* Yes. Well, it goes back to what you said. There are some areas in the country that do not have courts. Certainly, we have prosecutors in the major areas and provinces. And we have legal services. I believe they are working on trying to improve the court service in the smaller and rural areas.

*OM:* Can we shift a little bit on topic to the relationships between theory and practice? What do you think scholars could or should learn from the police and what do you think police should learn from scholars? What do you think should be their relationship?

*ES:* I believe, just from experience, from practicing policing, that we have a lot to learn from scholars because there are times that we, the practical police officers, are bogged down. We concentrate on just trying to do the work and don't have time to sit back and say, "There must be another way of doing this." And that is where scholars come in and say, "We've been doing it this way. Can we please ask you questions and help the police to think more outside the square on how to do something?" Probably, there could be a better way of doing the job; times have changed, people have changed, equipment has changed.

I see that the work of academics coming in to assist police officers, the practical police practitioners, will improve their work for the Solomon Islands. Because of the changes of our community in terms of computers, technology, and new ideas, the general duty policeman is also struggling to cope with these changes. But if we have academics show us that these are new ideas that will help us cope with the changes, I believe in some areas, especially in policing areas, we need the assistance of academics to help us through.

*OM:* What can academics do? What do they miss?

*ES:* Well, I think that theory needs to be put in practice; I think that academics need to really align their theory with what needs to be done. I think they need to learn from practitioners and in that way not only align theory to what is being done but also help improve what's being done.

*OM:* One of the basic questions we have as academics is to see what works.

*ES:* And how what works can be improved.

*OM:* If academics know how practitioners see what works or not, that would make research and evaluations more accurate and effective.

*ES:* Yes. And in this environment where we are, as you know, we're still way back. And we are still doing things because the law is still back there and the country has moved. So we need academics to take us from there to where we should be.

*OM:* You have to take yourself back to the university. Then you would not need to depend on the academics.

*ES:* Yes. Yes.

*OM:* I don't know how much time we have. To go back a little bit to when we were talking about local police and capacity building, do you think that point where the local police can take over effectively police services from the PPF is close at hand or not?

*ES:* I do not want to sort of put a time to it, but I think that in the next 4 years, if the RSIP and the PPF working together can accomplish what's in the plans already, I believe, the RSIP can start doing what is expected of them. Not necessarily what the PPF wants and what the people of the country want. So, for the RSIP, I think, with what we have now in the plans and with what resources we have to support those plans now, building houses and building office buildings and all that in the next 4 years, once we have those in place and the government framework in place, and our interaction with other government agencies and other state agencies within the country tied down properly, I think we can start looking at moving on our own and probably draw back some of the external resources.

*OM:* One of the big issues in police reforms is that there is not always a lot of trust between the public and the police. How do you go about restoring the trust? Through polite ways of interacting with the public? Through professional conduct? Through effective performance? What sorts of activities can the RSIP do which will begin to restore trust?

*ES:* We are going through a sort of reconciliation program. There are certainly identified areas within the country that do not want the RSIP and those are the areas where we have initiated programs. There could be other areas that don't want police. I think that we, within the next few years and backed by programs, will be able to help people and convince them that the RSIP is still the police force in the country. We need to build trust and work together and in terms of law and order see what we can do together.

*OM:* Who's conducting the reconciliation? Are other police involved?

*ES:* Yes, the ministry of reconciliation is coordinating the programs with the police and all who are involved. The ministry of reconciliation is doing all the negotiations and the mediation and all that.

*OM:* So you have meetings with people in the areas to try to help them resolve their conflicts?

*ES:* The consultation meetings with chiefs start on the 17th of this month. Police officers are going around with teams from other areas to meet with the people and with the chiefs.

*OM:* How well do you think this process will work?

*ES:* It will take time. I know there will be challenges to the process and I know there will be disagreements. But at least we meet. At least there is talking. And, I think that's ...

*OM:* ... Better than fighting?

*ES:* Better than keeping distance and not knowing what people are doing in the other area.

*OM:* Just to sort of sum up at the end: How optimistic are you about things getting better? Because sometimes people look at situations and they become pessimistic and cynical over time. Thinking about what will happen, are you optimistic? Reserved? Cautious?

*ES:* Right, this is what I wanted to say. There is probably a feeling that people don't want to return to the tensions. However, there are disgruntled people. There are people who just want to use the situation to continue to flare out issues. But in terms of policing, I am optimistic. I think the RSIP will grow and will be able to maintain law and order through the country, in time. And building up the right leaders, taking in the right people will be probably be the most effective change we can make.

*OM:* Thank you very much for taking the time to talk to me. I know you have a very busy schedule. I very much appreciate your willingness to talk with me and through me with other audiences.

*ES:* Thank you.

*OM:* OK, now I have to find out how to transfer this interview to my laptop.

*ES:* [Laughs]

## Endnotes

1. The police are still referred to, even by serving officers, as the Royal Solomon Islands Police Force (RSIPF). The official title has dropped "royal" from the name of the SIPF. Technically, the Queen of England is still the sovereign and is represented in the Solomons by a governor.
2. The Solomon Islands gained independence from Great Britain on July 7, 1978. The country comprises a few large islands (Guadalcanal, Malaita, San Schrisobal, Choiseul, Santa Isabel) with about 90 smaller ones scattered across the 900-mile length of the country. The two most important islands are Guadalcanal (a battle site during World War II where the Japanese southward thrust for control of the Pacific was halted and reversed in a series of naval and land battles between American and Japanese forces) and Malaita. The capital city, Honiara, is located on Guadalcanal, close to the former battle zones. About 10% if the country's population of about half a million people lives in Honiara. There are no other significant population centers in the country and most people live in villages that continue a traditional clan-based system (called "wantoks") as the basic form of governance.

   The government, a parliamentary democracy on the British model, has been extremely unstable, with repeated removal and reelections of the same leaders. Politics seems to be based on personalities and local identity ties. Most observers and the public at large assume that people in government are quite capable of looking out for their own material interests.

   The economic basis of the country is severely limited, with foreign companies exploiting timber, mineral, and ocean resources (often with minimal oversight from the government and limited financial returns for the country). The Solomons rank as one of the poorest countries in the world. About half the country's budget is provided by foreign assistance from regional donors and international organizations. The impact of poverty is alleviated for most people because villagers survive on subsistence agriculture and fishing, which, in a tropical climate and location, provide sufficient food resources.

   Tourism could be a major income earner—the scenery is spectacular and battle zones could attract veterans and their families—but there is little infrastructure designed for tourism. In addition, though the beaches could be a major attraction, saltwater crocodiles make swimming hazardous.

   The length of the island chain and the rugged topography of the larger islands make travel extremely difficult. The few roads are mainly along the edges of the islands. Many of the outlying villages are completely isolated and can only be reached by boats or helicopters. Even on Guadalcanal, no roads connect the capital city to the southern coastal villages on the so-called "weather coast." One man in a village on the weather coast told us that it took him 3 days' walking to reach Honiara to find a job. The terrain is extremely rugged—steep, heavily forested hills—and only footpaths traverse the interior. One consequence is that security is not provided effectively by a resource-depleted national police but rather depends heavily on traditional forms of conflict resolution and the authority of local chiefs and clan leaders.

Historically, by popular stereotypes and British colonial policies, people on Guadalcanal and Malaita are portrayed as culturally and temperamentally different and in conflict, with Malaitans described as aggressive and ambitious and "Gualies" as laid back and noncompetitive. The degree to which these stereotypes reflect reality is arguable, but they matter because much of the political discussion and dynamics in the country center on the presumed differences between peoples from these two islands, including explanations why the 2000 tensions and violence occurred and recommendations on how the Solomon Islands Police should deal with conflicts derived from cultural differences.

3. RAMSI is the regional effort, led by Australia but including members from 14 other Pacific Island states, to help establish stability, security, and peace in the Solomon Islands, following the tensions in 2000 that led to a collapse of the government's ability to provide stability and security for its populations. RAMSI was invited by the Solomon Islands government; it is led by a special representative and focuses mainly on restoring security; rebuilding capacity among security providers (basically the RSIP but reaching out to village leaders as well); and government competence in economic and fiscal budgeting, planning, and implementation, as well as addressing the issues surrounding integrity in national and local governmental performance.
4. The riot occurred in the Chinese commercial section of Honiara and led to the almost complete destruction of that section. A video created by the PPF shows serious confrontations between rioters and the police who tried to stop the burning and looting. The police initially were surprised and unprepared to confront the rioters and retreated but came back and imposed order.
5. The "tensions," or the "troubles," is the colloquial reference to the violence that happened starting in 1998 and peaked in 2000 and led ultimately to the request for an intervention force by the Solomon Islands government. The violence was basically between residents from the islands of Malaita and Guadalcanal. People from Malaita had moved into the jobs on Guadalcanal and were seen as depriving the local population of access to work. Both sides mobilized organized militias; the police were drawn into the conflict by their identities with islands and clans, participated in some of the violence, and finally collapsed completely. Only the entry of the RAMSI forces stopped the violence. Even in 2009, some of the leaders of the militias who engaged in murder and destruction were still on the run and could not be brought to justice, largely because of their support from local villagers.

# 18

# An Interview With Richard Monk, Police Advisor to NATO and Independent Consultant

## Interviewed by Kate Story-Whyte

**Contents**



**Introduction**

Richard Monk is an engaging, courteous man whose combination of humanity, intellect, humor, and strong will has led him from his early career as an English "bobby" to holding positions as UN police commissioner in Bosnia and Kosovo. In between these two appointments he was appointed by Kofi Annan to be a member of the high-level UN

Panel on Peace Operations and for 4 years was the senior police advisor to the secretary general of the 55 participating-state Organization for Security and Cooperation in Europe (OSCE), formulating police assistance programs for post-Soviet countries in Central Asia and the Caucasus. Since returning to the UK, he has been welcomed back to his university college in Durham and is a luminary within the City of London Livery Company of Security Professionals, which he helped to found in 1999.

He remains a leading international authority on police capacity- and institution-building in post-conflict states and states in transition. He also maintains a high interest and commitment to earlier work preventing the sexual abuse of children by supporting the need for clinicians to work with offenders in a residential setting. His preparedness to deal openly with hostile community leaders and disaffected young people for whom the police were a perpetual target confirmed the importance to him of carrying his uniform proudly and his authority lightly. He says:

> Most protesters are impressed by leaders rather than institutions. So the mode of intervention representing authority is important. It doesn't matter if they shout and swear at you personally so long as you go and meet them on their turf, you don't walk away, and you are sincere in what you say and do. That doesn't mean giving way to the threat of disorder or allowing spoilers to willfully misrepresent you because it's important that they afford you the same respect. It's always about reciprocal respect and courtesies.

In the course of a long and distinguished career, he has received honors and decorations from the queen, from overseas governments (in Bishkek, the crime investigation center is named after him), and, touchingly, from foreign police colleagues with whom he has worked. He is especially pleased to have been appointed by HM the Queen to be a Companion of the Most Distinguished Order of St. Michael and St. George (CMG). He said, "To receive that particular honor meant winning the approbation of the Foreign Office, which is not generally noted for a warm interest in police affairs."

**Career**

*From the Boys' Brigade to the Metropolitan Police Cadet Corps*

I started by asking Mr. Monk what initially had made him decide to join the police force. He explained:

> I first put on a uniform as a member of the Boys' Brigade when I was 12. The BB was an organization which provided young lads with interests and activities, gym, football, a silver band, and it gave us a first taste of self-discipline and a sense of belonging. My first ambition was to join the Royal Navy but a friend from the same BB Company was already a police cadet and he won me over.

He joined the Metropolitan Police Cadet Corps at aged 16. Cadet training had just undergone an extensive makeover by Colonel Andrew Croft, creator of the Army Junior Leaders Regiment at the behest of the then Commissioner Joseph Simpson, who was determined to change the image of cadets as tea-boys at police stations to a corps of proficient, well-prepared recruits for a seriously understaffed regular force. It was a formative experience, where the physical and educational work instilled in him the importance of "knowledge, teamwork, and fortitude" that he sees as essential elements in policing. One early activity where fortitude was tested to the limit was participation in the 125-mile Devizes to Westminster canoe race, the longest canoe race in the world. During the bad winter of 1962–1963, this meant training and camping in snow and ice.

> I realize now how enormously lucky I was to have 2½ years of further education, physical development, and professional studies in my teens. Much of the energy of youth is wasted today, so I'm pleased that youth organizations are beginning to reappear but disappointed that so many conditions are imposed on anybody wishing to work with children and young people.

About his instructors, he said:

> Many had a military background and some of them had fought in the war. They were formidable characters with a sense of humor—mostly

> enjoyed at our expense—but our respect for their experience and their ethics created a strong sense of identity and pride.

I asked him if there had been some cadets who had been unable to cope with discipline and the rigor of the work. He said, "One or two couldn't cope but we were made to realize that the convoy moves at the speed of the slowest ship. The important thing was to help one another keep going despite the tough physical tests and educational demands."

*First Postings*

His first posting as a constable in 1963 was to Kensington in West London, which he describes as having a bit of everything, from guarding Kensington Palace, the home of Princess Margaret, to patrolling the streets of Earls Court, well known for its frequently unruly Australian backpackers and an overtly gay community. "Drugs, mayhem and murder" were interspersed with long stints "being frozen to the pavement" standing outside embassies or consulates, testifying to their respective unpopularity with paint-daubing protest groups.

A natural driving ability meant that at the very young age of 22, he qualified to drive marked Jaguar "S" types and Wolsey 6/110s and a year later became the youngest top-class driver in the Met driving Q-cars and working with the flying squad. To achieve that distinction meant weeks of intensive driver training at Hendon and "rushing around the Home Counties in a wide variety of unmarked police cars being taught inch-perfect car control" as well as "banditing"—the skills of performing high-speed and above all safe pursuits.

Newly married, he realized that an ambition to work permanently with the Flying Squad would mean "marrying the job. You either got married, or you married the flying squad; you couldn't do both." Instead, he moved to London's traffic division, receiving more "superb tuition" to ride 650 Triumph motorcycles and by chance drive the Met's last Daimler Dart sports car. His delight in recalling these experiences is testimony to a lifelong love of driving and riding. He owns a classic Jaguar and Ducati and Triumph superbikes.

For the moment, the acquisition of skills which took others years to accumulate would be enough but within a year he needed a fresh challenge. He passed the sergeants' exam and stunned colleagues by asking to go back to ordinary duty—a decision nevertheless popular with his commander, who believed that officers at every level should do the same in order to be reminded of the realities of basic street policing. He asked for and got an inner London division and went to the police station covering Belgravia and Victoria—two polar opposites. It was a gamble. He had forsaken specialist status and the freedom to patrol a wide area of London to deal instead with celebrity tantrums, assaults, importuners, drug dealers, prostitutes, domestic disputes, luggage thieves in the railway and coach termini, and drunken vagrants.

> There was a cinema in Victoria close to the railway station where unsuspecting mothers and aunts would take young children to kill time before catching a train home. Unfortunately, the cinema was also a rendezvous for men committing lewd acts who were rather spoiling their afternoons. I remember taking a probationer constable to show him how to arrest these men, one of whom turned out to be a deaf mute. It was difficult to know what gestures to make to confront him with the evidence of his crime.

With 10 years' service, he sat the competitive inspectors' exam, which required vast amounts of material relating to police procedures to be learned by rote and answers to knowledge and reasoning questions to show a precise knowledge of criminal law definitions. After 9 months' perpetual study he was sixth out of 707 candidates: "That year, they made only 24 inspectors. The difference in marks of all 24 was very small. Imagine coming 25th."

### *The Shepherds Bush Shootings*

The Shepherds Bush shootings in 1966 were a watershed in the relationship between the public and the police in Britain. The cold-blooded killing of three police officers in an unmarked Q-car "Foxtrot One One" as they tried to stop three escapees from nearby Wormwood Scrubs Prison shocked the nation in a way never to be repeated. The chief superintendent who coped with the avalanche of media, government, and the service's internal demands would later move to Hounslow and it was from him that a newly promoted Inspector Monk would absorb a unique suite of practical leadership skills.

> He was an extraordinary character. He was tall and fit and walked with the familiar hunched shoulders of an ex-boxer. He never hid behind his rank and his leadership was very much based on his personal authority. If he thought problems on the ground were getting out of hand, he found the person with the influence to stop them and an accommodation was reached.

The person with the influence to stop them was not always a club, pub, or market owner:

> Hounslow had a rising Asian population and that's where I learnt to understand culture and the importance of face. I also learnt the need be your own man rather than trying to be popular—another of my boss's tips—especially in the face of police officers who were weak or idle. You end up feeling lonely for a time but suddenly you realize that the diligent officers are only too pleased to see you draw some lines.

His attendance of a residential inspector's course at the National Police Staff College at Bramshill provided an intellectual surge. "The dean of academic studies made a presentation about the political and religious ideas of the past 2,000 years. I was inspired." He won debating society competitions and spent hours by choice in the historic library of the College's Elizabethan Manor House, absorbing the language of critical political thought, and got down to some serious writing. His newfound "intellectual vitality" won him a Home Office scholarship and he chose to go to Durham University and to St Chad's College to read philosophy and politics.

*(His Studies at) Durham University*

He moved with his wife and three children to a small village high on a hill 4 miles south of the City, having decided that a whole change in lifestyle was as much a boon as a university education. "To be offered a place in the joint-honors school meant taking seven subjects in my first year. So there I was twice as old as most of the students doing twice as much work." He was soon regarded as a benign provider of food, alcohol, cigarettes, and occasionally advice to the younger students. Growing ever poorer as a result of his largesse and sharing the anxieties of other mature students, he founded and became the first chair of the Mature Student's Association—a counterpart to the Student Union—which was presided over by George Aligiah (later to become a distinguished BBC reporter and instantly recognizable newscaster).

> To go to university as a mature student means you are much keener to learn than most students who have slogged away at endless exams, assessments, and interviews to get a place but who are nevertheless quite tired of it and intent on discovering a wider world—and you're part of it. There were some familiar comments about police unfairness or corruption when they knew my background but you do learn how best to respond to them and it's as much the way in which you do, as what you say, that persuades people in your favor. At Durham, there was very little of that anyway. I found that philosophy is like medicine, difficult to swallow but good for you. It helps to clarify concepts and to use language correctly but after a year I decided on politics as my degree course, which incorporated political philosophy and left behind such things as aesthetics and epistemology.

His professor of politics helped refine his responses to difficult questions about tolerance.

> If your arguments are designed to convince, then I am bound to listen to them, but if your arguments are intended to win at all costs, then I think I have a perfect right to oppose you. Karl Popper wrote his book, *The Open Society and Its Enemies,* in the same year that I was born and his arguments against the notion of infallibility, which so accompanies political statements nowadays, has stayed with me.

We talked about the antipolice attitude, which can sometimes be nurtured at universities and which I had witnessed.

> This tends to occur among academics who are of questionable ability and/or who have a secondary agenda. They let down their students because they deny them the capacity to reason. I happen to believe that there is a need for far greater academic and intellectual input into policing and especially international police peacekeeping. There is a considerable

amount of excellent material which remains unread by leaders of international police missions and there are many reasons for this: difficulty in finding the work in the first place, not believing that it has a relevance to the job in hand, a suspicion that it is written by one academic trying to out-argue an academic rival and is written by academics who have only a short encounter with policing on which to base their opinion—or, too frequently, to substantiate their prejudices. That's why I would argue for links with academics who self-select themselves over a period of time and who become respected however critical their views, but who can help formulate persuasive arguments to counter unfounded criticism. I also think they may help set intellectual standards that may persuade poor-quality colleagues to choose another field of inquiry.

*Return to Active Service*

He returned to active service in Fulham in London and in 1981 was one of hundreds of police officers called to Brixton and to the worst race riot in London's history. The experience of being trapped in a firestorm in a London street and believing that his attackers were going to kill him was to remain with him when he was later appointed as head of policing in Brixton following another riot in 1985. Meanwhile, he was promoted to chief inspector and, after a year as head of the Traffic Unit covering the whole of West London, (an appointment that produced a wry smile on the faces of former colleagues), he was plucked from above to become staff officer to Geoffrey Dear (now Lord Dear), then an assistant commissioner at New Scotland Yard.

Geoffrey Dear was one of the most progressive police officers in the country. He was elegant in word and deed and it was a privilege to work with him. And it was with not solely for him and it was not solely for him—he would stress that. A good staff officer has a very privileged position. He sees and hears everything and moves subtly on his principal's behalf while of course claiming to know nothing about sensitive or personnel matters—if anyone is foolish enough to ask, Geoffrey Dear was one of the most progressive police officers in the country. He was k (British slang for knighthood). The secret, as Geoff taught me, is actually to be him and of course that's very akin to an official putting up a brief to a minister—something else I was to encounter later.

It was a time of momentous change within the Metropolitan Police. Margaret Thatcher became prime minister and there were requirements to open more and more doors to critics.

> There was a value to allowing greater access by journalists and academics but it was at a substantial cost. Many of them were of questionable quality and either saw a way to build lucrative consultancies, or they completely abused the access granted to them and produced TV programs that were smug and sneering. It became ever more "progressive" to question everything the police did both outside and inside the service. Too much emphasis was put on promotion candidates to project themselves as critical free-thinkers and business leaders and not enough on testing their policing skills as senior practitioners.

His insistence on retaining core policing skills and doing the job the public expected one to do was given a fresh impetus by winning selection to undergo the 3-month National Academy Associates' Course at the FBI Academy, Quantico, in the United States. Here, it was accomplished field agents who provided much of the teaching, complemented by the vast experience of law enforcement officers from all parts of America, all contributing to highly efficient networks of cooperation and knowledge.

On his return to London as a superintendent in 1985, he had a short stint at Kensington, free to devolve authority for local problem solving to his relief Inspectors and backed up by an information and intelligence unit seizing, collating, and dispensing information of any relevance to preventing and detecting crime.

> They were heady days. Devolving responsibility to the shift inspectors to prevent and clear up crimes was a cynical exercise unless you gave them the resources and the authority to do so. And when they took it, the success rate was extraordinary.

### *The Brixton Riots*

In 1986 Mr. Monk was appointed as chief superintendent and head of Brixton Division, which had just suffered a second major riot following the shooting dead by police of an unarmed black female resident.

He called all the church leaders around him, built a personal relationship with a militant borough council leader, invited lay visitors to inspect police cells unannounced at any time of the day or night, and sent rookie police constables to work in black youth clubs. He divided the area into eight smaller areas, assigned two uniform constables to each and made them the focus on all matters relating to operational policing, whatever the subject. He determined that police officers, including him, would walk anywhere unhindered by "no-go" areas but would carry their authority lightly and would know every community leader and opinion-formers on a first name basis. His boast by the time he left Brixton was that the queen's peace had been restored to such an extent he could not afford to buy a property in any of the earlier riot's street battlegrounds.

> The street where I remember thinking I was going to get killed by a mob is 3 miles from the Houses of Parliament. It struck me at the time that neither that nor anything else was going to help me. So I resolved to do whatever it took to address local problems to stop them ever escalating to that level again. The fact of asking protagonists to help and listening to what they say gets you started and, provided you're sincere, you pick up supporters on the way. I was indebted to one remarkable church leader, Pastor Nelson, whose proud boast was that none of the youths in his church had ever been involved in the riots. That was entirely as a result of his personality and presence, but he wasn't a pushover and if he thought you were going off track he wouldn't hesitate to say so. My predecessors started a lot of the work with community dialogues and consultative groups and I was privileged to carry it on.

He was appointed a commander at New Scotland Yard in 1988 responsible for seven departments dealing with crime and crime prevention and among which was the Obscene Publications Squad, universally known as the "dirty squad," which drew his attention to increasing seizures of pornography featuring young children. Creating the first police pedophile unit in the UK, he uncovered a network of child and ritual sexual abuse and took the unconventional step of sending investigators to talk to offenders at the Gracewell Clinic, the first residential treatment center of its kind in the world.

In 1990, at a major conference, he went public on the scale, persistence, and awfulness of the offending, stunning journalists and his colleagues alike about the damage done to people's lives by early sexual abuse and created a watershed in the willingness of government, media, and victims to address the subject openly. His belief that more than punishment was necessary to interrupt the distorted thinking of offenders led to his becoming a founding trustee and later chairman of Baroness Faithfull's Foundation to provide residential treatment to offenders and to work with the National Association for the Care and Resettlement of Offenders and with Victim Support. His proposals (made public) that courts should impose indeterminate detention orders and that there should be a minister with responsibility for children's affairs were loudly opposed. Today, both are taken for granted.

The controversy at the time raised the confidence of victims to speak out and it became evident that the scale of the problem was almost overwhelming. "Elderly people were telling phone-in programs or writing to me about how the abuse they had suffered as children had dogged them all their lives. It was with them every day." The Internet has made everything a whole lot worse. As he points out:

> Access to satanic Web sites is about four clicks away. [He stresses the need for realism about the ability of pedophiles to seduce young children in chat rooms and the revelation that young teenagers still meet men in their 40s despite the fact they have learned their seducer's age.]
>
> Investigators are still struggling to bring offenders to court that have abused very young children. If you want to evade conviction, put on a goat's head and think what the reaction of the court is likely to be when the child describes being abused by a goat. But the real issue is the failure to intervene in the distorted thinking of the abuser to prevent him—or her—reoffending. We have been totally unable to persuade governments of the need for residential treatment centers irrespective of the success of the Gracewell Clinic, now closed, or whether offenders are sent to prison. People just can't understand that pedophiles in these places aren't a threat because they're exposed and known. It's the abusive youth leaders, priests, and even policemen who are the threat because they go to great lengths not to be caught and, of course, the children don't tell.

In 1991, he took the unconventional step of moving sideways to become an assistant chief constable of Devon and Cornwall.

Three-quarters of the two counties are surrounded by sea, so when the visitors have left there is more time and opportunity to set up responses to local problems and to do this on a cooperative basis with the heads of Probation, Social Services, Health, and the Crown Prosecution Service from both counties. It was highly productive to be able to choose the priorities we would all agree on tackling. I also got the courts administrators to set up court user groups and that cleared away a lot of the acrimony that existed between court staff and the police.

*International Postings*

Eschewing the possibility of being considered for deputy and chief constable, Mr. Monk returned to London in 1994, appointed by the home secretary as assistant inspector of constabulary for England and Wales.

Michael Howard was home secretary at the time, and I was sent to New York to find out more about zero-tolerance policing from Commissioner Bill Bratten and whether it could be successfully introduced into Britain. Bratten's view was that "nobody's first crime is an armed robbery," so petty crimes such as graffiti, pick-pocketing, and criminal damage were targeted while he was head of the Transit Police. The subway was cleaned up and millions of dollars of extra revenue flowed in because people began using the transportation system again. When he became commissioner of the NYPD, he expanded the same strategy by insisting that his officers take back the streets. Also, his view was that he couldn't hold 33,000 police officers accountable but he certainly could 72 precinct commanders, which happened to be the exact same number of divisional commanders in London.

Different from London, he had the power of hire and fire and was vigorous about moving poor performers. If precinct commanders showed they didn't understand what was happening in their areas, they were gone by midday. Much of the turnaround in NYPD performance was attributable to Jack Maple, the principal deputy commissioner—one of the most extraordinary men I've ever met—who was full of practical ideas like cold casing and Compstat, and who had the authority to implement them. In a short time, Bratten and Maple were able to claim that there were about 3,000 people alive in New York, because of interventions by NYPD, who would otherwise be dead.

Richard mentions the larger salaries of the U.S. forces and particularly their forensic budgets, regretting that the UK does not have the same resources. I asked him what he brought back from the United States.

> Twenty years ago, one of the agents at the academy mentioned to me how they had just acquired an electron microscope which cost around a million dollars. The cost didn't seem to be a problem. I was impressed by the way the FBI maintained their network of information and skills. America is very good at answering the call to the flag and there is a pride among its federal agencies. The Hoover years were a bit of a tyranny, but the leadership of subsequent directors has raised their technical knowledge, skills, and resources and expanded their cooperation with police forces in the United States and abroad.

Increasingly called upon to review policing in oversees dependencies, he was a natural choice to be sent to assess the requirement for UK police to be deployed in Bosnia following the signing of the Dayton Peace Accords.

> At the time, I was advising the Ministry of Defense about handling indictments for war crimes and procedural issues for the Yugoslavia and Rwanda criminal tribunals. The home secretary wanted to know how to respond to constant demands by the Americans to add British police officers to the UN mission in Sarajevo. I remember being turfed-out [thrown out] of the nets and the back of a military plane at what was left of Sarajevo airport and within a few minutes everybody had cleared off. Eventually, I found a German soldier in a Land Rover and persuaded him to drive me to the UN headquarters, which was on Snipers' Alley. As I walked down a deserted first-floor corridor trying to find somebody, I noticed several very small holes in the corridor partition and on the other side of the corridor a corresponding hole, so you could line up the two to see where the sniper had been.
>
> After 3 days, I was convinced of the humanitarian need and that the UK was conspicuous by its absence. The foreign secretary was supportive but of course the trick was selling the idea to HM Treasury. We managed to raise 30 officers from UK police forces and subsequently another 30 after I had made an assessment of the effectiveness of the first. A few months later, I was summoned to the Foreign Office to meet

Kai Eide, the new head of the mission, who said, "Look, we need a new police commissioner and it's you."

### *Full-time International Career—Third UN Police Commissioner Bosnia and Serbia*

And that really was the beginning of my full-time international career. I had already been appointed in my own right to inspect the UK sovereign base area in Cyprus, so I knew something about overseas policing but this was a whole new experience. I found myself retiring from the police service on a Sunday in 1998 and on the Monday I was in Bosnia, where I became the third commissioner of the United Nations International Police Task Force (IPTF), responsible for rebuilding and reforming the police forces in the Republic Srpska and Federation of Bosnia Herzegovina.

The diplomatic community were trying to make up their minds about what the rule of law really meant and how the police forces were going to break free of the local political influence—which of course they wouldn't and as far as I know has still not been achieved. All the members of the police forces, many of whom had just dyed their army fatigues blue, had to be vetted against names held in The Hague of those allegedly involved in atrocities. On top of all the obfuscation, there was the baffling situation of the Federation of Bosnia-Herzegovina having 10 different cantons and therefore 10 ministers of interior and although the Republic Srpska had only one interior minister, his writ didn't really run in the eastern part of the country, which was more closely allied to Serbia.

As soon as you sorted out one awkward political situation, another would be presented and then another. I tried to match our response to people according to the degree of misery or injustice being suffered. For instance, there was a village named Bauci in Bosnia close to the border with Croatia around which Croatian police officers had created an exclusion zone, blatantly trying to annex a piece of Bosnia. I went there and found 16 women in a house outside the village—protected by only three exterior walls, UNHCR polythene sheeting at the windows, and no sanitation—clustered together in the bitter cold while their menfolk, all in their 60s, were clearing rubble from the only road leading back to their village, from which they had been forced to flee 4 years earlier.

People were being blatantly intimidated not to return and there seemed to be ambivalence to their wretched plight, which prompted me to ask the high representative administering Bosnia whether he was interested in actually knowing where Bosnia was. Irrespective of the high politics, I conspired with the high representative's military adviser, a Brit, to issue a directive to Com SFOR and to me to normalize the situation, which we did very easily. The test for me of whether the rule of law had been established became whether people could seek redress for their grievances, including against police officers for failing to respond as they should.

I kept questioning what it is that the international police force should be doing to stand the local police forces up while recognizing that the police officers were also living in fear of retaliation and brutal intimidation. If, for the same reason, judges at court were refusing to convict, what incentive could there possibly be for a police officer asked to live on 40 dollars a month to try to tackle ruthless thugs? So many of the fundamental policing needs had never properly been addressed, and allied to this was that, within some of the police contingents provided to me by 43 countries, there were international officers who behaved disgracefully.

Instead of talking about these matters I put them into recommendations in my closing report, which caught the attention of the French undersecretary of the Department of Peacekeeping Operations in New York and that probably led to my appointment by Kofi Annan in 2000 to a panel set up to look at the criticisms and failings of past peacekeeping missions, under Lakhtar Brahimi, a former foreign minister of Algeria. It was a very distinguished nine-member panel and it was the first time that policing had had a voice at that level. It wasn't difficult to convince distinguished colleagues of the importance of establishing the rule of law and that member states had to put greater commitment into choosing police officers that they were sending to missions as well as supporting them while they were there and also when they returned home. In short, policing had to be given much higher importance.

Kofi Anan put our report on the table at the Millennium Summit and all the ambassadors threw their hats in the air and said, "This is wonderful, absolutely outstanding, our guide for decades to come," but failed to mention that, unfortunately, they hadn't got time to read it. However, it was very well written by Bill Durch, a leading academic on peacekeeping, so critics and other academics read it and it is still waved in the air to remind officials and politicians of what they should be doing.

*OSCE Plan for Policing Kosovo, and Follow-on Report* After a year in Bosnia, he was asked to quality assure the OSCE plan for policing Kosovo and simultaneously provide an assessment for Foreign Secretary Robin Cook on the actions necessary to establish the rule of law. Shortly after that, he was asked to write a report on a follow-on mission to the UN mission in Bosnia and then to go to Belgrade to make a study of the police in the former Republic of Yugoslavia just weeks after the cessation of the NATO bombing.

> I started working with a table and a chair in a garage of a house that was to become the OSCE's headquarters in Serbia—a fairly typical beginning for anything to do with policing in diplomatic missions. I was there before Milosevic was arrested and got to know Dusan Mihailovic, the interior minister who gave the order for him to be seized. Although I had recruited an interpreter/translator, I was finding it very difficult to get Serbian police officers to talk to me. Mihailovic didn't respond immediately, but a few days later I was taken to meet him in his summer retreat in the mountains and through his personal assistant, who was an accomplished simultaneous interpreter, we had an enlightening exchange. A few days after that, police officers started to open up to me and it was obvious from what they knew about me that I had been researched and approved of.
>
> After 4 months, of which every day was spent gathering information, I started to write my report. I sat in a spare bedroom of my bohemian apartment in the center of Belgrade City for 16 days typing on a laptop, during which time the temperature stayed at 40° and I had no air-conditioning. All the papers and notes I referred to were laid out on the floor of the living room and, by sticking to a rigid daily routine, I gradually incorporated my findings into the report. It was probably the hardest job I've ever undertaken. I had to do my own shopping and laundry and also help the OSCE head of mission to set up a police assistance unit. My talented interpreter translated the entire report, although there was no budget to pay her. It was instructive that nobody thought that the people I was talking about should be able to read it. I made over a hundred recommendations and I really didn't want them to be presented in a dictatorial fashion. Actually, the Serbian government wholeheartedly accepted what I had written and used my report[1] repeatedly in future years to validate their demands for assistance from the international community.

The rapport that Richard Monk had won with senior police officials was to prove helpful in the future when relationships between Kosovo and Serbia reached a dangerous low following Kosovo's declaration of independence.

*Kyrgistan*

Very soon after I returned to the UK, the OSCE decided that crime and organized crime were of sufficient importance in the work they did that they ought to have a senior police adviser. Fifty-five countries had to approve my appointment, which should have warned me there and then that bureaucracy was going to play a big part in my work. The early experience was typical. I had to start with not very much, build up a case to have a secretary, and then formulate successive cases to recruit police officers and give everybody a vision and justification about the value of police assistance programs.

In some countries, this was what we were able to do, notably in Kyrgyzstan, and it was Kyrgyzstan which seemed to be the Central Asian state which was most prepared to accept outside assistance while resonating with Russian influence. I was profoundly stirred by the dilapidated state of the academy in stark contrast to the energy and smartness of the staff, particularly those working in the crime investigation center with the bare minimum of teaching aids. I persuaded some countries to put money into an assistance program, on the basis of reforming the culture, which could be part of the better training we had envisaged, and from that there grew a relationship between my unit and the Kyrgyzstan Police which is there to this day. Kyrgyzstan's police were desperately short of every item of equipment and their forensic capacity, scenes of crime procedures, and management of exhibits were dire. Furthermore, it may be very gratifying to a donor state to provide a sophisticated gas chromatograph or a fleet of new scenes of crime officer's vehicles but within a short space of time they're all pretty worthless if you don't provide the finances to purchase the gas or the spares to repair the vehicles.

Reforming the culture of policing is a long haul. It's got to be driven from the top and any interior minister brave enough to do it will be attacked by political die-hards as much as senior officers who can't or won't grasp the need for it. In the former Soviet states there are very strong links between political parties and police officers, so depoliticization and decentralization are among the first steps to be tackled.

In 2003, I commissioned a cup to be made and presented annually to the student who, over the preceding year, had shown most the quality of endeavor. This is a characteristic I greatly value because the naturally gifted are not always the most reliable or hardworking. I've just returned from presenting the cup at the academy's passing-out parade in Bishkek at the invitation of the minister of interior. That's a measure of our mutual regard for one another.

The important thing for me is always trying to build up policing into a profession. To do that requires a long-term commitment. During my time with the OSCE, most countries could only give assurances of support for a year because they were hamstrung by annual budgets. Others made promises and just broke them, whereas some countries—and notably Norway—would make an enduring commitment and stick to it. Political, social, and economic development is a slow process dependent on internal security and being free from corruption. Too often in the past we've believed that we can deliver on everything in a year and retreat. This links to one of my long-held beliefs that instead of the United Nations or the OSCE at the conclusion of a mission handing over to another large international agency like the EU, it would be better to arrange for four or five different countries to form links on topics in which they are internationally recognized to be preeminent. In some cases, this could include the Russian Federation, which has some very accomplished forensic scientists. One of the things I was able to do was to persuade the permanent council of the OSCE to waive the requirement for external experts being seconded to an OSCE assistance program to speak English. So, I could use Russian fingerprint experts in Kyrgyzstan who didn't speak a word of English but of course were understood by the practitioners they were instructing.

The point is to understand the culture and then find not just the expertise but also a cultural similarity because if you can achieve that (and while there may be all sorts of political issues to be sensitive to), police officers are happy to come without all that baggage. There really is a fraternity and a willingness to share information among good police officers across the world because they recognize that criminals have absolutely no compunction about dealing with one another irrespective of national or ethnic boundaries. Sadly, despite that willingness, they are frequently confounded by national data protection laws and a prohibition on intelligence contributed to one international agency being passed to another. This is immensely frustrating. Radical opposition is frequently financed by cross-border crime and while there may be extremists who will never be reconciled, criminals have absolutely no qualms about who they deal with as long as it contributes to the pot. This is particularly true where drugs are concerned. I have learned that in some cases the amounts of money are incredibly large—so much so that, in some countries, governments aren't powerful and the powerful don't govern. The criminals have stolen the state.

*UN Police Commissioner for Kosovo*

In 2006, Mr. Monk was persuaded by the U.S. Institute of Peace to facilitate work between police, NGOs (nongovernmental organizations), and politicians in Nepal and it was while there, in early 2007, that he received a call from UN New York to take over at very short notice as the police commissioner of both the 9,000-strong Kosovo Police Service (KPS) and the 2,000-member UN International Police following the shooting dead of two protesters by a Romanian-formed police unit and the political crisis that followed.

What made the situation so serious was that both had been shot in the back of the head with rubber bullets, which aren't supposed to cause that degree of damage or injury. Unfortunately, the bullets were out of date by 13 years and the rubber had gone rock hard.

What struck me forcibly was how little we, the internationals, had done after 8 years to stand up the Kosovo Police Service in terms of preparing it to become the future single law-enforcement authority for Kosovo. We had over 2,000 police officers from 43 countries pursuing one agenda and about 9,000 Kosovo police officers pursuing another. I took very seriously my role as the commissioner of the Kosovo Police Service and I determined that my principal role was to put in place the vision, strategies, structures, and systems that would enable them to manage their own affairs.

I was very grateful for the input of internationals that "got it" and who understood what needed to be done but, sadly, they were in the minority. Most UN missions are like that. The imperative was to show the KPS at senior level how to make policy; how to make difficult decisions about how to spend the very restricted budget; the importance of creating an institutional memory; how to put in place acceptable personnel procedures for recruiting, selecting, training, and promoting staff; and how to plan on the basis of what the policing requirement truly was rather than what they thought it was. In addition, the minister of interior, who I discovered had not been appropriately informed or consulted on anything previously, had to contribute to and then own the vision of what policing in Kosovo should be like in 5 years.

I was only supposed to be there for 5 months and my contract overran by another 7 months while we waited for the EU to take over. But I had invested such a huge amount of effort into the development of the KPS that I wanted to stay and see that it didn't unravel. I had become quite proud of being in charge of the Kosovo Police (which, for 80% of my time, the top team of generals touchingly let me believe I was). When the time came to leave, it was quite an emotional parting.

But back we come to the vexing issue about the willingness of UN member states to provide adequately prepared and committed police officers for the staff of the Police Division in the Department of Peace Keeping Operations (DPKO) in UN New York to deploy to field missions. Critics frequently overlook the fact that the UN does not exist independently of its member states. And it is their domestic agendas and political rivalries that frequently dilute the effectiveness of what the secretary general is able to do. In the past when the UN set up a new mission, it was the military that generally did most of the planning. Recently, there is an acceptance that the aftermath has also to be planned for. Policing and the administration of justice are very important factors and that's not what the military are there to do.

The real issue for me is not just a commitment to policing, but a commitment to the whole criminal justice system. Unless you have that—and frequently we don't—it's impossible to make policing effective or persuade police officers to arrest people who shoot at them if, when they go to court, the attacker is promptly released within hours. Not surprisingly, after being shot at for a third time, the police officer rather loses interest. And if the judges are being bought off or intimidated to such a degree that they cannot hear a case because, whichever way it goes, their lives are in danger, then we need to bring in and protect international judges and prosecutors until the place has been cleaned up. That also requires a penal system that's fit for purpose—something that's always at the bottom of anyone's list. Fortunately, we've spotted the importance of clarifying whose authority, laws, or criminal codes we are operating under.

### Concluding Remarks

I realized during the interviews that I had listened to brief recollections of a career in and around policing spanning almost 50 years. Very evident was a settled view of policing as a profession demanding the highest standards of behavior and performance in return for which society would accept its co-relative obligation to support its police. Knowledge-based policing was a recurring theme of his discourse as well as a compassion for people under duress but unable to defend themselves. I wondered how he would summarize his outlook. He said:

> Well, I've mentioned my belief that the initial basis for most interaction is reciprocal courtesy and respect. I wholly reject political interference in operational policing and I don't like the imposition of policing by numbers as an alternative to inculcating knowledge, judgment, and discretion. In this country, I lament the damage done to the dignity of the office of constable, which is what so many foreign police forces admired about us. As a personal credo, I suppose it's that you only truly fail when you stop trying.

Leaders like Richard Monk never "stop trying"; their contribution to both domestic and international policing has ensured the development of late twentieth and early twenty-first century policing as a truly ethical and "moral profession with unflinching adherence to the rule of law and human rights as the embodiment of humane values."[2] Enforcing the law must be seen as an essential part of social stability, but it is also essential to ensure that the law is enforced fairly and with respect for the society—both as a whole and as individuals—in which it operates. This is no easy task. The vital early lessons in self-discipline and self-reliance, teamwork, and the development of a sense of belonging and the ability to respect others—no matter what their background—from which Richard benefited can be difficult to inculcate in settings of severe social or emotional deprivation or outright conflict.

Modern policing requires a balance between tolerance and a strong commitment to values, between procedures and discretion, and between the real and the ideal, the practical and the academic. Domestically, policing works when officers are known, trusted, committed, and respected; internationally, policing works when the donor countries are known to be reliable, committed, and competent. Richard Monk has worked tirelessly and with unparalleled effectiveness in both arenas to raise the profile and the efficiency of policing as an integral part of modern social justice.

## Endnotes

1. OSCE Study of Policing in the Former Republic of Yugoslavia. (2001).
2. Cited from International Police Executive Symposium (IPES) Mission Statement, at www.ipes.info.

# 19

# Interview With Stephen White, Former Chief Police Officer and Current Head of "EUJUST LEX"

## The European Union's Integrated Rule of Law Mission for Iraq

INTERVIEWED BY RICHARD MEARS

**Contents**



### Introduction

I first met Stephen White in 2007 in Amsterdam. At the time I was the chair of the International Managers of Police Academy and College Training (IMPACT) section of the IACP, and we had invited Stephen to present an overview of the EU Justice Lex mission he was managing in Iraq. Stephen accepted our invitation and he also brought a couple of high-level Iraqi justice officials with him to participate in the IACP European Executive Leadership Conference as well.

I had never had contact with Stephen before; however, we have met several times since and he has also become a member of the IMPACT advisory board and a personal friend. Stephen has had an outstanding career in police work and he is a very personable and approachable man in spite of his busy schedule. He and I quickly connected via our respective police backgrounds and over the last few years we have had the occasion to tip a few beverages together and reflect on the many changes in policing since we became police officers in the mid-seventies. I have asked Stephen to respond to a number of questions in order to capture his ideas and impressions and in hopes that they will serve as a source of inspiration for the many officers that will follow us into one of the most challenging and rewarding professions in the world.

## The Interview

*RM:* Tell me a little about your career, length of organizations worked in, movements, and specializations. What surprised you about your career development? Did your work prove as interesting or rewarding as you thought it would?

*SW:* I have had quite a varied set of opportunities and experiences despite being based in Northern Ireland for most of my police career. I was very fortunate to have been entrusted with some important positions of responsibility and I feel this all stems from having a solid foundation based on some excellent educational and training opportunities and in terms of "lifelong learning." That is why I am so passionate about leadership and training. I benefited greatly from some excellent mentoring, exemplary leadership, and formal training and I think all current and future leaders in law enforcement have a key role to play in that respect.

### *Career Highlights and Beliefs*

*SW:* As a young man growing up in 1970s Belfast and the son of a police officer, I experienced a firsthand the demands on police officers serving the community—especially one that is divided, in conflict, and suffering daily terrorist atrocities. As soon as I was old enough, I joined the local British Army regiment (Home Service), which meant that during the day I was studying (economics and business administration) at university while, at night and weekends, I was on patrol deterring and detecting terrorism. The decision to join the security forces at that time was life changing. I had an aptitude for the work, enjoyed being part of something which I believe was totally noble (serving all the communities in Northern Ireland and trying to prevent whole-scale civil disorder) and I was very quickly asked to accept leadership roles. I came to see it as my duty and responsibility to devote my efforts in this direction.

As soon as I graduated from Queen's University, Belfast, I joined the police—the Royal Ulster Constabulary (RUC)—following in my father's footsteps. In the RUC, like all UK police services, all sworn officers must join at the bottom tier. I think the requirement of having to experience policing at all levels and gaining promotion through the ranks solely on merit results in senior officers understanding the challenges their subordinates face and, hopefully, gains their respect. I saw service as a young (part-time) soldier and as a police constable in some of the most bloody and violent years of the Northern Ireland conflict. Memories of those years provide me with the motivation to do everything possible to ensure my own country never returns to those times and to support conflict resolution efforts in other parts of the word, most notably Iraq.

In 1982 I was selected to take part in a UK-wide accelerated promotion scheme. For 1 year, as a young sergeant, I was posted to the UK Police Staff College at Bramshill. It proved to be another life-changing experience. Along with some of the UK's (current) most senior police officers, I was exposed to some of the best academic and professional training opportunities available. The ability to interact with senior police officers and experts from all over the world opened my eyes and gave me an appetite for learning and advancement. I was enabled to visit other countries and experience other law enforcement organizations and, during this time, with some assistance from other agencies including the FBI, completed a thesis on police suicides and post-traumatic stress disorder.

This was prompted by the increasing rate of police suicides in Northern Ireland at the time and led to me doing more work in this area at various times in my career. I strongly believe that most police officers are ordinary human beings, often exposed to exceptional experiences and asked to complete extraordinary tasks. They require, and deserve, a form of leadership which combines professional excellence with an understanding of, and adequate response to, the stresses and demands on individual officers and their families. Throughout my career I have always attempted to address morale, human resource management, and occupational support from an organizational and individual perspective.

Returning to Northern Ireland in 1983, I served at the sergeant, inspector, and chief inspector ranks mostly in uniformed operations. My preference was always for local policing—providing a normal police service during abnormal conditions. I enjoyed all aspects of "community style" policing, albeit having to carry it out in armored vehicles, accompanied by military resources and taking measures to minimize terrorist impact. During these years (1980s) I saw a lot of violence firsthand, with colleagues murdered and police stations destroyed in bomb attacks. Nevertheless, my interest was always centered on the role of leadership. My specialty was training—all aspects of training: needs analysis, curriculum design, delivery, and, evaluation. I designed stress prevention interventions and leadership courses working in partnership with a whole range of experts specializing in the subjects.

I developed and introduced community awareness training for the first time in Northern Ireland when, in 1992, I was appointed as one of the youngest ever commandants of the RUC's Police Training Centre. Around the same time, my force had sponsored me to complete an MSC thesis on police training and enabled me to examine training practices and exchange ideas with North American agencies such as the FBI, DEA, NYPD, LAPD, and RCMP. Such experiences have left me totally committed to the view that policing must be seen as an international activity and we must all support networks and organizations which facilitate exchanges of intelligence, information, and best practices.

In the summer of 1993 I was transferred to another posting which opened my eyes to another aspect of policing—the most political and strategic position: that of the chief! For almost 3 years I served as staff officer to the then chief constable (of a police service which at that time had almost 16,000 employees—13,000 sworn and 3,000 unsworn). I accompanied and staffed the chief at many important, historic and poignant events, from U.S. presidential visits to a series of police funerals as the force suffered multiple casualties and from executive board meetings of Interpol to discussions around police responses to terrorist ceasefires with government and nongovernmental organizations (NGOs). The job was one of the most stressful, demanding, and difficult I have ever had, but, if I am honest, it is the one where I learned most. I saw how chiefs of police must balance operational independence with accountability to the law, the community, the media, and the formal oversight authorities. It helped form my view that chiefs need to possess skills that include visionary, strategic, change managers, not just good operational managers. They need to have one eye on the immediate organizational challenges they face, but the other needs to be scoping the future and preparing for it. Today's world is no place for reactive police leaders; we all need to be proactive.

In 1996 when I left the chief constable's office on appointment to area commander in North Belfast, I felt privileged to have been given an insight into leadership at the top level. I faced many challenges in the new post: ongoing terrorism, wide-scale riots and disorder as Northern Ireland's conflict deteriorated into territorial disputes over traditional marching rights and protests, organized crime, and major organizational reforms. Thankfully, the HQ experience, to which I had just been exposed, guided me as I concentrated and targeted efforts on delivering modern, consultative, community-based policing (combined with an analytical and intelligence-led approach). My main aim was to gain public trust and confidence—the essential elements required to successfully fight any war against crime, terrorism, and disorder.

During my less than 2 years there (I was selected to attend another promotion course to prepare me for chief officer roles and responsibilities), my area and its local population suffered a lot of intercommunity strife. There were sectarian murders and large-scale riots and I commanded many major operations to deal with parades, demonstrations, riots, and terrorist incidents. My officers and I literally came under fire (not for the first time, in my case) and I witnessed, firsthand, bravery and professional restraint as my colleagues and I regularly faced very violent situations.

These events and others, before and since, helped me formulate my ideas and concerns about police use of force. Appropriate training, suitable equipment, a wide range of tactics, proper command and control systems, evidence gathering, community consultation, independent oversight, strategic planning, and visible leadership—they are all essential to ensure that police responses to violence are authorized, justified, legal, proportionate, and accountable. These are areas I have addressed many times when providing guidance and advice to other police bodies around the world. I am also passionate about supporting officers who have been involved in fatal and nonfatal shootings. From personal experience, I know that people react very differently. Nevertheless, there are good practices and principles which, if followed, will minimize inevitable difficulties.

From 1997 to my (early) retirement from policing I held some of the most unique and interesting posts in UK policing. After another spell at the police college and at Cambridge University, where I gained a postgraduate diploma in applied criminology and a second master's degree, I was given responsibility to develop a countrywide community policing strategy and to lead the police service's Community Affairs branch. These duties in turn led to an invitation to lead a joint NI-USA initiative to enhance policing in a divided society. This entailed partnerships with NGOs and major U.S. police departments (Atlanta, New York City, and San Diego), where we examined the role of police in society and a range of approaches and strategies to engage communities and, particularly, excluded and minority groups.

At around the same time, I was invited to support justice and police reforms in Mongolia. I worked there on seven occasions during 1998–2000, recommending and then supporting community policing strategies suitable for that country and its culture. I found myself from that point on being requested and permitted by my authorities to provide consultancy and training in various countries that were interested in Northern Ireland's conflict resolution process and the community policing model which I was charged with developing. The countries I visited and worked in included Serbia, Indonesia, and Bulgaria. As I visited each country I learned more about and became more interested in international policing. Just as I believe that there are many lessons to be learned from the reconciliation process in Northern Ireland and the role which policing played, I also believe that exposure to other models of policing in different cultures enhances any police chief's professional understanding and experience.

During 1998 and 1999, under terms of reference defined in the "1998 Belfast Agreement," an independent commission (under the chairmanship of Chris Patten, former governor of Hong Kong) was established. Its task was "to inquire into policing in Northern Ireland; to consult widely; and to make proposals for future policing structures and arrangements, including the police force composition, recruitment, training, culture, ethos and symbols."

The aim of the proposals was to create a police service that would be effective, operate in partnership with the community, cooperate with other police forces (including the Garda Siochana—the Republic of Ireland's police department), and be accountable to both the law and the community it served. On September 9, 1999, the commission produced its report, entitled "A New Beginning: Policing in Northern Ireland." Popularly known as the Patten Report, it contained 175 symbolic and practical recommendations and I would recommend it as a good reference document to anyone interested in police reform and management. In my opinion it is an excellent example of a comprehensive approach to police reform.

From 1999 to 2001, I was the program director of the Northern Ireland police's Change Management Program. This comprehensive program was the police service's response to the report's recommendations. Previously, during the research period, I had the privilege of presenting to the commission the RUC's own vision of community policing and our views on a number of issues concerning justice and community reconciliation.

The international commission's report and all of its recommendations (including a name change) were accepted in full by the RUC (soon to become the Police Service of Northern Ireland [PSNI]). New legislation, political will, resources, community support, and good leadership were some of the factors which allowed the process of modernizing Northern Ireland policing to take place. An improvement in the security situation, with reductions in terrorism and public disorder (due in large part to effective policing in previous years), was also an essential element. During this time, I completed a thesis on the role of community-based policing in conflict resolution. My conclusion, while not Earth shattering, was one which I still firmly hold to and frequently use as a reference point.

In essence, I believe that a police service cannot enjoy the support of all sections of a community while intercommunity conflict is ongoing and, *similarly,* that intercommunity conflict cannot be effectively resolved while a police service does not have support from all sections of the community.

Therefore, efforts to address these issues must be taken *simultaneously*. In other words, community reconciliation/political development and police improvements are inextricably linked. Therefore, both issues must be strategic priorities for government, for communities, for police leaders. This, surely, is common sense.

However, in the midst of violent conflict and public unrest, often the "blame game" is played out and a stalemate occurs. Police become frustrated with politicians and community leaders; ordinary members of the community often blame their representatives and the police for not resolving local enmities; and politicians and the community often expect the police to shoulder more than their share of responsibilities with social issues not of their making. The solution is to drive forward significant, incremental changes on all sides—politics, policing, and community developments. As this occurs, each individual improvement enables other positive changes to take place and then the whole process moves forward. There will be setbacks (often major ones). The main thing is to focus on the big picture.

Political settlement in Northern Ireland and an easing of community tensions allowed changes (many of which were welcomed and initiated by the local police) to improve the police to a better position in society. The aims of the reform package for the Northern Ireland Police were to make it more accountable, representative, impartial (from partisan political control), fair, effective, and efficient. There is no doubt in my mind that it has been successful in many of these areas.

I am proud to have played a major part in this process, but it is not perfect and many lessons have been learned. As policing entered a new era, the PSNI was massively downsized (to make room for new recruits more representative of society in terms of religion, ethnicity, gender, etc.). This inevitably led to a lot of expertise being lost and some vulnerability has now been exposed in terms of crime-fighting capabilities. However, attainment of the "great prize"—that is, public trust and confidence in the police service—appears evidently more achievable.

My involvement in such a massive undertaking (national police reform) led me to form strong views concerning *critical factors which ensure a successful change process*—a list which I still refer to when debating Iraq or indeed any other major challenge. *These factors include an agreed vision of success, political will, a strategic plan, clear priorities and guiding principles, adequate resources, security, community involvement, and enabling legislation—and, of course, the other key ingredient: successful LEADERSHIP!*

In 2001, as a newly promoted assistant chief constable, I was given territorial command of the south region of Northern Ireland. It was a large geographical area (by national standards) requiring massive military support to include five battalions of the British Army with their specialist units and equipment. For example, Special Forces, border watchtowers, helicopters, bomb disposal experts, and military engineers and their heavy plant assisted me and my 3,000-member staff in dealing with infrequent but nevertheless violent and large incidents of disorder and cross-border crimes. These crimes included acts of terrorism committed by the residual dissidents from terrorist organizations that did not support the peace process. The challenge to me, my local police commanders, and the military supporting us was to avoid overreaction, thereby maintaining the support of the majority of the community. Fortunately, by the time I left to go to Iraq in the summer of 2003, things had improved dramatically—again, due to an appropriate balance having been struck between political development, good policing, and, hopefully, effective leadership and strategic direction provided by myself.

*International Experiences and Beliefs*

*SW:* After Saddam Hussein had been removed from power by U.S.-led coalition forces, the British government sought a senior UK chief police officer to go to Iraq to lead law and order reforms in the four southern provinces. Iraq has a total of 18 provinces, so the task entailed a sizeable portion of the country and its complex communities. I had no hesitation in volunteering and within days was deployed to Basra (Iraq's second biggest city). I believed that my unique CV (with over 4 years in the army and 25 years' Northern Ireland police experience) equipped me for this role. I had spent my career dealing with terrorism, working alongside the army and other security forces, delivering community policing in a sectarian and divided country, designing and delivering leadership and specialist training, and focusing on police community relationships at home and abroad. All this experience provided me with the self-confidence and professional background to grasp the challenges Iraq presented.

In my first 6-month tour as director of law and order (southern Iraq), I learned a lot—not least that leadership alone (in the absence of the other aforementioned critical success factors) can only do so much. In Iraq my small team and I did make a difference (for example, building, opening, and operating the first regional police academy in Iraq), but, in the absence of an agreed national plan and with shortfalls in expert civilian resources, life was difficult and professionally frustrating. That is why I was pleased to be given another opportunity to help Iraq in my current position, since March 2005, as head of the European Union's rule of law mission for Iraq: EUJUST LEX.

Just prior to that, on return from my first senior role in Iraq (in 2004), I had led the UK Senior Police Leadership Development Program based at the Police Staff College, Bramshill, England. I felt that it was a fitting end to my formal police career. In a sense, at Bramshill, I concluded my personal journey in British policing by mentoring and training others based in the same location where I had begun my own career development as a young sergeant on the accelerated promotion course. This final UK police role required me to oversee the design and development of appropriate training for all future chiefs of police in the UK. While in this role, in late 2004, aged 49, due to downsizing of the

PSNI, I was afforded and accepted the opportunity to take early retirement.

This in turn led to my current civilian role as special advisor to the secretary general of the Council of the European Union (EU) and "head of mission" for the EU rule of law (ROL) mission for Iraq. The mission is named EUJUST LEX. My latest role has been very fulfilling in all sorts of ways and is one I could never have imagined holding even a few years ago. My career has led me to many difficult and demanding places, to meeting many interesting people, and to taking on many challenging responsibilities. The current one is, by far, the most interesting and most challenging post to date!

During the time I have been head of mission (and 2 months prior to it, when I was employed to research the Iraqi criminal justice system [CJS] and propose possible interventions for the EU to support the ROL and human rights), I have had some wonderful experiences professionally and culturally. I have met literally thousands of Iraqi people: men and women, religious and secular, Sunni, Shia, Kurdish, Christian, Turkmen, Arab and non-Arab, police officers, judges, lawyers, and penitentiary officials, as well as senior political figures from prime ministers and ministers to ambassadors and officials. I have flown around the country in military aircraft and helicopters and driven through deserts, mountain ranges, famous historical cities, and breathtaking locations. I have met fellow professionals whose dedication and courage have impressed me greatly and, sadly, I have seen examples of cruelty, lawbreaking, and abuses of human rights which have affected me deeply.

As a result, I consider it a great privilege to lead a mission whose aim is to address the urgent needs of the Iraqi CJS by providing its leaders with professional development opportunities throughout Europe, the Middle East, and in Iraq. Almost 3,000 Iraqi judges, prosecutors, senior police officers, and prison managers have participated in the training events which my team and I have designed, developed, and coordinated with judicial institutes, penitentiary academies, and police colleges throughout the EU and the region. In so many ways, they have taught me as much as I have taught them—not only about the culture and history of Mesopotamia, but also about justice and the role of police in societies other than Western democratic states. Throughout all of this experience, I have been delighted to learn that the *mission's guiding principles,* which I set immediately on being appointed, have proved to be appropriate and necessary. To a large degree they epitomize my own principles:

*Security is paramount.* At all times, the health and safety of my own staff and the Iraqis we support must be the first "agenda point." As a consequence, this drives us to address many issues, such as operational tactics and performance, stakeholder and partner analysis, selection and training of suitable staff, equipment and technological needs, confidentiality policies, the media and public information strategy, accommodation and transport needs, close protection, briefings, and many others.

*Iraqi involvement at every stage.* This is an obvious priority, especially for a training and support mission. Yet, it is amazing how many times the international community, in one form or another, attempt to dictate to host countries and their police services what is good for them without any consultation, ownership, or buy-in. It is no wonder that often there are disappointing outcomes to support missions and, in some cases, absolute failure. At every stage of my mission, we have consulted and involved Iraqis in such issues as training needs analyses, curricula design, program implementation, monitoring of performance, and evaluation of outcomes.

*Flexibility and responsiveness to Iraqi needs.* Again, such a principle may seem obvious. However, when large bureaucratic institutions and legal mandates necessarily impose tight parameters to determine mission's budgets, resource allocations, and measures of success, it is imperative, when supporting police reform in conflict and postconflict situations, that support programs are designed and led in such a way that there is sufficient flexibility to react to changing situations.

The government of the Republic of Iraq, its ministries, its CJS institutions, and their individual leaders appreciate the adherence to such principles. Together with political astuteness, community sensitivities, and cultural respect coupled with professional expertise, they form a *best-practice checklist* for any international police support program.

The EUJUST LEX mission started with a very modest program, time frame (1 year), and budget with tight restrictions limiting its activities in Iraq. Since its inception, I have been delighted to see it evolve and grow into a much more meaningful intervention—one which the Iraqi prime minister and his cabinet have greatly valued as evidenced by their requests to the Council of Ministers of the EU to extend and expand it (three times to date). Recognition, on worldwide scale, by my fellow practitioners (for example, with the IACP's Webber Seavey Motorola Award in 2008) is also very heartening and indicates that there is something of significant merit in what the mission achieves.

I have been very fortunate in my professional life. I have been afforded some very special, unique, and challenging opportunities and have worked with some excellent colleagues and partner agencies through the years. Organizations, units, and missions I have worked in have been rewarded and recognized in many ways. For example, the Royal Ulster Constabulary and all its officers were collectively presented the UK's highest civilian gallantry award, the George Cross, by Her Majesty, Queen Elizabeth. My work in Mongolia received the president's award from the International Society of Crime Prevention Practitioners and, as mentioned, the EUJUST LEX mission has been recognized by the IACP.

At a personal level, I have received a number of awards, not least the honor of being appointed as an Officer of the Most Excellent Order of the British Empire (OBE) by Her Majesty, the Queen, at Buckingham Palace. However, what really counts—what really motivates me—is how policing and the role of police leadership are viewed by the general public at the individual and the macro levels nationally and internationally.

*RM:* What do you see as the most important changes which have occurred in policing over the course of your career, such as philosophies, organizational arrangements, specialization, policies and programs, equipment, personnel, diversity, etc.? Overall, has the quality of policing improved or declined and, in general, is it more or less difficult to be a police officer (street manager) now than in the past?

*SW:* It would be relatively simple to compile a list of the important trends, philosophies, priorities, and practices which have taken precedence during my 30 years in policing.

*Changes, Trends, and Developments in Policing*

*SW:* The list of changes, trends, and developments would, of course, include:

The challenge of terrorism (at home and abroad) and the internationalization of organized, cross-border crime. This has led to the requirement for police organizations and security services to work transnationally and internationally in a more coordinated fashion.

The accepted wisdom of transition from a model of law enforcement and *police force* toward a model of community protection, crime prevention, and *police service.*

The advances in technology and coming of the "information age" as threats in terms of new crimes and advanced criminal techniques and also as an opportunity for crime reduction and detection.

The focus on more analytical, problem-solving, community-based approaches to crime detection and reduction.

The movement toward more independent oversight and accountability (e.g., to the law, to the public and its representative bodies, and to the media).

The challenge to make best use of intelligence while recognizing and balancing legitimate demands for openness and transparency. Tensions exist when police carry out (even essential and lawful) secret actions in open societies. Consequently, I believe, police commanders need to carefully manage the protection of individual liberties and collective security. This is particularly pertinent in times of crisis when the work of intelligence agencies is critical. Police departments and partner agencies must recognize that democratic oversight and transparency in more general activities will enable the public to more readily accept the need for some secrecy and have confidence in use of intelligence.

The requirement for police departments to be more strategic and proactive when dealing with important issues such as human rights, diversity, and inclusiveness. These issues impact both inside and outside police organizations (e.g., internal human resource strategies and external interactions with every individual and society as a whole).

The need for police executives to consider "value for money," effectiveness, and efficiency as police departments compete for and make use of scarce public finances and resources.

The professionalization of police (evidenced, for example, by specialization, profession-centered education and training, and interactions with other criminal justice professionals and associations).

The requirement of police chiefs to be multitalented, multidimensional strategic leaders with an understanding of the political and cultural worlds they operate within and the diversity of stakeholders and partners they interact with.

This list is by no means exhaustive, but these are issues which have impacted significantly on my career and the organizations I have worked for. For the purposes of this discussion, I wish to focus on only a few in particular.

*The Challenges of Leadership*

*SW:* First is the challenge of *the role of modern police leaders* and the range of responsibilities and requirements they now must fulfill. During my career, police chiefs (particularly those in command of large organizations), in order to be successful, have become ever more adept at handling a wide range of situations and demands. The ability to detect and investigate crimes will always be a central part of police officers' skill sets. However, today, more and more, police officers need to be culturally sensitive, possess community awareness, demonstrate political astuteness, and show media savvy when dealing with stakeholders outside the police department.

Also, within the organization, police chiefs need to possess managerial skills in areas such as IT, finance, human resources and diversity, legal issues, and change management, in addition to their operational skills to deal with terrorism, public disorder and police use of force, critical incident management, contingency planning, and modern investigation techniques. It is for these reasons that I have always supported the concept of "lifelong learning," the importance of training in organizations (especially leadership development), and events, associations, and programs which enable senior law enforcement officials to share knowledge and experiences.

*International Police Reform*

*SW:* The second topic or trend which I wish to highlight is *the need for a strategic, comprehensive approach to police reform programs.* "Police experts" come in many forms and, in my experience, some so-called experts fail to display sufficient expertise when it comes to their ability to see the "big picture." This is potentially very damaging—not just to the credibility of the "expert," but particularly to the host organization or country when supporting a police reform program. Sadly, some advisors simply wish to apply what worked in one department, or even in one country, to a completely different and unique situation. Often they do not understand that some cultures and contexts have different priorities; for example, in Iraq, following the dictatorship and police brutality, a clear priority is to provide a style of policing and methods for the investigation of crime which protect human rights and move away from confession-based prosecutions (which were often the results of torture and abuse).

While all police departments share some similar priorities (e.g., to be effective, efficient, inclusive, transparent, accountable, fair, and impartial), they do not share the same historic, political, and cultural context; the same leadership, managerial and resource issues; the same legal framework and justice systems; or the same security, crime, and disorder challenges. For these reasons and many other obvious ones, close attention and specific research is needed in respect of the context in which reforms take place in order to avoid adopting a "one size fits all" approach. Only on completion of in-depth and comprehensive consultations can any meaningful set of recommendations or plans be offered to an organization.

This topic is very close to my heart and I can illustrate my views with examples of good and bad practices from many scenarios, including Iraq, South Africa, Mongolia, and Northern Ireland. Suffice to say that when I look for expertise and advisors, I value most those who take the big picture into account and take time to learn the culture and context of any proposed reforms.

There is an increasingly important role to be played by civilian police experts in overseas missions, in rule of law reforms and reconstruction processes in conflict and post-conflict situations. I believe that it is imperative to distinguish clearly the respective roles of the army and the (civilian) police. In conflict zones around the world, I detect that some assumptions are made that military power and even greater numbers of troops can solve all problems. In my view, the military are often tasked to deal with symptoms rather than causes, whereas good policing takes a more analytical, long-term viewpoint.

As I mentioned earlier, it is often the case that reconstruction efforts to rebuild civilian infrastructures (including policing) take place as other reforms occur. Often, it is inappropriate or impossible to wait for conflict and all aspects of a security situation to be solved before work on reconstruction takes place. However, if the two are tackled simultaneously, military assets should be focused on the security task and police reforms should be led and supported by civilian police experts.

Now, I will offer some personal insights and experiences in respect of two major trends which took place on my watch: the debate between community policing and other crime-fighting philosophies and the increasing demand for accountability and independent oversight.

### *"Competing" Police Philosophies*

#### *Community Policing, Law Enforcement, and Crime Fighting*

*SW:* I find it somewhat disheartening when I reread some of the coverage given, at the time, to whichever favored approach to policing was being advocated by various police commissioners and administrations during my career. It was not only in New York, but also in many other cities around the world, that "community policing" was labeled by some as "social work" while being lauded by others as the only way forward to tackle crime. Similarly, the policy of enforcement and "zero tolerance" (to low-level crime and misdemeanors) was the subject of much discussion among academics and practitioners in many quarters. I recall debates when advocates of one particular philosophy or another argued as if they were in competition with each other.

I was never convinced that one's approach to policing had to be based on a "single choice" from the menu. It has long been my opinion that policing strategies are not mutually exclusive or necessarily in competition with each other. Often the smart police officer is aware of the many different approaches which exist and applies them as and when it is appropriate. The trick is not to lose sight of the primary duties of a police officer and a police service. There are various forms of words to describe the list of main police responsibilities but usually they comprise the following duties: to protect life and property, to prevent and detect crime, to preserve the peace and public order, and to do so in a way that garners public support and instills community trust and confidence.

Depending on the context, crime problem, community, culture, etc., the best way forward may be problem-oriented policing, intelligence-led policing, crime pattern analysis/hot-spotting, proactive policing, community policing, or some other title. But in essence they are simply titles and labels to assist practitioners communicate plans and priorities. To me, it is abundantly clear that they all have a place in the modern police officer's repertoire; they all recognize that the days of aimless patrol, "police-alone" attitudes, and reactive responses are gone. What is important is the need to recognize that crime and criminals require coordinated planned responses making best use of all available resources—human and technological—and that individual police responses have an impact beyond the particular action taking place at that time.

Let me conclude this section by stating that I fundamentally disagree with those who feel that community policing is some soft option—not real policing. I have spent almost all my adult life dealing with terrorism and trying to keep fellow police officers alive along with the general public, whom we are duty bound to protect. If, by our actions, we gained their support and confidence and later a member of that same public supplied a piece of information which saved a life, improved the quality of life for a community, or was instrumental in gathering evidence which led to a successful prosecution of a terrorist or criminal (and I know it has happened many times), then I am a proud advocate for community-centered policing strategies.

*Public Accountability and Oversight*

*SW:* I have known very senior police colleagues who have calmly, professionally, and courageously faced terrorism, violence, criminality, cruelty, chaos, and all the operational challenges which policing can throw at them, but who wither and worry when a TV camera appears or a press conference is called for. I have witnessed officers who are masters of the written word or very competent performers in police briefing rooms suddenly lose their nerve when asked to account for police actions at public meetings or open forums. I do not believe it is due to inadequate training or a lack confidence in their own abilities or grasp of the subject at hand which lies at the root of this problem. It is something more complex, related to police culture. During my time as a police officer, I encountered many police officers who feared the media and who distrusted giving information to others outside police circles. Some preferred to remain anonymous and unanswerable even when given opportunities to account for or explain the rationale behind decisions which were being criticized (often, unfairly, out of incomplete knowledge).

In my opinion, those days are long gone, or they should be. We (the police) are public servants. It is often written on our badges and logos: to protect—*and serve.* Why it should be seen as unreasonable for those we serve to know how and why we serve in particular circumstances, how we use public funds, and what our priorities are is beyond my comprehension. In these days of instant media—with Internet, cell phones, and other means of immediately portraying police words and deeds around the world in seconds—it is even more important for police officers to realize that accountability to the public in general and via the media (in the widest sense) is important. We are also accountable to the law and more and more often to official independent oversight bodies.

The media should be made use of wisely and proactively to ensure that the police side of any story is accurately conveyed by the police themselves. In addition, the trend for more independent, formal oversight and public accountability should be positively and proactively responded to by police.

For centuries, the question of "Who guards the guards?" has been debated in one form or another. In recent decades, the question has frequently taken the form of "Who polices the police?" There are those who believe that police organizations (in the shape of their "internal affairs" branches and "complaints and discipline" departments) are better equipped to detect wrongdoing, negligence, and corruption.

The argument goes that cops know how the system works and are better skilled at investigation. However, in these days of increasing demands for public accountability and transparency, it is an argument less likely to be understood and accepted—especially by critics of police tactics and performance. During my police career I observed a firsthand the growth of and response to demands for oversight.

The Northern Ireland example is worthy of close study. In addition to the normal laws and discipline codes regulating police officers' behavior, a number of new measures were introduced, in the past 10 years or so, to enhance public consultation, participation, and confidence in policing. As part of the community policing strategy, local community forums and district policing partnerships were formed; to appoint senior officers and call the chief to account at a national level a Policing Board for Northern Ireland was formed. All these bodies comprise local elected and nonelected community representatives.

In addition, an independent Police Ombudsman for Northern Ireland, with wide-reaching powers, was established to investigate not only complaints against the police, but also contentious issues such as police traffic accidents involving members of the public, all use of firearms, and matters deemed to be of public interest. Other unique bodies were launched, such as an independent Oversight Commission to measure progress and performance against the change-management plan and an independent Parades Commission to rule on matters relating to contentious parades and demonstrations. The critical factor is the independence of these bodies, along with their specific mandates, legal powers, and composition in terms of experience, skills, and community representation.

Although they were initially distrusted, resisted, and criticized by police, these bodies have evolved and matured into their current roles. Importantly, police chiefs have realized that there are many advantages—to the police organization as a whole as well as to individual commanders—in the rigorous scrutiny their plans, decisions, and operations are now subjected to. Public confidence in these bodies and the police is at high levels and "accountability" is accepted as a norm. The role of oversight bodies is introduced in early training and is deemed to be an aid to discipline and standards. In summary, I believe the trend will continue globally in all aspects of policing and smart police officers will work with it and see benefits, not difficulties, and opportunities, not threats.

**Conclusion**

*SW:* To conclude this interview, I have been asked to offer my views on the role of police and whether or not it is better today than when I joined. My answer is a positive one. I firmly believe that policing is more complex, more skillful, more specialized, and more demanding and entails more oversight and scrutiny from the media and increasingly "intelligent users"—a much better informed public. Thankfully, the police response has often been entirely appropriate and equally comprehensive. I am proud of the energy, flexibility, and professionalism displayed by police organizations in rising to the challenges—not least of all my own organization.

First, the RUC and then the PSNI responded with visionary leadership, strategic planning; comprehensive restructuring; better selection procedures; improved training and leadership development; more effective, interagency partnerships; and an overall positive attitude to change. The target was kept in sight—the "great prize" of public trust and full community involvement in policing, reconciliation, and conflict resolution. When I joined the police, the average age of a recruit was 18½; now it is 27. I was one of a few recruits with a university degree; now many join with postgraduate qualifications. Women and all the underrepresented groups are recruited in much more proportionate numbers—in particular Catholics from Northern Ireland's complex divided society.

Policing can no longer be seen as simply a local matter. There are many organizations, associations, bodies, and international forums which enable police chiefs, public oversight officials, academics, and researchers to share information and best practice. Their contributions and potential aid should not be overlooked. The world of policing is complex and it is up to all leaders to ensure that developments and best practices are shared and to provide mutual aid and international support.

My conclusion, about the changes, trends, and pressures (only some of which I have identified in this interview) is that they have undoubtedly resulted in the general betterment of policing, more public trust, and safer communities. Therefore, when asked if I am confident about the future of policing and how it is developing, my answer is without doubt a resounding "yes!" The world is a dangerous, difficult, and demanding place for all the men and women brave enough to provide it with policing services. With good leadership, of the caliber they deserve, policing will be in good hands.

# 20

# Interview With Andrew Hughes, Police Advisor to the United Nations

## INTERVIEWED BY JAMES E. MCCABE

**Contents**



**Background**

In August 2007, Andrew Hughes was named the police advisor to the United Nations by Secretary General Ban Ki-moon. As the police advisor, Mr. Hughes is the director of the police division in the UN's Department of Peacekeeping Operations and is responsible for the deployment and operations of more than 11,000 police officers from around the world who are engaged in 16 operations in Africa, Asia, Europe, the Middle East, and the Americas. He was appointed to this position after more than 30 years of policing, serving as the chief police officer in the Australian Capital Territory Police and the commissioner of police in Fiji.

The first UN peacekeeping operation began very soon after the United Nations came into existence. The first UN peacekeeping mission was established in 1948, when the Security Council authorized the deployment of UN military observers to the Middle East to monitor the armistice agreement between Israel and its Arab neighbors. Since then, there have been a total of 63 UN peacekeeping operations around the world. The 16 missions currently in existence are considered "multidimensional" and an evolution of the traditional peacekeeping efforts of the past. The current missions, with regard to the UN police officers, are seen in support of the military efforts to sustain the peace in the host countries and help them reform, restructure, and rebuild the whole system of courts, prisons, prosecutors, public defenders, and civil society.

### The Interview

This interview took place on October 20, 2008, in Mr. Hughes's 36th floor office in the United Nations in New York. The impressive views he enjoys from high atop the Manhattan skyline symbolize the broad view he has of policing and the lofty responsibilities he shoulders as the leader of UN police officers deployed around the world. Our conversation was wide-ranging and candid, and Mr. Hughes shared his philosophy on policing in a direct and clear manner. His enthusiasm for and interest in the project were clear as he made himself available almost immediately after returning from a demanding international trip visiting several of the UN police deployments.

While his portfolio of experiences and responsibilities is broad, his approach to policing is brilliantly simple. Two clear themes emerged out of our conversation: adherence to the "rule of law" and the importance of "partnerships." The effective combination of these themes is the foundation of policing for Mr. Hughes, and they are the ingredients for dealing with a myriad of policing issues from terrorism to leadership to crime control. These concepts seem to flow naturally from his laid-back, yet engaging, style and clearly serve him well as he directs thousands of officers hailing from hundreds of countries and deploying them in diverse and volatile areas around the world. The following is a transcript of our meeting:

*JEM:* Can you tell me about your career?

*AH:* I have 31 years on the job. I joined a small force of 550 in 1977 in the Australian Capital Territory [ACT]. Then, in 1979, the ACT police amalgamated with some federal bodies and became the Australian Federal Police. At that stage I was a young detective working on criminal investigations in the nation's capital, doing a wide range of investigations that you might find in any city. The amalgamation opened up many opportunities and I was given a lot of responsibility early on. In 1993 I moved to the international side and to one of the cities in northern Australia. I worked there a couple of years and through a series of internal moves I moved up the chain and I ended up in London for 3 years working for the Australian High Commission with UK and European counterparts in law enforcement, primarily on organized crime investigations.

I went back to Australia on promotion to an executive level and then on to the senior executive level as the commander of the Australian Federal Police in the international network as well as the federal operations, performing two different roles: international investigations and the federal operations, which dealt primarily with complex frauds. Then I was promoted to assistant commissioner, where I had a similar portfolio of responsibility, but larger; it included international investigations, peacekeeping, and all of the AFP's national operations. During that time I was also selected to be on Interpol's Executive Committee, which was part time for a couple of years. Then I had a sideways move at the same level but as a deputy chief police officer in the Australian Capitol Territories where I first started.

I had been there for about 18 months when I was selected as Australia's nominee for the Police Commission for Fiji, which is an independent country, but after a series of coups they wanted an independent police commissioner. There were persistent allegations about the previous police commissioner—that he had been complicit in one of those coups—so they wanted an outsider, and I was selected. I worked there for 3½ years until the last coup, which occurred in December 2006. I left the country under less than favorable circumstances because we had criminal complaints against the military commander and his senior officers. There was quite a standoff there for a period of time, but it became "rule of law" versus "rule of the gun" and I'm sorry to say that rule of the gun prevailed. We came very close to stopping it, which would have been a first for Fiji, but we didn't have enough political will in the region to take a strong stance.

My family was evacuated. I was going to be taken in by the military, but I got quickly on a plane to New Zealand and decided not to go back. I had the Australian Navy standing by just in case I needed them to come in and get me. Then I went back to Australia and took over as the chief police officer for the ACT. Meanwhile, the position here at the UN had come up and my name was put forward for the selection process; I was successful and have been here now for 13 months as the police advisor.

*JEM:* What actually is your role as the police advisor to the UN?

*AH:* The best way to understand it is that I am the director of the police division in the Department of Peacekeeping Operations. Peacekeeping Operations has a number of components. They have the military, the police, and a civilian component. Of the police components of our peacekeeping operations, there are 16 at the moment around the world, and we have more than 12,000 police in the field, from 98 contributing countries, against a mandated strength of 16,900, with the gap largely from Darfur because we are struggling to fill Darfur.

They provide a wide range of policing activities like interim law enforcement, as in Kosovo and Timor-Leste, where the UN police have law enforcement powers and responsibilities. Also, they provide operational support, as in Haiti and Liberia, where the police work shoulder to shoulder with the national police. And then there is the reforming, restructuring, and rebuilding role, where they either rebuild a police department from scratch, or we assist an existing police force, one that might have been decimated by conflict, to get back up to strength again; this would be driven by a mandate to perform the restructuring and rebuilding component. That is a growing area, and an area where we struggle, but it is an area where the Security Council is giving us mandates.

Also, my division has the global lead for all policing activities across the United Nations. So anything to do with policing, we are the lead. Whether it is an UNDP project or a humanitarian effort, we are the lead for all police programs. It is easier said than done because it is a big role. Also, in theory, I am the police advisor to the secretary general of the United Nations and the undersecretary general for peacekeeping.

*JEM:* This must be an enormous challenge dealing with the diverse countries and cultures around the world. It seems that there are three dimensions to your mission: interim law enforcement, operational support, and restructuring. How is the approach selected or is there one uniform approach that applies to a police model in the host countries?

*AH:* There are really two strands to the answer to that. One is that local ownership is crucial. We don't come in and impose any systems of a preconceived policing model onto a country. We have to look at their norms, their cultures, their values, their religious beliefs, and so on, and look to see, historically, what systems they are familiar with. Five of the missions are in post-French colonies where they adopted a French model of policing. The others have a range of systems. Many are predominantly a British model, so we have to take that into account. The local ownership, however, is first and foremost.

There is also a need for a more uniformed UN policing model and this is a major project which we are embarking on at the moment. Essentially, this project asks, "What does it mean to put a blue beret on?" Most of our UN police are drawn from developing countries in Asia and Africa. That's fine and we welcome the contributions of all countries; however, it does bring a range of challenges. Not all of the countries have democratic policing and not all of the police officers understand that. Many of our contributing countries have authoritarian systems. Some of them have systems where the police are perceived as forms of oppression. But when they put the UN beret on, in the absence of us explaining what doctrine we want applied, they fall back to what they know from home, and that is unacceptable. The UN is very specific and strong on various principles like human rights, gender mainstreaming, and the rule of law; we are in the process now of looking at all the guiding documents and policy statements that are out there to define what UN policing model ought to look like, and that model is emerging exactly as a model of democratic policing.

*JEM:* So, in theory, you have a foundation of democratic policing, and you enter the country with this in mind and then the values, norms, and cultures shape this model into a workable system for the country. Is this an accurate description of the approach?

*AH:* That's the theory, but it's never as refined as that. You're dealing with human beings from many different cultures and backgrounds. It's not an easy thing to do, but the commissioners in the field, the UN police commissioners, are the senior police advisors in the field, and have the primary function and the responsibility to gel all of that. Here at headquarters we have the responsibility for creating the framework to allow this effort to take place strategically.

*JEM:* So how do you pick your police commissioners in the field and what does the organization look like?

*AH:* It's a matrix relationship, where I don't have any supervisory responsibilities on the police commissioners, but there's a line of reporting to me where I monitor their performance. I do have input into whether we renew their contracts, and we also select them here at headquarters. But it's a matrix arrangement, as I've said. I have a division here, an operational arm called the Standing Police Capacity; the missions are not quite autonomous, but do enjoy a degree of delegated authority. I have a strategic overview, and can terminate the commissioners if necessary.

*JEM:* Do the police commissioners come from the host country?

*AH:* No they don't. They are recruited internationally. Most of our police in the field are incumbent officers. That means they are already serving on a police force. There are some exceptions, but for the most part they are officers already serving. Once the Security Council mandates a particular mission, we then send a notice to all the permanent missions here in New York, the representatives from member countries, seeking nominations for police officers. Separate notices are sent out for commissioners and deputy commissioners, and so on, and applications are collected.

*JEM:* That process has to be a challenge in itself.

*AH:* Recruitment is massive; it's one of the major activities here at headquarters. We recruit nearly 10,000 police officers each year because they only go for 12 months, so we are continually recruiting 10,000 to 12,000 officers each year. We actually have a backlog; we have nearly a thousand police officers to deploy, but it's slow because of Darfur. They don't have anywhere to accommodate them, feed them, water them, transport them, and so on.

*JEM:* Do you make it a habit of visiting all the countries where UN police officers are deployed?

*AH:* I've been to a few, but not as many as I'd like, and I'd like to visit more. But it's a matter of judgment because when I'm here I can't be there, and when I'm there, I can't be here. I've got a deputy now; in fact she's out in Liberia and Cote d'Ivoire. She's from Sweden, and she's been a big help. We try to manage our time so we can spread the load a bit and share the burden of travel.

*JEM:* What motivated you to go into police work in the first place?

*AH:* I got accepted in the university to marine biology. You see I always had a fascination with the sea, but I couldn't afford to live in the town near the Great Barrier Reef where the marine biology and fisheries program was located. So I came back and decided the next best option was to be a fisheries inspector. But to be a fisheries inspector you needed to be 21. When I turned 21 they weren't recruiting, but the ACT Police was, and I thought that would be a good background. So I figured I would do that for a couple of years and then slide across. I joined the cops and I loved it, particularly when I went into investigations. Then I moved up through the ranks, and here I am.

*JEM:* Is there anything in your career that has surprised you?

*AH:* Well, the whole thing has been sort of a surprise! I joined as a rookie cop, and if you had asked me 31 years ago, "Do you think you'd be sitting in the UN as the police advisor?" I would have laughed it off. But I was the commissioner of another national police force, and all these things that seem to have come my way, and I've been very fortunate to grab challenges as they've come. I have seen a few surprises, almost in a structured way. There were too many in a row to think that they were all by chance. I think you've got to make your own luck. I've always tried to manage my career and not let it wash over me. I have no time for officers who for the moment think they are stuck in their careers, and say, "Look at that guy. I'm better than he ever was. And why is he doing 'this' and 'that'?" And when you actually look, you see they were quite happy to sit on their backsides and do nothing, and that's the reality of so many cops these days.

My advice to any young cops is to make sure you manage your career ... where do you want to be in 5 years, 10 years, 15 years, 20 years? You might be very happy riding a traffic bike around, and who wouldn't be at 21 years of age? But do you want to do that forever? No, you should do it for 2 or 3 years, have a good time, and move on. You have to ask, "Where do I want to be?" "How long do I want to do this for?" You see guys my age riding a motorbike and you say, "Goodness gracious!" Maybe they're happy, and good on them if they are, but that's probably not the place they want to be. You've got to be ready. You've got to have all your certificates in the draw and your experiences behind you and when the opportunities come up, you grab them.

*JEM:* Can you tell me about your personal philosophy on policing?

*AH:* I've always maintained that the people are the police and the police are the people. And the closer you can get to that policing philosophy the better. Any notion that we are somehow separate or somehow divorced, or elite, or an instrument of politics, is wrong. Although we have political masters, our overall master is the law. And I think if you follow that guide through, even though politicians will try and influence the police to make a decision in a particular way—it can be overt or it can be quite subtle at times, but it's there; you can feel it—the overarching and overriding allegiance must be to the law. So I think if you follow that and understand that people are helped at the end of the day, that's really what we're about. I'm sure I've locked up countless villains in my day, but I think in the end I've helped more people than I've hurt, and that's one thing that I get a lot out of this job.

When I go out on my field missions, I see the people who are impoverished, who literally have nothing, I mean nothing, and a bundle of firewood means a good day's work for them, and we're just trying to help these poor folks. And I think keeping that constantly in your mind, whether you're doing this sort of work (with the UN) or working here in New York with the NYPD, or in my home country, or wherever, keep your eye on yourself and never lose sight of the fact that we are there to help people and to uphold the law. It's not to apply any persuasion and sometimes you have to do what's unpopular and sometimes you have to stand up to the military, but it's all about upholding the rule of law.

And I've seen what happens when the law is gone. This is where it is good for so many police from developing countries to get engaged in the UN missions. Many critics say that we shouldn't do it because they have enough problems in their own countries—"Why are they going around spreading their views of the world?" But the reality is that when they go and they see what happens when that thin blue line breaks down, it just drives it home that the rule of law is key. I've spent some time in Fiji, and they've had a troubled political past, but to go and actually see Darfur, see Sudan, see Liberia, see Kosovo and what happens when it breaks down, you see genocide and you see the most unthinkable things humanity can wreak upon itself. It does have a very strong reinforcing effect to uphold those values of the rule of law.

*JEM:* Can you discuss the internal and external pressures that create tension for you as you apply the rule of law and the democratic police model during the UN police missions?

*AH:* I think my experience in Fiji is the best example of that. In that case we had the Fijian military [which had staged a coup], which was physically intimidating because it is an island-nation with 300 islands in a very large area, and there was no question that there was outside help coming, so it was a matter of knowing what's right and what's good and sticking with it; it's principled policing. I had a lot of public support, and I didn't know what was going to happen, but there was a lot of support for what the police force was doing. It was a difficult thing to do, to stand there against the military, and my officers lived there, so there was no going back. So I think you have to stand by no matter what, and it can lead you to danger, but you just have to stand by, stand by the rule of law. If you can't do that, then you shouldn't be on this job, you shouldn't be wearing the police shield.

*JEM:* So how do you, as a manager or as the police chief, deal with the officers who are not willing to stand up and protect the rule of law? How do you identify those not suitable to wear the shield and sanction them?

*AH:* The old claim about the police culture! There's been a lot written about that, and there are both negatives and positives. Unfortunately, it is a double-edged sword. That very same sense of loyalty—that comradeship—that means that officers will put their own lives on the line to protect their fellows also at times goes over the boundaries of the law and protects them against wrongdoing. As an officer, you have to think right from day one, you have to make your mind up, which side of the fence you are on. Those officers that can't or who go the wrong way—as far as I'm concerned, I don't have time for them. I've been involved in a number of internal investigations where officers have gone the wrong way. I remember one officer got corrupted and rolled with "bikies" [outlaw motorcycle gangs]; he was totally out of control, and he was taken down and did 3 years in prison.

*JEM:* How can the profession of policing strengthen itself against corrupt officers like that?

*AH:* I think there have been huge inroads into this sort of thing in the last 10 or 20 years, into systemic police corruption. It's not perfect, but it's a whole lot better than it once was, and I think it's a lot cleaner environment now. I think the reasons for that are many, but it has a lot to do with whom you recruit and the screening process. It has a lot to do with internal control mechanisms. I am a great believer that police integrity is a managerial issue. Rather than it being a punitive process, we need to take a holistic approach, so that you reward good behavior as much as you punish bad behavior. And there has to be an organizational culture that supports these things. It is a difficult task, but it can be done. It's a matter of constantly reinforcing the message, and giving examples of those who have fallen over and how they've been dealt with, and those that shine and have done the right thing and how they are protected and rewarded. So the "whistleblower" side is very important. I think that when you look at all of that over the last 10 or 20 years, there's been a huge step forward, but we've still got a way to go and we're not there yet, but there's been massive improvement in police integrity.

The whole organization needs to be looked at: hiring, training, education, supervision. There's a whole suite of solutions that you bring to the trouble, not just one. The officer's wrongdoing is a symptom that something is not right with the organization. When you have corruption with one officer, it can be an isolated thing; these things happen, but you need to look at the whole system and think you have a problem somewhere. So you have to analyze that officer. What happened, when did he or she turn over the wrong way, what triggered it, was it a cumulative thing or a single event, and where was the supervision? It takes a lot of work, and a lot of work has been done to analyze these cases, but you need constant reinforcement.

*JEM:* What is your opinion of the various management strategies governing policing? For example, what do you think of community policing versus zero-tolerance policing versus intelligence-led policing? Can you give us some of your insights on these approaches?

*AH:* They all have their strengths. And I think when you look at it, they all came about at the right moment. We talked about making the opportunities within your own career, it is similar here. The times were right for these approaches to emerge and they were the right approach for the particular time. They came out at the right moment, there was a need. Look at "Broken Windows." There was a need. Something had to be done about disorder. Even though Bill Bratton doesn't like to call it zero tolerance, there was a lot of that surrounding that approach. Deal with the low-level stuff; fight that and make sure there are no dark alleyways and that broken windows are fixed. So that was the right strategy for the time.

Maybe now, for the moment, a new strategy is required. Now our focus needs to change after 9/11, and maybe now we have to focus on communities with our programs. I think we've run the risk of marginalizing and alienating large sections of society, not so much in the United States, but in other countries that have taken in a larger number of Muslim immigrants with their migration programs. The Muslim communities have been left in enclaves and this has led to a great deal of outrage. I know this is occurring in London and in parts of France, and it's starting in my own country. So you've got to reach in there, to the young people particularly, and combat these feelings of marginalization and outrage. I think we are about to start the new era of community policing, and this time it will be more robust and more earnest than it's been previously. Community policing projects in the past have been much more about break-ins and muggings and things like that. Now I think community policing will be much more fundamental to dealing with communities and these deep-seated issues that have evolved since 9/11.

And this goes back to what I said in the beginning that the people are the police, and the police are the people. It's really about that, and it's about making them understand that the police are not agents of oppression. Maybe they come from countries where the police are agents of oppression, and we need to make them understand that the police are different, and that we will deal with their problems in the same way we deal with everyone else's problems. So our outreach programs become very important.

*JEM:* This sounds like a way of combating both terrorism and crime. Can you do both with the same approach?

*AH:* Yes, I think so. Any sort of recalcitrant behavior can be addressed by this approach. But being overly broad is a little over the top and there needs to be a lot of refinement in all of that. Obviously, you've got to focus your sights carefully and not take a blanket approach. You need good ambassadors out there. You need good people that you can trust than can develop an understanding with the community, and you know it's all based on trust.

*JEM:* It's almost unfair to call that sort of an approach community policing. Is that a broader approach than community policing?

*AH:* Yes, but it's got a lot of community policing elements in it and the guiding principles are sound and valid.

*JEM:* How would the police need to change to accommodate such an approach?

*AH:* Well, there are a lot of problems that we face, and will always face. There is a hard edge of policing and a soft edge. The hard edge of policing, unfortunately, is sometimes inevitable. That is, you've got to make hard decisions; you have to deal with the angry crowd by responding with greater force, or whatever, and that makes great TV. But, unfortunately, that actually undermines what we are doing. In 1 minute we are saying we're your friend and we're here to help, and the next minute we're shown with black gear on carrying batons, throwing gas at you. It just doesn't add up in people's minds. So this is the dilemma: the dichotomy of policing, managing both sides of this issue. I'm not sure there's anyone around policing that's tried to separate the roles: the gendarme style and the more community style of focus. You know a cop's a cop as far as the people are concerned and there's no getting around this dilemma. This brings up an important role for the media, and it really amounts to getting the positive message out and getting people to understand that, yes, we did it, but we had to do it. It's not that we wanted to do it, but we had to.

*JEM:* But don't we train and socialize officers initially into performing that "hard-edge" policing style and then ask them to use a "soft edge" after the fact?

*AH:* I think recruiting is very critical to get the right people to do both these styles. You know, when I went on the police, I was 5 ft, 11 in. I think I'm 5 ft, 10½ in. now, but I was short, and you had to be 6 ft+ and play rugby, Australian football, or some body-contact sport, and maybe there were one or two women in every cohort of 25 or 30 recruits. It was very much about the brawn, the physical side of the job. The mental side of the job was important, but not stressed.

Now, it's quite the opposite. Now, size is not important at all because the men and women hired now, while not as tall as before, have got the smarts to be good cops. They have the right attitude and the right mental outlook to carry out the job. So I think softening the hiring approach, looking for brains as opposed to brawn—particularly hiring more women into the force—is the right approach. Women bring a softer image to the job, and we need that. They are better negotiators, they're more tolerant, and don't overreact to things as quickly as men do; they are more reasoned in their approach to things. They're quite happy to talk and work things through to a peaceful solution more than men, and if they have to "go off"—and sometimes they do—they can give as good as they get and are just as formidable as men.

*JEM:* Looking at the publications of the UN Police Division, it appears that you are actively recruiting women officers for your missions.

*AH:* Yes, this is a major push for us. We've been able to increase the number of female UN police officers from 4% to just under 8% of the total deployment in the last 3 years. One quarter of our standing police capacity [police trained and ready to be deployed overseas] is female, so we are making huge inroads. But the problem is, of course, that policing has been and, in many countries, continues to be a male-dominated profession. So when we look for senior officers, when we look for commissioners and deputy commissioners, you are looking somewhere in the 20+ years of experience cadre and, unfortunately, there aren't a lot of women out there in that category. We're fishing in a very restricted pool.

*JEM:* Earlier you raised the issue of the media in policing. Can you discuss the role of the media in contemporary policing?

*AH:* I can't overemphasize the importance of the media. It's one of those things where you live by it and you die by it, but it's getting that balance right that's so important. One of the challenges for us is ... well, first of all, the ability of the modern media is tremendous. They can be on the scene, even at times before the cops get there; whether it's Brooklyn or downtown Bagdad, they'll be there, and they're filming and they'll be showing that on the news. They're not constrained by the laws of evidence, nor are they constrained by investigative processes or procedures and so on. They can just go in and get their footage and their jobs done. Then they can go away and everyone's happy. But that makes us look slow and it makes us look cumbersome; it makes us look guarded, when we're asked things about the incident. We've got an end-game: a successful prosecution. We've got to find the villains that did whatever it is we're responding to, so we've got to be much more guarded, and this comes across as if we don't know what we're talking about or even that we are unnecessarily secretive. So we are at a distinct disadvantage in the information game.

So how do we deal with this? I think we have to be absolutely as honest as we possibly can be. And if that means occasionally saying something that, maybe in hindsight, we'd rather we didn't, so be it. Often, the costs of being too guarded or too protective of what we're about can be so counterproductive that you get the media to turn on you, and then no matter how good a job you actually do, it's too late. Then the public will see how it's portrayed, and there will be negative consequences. So dealing with the media, managing the information, and projecting a positive image are so important. This is a thing that many police forces don't do very well. Some of them do it extremely well, but not enough.

I know that in my own country, my police force went through a period where we were managing the media very well, and we're going through a period now where it's not managed very well, and there are a number of underlying factors for that. I'd say that in some of the smaller police jurisdictions, where they have a very close relationship with the media, it's going well, and they can generally get away with more than the big city forces can, where they have a more aggressive or more competitive media environment. There are more TV channels out there competing for the same stories; there are more news sources grabbing for the headlines. But recognizing this competition is half the battle. If you can give them what they need to be able to run their story, they will generally not be so aggressive as long as they have something to run with. If you give them nothing, they'll either make it up or attack you until they get something. I make a point to talk to junior officers to tell them to give the media something—don't spoon-feed them, but give them as much correct information as you can and recognize that they have a valid role in society too, whether you like it or not. They're out there and never going to go away, so we have to look after them as best we can.

*JEM:* This sounds very much like the approach you recommend to deal with communities: Be proactive with them. Is this right?

*AH:* Yes, it's pretty close. You have to recognize their need: What drives them? What are they after? What do they need? Then you try to accommodate this need as best you can. You can't be all things to all people, but at least we can be seen to be trying, genuinely, honestly, hand-on-heart trying. I think that counts for a lot. You know the history of policing is littered with problems where the police and the community did get on very well. So dealing with these problems head-on, in an honest way, can help in the long run.

*JEM:* Can you speak about some of the greatest challenges that the profession of policing faces now?

*AH:* Right now, the current world financial crisis may potentially increase our work. I am not convinced that there is an ordinary nexus between unemployment and crime, but it stands to reason that if someone can't put food on their table they may resort to other ways. This doesn't mean that they will necessarily resort to crime, but as financial pressures mount and if people feel that they have no other options, anything can happen. I think this can be an issue for us.

Another major issue is in the area of after 9/11. Somewhere along the line we got it very wrong, and I think now it's time to unravel that. We're still dominated by cold war thinking with regard to intelligence gathering and that plays into the way law enforcement reacts and manages and responds to threats, with a cloak of secrecy. Prevention is what this is all about with regard to terrorism. We can't afford to have a mistake. Prevention is everything. You move into that paradigm of prevention rather than pure investigation: When you are doing pure investigation secrecy is important because you don't want the bad guys to know you're onto them. When you're on the prevention side of it, it's all about exposure; it's about shining sunlight into the dark crevices and exposing all of that.

To me, I think, that's how we may have to look at it; rather that it just being cloaked in secrecy and the history of the cold war, there's got to be a shift. It's going to involve building trust; it's going to involve complete change in mind for people in jobs like mine, and my peers that run large police agencies are going to have to recognize this, but I don't think many do. I'm talking about trust between officers, between law enforcement agencies and intelligence communities, between law enforcement agencies and military organizations, no matter which way you slice it. It's not trust like we used to know, like "I'll tell a secret because I know you might tell me one anyway." Rather than starting from the point that we're not telling anybody anything, we need to think, "Okay, why can't we tell them that? Why can't we say we've got these problems in this particular borough with this particular group? Why can't we tell them that, so that the others in the borough can say we've got problems and concerns with that group too, and then do something about it." Instead of keeping information in a shadowy world, it should be out in the open where people can do something about it. But there are people who come from a culture or worked for decades in secrecy, and they tend to be guarded. And the military, with the element of surprise, it's counterintuitive to share information, but I think we have to and it comes back to the trust issue.

*JEM:* How can this be done in policing today?

*AH:* You're going to have to get down to a common understanding of the political motives, and you need to chisel away at the stalwarts of the old way of doing business and, maybe, as they fall off the perch and new blood comes in, things can change. Part of the plan is to get good people, to recruit people who are more frank and open-minded about looking for solutions and not just locked into the idea that "I will be a cop forever and that's how I see the world." There needs to be a more holistic way of looking at intelligence, developing partnerships, and developing trust. This is not going to be changed overnight. There needs to be a fundamental shift in the way we deal with these new security threats. It will be generational. It will mean recruiting people to work against the secrecy. Sure, sometimes there will need to be secrecy, but even in the investigation side of it you need to be ambidextrous, and you need to make judgment calls along the way, rather than just getting locked into a way of doing things. It's like we were talking before about hard-edge and soft-edge policing. You've got to be able to do both, and you've got to be able to do both in a way that they don't compromise each other. It's not easy, but necessary.

Also, the quality of the intelligence gathering by the police is high, particularly because we have so many men and women in the grassroots that the information will be superior to what any cloak and dagger organization could even hope to get. It's the conversations we have over coffee with people and not the satellites picking up tanks on the border. When someone works their beat well, they can get that gut feeling that something's not right: from the way they're being spoken to and the way they're being treated by the young kids. After about 5 to 7 years of working, you should be able to get that "internal radar" going off. But then how do we manage this, and how do we react to it? What do you do with it? Do you cover it and guard it, or do you develop a strategy which would put sunlight onto the problem so it becomes a community problem?

*JEM:* So, if you had a clean slate, how would you accomplish this information sharing? How would this all unfold?

*AH:* Well, it wouldn't be in my lifetime, but I think you'd start by changing the way you recruit people, by the way you train people, developing community outreach programs, getting more engaged with community leaders to make decisions at the local level about what is important and what's not important. I know these things are happening already, but they are happening in an incremental way, and there's no overarching strategy. It's like treating the corruption issue with police. There's no single strategy; there's a holistic approach, a shift in the way we see the business of protecting a community. It's not just us; it's everybody's responsibility. We are the conduit; we are the mechanism to promote it happening. The way we've been doing it has been driven by cold war philosophies of secrecy and the military, the philosophy of surprise and attack. Whereas I think we need a new style, to give us an opportunity to actually undermine terrorist cells and the way they operate. We can expose them and make it harder for them. It's like fighting cancer or another disease: Find the weakness and expose it, but not in a way that's going to alienate the community.

*JEM:* Again, the approach to intelligence sounds very much like your community policing philosophy in general: dealing with the community to provide service and collect intelligence. Does this sound right?

*AH:* It's not a foreign approach, no, and it has many similarities. But it's almost unfair to call it community policing because it's more than that. You may need to deal with operational issues or deal with integrity issues with the police, all of it. You've got to get these all right. You've got to get intelligent, smart, young officers in there, and you've got to recruit from those communities that seem to be the problems and break down those barriers altogether. But it's not going to happen overnight.

*JEM:* What about the responsibilities regarding rapid response to 911 calls and the traditional police role in crime control, investigations, and so on?

*AH:* Well, we're still going to have to deal with that, no matter what. I mean that's the nature of the beast.

*JEM:* It sounds like today's police officer has an enormous challenge juggling all of these competing roles. Can you talk a little bit about how today's generation of potential police officers, with their different expectations and familiarity with technology, can handle these diverse responsibilities?

*AH:* Yes, the new officers coming in are a new generation. It's all about them: "What's in it for me?" It's not so much about the money; it's about the opportunities. Education is going to be important; travel will be important, stimulation, variety, providing them with jobs where they have an interest. Technology has to be cutting edge. The police force has to get "techno savvy" and have all those gadgets and toys. Whether they work or not, you've got to get them, just to get people focused and interested. When I first started, all we had was a pad, a pen and a typewriter. Now we're doing "flash" video interviews, and that's the way it goes. Technology is moving so fast, and we've got to move with it.

I also think a strong sense of purpose is important and will be of real value. You know we've got to deal with the Hollywood image of policing and keep the new generation interested.

*JEM:* In order to keep new officers satisfied with their jobs and interested in their career, does a police organization have to manage the expectations of new officers better or change the organization to meet those expectations?

*AH:* Probably, a bit of both. Somewhere in the middle of those two [manage expectations vs. restructure agency]. You obviously can't give everyone a promotion when they want it or a new car and computer all the time. But you do have to manage those expectations. You have to illustrate to people that there are rewards: "If I do this, I get that." This will force positive behavior and encourage ideas. I firmly believe that the best ideas within an organization are down at the bottom. So developing ways to make sure those ideas "bubble up" is really important.

*JEM:* Have you ever done that in your organization—solicited input from line officers?

*AH:* Sure, I do it all the time. The board of management meetings I had in the Fiji police, where it wasn't just the assistant commissioners or regional commanders, we'd bring in junior officers and we'd debate about the attributes of certain issues. Culturally, this was new to them, but once they realized that this was not threatening, they were generally interested in participating and gave up some great ideas. Young, smart, bright officers don't have any problems with this because they are used to being challenged at the universities. It's harder in this organization because there is such turnover. In the UN police, everyone leaves after 1 or 2 years and the organization gets a new face.

*JEM:* As you were describing this participatory management philosophy, I couldn't help but see a corollary with your community policing strategy. With the community you go in and get familiar and essentially ask them how they want the police to operate. And with the management, you ask the lower level employees how the police department can be run. Do you see similarities here?

*AH:* Definitely. Any major project I think that a police force embarks on should have representatives from whoever will be running it, not just senior executives. You need their input and this is a tremendous motivating factor. Remember we talked about the new generation of police, the "generation X" officers. This is a major opportunity to motivate them and give them really challenging projects so they will show an interest in and be invested in the organization. They are the future and this can help that.

*JEM:* But in most police organizations, salary and compensation for police officers is equalized. So, if the financial motive is not there, how else can officers be motivated to engage in this challenging project?

*AH:* Well, there's the mental stimulation of engaging in such work. You can offer them the possibility of travel, to look at other systems around the country—maybe provide them with equipment, let them get a laptop out of it. I think it's not surprising that most people will rise to the occasion if given the opportunity. Not everyone will of course. Some officers will be content hiding around on their "Harleys." The other thing comes back to management style. We all know that in a time of crisis, command and control is the best management style. But when we are not in a time of crisis, this participatory, all-inclusive, or democratic style is more conducive to effective management than command and control. In fact, one of the challenges for management is the ability to switch from one style to the other. And the best leadership training is where you have that, where you're given training on command and control, and you're given training on the democratic management style and how to switch from one to the other.

We had one of Australia's major bush fires when I was a deputy police chief and the government gave executive powers to the police. We ran the ACT for 2½ weeks. So the chief was the executive officer during the day and I was the executive officer at night. We had incredible power. We could commandeer anything we thought that we'd need to fight this massive fire. But that was only for a short period of time and after it was over we had to switch back; you've got to be able to do that. You've got to be able to take command, but you've also got to be comfortable with getting with your people, coming up with ideas, and genuinely listening to them. You've got to know command and control. There's no getting away from it. Because you can't have a group hug while you're trying to put out the fire.

*JEM:* As you discussed, being able to switch management styles is important, as is the application of sound leadership. Do you think that there's a benefit to providing leadership training to entry-level police officers?

*AH:* Absolutely. The first job that rookie officers go to, let's say a traffic accident: What are the people looking for? They're looking for leadership. They're in shock, they might be injured, their cars are broken, so what do they want when the police arrive, and why do they want the police in the first place? Because someone's going to take control of this mess; it's leadership. So we don't teach them how do be leaders. In fact, we teach them how to obey orders, walk within a uniform, but we don't teach them to police freely. That's where we have to break away from the military style of training. It's important to teach the command and control side of it, but it's more important to show them that they are all leaders. When they go to a situation, a domestic dispute, a traffic accident, whatever it is, they've got to show leadership; they've got to take command, even if they're 18 years of age. They've got to take command and lead people out of their crisis. So, leadership training is essential.

It starts at day 1. They have to know the importance of service, and what their job means: what it means to put that badge on and that uniform on, and the expectations of how to behave as an individual, and how you conduct yourself, and how you react in command and control situations. Sometimes there will be situations where you'll exercise command and control and then there'll be situations where you'll have to use the softer side, negotiate with people, influence them without resorting to your authority, through simple human interaction. We have to teach them a whole set of different sets of solutions.

I really do admire experienced patrol officers that can do this with such aplomb. Within seconds they can go in and automatically know what's going on and what needs to be done, and everybody knows how to fall in line: "Don't touch that" or "Please stand over there, sir." They control the scene and then go over and talk to everybody and regain a sense of authority over things. It's amazing the skill they've got, and this is leadership.

*JEM:* Was there any particular training in your career that was instrumental in developing those leadership skills and techniques?

*AH:* There was a training course I attended that was run between the Northern Territory Police and the Northern Territory University called the "National Police Leadership Program." We got 1 week of the command and control style leadership and then 2 weeks of the democratic, or participatory, leadership training. But I also have a graduate diploma in executive leadership and a graduate certificate in applied management, which emphasized more about modern management principles than command and control.

*JEM:* Speaking about the world of higher education, there is often a divide between the world of theory, predominantly found in the academic community, on the one hand, and the practical world, on the other hand. Can you envision a better integration of those two worlds and, if so, how?

*AH:* I think they're coming together. For example, Princeton University is working with the UN to do a project on the history of the UN policing program. I've been interviewed and other senior officers have been interviewed. As one of my senior officers said, "You can trace military history back to Hannibal riding the elephants, but you can't trace police history. It's not written." So there's one project involving the UN police: to speak with the people that have been involved with it to provide a living record. And that will be a resource that will come into play later. So in the future, someone could say, "I wonder what Hughes's thoughts were on that in 2008?" It will be a great resource. I think there are bridges being built, and this has been under way for a long time, as others have, particularly since universities have realized that policing is a rich and fertile field for research. So there are guys like you [JEM] that have crossed over to the academic side, and some academics have become police officers themselves.

*JEM:* There are many programs in the United States, and I suspect around the world, that are very engaged in police theory and practice. But, it also seems that a lot more needs to be done to merge the two worlds. Do you see this as an issue, and how should this be addressed?

*AH:* Maybe I am looking at this from an Australian perspective, but I don't see the divide. A number of universities in Australia have quite mainstream policing programs, where you can get right up through a PhD in policing. Universities offer master's degrees in transnational crime prevention, MBA degrees, and degrees in public administration in policing as well. So, quite apart from the technical areas like forensics and ballistics, the relationship in Australia between the universities and the police is maybe closer than anywhere else.

You'd be able to go online and get a look at all the programs available at Australian universities. You'd be surprised; it's quite good.

*JEM:* Besides Princeton, are there any other academic organizations that you partner with?

*AH:* Yes, there's the National Police Institute in Washington, D.C. We've just conducted some major reviews and they've provided some assistance in that with the research and writing.

*JEM:* Can you speak about the various crime threats and the threats to public safety that exist around the world in the countries where you operate?

*AH:* Every country has its particular issues and its particular moments. In Haiti, you have a tremendous gang problem. It's large enough where it's a threat to the military. A robust police response was necessary, and that's been effective. Then you have militias in Darfur, in Sudan, and in Chad creating a problem. One minute they are a military force, and the next minute they are doing banditry. We're dealing with guys that are battle hardened, 20 to 30 years of war, 50-caliber [guns] on top of their shoulders, probably killed hundreds of people themselves, so it's a villain that most cops are not used to dealing with at home. We would need a military response to that, but we are being pushed into dealing with that. The military does not want to get involved with banditry because it's a police issue and they want the police to deal with it. But we constantly have to say, "Look at the nature of the criminal: They are a militia. Yes, they robbed a World Food Program convoy and that's banditry, sure, but look at who they are. You can't send lightly armed police officers to confront them. There needs to be a military response."

*JEM:* In general, how satisfied are you with the state of policing in the world in 2008?

*AH:* Well, I think if you look at it globally, it's quite diverse. In some countries there has been massive improvement and great strides ahead. In other countries they're mostly where they were without any signs of improvement. So it's very difficult to generalize. But if you look at the countries in my sphere now, well, you can't get much worse; they're at the bottom and there's nothing but great improvements to be had. And if you look at Australia, well, Australia is a very progressive country as far as the police are concerned, and the police there are responding really well to society. And there is a whole range of countries in the middle. There is an entire continuum of how well the police are doing, and it's too hard to say because the picture is mixed.

*JEM:* Does it go back to your initial philosophy that if we do a better job dealing with or managing the communities there will be improvements in policing?

*AH:* Yes, I think that's it, no matter where you are. Remember, too, we are also talking about many Communist countries and that approach is not going to work there because of the political motivations. Some countries are extremely radical in their religious beliefs and the culture is very strict. So we are talking about the liberal democratic countries, and that's not everywhere. So one solution won't fit all, but when you look at the microlevel, at the personal level, at the end of the day people are people, and they want to be treated well. Even if you don't like the outcome, if you've been treated fairly, then you'll generally accept the outcome. I think there's a lesson to be learned here and it can be applied anywhere.

*JEM:* So, even in the Communist or other "nondemocratic" countries, the democratic policing model can still apply?

*AH:* It does. We're introducing community policing programs in Sudan and they're popular. The Sudanese police are right behind us with it, the people like it, and the government is on board with it. So even though at times they can be guarded, they're on board with it. Similarly, in Chad, we're dealing with internationally displaced persons, the IDP camps. We are in the process of selecting 900 officers to police the IDP camps, and guess what principles we're espousing? Community policing is being rolled out and the new officers are getting trained in it. Hopefully, it will rub off, and when they go back to their "day jobs" in their home countries, they'll take some of these ideas with them.

In some places it will take longer than in others, but this is the general direction which the world is lurching toward. It's not coordinated or moving in any universally planned way, but as more and more police get involved in UN policing—and we're turning over more than 10,000 per year—we send them back with a new way of looking at things. They worked alongside American officers and Australian officers and they see a different approach. They didn't have to hit the guy over the head to find out certain information. They can talk to him like a human being and get better information than by using the butt of a gun. And I think as we replace 10,000 men and women each year (and that's increasing to 15,000 each year) and this approach begins to rub off, it has to add up somewhere.

There's some thinking that this will be the millennium of the UN police officers, as opposed to the UN military forces. As time goes on, the UN police increase in numbers, and we are catching up to the military. The UN police model has been around since the 1960s. The first mission was monitoring and we were joined at the hip with the military. There was no way of telling the difference between the military and the police. But it's taken on a new role now. We're very much in the fore with justice issues, police, corrections, prosecutors, and courts. The military goes in and creates a security envelope, and then we go in. Some of the police units are heavily armed and assist in establishing order.

Then, inside that security envelope, what do you do? You've won the war; now how do you win the peace? We then bring in some police, prosecutors, public defenders, correction officers, to rebuild so that when we leave there's something sustainable. So when there's a grievance between party "A" and party "B," whether it's at an organizational level, an individual level, or a political level, there is a means of redress. There are courts where the parties can bring their grievances and the courts are open and accountable, and the rule of law prevails. So that's what we are trying to do; that's the new direction of peacekeeping.

*JEM:* Changing gears a little bit; when you look at policing as a profession, do you see any major setbacks or failures that we've encountered over the years? If so, how could have we avoided them and how do we move on from them?

*AH:* Yes, I think the participation of women needs improvement. We are marginalizing a resource that we push away, when we should be pulling people in.

*JEM:* Is there anything easy about policing?

*AH:* Dealing with people is easy. If you approach it the right way, most people are decent people. So dealing with most people is easy. From time to time you might get the hardened criminal, the irate, the deranged, or the drunk or drugged up people, and they create problems, but most people are happy to see the police around. So it's not hard at all.

*JEM:* Do have any final comments, perhaps on something we didn't cover or something you'd like to add?

*AH:* Well, this has been pretty wide-ranging, but I would just like comment on this new approach to policing. It's not going to be easy, I don't pretend it to be easy, and if I were sitting in a police commissioner's shoes I know it would be a difficult task. It's easy for me to say, while sitting here in the UN, about these wonderful principles, but we've got to try something and I think working with the community offers the most promise.

*JEM:* Thank you for taking the time to talk to us.

## Summary

Mr. Hughes's vision for twenty-first century policing is remarkably similar to the vision for civil police when it began in the nineteenth century. To use the expression of Sir Robert Peele, as repeated by Andrew Hughes, "The police are the people, and the people are the police." It seems, according to Mr. Hughes, that this principle is alive and well today. Dealing with the wide-ranging constituencies facing police organizations—communities, the media, elected officials, internal ranks and units, etc.—calls for a universal approach. Remembering that we are partners in creating public safety, order, and peace, recognizing and addressing each other's concerns, and then delivering on these concerns were the hallmarks of modern policing as envisioned by Sir Robert and clearly underlie the driving vision and philosophy of Mr. Hughes. It is comforting to know that the world has a leader that is passionate about and committed to these principles as he spearheads the UN policing efforts around the world. The road he travels is difficult, but the map being used as a guide is sound.

# Suggested Guidelines for Interviewers

**Contents**



## General Remarks

The general goal of the interviews is to present the views and interpretations of policing developments and current issues *by experienced practitioners.* What do they see happening in policing in their countries and internationally, and how do they evaluate or interpret developments? We have many analyses and interpretations of policing by scholars and policy makers from outside the police organization. What we would like to have are views and interpretations from within the organization. What do police leaders who do the work see happening in policing? What are the issues they consider important? What changes do they see as successes or failures? What are likely lasting futures or passing fads?

The basic goal of the interviews is to capture the views of police officials. Your role should not be to be too critical or interpret what the officials meant to say, but to write as accurately as possible what the officials told you. It is their views, based on their experience and thinking, that we are interested in. We know what scholars think about policing, but we know less what the people who do policing think about and how they evaluate trends, developments, and issues in policing. That is the important goal.

The basic reason for doing the interviews in the first place is our firm belief that police officials know a lot; that practitioners can make significant contributions to our understanding of the prospects and problems of policing today. It is that knowledge and their judgments of policing that we are after. But that knowledge is not easily captured.

The practical reason for the interviews is that police leaders do not have the time to write and reflect on their experiences, views, opinions, and perspectives. We think interviews are one means to capture that knowledge and that is why we are requesting researchers like you to record their views.

We want to reemphasize one major point. We *do not want the official rhetoric (or the official success stories)* that high-level people sometimes fall back on during interviews; we want their *personal views and thinking*. If you have the sense that you are getting the formal language and official views of policing and reforms, see if you can get the officials to go beyond that and push them for their own views. The interviewer should seek to get the person interviewed to move beyond simple answers and get him or her to analyze and reflect on experiences and knowledge. That takes skill on the part of the interviewer—but that is why you were asked to do an interview.

**Topic Areas That Should Be Covered**

These are the basic areas we would like to cover. In some cases, there may be other areas of importance in "your" country or community and you should ask about those areas as well. For example, questions of police leaders in transitional countries will likely deal more with changes in policing philosophies and organizations than questions for leaders in stable democracies will. When asking you to conduct an interview, we know that you are quite familiar with the policing situations in "your" country and that you will tailor your questions toward the dominant local issues with which the leaders have had to deal. Be creative but not overly so.

We have listed a number of topics that should be covered in the interview. Please try to cover the following topics as the conduct and flow of the interview dictate. And add, elaborate, and follow up as you see fit and necessary to clarify points, expand on ideas, or pursue an insight offered.

All the topical areas should be covered, but the specific questions that follow for each topical area are suggestions. Interviews have their own dynamics. Follow them down their most fruitful avenues. Because each of you will be interviewing officials within different organizations, the list and sequence of questions will have to be adjusted in any case.

The wording of questions is, of course, your own. In follow-up questions, try to get specific examples or details of generalizations made. (Examples are probably among the most useful pieces of information to readers.)

*Suggested Questions*

*Career*

"Tell us a little bit about your career: length, organizations worked in, movements, specializations, etc. Basically standard stuff."

Other questions could include:

"What motivated you to enter police work?"
"What about how your career developed surprised you?"
"Did your work prove as interesting or rewarding as you thought it would?"

*Changes Experienced*

"What do you see as the most important changes that have happened in policing over the course of your career (philosophies, organizational arrangements, specializations, policies and programs, equipment, personnel, diversity, etc.)?"

"What changes in external conditions (support from communities, legal powers, judicial relations, relations with minority communities, resource provision, political influence, etc.) have had a significant impact on policing?"

"Overall, has the quality of policing improved or declined (street work, specialized units, managerial capacity, self-evaluation, interagency cooperation, etc.)?"

"In general, is it more or less difficult to be a police officer (street, manager) now than in the past?"

*Personal Policing Philosophy*

"What do you think should be the role of the police in society?"

"What should be their jobs, functions, and roles? What should be left to other people or organizations?"

"Which organizational arrangements work and which do not?"

"What policies on relations with the community, with political groups, with other criminal justice organizations work well? What hampers cooperation with other agencies and groups?"

"How should policing be performed? What should be the preferred priorities and strategies: hard-edged crime control, prevention, services, order work; what mix for which types of problems: proactive–reactive, community policing–law enforcement, etc.?"

*Problems and Successes Experienced*

"In your experience, which policies or programs have worked well and which have not? Can you speculate why?"

"What would you consider to be the greatest problem facing the police at this time?"

"What problems in policing do you find are the most difficult to deal with? What would be easy to change? Internal problems (culture of the organization, managerial deficiencies, allegations of corruption or gender-related problems, etc.) or externally generated problems (resources, community support, etc.)?"

"Is anything about policing easy?"

*Theory and Practice*

"What should be the relationship between theory and practice? What can practitioners learn from theory and what can theory builders learn from practitioners?"

"What is the relationship right now? Does it exist? Does it work? What holds collaboration or interactions back?"

"What kind of research, in what form, on what questions would you find most useful for practice? If not very useful, what could or should theory builders do to make their products more useful to you?"

"Where do you find theory-based information? Where do you look: journals, professional magazines, books, publications, reports?"

"Does the organization do research on its own? On what types of issues or questions?"

*Transnational Relations*

"In the work of your organization, have you been affected (and, if so, how) by developments outside the country (human rights demands, universal codes of ethics, practical interactions with police from other countries, personal experiences outside the country, new crime threats, etc.)?"

"Have those interactions been beneficial or harmful? What kinds of external international influences are beneficial and which ones less so?"

"How have developments after September 11 affected your work?"

*Democratic Policing* (There has been much discussion of what this phrase means and how it can be achieved.)

"How would you define democratic policing?"
"What practices would bring democratic policing to life?"
"Can democratic policing be achieved in your country, or not, and what obstacles stand in the way?"
"Should democratic policing be the goal of reforms?"

*General Assessments*

"Are you basically satisfied or dissatisfied with developments in policing?"
"Which are the most likely developments you see happening and which would you like to see happening?"
"What is most needed now to improve policing?"

**What to Do Before and After the Interview**

*Before*

Get a sense of how much time you are likely to have and what questions you can get to during that time. In no interview will you be able to ask all the questions you want. And, when you write up the interview, you will have space for about 6,000–8,000 words (on the average). Choose your priorities. The top priorities for us are the reflections by the officials interviewed on changes experienced during their careers, how they evaluate those changes, and the interrelations of theory and practice. These are high priorities for the interviews.

*After*

1. Please write a short introduction to the actual interview.
    a. Briefly describe the basic structure of policing in "your" country. You have to be the judge of how much an informed reader is likely to know about the country and how much should be explained.
    b. Describe, briefly, the interview itself: where and when it was conducted, how long it took (multiple sittings?), how honest and open you feel the discussion was.

2. You should, if at all possible, tape record the interview. For publication, edit the interview to bring out the most important discussion and answers. Chances are you will have much more information than we will have space for in the proposed book.
3. Write a short conclusion on your impression of the interview: what the major themes were, how well the views expressed accord with the known literature (but do not be overly critical on this point, please). Again, briefly.
4. Write a glossary of terms or events mentioned in the interview with which a reader might not be familiar (e.g., if you interview a German official and *Bundeskriminalamt* is mentioned, describe very briefly what that is; if you are interviewing a South African official and SARPCCO is mentioned, describe that). Just select the most likely items that inexperienced readers might not know.
5. We have had two basic styles in writing up interviews. Both are acceptable, but we prefer the second style. One style is simply to transcribe the interviews: questions asked, answers given. The second style, which requires more work, is to write short statements about the topic of a question and then insert long excerpts from the interviews. The main point is to have the voice and views of the leaders being interviewed, not your own.
6. Send the completed interviews to Dilip and me.

The total interview, with intro, conclusion, and glossary, should be about 6,000–8,000 words.

# International Police Executive Symposium (IPES) www.ipes.info

The International Police Executive Symposium (IPES) was founded in 1994. The aims and objectives of the IPES are to provide a forum to foster closer relationships among police researchers and practitioners globally, to facilitate cross-cultural, international, and interdisciplinary exchanges for the enrichment of the law-enforcement profession, and to encourage discussion and published research on challenging and contemporary topics related to the profession.

One of the most important activities of the IPES is the organization of an annual meeting under the auspices of a police or educational institution. To date, meetings have been hosted by the Canton Police of Geneva, Switzerland (Police Challenges and Strategies, 1994), the International Institute of the Sociology of Law in Onati, Spain (Challenges of Policing Democracies, 1995), Kanagawa University in Yokohama, Japan (Organized Crime, 1996), the Federal Police in Vienna, Austria (International Police Cooperation, 1997), the Dutch Police and Europol in The Hague, The Netherlands (Crime Prevention, 1998), and Andhra Pradesh Police in Hyderabad, India (Policing of Public Order, 1999), and the Center for Public Safety,

Northwestern University, Evanston, Illinois, USA (Traffic Policing, 2000). A special meeting was cohosted by the Bavarian Police Academy of Continuing Education in Ainring, Germany, University of Passau, Germany, and State University of New York, Plattsburgh, USA, to discuss the issues endorsed by the IPES in April 2000. The Police in Poland hosted the next meeting in May 2001 (Corruption: A Threat to World Order), and thereafter the annual meeting was hosted by the Police of Turkey in May 2002 (Police Education and Training). The Kingdom of Bahrain hosted the annual meeting in October 2003 (Police and the Community).

The 2004 meeting in May of that year (Criminal Exploitation of Women and Children) took place in British Columbia in Canada, and it was cohosted by the University College of the Fraser Valley, Abbotsford Police Department, Royal Canadian Mounted Police, the Vancouver Police Department, the Justice Institute of British Columbia, Canadian Police College, and the International Centre for Criminal Law Reform and Criminal Justice Policy. The next meeting (Challenges of Policing in the 21st Century) took place in September 2005 in Prague, The Czech Republic. The Turkish National Police hosted the meeting in 2006 (Local Linkages to Global Security and Crime). The 14th IPES was held in Dubai on April 8–12, 2007 (Urbanization and Security). The 15th annual meeting was hosted in Cincinnati, Ohio by the City of Cincinnati Police and the Ohio Association of Chiefs of Police in Cincinnati on the theme of "Police without Borders: The Fading Distinction between Local and Global." The 16th annual meeting was hosted by the Republic of Macedonia in Ohrid on June 9–14, 2009 on the theme of "Policing, the Private Sector, Economic Development, and Social Change."

The majority of participants of the annual meetings are usually directly involved in the police profession. In addition, scholars and researchers in the field also participate. The meetings comprise both structured and informal sessions to maximize dialogue and exchange of views and information. The executive summary of each meeting is distributed to participants as well as to a wide range of other interested police professionals and scholars. In addition, a book of selected papers from each annual meeting is published through Prentice Hall, Lexington Books, the Taylor & Francis Group, and other reputed publishers.

Closely associated with the IPES is *Police Practice and Research: An International Journal* (*PPR*). The journal is committed to highlighting current, innovative police practices from all over the world; providing opportunities for exchanges between police practitioners and researchers; reporting the state of public safety internationally; focusing on successful practices that build partnerships between police practitioners and communities, as well as highlighting other successful police practices in relation to maintaining order, enforcing laws, and serving the community. For more information visit our Web site, www.ipes.info.

The IPES is directed by a board of directors representing various countries of the world:

**President**

Dilip K. Das, 6030 Nott Road, Guilderland, NY 12084, USA; Tel: 318 274 2520, Fax: 318 274 3101, e-mail: dilipkd@aol.com.

**Vice President**

Tariq Hassan Al Hassan, P.O. Box 13, Manama, Kingdom of Bahrain; Tel: (973) 17 756777, Fax: (973) 17 754302, e-mail: Ropac@batelco.com.bh.

**Treasurer/Director**

Jim Lewis, 406 Quail Lane, Ruston, Louisiana 71720, USA; Tel: 318 413-0551.

**Directors**

Rick Sarre, GPO Box 2471, Adelaide 5001, South Australia; Tel: 61 8 84314879 (h), 61 8 83020889, Fax: 61 8 83020512, e-mail: rick.sarre@unisa.edu.au.

Tonita Murray, 73 Murphy Street, Carleton Place, Ontario K7C 2B7, Canada; Tel: 613 998 0883 (w), e-mail: tmurray@ca.inter.net.

Mark Chen, Professor, Central Police University, Taiwan, e-mail: mark@mail.cpu.edu.tw.

Snezana (Ana) Mijovic-Das, 6030 Nott Road, Guilderland, NY 12084, USA; Tel: 518 452 7845, Fax: 518 456 6790, e-mail: anamijovic@yahoo.com.

Horace Judson, P.O. Drawer 607, Grambling, LA 71245 USA; Tel: 318 274 6117, Fax: 318 274 6172, e-mail: judsonha@gram.edu.

Paulo R. Lino, 111 Das Garcas St., Canoas, RS, 92320-830, Brazil; Tel: 55 51 8111 1357, Fax: 55 51 466 2425, e-mail: paulino2@terra.com.bv.

Rune Glomseth, Police Superintendent, Norway Police University, Slemdalsveien5, Oslo, 0369, Norway; e-mail: Rune.Glomseth@phs.no.

Mustafa Ozguler, Chief of Police, Ankara, Turkey; e-mail: Mustafaozg@hotmail.com.

Maximillian Edelbacher, Riemersgasse 16/E/3, A-1190 Vienna, Austria; Tel: 43-1-601 74/5710, Fax: 43-1-601 74/5727, e-mail: edelmax@magnet.at.

IPES operates through active support, cooperation, and subscriptions of Institutional Supporters:

1. Dubai Police Department (Dr. Mohammed Murad Abdulla, Director), Decision-Making Support Center, P.O. Box 1493, Dubai, United Arab Emirates; Tel: 971 4 269 3790, Fax: 971 4 262 3233, e-mail: dxbpolrs@emirates.net.ae.
2. Bahrain Police (Lt. General Shaikh Rashed Bin Abdulla Al Khalifa, Minister of the Interior), P.O. Box 13, Manama, Kingdom of Bahrain; Tel: 973 17 270800, Fax: 973 17 253 266, e-mail: Colonel Tariq Hassan AL Hassan, Ropac@batelco.com.bh.
3. Fayetteville State University (Dr. David E. Barlow, Professor and Dean), College of Basic and Applied Sciences, 130 Chick Building, 1200 Murchison Road, Fayetteville, North Carolina, 28301 USA; Tel: 910-672-1659, Fax: 910-672-1083, e-mail: dbarlow@uncfsu.edu.
4. University of Hull (Dr. Bankole Cole, Director of Undergraduate Programmes, Department of Criminology and Sociological Studies), Cottingham Road, Hull HU6 7RX, UK; Tel: 01482 465669, e-mail: B.Cole@hull.ac.uk.
5. National Institute of Criminology and Forensic Science (Mr. D. M. Mitra, Inspector General of Police) MHA, Outer Ring Road, Sector 3, Rohini, Delhi 110085, India; Tel: 91 996 826

2008, Fax: 91 11 275 10586, e-mail: Johndm_mitra@yahoo.co.in.

6. Birmingham City University (Mike King), Center for Criminal Justice Policy and Research, Perry Barr, Birmingham B42 2SU, UK; Tel: 0121 3315163, Fax: 0121 3316938, e-mail: Mike.King@bcu.ac.uk.
7. Defendology Center for Security, Sociology and Criminology Research (Velibor Lalic), Srpska Street 63,78000 Banja Luka, Bosnia and Herzegovina; Tel and Fax: 387 51 308 914, e-mail: lalicv@teol.net.
8. University of Maribor (Dr. Gorazd Mesko), The Faculty of Criminal Justice and Security, University of Maribor, Kotnikova 8, 1000 Ljubljana, Slovenia; Tel: 386 1 300 83 39, Fax: 386 1 2302 687, e-mail: gorazd.mesko@fpvv.uni-mb.si.
9. Florida Gulf Coast University (Charlie Mesloh, PhD, Director), Weapons and Equipment Research Institute, 10501 FGCU Blvd S., Fort Myers, Fl 33965, USA; Tel: 239-590-7761 (office), Fax: 239-229-3462 (cellular), e-mail: cmesloh@fgcu.edu.
10. Ohio Association of Chiefs of Police (Chief Michael Laage), 6277 Riverside Drive, #2N, Dublin, Ohio 43017, USA; Tel: 614 761 0330, Fax: 614 718 3216, e-mail MLaage@springdale.org.
11. Kent State University Police Services (John A. Peach, Chief of Police), P.O. Box 5190, Stockdale Safety Building, Kent, Ohio, USA 44242-0001; Tel: 330 672 3111, e-mail: jpeach@kent.edu.
12. Abbotsford Police Department (Ian Mackenzie, Chief Constable), 2838 Justice Way, Abbotsford, British Columbia V2 T3 P5, Canada; Tel: 604-864-4809, Fax: 604-864-4725, e-mail: bobrich@abbypd.ca, swillms@abbypd.ca.
13. Department of Criminal Justice, North Carolina Central University, 301 Whiting Criminal Justice Bldg., Durham, NC 27707 USA (Dr. Harvey L. McMurray, Chair); Tel: 919-530-5204, 919 530 7909, Fax: 919-530-5195, e-mail: hmcmurray@nccu.edu.
14. University of the Fraser Valley (Dr. Darryl Plecas), Department of Criminology & Criminal Justice, 33844 King

Road, Abbotsford, British Columbia V2 S7 M9, Canada; Tel: 604-853-7441, Fax: 604-853-9990, e-mail: Darryl.plecas@ucfv.ca.

15. National Police Academy, Japan, Koichi Kurokawa, Assistant Director, Police Policy Research Center, Zip 183-8558: 3-12-1 Asahi-cho Fuchu-city, Tokyo; Tel: 81 42 354 3550, Fax: 81 42 330 1308, e-mail: tcr01@npac.jp.
16. Canterbury Christ Church University (Claire Shrubsall), Department of Crime and Policing Studies, Northwood Road, Broadstairs, Kent CT 10 2 WA, UK; Tel: 44 (0) 1843 609115, Fax: 44 (0) 1843 280700, e-mail: Claire.shrubsall@canterbury.ac.uk.
17. Police Standards Unit, Home Office (Stephen Cahill), 4th Floor Fry Building, 2 Marsham Street, London SW1P 4 DF, UK; Tel: 44 20 7035 0922, Fax: 44 870 336 9015, e-mail: Stephen.Cahill@homeoffice.gsi.gov.uk.
18. Royal Canadian Mounted Police (Gary Bass, Deputy Commissioner, Pacific Region) 657 West 37th Avenue, Vancouver, BC V5Z. 1K6, Canada; Tel: 604 264 2003, Fax: 604 264 3547, e-mail: gary.bass@rcmp-grc.gc.ca.
19. Eastern Kentucky University (Dr. Robin Haarr), Stratton Building 412A, Stratton Building, 521 Lancaster Avenue, Richmond, KY 40475 USA; Tel: 859-622-8152, e-mail: robin.haarr@eku.edu.
20. The Faculty of Law, University of Kragujevac, Serbia, (Prof. Branislav Simonovic), Str. Jovanba Cvijica 1, Kragujevac, Serbia 34000; Tel: 381 34 306 580, Fax: 381 34 306 546, e-mail: simonov@EUnet.yu.
21. Marc Dann, Attorney General, State of Ohio, (Jessica Utovich) State Office Tower, 30 E. Broad Street, 17th Floor, Columbus, OH 43215-3428; Tel: (614) 466-4320, e-mail: mdann@ag.state.oh.us, JUtovich@ag.state.oh.us.
22. The Ministry of Interior, P.O. Box 13320, Doha. Qatar (Contact Brigadier Al Kaabi Nasser Rashid); Tel: 250 552 6009. e-mail nasser55@windowslive.com.
23. The Cyber Defense & Research Initiatives, LLC, P.O. Box 86, Leslie, MI 49251 (Contact James Lewis); Tel: 517 242 6730, e-mail lewisja@cyberdefenseresearch.com.

24. Audiolex (Contact Kate J. Storey-Whyte, PhD), 9-10 Old Police Station, Kingston, Hereford, Herefordshire HR53DP, England; Fax: 44 154 423 1965, Mobile 44 7833 378 379.
25. The Department of Criminal Justice, Molloy College, 1000 Hempstead Avenue, P.O. Box 5002, Rockville Center, NY 11571-5002, USA (Contact Dr. John A. Eterno, NYPD Captain-Retired); Tel: 516 678 5000, Ext. 6135, Fax: 516 256 2289, e-mail: jeterno@molloy.edu.
26. The Senlis Council, Center of Excellence on Public Safety (George Howell) Rua Maria Queteria, 121/305, Ipanema, Rio de Janeiro, RJ 22410040, Brazil; Tel: 55 21 3903 9495, Cel: 55 21 8156 6485, e-mail: howell@senliscouncil.net.
27. The Department of Applied Social Studies, City University of Hong Kong (Li, Chi-mei, Jessica, PhD, Lecturer), Tat Chee Avenue, Kowloon Tong, Hong Kong; Tel: 2788 8839, Fax: 2788 8960, e-mail: jessica@cityu.edu.hk.
28. University of Maine at Augusta, College of Natural and Social Sciences (Professor Richard Mears), 46 University Drive, Augusta, ME 04330-9410, USA; e-mail: Rmears@maine.edu.

# Index

## J

www.ingramcontent.com/pod-product-compliance
Ingram Content Group UK Ltd.
Pitfield, Milton Keynes, MK11 3LW, UK
UKHW020024200926
475702UK00014B/2047
* 9 7 8 1 1 3 8 1 1 3 2 1 3 *